THE CITY IN CENTRAL EUROPE

The City in Central Europe

Culture and Society from 1800 to the Present

Edited by Malcolm Gee, Tim Kirk and Jill Steward

LONDON AND NEW YORK

First published 1999 by Ashgate Publishing

Reissued 2018 by Routledge
2 Park Square, Milton Park, Abingdon, Oxon, OX14 4RN
711 Third Avenue, New York, NY 10017, USA

Routledge is an imprint of the Taylor & Francis Group, an informa business

Copyright © The individual contributors, 1999

The contributors have asserted their moral rights.

All rights reserved. No part of this book may be reprinted or reproduced or utilised in any form or by any electronic, mechanical, or other means, now known or hereafter invented, including photocopying and recording, or in any information storage or retrieval system, without permission in writing from the publishers.

Notice:
Product or corporate names may be trademarks or registered trademarks, and are used only for identification and explanation without intent to infringe.

Publisher's Note
The publisher has gone to great lengths to ensure the quality of this reprint but points out that some imperfections in the original copies may be apparent.

Disclaimer
The publisher has made every effort to trace copyright holders and welcomes correspondence from those they have been unable to contact.

A Library of Congress record exists under LC control number: 98053573

Phototypeset in Palatino by Intype London Ltd

ISBN 13: 978-1-138-33814-2 (hbk)
ISBN 13: 978-1-138-33815-9 (pbk)
ISBN 13: 978-0-429-44190-5 (ebk)

Frontispiece: map of central Europe:
Roger Newbrook

Contents

List of figures	vii
Contributors	ix
Acknowledgements	xi
Introduction	1

1. A city in distress?: Paul Bröcker and the new architecture of Hamburg, 1900–1918
   Matthew Jefferies — 9

2. From the garden to the factory: urban visions in Czechoslovakia between the wars
   Jane Pavitt — 27

3. Networks and boundaries: German art centres and their satellites, 1815–1914
   Robin Lenman — 45

4. The Berlin art world, 1918–1933
   Malcolm Gee — 63

5. Cultural institutions as urban innovations: the Czech lands, Poland and the eastern Baltic, 1750–1900
   Lud'a Klusáková — 85

6. Castles, cabarets and cartoons: claims on Polishness in Kraków around 1905
   David Crowley — 101

7. 'Gruss aus Wien': urban tourism in Austria-Hungary before the First World War
   Jill Steward — 123

8 Big-city Jews: Jewish big city – the dialectics of Jewish
    assimilation in Vienna c. 1900   145
    Steven Beller

 9 Popular culture and politics in imperial Vienna   159
    Tim Kirk

10 'Making a living from disgrace': the politics of prostitution,
    female poverty and urban gender codes in Budapest and
    Vienna, 1860–1920   175
    Susan Zimmermann

11 Coping with social and economic crisis: the Viennese experience,
    1929–1933   197
    Gerhard Melinz

12 Walter Ruttmann's *Berlin: Symphony of a City*: traffic-mindedness
    and the city in interwar Germany   209
    Anthony McElligott

13 Wim Wenders and Berlin   239
    Sabine Jaccaud

Select bibliography   255

Index   267

List of figures

Frontispiece:
Map of central Europe: Roger Newbrook.

1 A city in distress?

1.1 Mönckebergstrasse development, Hamburg: From Fritz Schumacher, 'Das Entstehen einer Großstadtstraße', *Fragen an die Heimat Heft 3* (Brunswick and Hamburg, 1923).

1.2 The 'Chilehaus' Hamburg (1922–4, architect Fritz Höger): photo Matthew Jefferies.

1.3 Cover by Ferdinand Sckopp to Paul Bröcker, *Über Hamburgs neue Architektur* (Hamburg, 1908).

1.4 Commercial building, 1910: design by Fritz Höger, drawing by Ferdinand Sckopp from Paul Bröcker, *Die Architektur des Hamburgischen Geschäftshauses*.

1.5 Commercial building, 1910: Design by Fritz Höger, drawing by Ferdinand Sckopp from Paul Bröcker, *Die Architektur des Hamburgischen Geschäftshauses*. Built as the Niemannhaus (1909–10).

2 From the garden to the factory

2.1 Jan Kotěra, workers' colony at Louny: illustration from O. Novotný, *Jan Kotěra – A Jeho Doba*, Státní Nakladatelství, Prague, 1958, plate 213. British Architectural Library, RIBA, London.

2.2 Ořechovka Garden Suburb, Prague: photo Jane Pavitt.

2.3 Spořilov Garden Suburb, Prague, 1920s: postcard from author's collection.

2.4 Family house, 1930s, in Zlín: photo Jane Pavitt.

2.5 'The Modern Flood': from K. Honzík, *Tvorba Životního Slohu*, Václav Petr v Praze, 1946.

3 Networks and boundaries

3.1 Darmstadt: Mathildenhöhe artists' houses, c. 1905: postcard from author's collection.

4 The Berlin art world

4.1 National Gallery Berlin, 1866–76 (Arch. August Stüler, Heinrich Strack): from *Album von Berlin*, Berlin: Globus Verlag, c. 1910.

4.2 National Gallery Berlin, Impressionist Room (3rd floor, room 6, 1908): Staatliche Museen zu Berlin Zentralarchiv: Preußischer Kulturbesitz.

4.3 Viktoriastrasse (Tiergarten), c. 1935: Landesbildestelle, Berlin.

4.4 Interior of Alfred Flechtheim's house, c. 1925: Landesbildestelle, Berlin.

4.5 Felix Nussbaum, *Der tolle Platz*, 1931 (oil on canvas, 97 × 195.5 cm): Berlinische Galerie, Berlin.

4.6 New section of the National Gallery, Crown Prince's Palace, top floor, 1929–30: Staatliche Museen zu Berlin Zentralarchiv: Preußischer Kulturbesitz.

5 Cultural institutions as urban innovations

5.1 Wilhelm Stavenhagen, *View of Dorpat (Tartu)*: from *Album Baltischer Ansichten, vol. 3, Mittau,* 1867.

6 Castles, cabarets and cartoons

6.1 Karol Frycz, *Zawiejski's Wawel*, 1905: State Collection of Art at Wawel.

6.2 Karol Frycz, *Manggha's Wawel*, 1905: State Collection of Art at Wawel.

6.3 Karol Frycz, *Project for the restoration of the Castle by the City Council*, 1905: State Collection of Art at Wawel.

6.4 Karol Frycz, *Wawel in the 'Zakopane style'*, 1905: State Collection of Art at Wawel.

6.5 Karol Frycz, *Socialist Wawel*, 1905: State Collection of Art at Wawel

7 'Gruss aus Wien'

7.1 *Führer durch Wien*, c. 1908: postcard guide from author's collection.

7.2 Vienna, 1904. Advertisement for the Hotel Wimberger in Fünfhaus: postcard from author's collection.

7.3 'Gruss aus Wien', 1905: postcard from author's collection. Collaged photograph with drawing of 'Viennese Types' by Ch. Scolik, printed by Popper and Lederer, Prague. A version of the same image appears in the *Wiener Cicerone: Illustrierter Fremden-Führer durch Wien und Umgebung* (15th edn), 1907, p.112.

7.4 Souvenir of the 1891 Prague exhibition: postcard from author's collection.

7.5 The Lukásbad, Budapest, c. 1900: postcard from author's collection

12 Walter Ruttmann's *Symphony of a City*

12.1 Chemnitz zone map: Verein für Fremden-Verkehr in Chemnitz (hrsg.), *Chemnitz und Umgebung. Führer durch Chemnitz* (Chemnitz, Dritte Auflage, 1914–16).

12.2 Berlin transport networks, 1931: Berliner-Verkehrs-A.G. (March 1931).

12.3 'Roads of the Führer': i. *Der Grundstein* [No. 7], July 1939: 'Kernstück aller Reichsautobahnen. Der Ring um Berlin'; ii. *Frankfurter Zeitung*, 8 April 1938: 'Der Spatenstich'.

12.4 Competition entry 1933: Alexanderplatz: from *Berlin, Berlin. Die Ausstellung Zur Geschichte der Stadt*, exhibition catalogue edited by Gottfried Korff and Reinhard Rürup (Berlin, 1987), p.475.

12.5 'Mercedes Benz, Deeds of World Renown': from Michael Kriegeskorte, *100 Jahre Werbung im Handel* (Cologne, 1995), p.99.

12.6 Still from *Berlin: Sinfonie der Grossstadt*. Deutsches Institut für Filmkunde, Bildarchiv.

13 Wim Wenders and Berlin

13.1 Still from *Der Himmel über Berlin*: Homer and Cassiel in the library. Bibliothèque du Film, Paris.

Contributors

STEVEN BELLER is the author of *Vienna and the Jews 1867–1938* and has recently published biographies of Theodor Herzl and the Emperor Franz Joseph.

DAVID CROWLEY teaches visual culture at the University of Brighton. He is the author of *National Style and Nation State. Design in Poland from the vernacular revival to the international style* (Manchester, 1992).

MALCOLM GEE teaches art history at the University of Northumbria. He edited the volume *Art Criticism since 1900* (Manchester, 1993) and is currently working on the history of the European art market between 1900 and 1939.

SABINE JACCAUD is currently working as a writer and editor in London. She has published on architectural theory in the work of Wim Wenders, Peter Modiano and Peter Ackroyd. Her most recent research is on contemporary Swiss writing in French.

MATTHEW JEFFERIES teaches history at Manchester University. He is the author of *Politics and Culture in Wilhelmine Germany: The Case of Industrial Architecture* (Berg, 1995).

TIM KIRK teaches history at the University of Northumbria. He is the author of *Nazism and the Austrian Working Class* (Cambridge, 1996) and is currently working on cultural competition and the Nazi new order.

LUD'A KLUSÁKOVÁ teaches history at the University of Prague.

ROBIN LENMAN is senior lecturer in history at the University of Warwick. He is the author of *Artists and Society in Germany 1850–1914* (Manchester, 1997) and is currently working on a social history of photography.

ANTHONY MCELLIGOTT is lecturer in modern history at the University of St Andrews. He is the author of *Contested City. Municipal Politics and the Rise of Nazism in Altona 1917–1937* (Ann Arbor, 1998) and is currently researching rape and murder in Munich between the wars.

GERHARD MELINZ teaches history at the University of Linz. He is co-author of *Wohlfahrt und Krise. Wiener Kommunalpolitik 1929–1938* (Vienna: Deuticke, 1996).

JANE PAVITT is the University of Brighton/V&A Senior Research Fellow in Product Design and Museology. She is the author of *Buildings of Europe: Prague* (Manchester, 1999).

JILL STEWARD is senior lecturer in cultural history and theory at the University of Northumbria. She is currently working on the history of tourism and travel writing before the First World War.

SUSAN ZIMMERMANN teaches history at the Central European University, Budapest, and is also based at the Institute for History and Contemporary History, University of Linz. She is the author of *Prächtige Armut. Armenfürsorge, Kinderschutz und radikale Reform in Budapest im Zeitalter der Donaumonarchie. Im Vergleich mit Wien* (Sigmaringen,1996).

Acknowledgements

This book had its origins in the first conference held by the European Urban Culture Research Group at the University of Northumbria at Newcastle in 1994. The editors would like to thank the Austrian Institute, the British Academy and the University of Northumbria for supporting the original conference. Thanks are also due to the Department of Historical and Critical Studies at the University of Northumbria, which provided important technical and administrative support.

Introduction

Es soll also auf den Namen der Stadt kein besonderer Wert gelegt werden. Wie alle große Städte bestand sie aus Unregelmäßigkeit, Wechsel, Vorgleiten, Nichtschritthalten, Zusammenstößen von Dingen und Angelegenheiten, bodenlosen Punkten der Stille dazwischen, aus Bahnen und Ungebahntem, aus einem großen rhythmischen Schlag und der ewigen Verstimmung und Verschiebung aller Rhythmen gegeneinander, und glich im ganzen einer kochenden Blase, die in einem Gefäß ruht, das aus dem dauerhaften Stoff von Häusern, Gesetzen, Verordnungen und geschichtlichen Überlieferungen besteht.
Robert Musil, *Der Mann ohne Eigenschaften*. 'Eine Art Einleitung', 1930.[1]

The name of the city, then, is not particularly important. Like all big cities, it consisted of irregularity, change, sliding forward, falling behind, collisions of things and affairs, and fathomless silent places in between, of tracks and trackless territory, of one great rhythmic beat and the constant discord and dislocation of all rhythms against each other, and as a whole resembled a seething bubbling fluid within a vessel made of the solid stuff of buildings, laws, regulations, and historical customs.

The 'great rhythmic beat' of Musil's modern city, its 'perpetual discord and dislocation', was becoming increasingly familiar to central Europeans by the turn of the century as the tide of economic modernization swept across the continent. Existing cities had experienced historically unprecedented growth during the nineteenth century, and new ones were thrown up around them on the sites of small market towns and country villages. At the end of the eighteenth century the vast majority of people lived in the countryside, and sizeable towns were few and far between, especially in the relatively under-developed east of the region: Vienna, the largest city in central Europe at the time, had barely 200 000 inhabitants. Within a hundred years its population had increased almost tenfold and it had already been overtaken by Berlin. The Prussian capital had around 173 000 inhabitants in 1800, while the 'Greater Berlin' of the Wilhelmine empire had some three and a quarter million by 1910. Similarly, Hamburg grew from 128 000 at the end of the

Napoleonic Wars to 931 000 in 1910; Munich from 54 000 to almost 600 000; Prague from some 74 000 (within the city walls) in 1805 to some 400 000 a century or so later; and where Pest had been a small town of 29 560 in 1802, the Hungarian capital Budapest had grown to almost 900 000 by the eve of the First World War.[2]

The relentless and overwhelming influx of migrants into the expanding cities from a diversity of social and ethnic backgrounds generated class and racial tensions confronting politicians and policy-makers with new types of political problems. It also dramatically altered physical and mental landscapes. Urbanization posed new challenges for the architects and planners charged with constructing the built environment, and affected cultural production and consumption at all levels, from the art galleries and theatres patronized by the social elites to the bars and funfairs frequented by workers and tourists. Just as London and Paris had given rise to new kinds of writing and visual representation, so central European cities such as Berlin and Vienna now dominated the 'urban' novels of writers such as Musil, Theodor Fontane and Alfred Döblin, and became a principal theme in the work of visual artists from the Berlin caricaturist Heinrich Zille to George Grosz. Indeed, the earliest film-makers, working with the quintessentially modern medium of moving pictures, found that simple footage of local streets was often enough to draw an audience and hold its attention, and the 'city-scape' became the staple subject of popular genres such as watercolours, photographs and postcards, popular fiction and journalistic reportage which 'documented' the city.[3]

The documentation of urban life was also a preoccupation of contemporary academic commentators. And while the notion of cultural modernity generally, particularly in the visual arts, has been associated above all with Paris, key elements of our understanding of urban modernity in particular were formulated by early German sociologists such as Max Weber, Georg Simmel, and Ferdinand Tönnies and there was already an extensive and sophisticated literature in German on urbanization and the nature of urban society by the turn of the century.[4] Much of this early work adopted a qualitative approach which took into account the cultural dimension of urban experience as well as other, more directly quantifiable data.

Most modern accounts of urbanization in the region have been written by German scholars dealing exclusively with Germany, and focus on the social, economic and institutional history of German cities.[5] Works dealing with the urban cultures of the region have tended to concentrate on one or two specific cities, often addressing a particular 'episode': *fin-de-siècle* Vienna, for example; imperial or Weimar Berlin.[6] Those works which have the broadest focus, embracing a range of cities in both Germany *and* the Habsburg empire and its successor states, have tended to come above all from Austrian scholars and their colleagues in Prague and Budapest.[7]

It is this broad definition of central Europe which has been adopted in the present volume. Despite the well-documented rise of nationalism in the region during the early nineteenth and twentieth centuries, Germany and the Habsburg empire constituted a recognizably common cultural space, which persisted beyond the wars of German unification and the collapse of the two states in 1918. This 'cultural community' was nowhere more evident than within the towns and cities of the region. City-dwellers were inclined to look beyond the local hinterland to other urban centres in an extended network on which they relied for cultural as much as for economic or political contacts. It was not only that Viennese artists and intellectuals were, as might be expected, more closely engaged with what was happening in Berlin than in provincial Austria, but that the everyday experience of people in towns and cities was shaped by an infrastructure of urban institutions which was common to much of the region. The shared experience of urban life transcended the political and even to some extent the ethnic and linguistic boundaries which divided the region, and often ran through the cities themselves.

The essays in this collection examine aspects of the social and cultural history of the cities of central Europe from a variety of disciplinary perspectives. Despite their differences of approach and specific subject matter the individual contributions to the volume are broadly informed by an overarching theme: the shaping of modern urban culture – of modern 'urbanity' – by members of the dominant classes or other social groups, by the local or national political authorities, commercial interests, or ideological forces or political parties. These forces structured the urban environment, promoted cities as centres of culture, and regulated their societies. Finally, urban identities themselves were reinvented by means of a process of interaction and negotiation between different agents according to the specific context. This process occurred much earlier in the industrially advanced west of the region than in the east. Matthew Jefferies and Jane Pavitt discuss particular planning initiatives at different stages of this process. Matthew Jefferies's essay on Hamburg addresses a specific case of the way in which initiatives for commercial urban development in the early twentieth century raised questions about the choice of architectural forms deemed most appropriate for the expression of a modern urban society which saw itself as part of a distinctive historical tradition but which also looked to the future. The architectural critic Paul Bröcker and his collaborator, the architect Fritz Höger, intervened with some success in debates over the redevelopment of the historic centre of Hamburg, which they felt was in danger of being carried out in a tasteless and unhistorical manner as the commercial elites of the city benefited from

Germany's prosperity at the turn of the century. Dealing with a slightly later period, Jane Pavitt's essay on architectural practice in Czechoslovakia presents the adoption of the garden city concept, originally developed in England, as a form of urban planning suitable for a modern industrialized society. She shows that in the specific case of Zlín in Moravia, the Bata shoe company, a self-consciously modernizing, but at the same time socially conservative enterprise, allied a progressive attitude towards design with a reactionary, patriarchal attitude towards its workers.

Urban elites were also instrumental in promoting institutions of high culture. Robin Lenman examines the character and function of German cities as art centres in the nineteenth century. This involves the consideration of institutions and commercial practices associated with the creation of a modern art market, and particularly museums, art galleries and art academies. By 1914 Wilhelmine Germany possessed a complex and highly developed infrastructure for the promotion of art that was concomitant with the emergence of wealthy, ambitious and sophisticated middle-class elites for whom cultural consumption was an important element in their way of life. Cultural matters both for them and their rulers acquired political significance in the context of contested definitions of German national and regional identity. In the latter half of the nineteenth century the Prussian monarchy invested heavily in public cultural institutions particularly in Berlin, creating some of the city's most imposing buildings. Malcolm Gee's essay on the Berlin art world examines how different groups and individuals sought to adapt cultural practice and its institutions to the difficult conditions that prevailed after 1918. Housed, appropriately, in a redundant Hohenzollern palace, the 'new section' of the Prussian National Gallery became an important site for the promotion of modern German art as, despite economic and political difficulties, Berlin reasserted itself as a dynamic cultural centre. In the case of the visual arts key roles in this process were played by artists' exhibiting associations and commercial galleries, as well as the official institutions of the state.

Luďa Klusáková is concerned with the development of urban centres in less developed parts of central Europe over a relatively long timescale, including the period of proto-modernization in the late eighteenth and early nineteenth centuries. This essay raises the question of what the minimal conditions for the presence of an urban culture might be. These include the presence of a critical mass of population not dependent on the land, and forms of commercial activity which are registered in the physical fabric of the place, accompanied by modes of sociability characterized by regular and high levels of interaction which occur in buildings and spaces provided for the purpose (such as pubs and cafés). As we have already seen, these conditions were fulfilled much earlier and more comprehensively in the towns of the western regions of central Europe than the east. Although at the end of the nineteenth century many of the towns in this area, including Tallinn, Riga, Kraków and Lvov, had acquired several of the features of modern urban culture such as theatres and opera houses, museums and transport and lighting systems, only Prague resembled Budapest and Vienna in possessing the dense and complex urban culture of a major city. The factors underlying these disparate rates of development were both political and economic. David Crowley examines the particular case of Kraków, a city with a privileged place in Polish national history that, as a result of partition, was a neglected backwater of the Habsburg empire relatively untouched by modernization. Crowley is concerned with the relationship between ideas about the 'stuff of buildings' and conceptions of identity and the role that artistic representation could play in both affirming and criticizing this. Through the loss of Polish national statehood, cultural practice in this part of the region took on a particular importance as it became identifed as the repository of Polish heritage and of exemplars of 'Polishness'. In 1905, in the context of the return of the historic site of Wawel Hill in the city to the Polish nation, the artists associated with the 'Green Balloon' cabaret amused themselves with a series of satirical representations of competing 'visions' for the development of this national shrine – asserting, as they did so, their own affiliation with a modern, critical view of art that was essentially urban.

Life in Kraków was also characterized by another form of cultural consumption associated with modern urban life in the new centres of nationalism in central Europe: the appearance of streams of tourists gazing at its national monuments through the windows of the new electric trams as they passed on their way to Wawel Hill. Another city whose urban transport system developed as a response to the modern phenomenon of urban tourism was Vienna, by far the largest centre of tourism in Austria-Hungary. Jill Steward's essay on the growth of a specifically urban form of tourist culture in the city discusses the way in which the old city core was well suited to the modern tourist's taste for picturesque urban scenery. The influx of tourists from all over the empire helped to reinforce an experience of the city which focused on the picturesqueness, glamour and *Gemütlichkeit* of 'old Vienna'. This served to conceal many of the more disturbing aspects of the city's social and political life as its effective power as a capital began to slip away to the new regional centres of nationalism in Prague and Budapest. As in Kraków, nationalists in these cities tried to use cultural tourism as a means of establishing forms of regional, national and cultural identity.

The use of culture for socially strategic purposes, by both old and new elites, was an important feature of cultural life in all the major cities of central Europe: all forms of cultural consumption played a role in the way in which people sought to identify themselves socially as well as politically.[8] In the case of Vienna aristocrats were foremost among the consumers of culture for this purpose: their patronage of traditional forms of 'high' culture generated the 'culture of grace' which, as Carl Schorske has argued, provided a model for the newly enriched 'second society' in the city.[9]

The centrality of aesthetic and intellectual modernism to the culture of *fin-de-siècle* Vienna is well known.[10] A major role in this development was played by the city's Jewish elites, not least as patrons of modern art and design.[11] Steven Beller argues that the specific form of central European urbanity that developed in Vienna was the product of a 'remarkable process of osmosis' between the traditional culture of Vienna (and, beyond that, the whole German enlightenment tradition) and educated Jews who saw the assimilation and development of those cultures as a route towards integration and self-improvement.

Cultural self-improvement – the acquisition of *Bildung* – was an important element in the approach of the Social Democratic Party in Vienna to questions of culture. Tim Kirk shows that it was not only the state authorities and cultural critics which worried about the effects of the new commercial 'mass' culture, but the representatives of the working class themselves. Party leaders in Vienna before the First World War were only too aware of the political importance of culture in reinforcing social and political authority, and sought – albeit without great success – to educate their members away from mere 'entertainment' or 'leisure' and towards more edifying and socially empowering forms of cultural consumption.

All classes of urban immigrants came because the 'big city' was a site of economic and social opportunity. However, the phenomenal growth of big cities gave rise to new problems of regulation and control, particularly in relationship to poverty. Susan Zimmerman describes the way in which attempts to deal with poverty in Vienna and Budapest around the turn of the century were 'gender-coded', and argues that the problems of poverty and female prostitution were inextricably bound together. Attempts were made to control female lifestyles by regulating the behaviour of women on the streets. The authorities wished to remove obvious signs of abject poverty from public spaces, but saw prostitution as a necessary evil that needed to be controlled through inspection, registration and zoning. For socialists, both vagrancy and prostitution were products of capitalism that would be overcome in a properly organized society. After the First World War the Social Democratic city authorities in Vienna sought to implement policies that would overcome the deficiencies of the capitalist system through welfare and shape the working class for a better future. Gerhard Melinz's essay is a study of the slow shipwreck of the project of 'Red Vienna' in the late 1920s and 1930s, as Austria experienced the impact of the world economic slump.

The growth of cities generated new forms of urban hazard which the authorities felt impelled to regulate. Urban life was profoundly affected by the development of transportation systems from the electric trams to the individual motor car. Essential prerequisites to the rapid circulation of goods and people, they added to the quality of life. Both the tourists described by David Crowley and Jill Steward, and the ordinary citizens of the new 'Grossstädte' experienced the city through the windows of trams and the new urban railway systems. But traffic made the over-crowded streets even more dangerous and difficult to negotiate. Anthony McElligott argues that the experience of traffic emerged as the 'defining paradigm' of modernity in Germany between the wars, and prompted regulatory procedures from planners and policemen. Traffic provided emblematic material for the depiction in literature and the visual arts of the quotidian rhythms of urban life, most notably in Walter Ruttman's *Symphony of a City*. Superficially, the film evokes a chaotic experience of the modern metropolis, but underlying this are elements of control, evoked by the director's use of montage: the rhythms of the city it presents constitute in fact 'a single pulsating flow of order'.

The urban cultural environments created by modernization proved ephemeral. The socialists who had dominated the municipal politics of most of the region's major cities were swept aside by the political consequences of the depression. Vienna – the Jewish 'big city' – became a provincial town in the Third Reich. With the Cold War, the Potsdamer Platz, symbol of Berlin's modernity since the turn of the century, became a wasteland at the heart of a divided city. Sabine Jaccaud's essay, which closes this collection, examines Wim Wenders's use of the Potsdamer Platz as an emblem of the city's tragic fate in the film *Wings of Desire*. The new library adjacent to the square is a repository of the city's cultural memories embodied in the figure of the old man Homer, who 'cannot find' Potsdamer Platz in the contemporary city. The city as a whole is treated by Wenders as a 'palimpsest', a surface on which is inscribed – in buildings, streets and monuments – the myriad layers of the past. The cities of central Europe with their complex past and contested histories also form a vast cultural palimpsest recording traces of the urban experience, some of which these essays have sought to recover.

Notes

1. Robert Musil, *Gesammelte Werke. 1. Der Mann ohne Eigenschaften*, Reinbek: Rowohlt, 1978, p.10.
2. See Renate Banik-Schweitzer, 'Berlin-Wien-Budapest. Zur Sozialräumlichen Entwicklung der drei Hauptstädte in der zweiten Hälfte des 19. Jahrhunderts' in Wilhelm Rausch (ed.), *Die Städte Mitteleuropas im 19. Jahrhundert*, Linz: Ludwig-Boltzmann-Institut für Stadtgeschichteforschung, 1983, pp.139–54. Here p.140; Jürgen Reulecke, *Geschichte der Urbanisierung in Deutschland*, Frankfurt: Suhrkamp, 1985, p.203; Jan Havránek, 'Prag in der Zeit der Industrialisierung' in Monika Glettler, Heiko Haumann and Gottfried Schramm (eds), *Zentrale Städte und ihr Umland. Wechselwirkungen*

während der Industrialisierungsperiode in Mitteleuropa', St. Katharinen: Scripta Mercaturae Verlag, 1985, pp.98–105. Here, p.99.

3. See Peter Fritzsche, 'Vagabond in the Fugitive City: Hans Ostwald, Imperial Berlin, and the Grossstadt-Dokumente', *Journal of Contemporary History,* 29, 1994; and *Reading Berlin 1900*, Cambridge, Mass. and London: Harvard University Press, 1996.

4. See above all Weber, *Die Stadt*, and Simmel, 'Die Grossstadt und das Geistesleben' in T. Peterman (ed.), *Die Grossstadt*, Dresden, 1903, and widely reproduced in English as 'The Metropolis and Mental Life' in (e.g.) Philip Kasinitz (ed.), *Metropolis. Centre and Symbol of our Times*, London: Macmillan, 1995, pp.30–45. This early literature, some of it polemically anti-urban, is widely discussed in the secondary literature. See, for example, Reulecke, *Urbanisierung*, pp.139–46; also Andrew Lees, *Cities Perceived. Urban Society in European and American thought, 1820–1940*, Manchester University Press, 1985.

5. See, for example, Reulecke, *Urbanisierung*; and Horst Matzerath, *Urbanisierung in Preußen 1815–1914*, Stuttgart, Berlin, Cologne and Mainz: Verlag W. Kohlhammer/Deutscher Gemeindeverlag, 1985; Wolfgang R. Krabbe, *Die deutsche Stadt im 19. und 20. Jahrhundert. Eine Einführung*, Göttingen: Vandenhoeck und Ruprecht, 1989.

6. See, for example, Carl E. Schorske, *Fin de Siècle Vienna. Politics and Culture*, Cambridge University Press, 1981; Helmut Gruber, *Red Vienna. Experiment in Working Class Culture, 1919–1934*, Oxford University Press, 1991; *Berlin um 1900*, Berlin: Berlinische Galerie, 1984; J. Boberg, T. Fichter and E. Gillen (eds), *Die Metropole: Industriekultur in Berlin im 20. Jahrhundert*, Munich, 1986; Charles W. Haxthausen and Heidrun Suhr (eds), *Berlin: Culture and Metropolis*, Minneapolis and Oxford: University of Minnesota Press, 1990; Peter Alter (ed.), *Im Banne der Metropolen. Berlin und London in den zwanziger Jahren*, Göttingen and Zürich: Vandenhoeck und Ruprecht, 1993; Walter Prigge, *Urbanität und Intellektualität im 20. Jahrhundert. Wien, 1900, Frankfurt, 1930, Paris, 1960*. Frankfurt and New York: Campus, 1996; John Lukacs, *Budapest 1900: a historical portrait of a city culture*, London: Weidenfeld and Nicolson, 1989.

7. See above all *Beiträge zur Geschichte der Städte Mitteleuropas* (8 vols, 1981–7), Linz: Österreichischer Arbeitskreis für Stadtgeschichtsforschung and Ludwig-Boltzmann-Institut für Stadtgeschichtsforschung. See in particular Wilhelm Rausch (ed.), *Die Städte Mitteleuropas im 19. Jahrhundert*, Linz: Österreichischer Arbeitskreis für Stadtgeschichtsforschung and Ludwig-Boltzmann-Institut für Stadtgeschichtsforschung, 1983; and *Die Städte Mitteleuropas im 20. Jahrhundert*, Linz: Österreichischer Arbeitskreis für Stadtgeschichtsforschung and Ludwig-Boltzmann-Institut für Stadtgeschichtsforschung, 1984.

8. See for example Dolores L. Augustine, *Patricians and Parvenus: Wealth and High Society in Wilhemine Germany*, Oxford: Berg, 1994.

9. Schorske, *Fin de Siècle Vienna*.

10. For example, Allan Janik, Robert A. Kann Memorial Lecture (1995), 'Vienna 1900 Revisited: Paradigms and Problems,' *Austrian History Yearbook* 28, 1997, 1–27.

11. For a discussion of patronage, see Jane Wiegenstein, *Artists in a Changing Environment: the Viennese Art World 1860–1918*, PhD thesis, Indiana University, 1978.

A city in distress?: Paul Bröcker and the new architecture of Hamburg, 1900–1918

Matthew Jefferies

Hamburg has never been a city noted for its architecture. Despite its size and importance,[1] Germany's leading port was slow to develop the architectural characteristics of a major urban centre. The absence of a royal court meant that Hamburg not only missed out on palaces and pleasure gardens, but also on the theatres, galleries and grand avenues which came to grace even the smallest *Residenzstädte* like Karlsruhe and Weimar. Of course, Hamburg's proud hanseatic traditions left other monuments, but as a city of work and a city of trade, commerce always came before culture.

Moreover, the 'celebrated philistinism'[2] of the patrician families who for centuries controlled Hamburg's fortunes ensured that no building, however grand or venerable, was allowed to stand in the way of the port's prosperity. The city's Gothic cathedral, for instance, was pulled down in the 1800s and five more medieval churches followed between 1807 and 1837.[3] As the famous long-serving director of the city's art gallery, Alfred Lichtwark (1852–1914), bemoaned in 1912: 'No other city in the world has ever developed such a lust for self-destruction as Hamburg. Hamburg could have been the city of the Renaissance, the Baroque and the Rococo – yet all these treasures were consistently and enthusiastically sacrificed in the name of commerce.'[4]

Of course, not all Hamburg's architectural wounds were self-inflicted: the 'Great Fire', which raged for four days and nights in May 1842, destroyed over three hundred hectares of built-up land and nearly all the city's major public buildings. However, those parts of the old city which did survive the 1842 conflagration then disappeared in two further waves of municipal destruction: in the 1880s the development of the city's new free port necessitated the demolition of the old merchants' quarter and the eviction of more than 20 000 people; then, in response to the 1892 cholera epidemic, in which some 8 000 died,[5] slum clearance programmes reduced what little remained of the old city to rubble.

In the aftermath of each of these upheavals major building projects were undertaken, but the architects and architectural styles employed were often out of sympathy with the Hamburg townscape, hitherto typified by red bricks and tall gables. For Lichtwark and others, the stylistic diversity which resulted was a cause of profound regret:

> All the styles of the civilized world held a rendezvous in our backyard. One could call it an architectural masquerade in cement. English country-house Gothic, Flanders Gothic, Berlin Hellenic, French classical, Venetian and Munich neo-Romantic, all stand alongside the few attempts to take up the local brick Gothic, or at least ... to show the local material to advantage.[6]

The first of the city-centre redevelopments had come in the 1840s, when a series of classical arcades with gableless roofs and white plastered walls were built in the vicinity of the Alster lake, and a generously proportioned square, inspired by St Mark's in Venice, was laid out as a focal point for the city's new public buildings. It was here that the new town hall, in pompous neo-Renaissance style, was built some fifty years later. An even more monumental undertaking was the construction of a vast complex of warehouses – the famous *Speicherstadt*[7] – in the 1880s, under the agreement by which Hamburg joined the German Customs Union but retained a free-port zone in which the city's merchants could continue to enjoy the benefits of free trade. The towering warehouses which line the channels of the free port, and which remain to this day Hamburg's most imposing and controversial architectural ensemble, were built of brick, but in the neo-Gothic style of the Hanover school.

It was the slum-clearance programmes at the turn of the century, however, that most changed the character of the city. Despite the Great Fire and subsequent redevelopment, much of the city centre had remained a warren of picturesque but overcrowded alleyways, in which disease and crime were rife. The Slum Clearance Commission, established by the city authorities after the 1892 cholera epidemic, identified three inner-city districts in need of renewal. In the first area to be tackled, the southern *Neustadt*, the authorities proceeded with some caution, removing buildings which were identified as a threat to health, but leaving others standing. When the Commission came to tackle the alley quarters (*Gängevierteln*) of the eastern *Altstadt*, however, it was decided to raze the whole district to the ground and begin from scratch.

Initial assurances that new housing would be provided in the cleared area were quickly forgotten as the city fathers began to recognize the commercial opportunities presented by the development sites: displaced dock workers could, after all, be re-housed in the suburbs, now linked to the city by an expanding electric railway network. The centrepiece of the eastern *Altstadt* redevelopment was instead to be a wide thoroughfare of offices and shops, below which an underground railway would run, linking the central railway station with the town hall square (see Figure 1.1). This new transport artery, laid out between 1904 and 1908, was named after the long-serving chairman of the Slum Clearance Commission, Johann Georg Mönckeberg (1839–1908). Today, of course, the Mönckebergstrasse is Hamburg's principal shopping street, still channelling thousands of people daily into the heart of the city.[8] To the south of the Mönckebergstrasse stands another legacy of the slum clearance programmes of the 1900s: a much quieter, but equally prosperous area of bulky, angular office buildings, forming a fortress-like wall between the shops and the docks. This monofunctional office quarter, which shot up in the two decades between 1910 and 1930 on the site of Hamburg's most crime-ridden alleyways, lays claim to the title of Germany's first central business district. It is also here that one can find the only building in Hamburg to grace the pages of the architectural history books with any regularity, that vast, expressionistic ocean-liner of an office block, the 'Chilehaus', designed by Fritz Höger and built between 1922 and 1924 (see Figure 1.2).

Fritz Höger (1877–1949) was a close friend of the man whose work is the main subject of this essay, Paul Bröcker (1875–1948). Not only were they of a similar age and outlook; they also collaborated professionally, and the art historian Dörte Nicolaisen has written: 'The character and meaning of Höger's early office buildings can only be worked out if one attempts to understand them in the context of Bröcker's theories'.[9] Bröcker first made a name for himself as an architectural commentator in the mid 1900s, with a series of articles and pamphlets including *Hamburg in Not!* ('Hamburg in Distress' – see p.256), which was subtitled 'an urgent cry for help, and a suggestion on how to save the architectural culture of our hometown'. The impact of Bröcker's pamphleteering was considerable, but before assessing it in detail, it is worth looking briefly at what is known about his early life.

Paul Heinrich Bröcker was born in Hamburg on 2 July 1875. In the absence of any letters or diaries, however, one is left to search for further biographical details in the large body of literature he produced between 1905 and 1922 and in the files of Hamburg's political police.[10] Bröcker first came to their attention in the spring of 1900: whilst working as a clerk in the city's planning department, the *Baudeputation*, he entered a short-story competition run by the socialist publication *Der Wahre Jacob* to mark that year's May Day celebrations. His story – 'Ein Sterben' – was awarded first prize by a jury which included the SPD luminaries Bebel, Zetkin and Mehring, and was published in the May issue.[11]

Shortly after this success, Bröcker left his clerical job to become local news editor of a minor SPD paper, the *Harburger Volksblatt*. Things did not run smoothly, however, and on 1 October 1902 he left in rather acrimonious circumstances. Having spent several months on sick leave suffering from nervous exhaustion, Bröcker claimed he was forced out by the party's 'press commission' – a panel of 'bricklayers, tailors and factory workers' (Bröcker) – which had been putting constant pressure on him to attack the party's political opponents in a more forthright manner. Apparently the paper's printers were so irritated by Bröcker's 'soft' political line that they had begun to take matters into their own hands by altering his copy to include more colourful terms of abuse. For its part, the local SPD did not deny there had been political differences, but pointed out that the absent Bröcker could not expect to remain on the paper's payroll indefinitely, and questioned the seriousness of his 'illness'.

After leaving Harburg, Bröcker briefly wrote for the *Hamburger Echo* before joining another SPD paper in Solingen, but in 1904 a similar dispute – he was criticized for his 'spineless' style – led to his dismissal from that publication too. Soon he was to leave the party altogether, citing differences over naval and colonial policy. He returned to Hamburg where he continued to write on a freelance basis, including an essay for the revisionist *Sozialistische Monatshefte* and articles for the bourgeois *Hamburgischer Correspondent* and *Hamburger Fremdenblatt*. Bröcker's nationalism, which had been the root cause of his disenchantment with the SPD, was combined with a strong dose of Hamburg *Lokalpatriotismus*, and it was this sometimes sentimental but always deeply-felt attachment to his home town which came to dominate his writings for the next decade or more, as this extract from *Hamburg in Not!* indicates:

We squabble enough amongst ourselves about political and social things. Let us for once think sincerely about what unites us: our home; our hometown; and the beauty of the things produced by our labour, whether we are bricklayers or businessmen; the things which make life worth living...[12]

In one of his first articles back in Hamburg, written in September 1905 and entitled 'Old and New. In the Slum Clearance Areas', Bröcker wrote:

Old Hamburg is passing away ... After the fire and the customs union there now follows the slum clearance ... and this too is necessary, if our descendants are not to accuse us of serious negligence. It is just a pity that the new, which is being erected in place of the old, is so much worse, despite all the fancy decoration...'[13]

The characteristics of old Hamburg buildings – their functionality, their honesty in construction and use of materials – were, Bröcker argued, being lost in favour of the ostentatious and superficial. The sins of the *Gründerzeit*, the eclectic use of historicist motifs in what Bröcker called 'palace style', were still being committed thirty years later, only now motifs from English country houses and north German vernacular architecture were being appropriated too. Bröcker saw these new buildings as part of a much wider problem: 'He who has tradition also has soul.... Man has been alienated from the land. Even if he owns a piece of it, its only value is like that of the calf to the butcher: what did it cost? How much does it make?'[14]

There was, of course, nothing particularly original about these sentiments. Bröcker's words echoed those of many in the turn-of-the-century movements for architectural and land reform: they could well have been written by Paul Schultze-Naumburg or Ferdinand Avenarius or indeed Hamburg's own Alfred Lichtwark who had been attacking this 'epoch of cheap clutter and bombast' for more than a decade, and who was clearly a big influence on the young Bröcker. What makes Bröcker interesting is the much more specific things he had to say about architecture and planning in Hamburg, and the influence his ideas had.

A subject of particular interest for Bröcker was the Hamburg office building, the *Kontorhaus* or *Kontorhof*. Traditionally, Hamburg merchants had lived, worked and stored their goods in the same building, but over time such functions had become separated, and by the turn of the century the office building had become an established building type in its own right. Bröcker noted that just as the first cars had resembled horse-drawn carriages, so the first office buildings in Hamburg had looked like ordinary dwelling houses, until steel and reinforced concrete had opened up new possibilities. The first of this new sort of *Kontorhaus*, the 'Dovenhof' of 1885, had been followed by a whole series of purpose-built office buildings, each boasting electric lifts, central heating and large, uninterrupted floor areas, with movable partition walls to encourage multiple-occupancy.

Bröcker was always quick to celebrate the structural and aesthetic achievements of steel, concrete and glass – most notably in his eulogy to the great roof of Hamburg's main railway station[15] – but he was also anxious that the city should not lose its unique historical character. Thus, whilst Bröcker recognized that an international style of steel-framed office building was developing, he urged clients and architects not to succumb to the banal and the anonymous. Hamburg's new buildings for commerce and trade should instead combine the local with the international, the traditional with the modern. As Bröcker put it: 'The construction of the human skeleton tells us; this is a person! And the colour of the skin tells us; this is a paleface, a redhead, a Japanese! In the same way, the brick skin of an office block should tell us; this is a Hamburg building!'[16]

Bröcker saw in the humble brick not only a simple and honest building material, which could produce a pleasing aesthetic effect through its colour and pattern, but also a symbol of continuity running from the half-timbered houses of the medieval *Hansestadt* to the multistorey office blocks of the twentieth century, whose steel frames fulfilled much the same function as the wooden beams of old. Bröcker's admiration for brick architecture was by no means universally shared in turn-of-the-century Hamburg: for many, 'naked' brickwork was cheap and nasty, fine for factories and warehouses, but not well-suited for more representative building tasks. There were even many in the *Heimatschutz* movement, which Bröcker actively supported, who doubted the qualities of brick architecture.[17] One person who did share Bröcker's enthusiasm, however, was the architect Fritz Höger, a carpenter's son from Holstein who had set up his own architectural practice in 1907, and who later wrote: 'for me, every building in brick or clinker expresses something sacred and religious if it comes from the hand of a good masterbuilder'.[18]

It was perhaps inevitable, then, that the two men should become friends and – for a time – collaborators. The main result of their cooperation was the 1910 book *Die Architektur des Hamburgischen Geschäftshauses* (The Architecture of the Hamburg Commercial Building), for which Bröcker supplied the theoretical ideas and Höger the practical suggestions. It was illustrated by a third admirer of brick buildings, the self-taught artist Ferdinand Sckopp, who had made a name for himself with numerous drawings of Hamburg's rapidly disappearing *Altstadt*, and who had joined Höger's studio a year earlier. The book demonstrated a number of ways in which buildings could serve modern commercial and retail functions whilst at the same time enhancing the Hamburg townscape and remaining in harmony with Hanseatic traditions.

Höger's designs varied in the extent to which they borrowed formal motifs – like the tall gable – from Hamburg's past architecture, but all the façades emphasized load-bearing steel columns and brick in-fill. Some of the illustrated schemes were merely academic exercises (see Figure 1.4), but others had been submitted with real sites in mind: indeed, three of Höger's schemes were already under construction in Hamburg when the book appeared, and one of them, the 'Niemannhaus', was all but finished (see Figure 1.5). However, as the book's subtitle – *Ein zeitgemäßes Wort für die Ausbildung der Mönckebergstraße* (A Timely Word on the Shaping of the Mönckebergstrasse) – made clear, it was on the major new traffic artery through the *Altstadt* that the two men most wanted to make an impact.

They did not have long to wait. Following the publication of *Die Architektur des Hamburgischen Geschäftshauses* Höger picked up commissions to build a series of large commercial buildings on the Mönckebergstrasse, including the 'Haus Glass' (1910–11), the 'Rappolthaus' (1911–12), and the 'Klöpperhaus' (1912–13). Of these, the Rappolthaus was the most imposing: an office building with retail outlets on the ground floor, topped by a series of baroque gables. It was quickly followed by the Klöpperhaus, built as an office block but nowadays housing the Kaufhof department store, and designed by Höger after a competition in which the clients had specified that the building should have 'local character'. All three buildings were of course clad in red brick or clinker and conformed closely to the ideas expressed in Bröcker's book. Indeed, that the young and inexperienced Höger was able to tap such a rich seam of work owed much to Bröcker's brick evangelism, which reached a peak at around this time.

The Mönckebergstrasse had been at the heart of Bröcker's concerns for several years. From the beginning, the proposed route of the new street had caused controversy: the engineers who dominated the city planning department wanted to strike a straight line from the railway station to the town hall square, whereas Bröcker, and many local architects – no doubt inspired by Camillo Sitte's book on 'artistic' town planning[19] – argued for a less geometric approach. In this, the critics had enjoyed some success, but Bröcker was nevertheless shocked that such a major project could proceed without any serious consideration of its aesthetic impact. In his pamphlet *Hamburg in Not!*, written in 1907 and published at the start of 1908, he therefore called for the establishment of a *Künstlerkommission* (commission of artists) to judge major planning issues on aesthetic as well as technical grounds, along the lines of one that already existed in Munich. He suggested such a commission should include representatives from the architects' association, the *Heimatschutz* movement, the art galleries and museums, together with some practising artists and possibly representatives of property owners' and tenants' groups. It should be chaired by a senator or council officer.

In an article for the *Hamburgischer Correspondent* later in the same year, Bröcker repeated his call for a commission of artists but combined it with a plea for greater public involvement in planning and architectural issues, 'because a true architecture is impossible without the sincere participation of the people.'[20] To this end, he suggested measures to educate and inform the populace, including evening classes and easily understood pamphlets. Bröcker's own contribution to public enlightenment included a series of open lectures which he gave in 1910 under the title *Streifzüge durch die Baukunst* (Excursions in Architecture), and a new journal, *Der Hamburger*, which he launched as a monthly in December 1910, but which was appearing fortnightly by the middle of 1911.

Even though the journal boasted an impressive list of contributors, *Der Hamburger* was very much Bröcker's baby and reflected his own idiosyncratic range of enthusiasms: architecture and town planning, of course, but also local history, *Heimatliteratur* (including poetry and prose in Low German), interior design, gardening, education and high politics. Long essays on the Morocco Crisis or the colonization of East Africa would be followed by articles on the design of radiators or the department store of the future, and interspersed with illustrations, usually by the aforementioned Ferdinand Sckopp.

Bröcker published the journal with his brother Otto, a printer, who was responsible for the business side of the operation, including the sale of advertising space. This proved to be an unrewarding task, despite the journal's assertion that 'the readership of the *Hamburger* represents for the advertiser the pick of the leading intellectual and social circles, people who as consumers set the tone in matters of taste'.[21] The Bröckers' stated desire to accept only 'quality' advertising may have been over-ambitious; certainly, little revenue was gained from this source, and it was no real surprise that the journal ceased publication halfway through its second year.

Bröcker was unabashed, however, and continued to publish pamphlets at an alarming rate. Despite the failure of *Der Hamburger*, his efforts were certainly not falling on deaf ears. Bröcker's calls for the establishment of a commission to assess planning applications on aesthetic as well as technical grounds had received widespread support: a *Fassadenkommission* to vet the façades and roof lines of new buildings in the Mönckebergstrasse was established in 1908, and ensured that the finished street reflected an aesthetic unity sadly lacking in earlier roads through the slum-clearance areas.[22]

Later that same year a motion proposing a permanent commission to examine all important planning applications was introduced in the Citizen's Assembly. It took four years before legislation was in place, but the eventual *Baupflegegesetz* of 1912 owed much to Bröcker's tireless campaigning.[23] This law introduced an aesthetic dimension to Hamburg's planning procedures for the first time. The city's existing building code, which dated back to 1865 (although it had been revised in 1882 and amended on several occasions) was purely technical in character, limiting the height of buildings and dealing with such issues as fire safety and hygiene. The new law established a commission of three senators and six members of the Citizen's Assembly, together with an advisory committee of twenty-five professionals and laymen, to vet new building plans for their impact on their surroundings, and to advise on the preservation of existing buildings. The commission had the right to call in any building plans from the whole of Hamburg and to ask for alterations, though it could not block projects permanently. Even so, the commission subsequently achieved an impressive record of persuading developers to adapt their plans and the law made a considerable impact on the appearance of the city centre.

The *Baupflegegesetz* was only passed after much heated debate, in which such heady concepts as the freedom of art and the freedom of the individual were frequently invoked. Bröcker joined in regularly via pamphlets and the pages of *Der Hamburger* but the law's most important backer was Fritz Schumacher (1869–1947), who became the city's chief architect in 1909. In fact it is Schumacher, a founder member of the Deutsche Werkbund[24] and Professor of Architecture at the Technical High School in Dresden before his move to Hamburg, who is usually credited with both the *Baupflegegesetz* and the successful completion of the Mönckebergstrasse. Indeed, the very revival of brick architecture in early-twentieth-century Hamburg is invariably associated with his name. This reputation is by no means undeserved – as an architect and as a town planner he had a decisive influence on the appearance of the city for nearly a quarter of a century, and his red-brick municipal buildings and housing schemes are rightly admired – but one should not forget that much was under way before Schumacher's arrival in the city.

In his memoirs, Schumacher was dismissive of Bröcker's influence, remarking 'to the disappointment of its leaders, I kept my distance from the literary brick movement, which began around this time'.[25] Schumacher claimed his decision to use brick as the consistent feature of his Hamburg architecture was taken whilst he was still in Dresden, and had nothing to do with Bröcker and Höger's agitational efforts. Even if this is so, however, it is clear that the revival of brick architecture in Hamburg predated Schumacher's arrival in the city, and began with the commercial buildings of the redeveloped *Altstadt* rather than Schumacher's schools, hospitals and fire stations.

With Schumacher and the *Baupflegegesetz* both safely in place, Bröcker apparently felt that Hamburg was no longer a city in distress or danger: architectural and town-planning issues now slipped from the top of his agenda. After glorying in the spirit of national unity in August 1914, which prompted a militaristic essay entitled 'The Labour Movement as a Preparatory School for War',[26] and a pamphlet in which he supported the idea of forced labour for POWs,[27] Bröcker turned his attention from the local to the national stage. Bröcker's desire to see the end of class confrontation, and the reconciliation of internal conflict through national solidarity, was expressed after the war in the rhetoric of the *Volksgemeinschaft*, a concept vague enough to be embraced by both left and right in the early Weimar years. Between 1918 and 1922 he produced a stream of pamphlets[28] for the white-collar trade union, the *Deutschnationale Handlungsgehilfen Verband* (DHV), whose position in the political spectrum between the representatives of big capital and socialist labour appealed to Bröcker, as did its *völkisch* leanings, which became increasingly pronounced in the later years of the Weimar Republic.[29]

Although he was no longer writing on architecture, Bröcker had the satisfaction of seeing many of his ideas come to fruition as Hamburg's central business district developed in the 1920s. Under the planning legislation he had helped to inspire, brick was the prescribed material for the façades of office buildings rising in the *Altstadt*, whilst his old friend Fritz Höger was an architect greatly in demand. Höger's architectural style had evolved since the two men had worked on their 1910 book – tall gables had been replaced by stepped roofs – but he remained committed to a distinctively Hanseatic architectural vocabulary. Nowhere was this better illustrated than in the Chilehaus itself, a building intended to express the unshaken self-confidence of Hamburg traders in the aftermath of a lost war, and seen by the architect himself as a statement of the *große Wille* of the German people.[30]

Despite Höger's *völkisch* mysticism, architecture did not become as politicized in Hamburg as it did in other German cities during the Weimar Republic. Thanks to Bröcker's propaganda and Schumacher's pragmatism, brick was widely accepted as the most appropriate building material for the city, and was used by 'modern' and 'traditional' architects alike, thus lessening the shock of the new and limiting any political capital to be made from it.[31] Paul Bröcker retreated from public life in the mid-1920s and thereafter devoted himself to his family and the study of Low German dialects. He died in his house overlooking the River Elbe in 1948.

The popularity of brick architecture in Hamburg lives on, however, and the last decade has seen a large number of new office developments and shopping malls making a feature of brick cladding. In a recent article on Hamburg entitled 'Die neue Backsteinpracht', the architectural correspondent of *Die Zeit* concluded that Hamburg is a city 'held together by brick'.[32] It is a thought which would no doubt cheer Paul Bröcker, whose writings are now largely forgotten, but whose efforts to reconcile tradition and modernity, nationalism and socialism, crossed many of the cultural boundaries of his time, and made a lasting impression on the appearance of his hometown.

Notes

1. Hamburg was the second city of the German empire, with a population of 570 000 in 1890 and 1 030 000 in 1913. Between 1888 and 1914 the city's harbour area grew tenfold, and the amount of shipping quadrupled.
2. The phrase was coined by Richard J. Evans in *Death in Hamburg. Society and Politics in the Cholera Years, 1830–1910*, Oxford: The Clarendon Press, 1987.
3. R.J. Evans, *Death in Hamburg*, p.36.
4. A. Lichtwark, quoted in *Als Hamburg nobel war*, exhibition catalogue, Hamburg, date unknown.
5. See R.J. Evans, *Death in Hamburg*.
6. A. Lichtwark, quoted in D. Nicolaisen, *Studien zur Architektur in Hamburg, 1910–1930*, PhD thesis, Munich, 1974 (revised Hamburg, 1985), p.35.
7. See K. Maak, 'Die Speicherstadt im Hamburger Freihafen. Eine Stadt an Stelle der Stadt', *Arbeitshefte zur Denkmalpflege in Hamburg* no.7, Hamburg: Christians,1985.
8. See H. Hipp, 'Die Mönckebergstraße', in V. Plagemann (ed.), *Industriekultur in Hamburg. Des Deutschen Reiches Tor zur Welt*, Munich: Beck, 1984. Also H. Hipp, 'Heimat in der City. Die Wandlung

des Stadtbildes in der Hamburger Innenstadt um die Jahrhundertwende', in J. Ellermeyer (ed.), *Stadt und Hafen*, Hamburg: Christians, 1986.

9. D. Nicolaisen, *Studien zur Architektur in Hamburg 1910–1930*, pp.53–4.

10. Staatsarchiv Hamburg, Polizei Behörde Hamburg, Abteilung II Politische Section, No. 8053 Paul Heinrich Bröcker. This thick file contains a large number of press cuttings by and about Bröcker, together with handwritten observations by the authorities.

11. *Der Wahre Jacob*, No.359 (May 1900), pp.3232–4.

12. P. Bröcker, *Hamburg in Not!*, Hamburg, 1908, p.27.

13. P. Bröcker, 'Alt und Neu. Im Sanierungsgebiet', in *Über Hamburgs neue Architektur. Zeitgemäße Betrachtungen eines Laien*, Hamburg, 1908, p.9.

14. P. Bröcker, *Über Hamburgs neue Architektur*, p.16.

15. P. Bröcker, 'Der Zentralbahnhof als Kunstwerk', *Über Hamburgs neue Architektur*, pp.88–92.

16. P. Bröcker, *Die Architektur des Hamburgischen Geschäftshauses. Ein zeitgemäßes Wort für die Ausbildung der Mönckebergstraße*, Hamburg, 1910, p.52.

17. For the *Heimatschutz* movement see M. Jefferies, *Politics and Culture in Wilhelmine Germany: The Case of Industrial Architecture*, Oxford: Berg, 1995, chapter 2. Also C.F. Otto, 'Modern environment and historical continuity: the Heimatschutz discourse in Germany', in *Art Journal*, Summer, 1983, and S. Muthesius, 'The origins of the German conservation movement', in R. Kain, *Planning for Conservation*, London: Mansell, 1981. Bröcker was secretary of the *Verein Heimatschutz in Hamburg*, one of three conservation associations in the Hamburg area. In February 1911, when the three groups merged to form the *Verein Heimatschutz im Hamburger Staatsgebiet* (308 members) he became its vice-chairman, but left the post later that year. Brick architecture had been criticized by other *Heimatschutz* leaders, such as Paul Schultze-Naumburg.

18. F. Höger, quoted in C. Westphal (ed.), *Fritz Höger. Der niederdeutsche Backstein-Baumeister*, Wolfshagen, 1938, p.38.

19. C. Sitte's *Der Städtebau nach seinen künstlerischen Grundsätzen* was published in Vienna in 1891 and proved tremendously influential in pre-First World War Germany (and elsewhere).

20. P. Bröcker, 'Ein Vorschlag für die Berufung einer Künstlerkommission', *Hamburgischer Correspondent*, 20 November 1908, p.2.

21. 'An die Geschäftswelt von Hamburg!', in *Der Hamburger*, vol.1. no.8, p.189.

22. All available plots on the street were sold by the city authorities on the understanding that drawings of the planned façades would be subject to scrutiny, in order that a good overall effect could be achieved.

23. See K. Rauschnabel, 'Stadtgestalt durch Staatsgewalt? Das Hamburger Baupflegegesetz von 1912', *Arbeitshefte zur Denkmalpflege in Hamburg* no.6, Hamburg: Christians, 1984. Also G. Schiefler, *Eine hamburgische Kulturgeschichte 1890–1920*, Hamburg: Verein für Hamburgische Geschichte, 1985. Rauschnabel stresses the key role played by laymen in preparing the ground for the new legislation, since the architects' professional body, the *Architekten und Ingenieurverein Hamburg*, was reluctant to become involved in aesthetic issues. Faced with a conflict between its role as a professional body and its wider responsibilities, the AIV tended to favour the former, for fear of damaging the livelihood of members.

24. For the Werkbund, and Schumacher's role in it, see J. Campbell, *The German Werkbund. The Politics of Reform in the Applied Arts*, Princeton University Press, 1978. Also M. Jefferies, *Politics and Culture in Wilhelmine Germany*.

25. F. Schumacher, *Stufen des Lebens. Erinnerungen eines Baumeisters*, Stuttgart and Berlin, 1935, p.305.

26. P. Bröcker, 'Die Arbeiterbewegung als Vorschule für den Krieg', in *Der Kunstwart*, vol.27/2 (1914), pp.349–53.

27. P. Bröcker, 'Der Heimatschutz und die Urbarmachung der Oedländereien durch Kriegsgefangene', *Dürerbund Flugschriften* no.136, Munich, 1915.

28. Including: *Wertgutgedanken. Die Wertgutgestaltung als Problem der Ästhetik, der Wirtschaft und des Staates*, Hamburg, 1919; *Die Arbeitnehmerbewegung. Eine Darstellung ihrer geistigen Entwicklung und kulturellen Macht. Ein Beitrag zur Wiederaufrichtung der deutschen Arbeit*, Hamburg, 1919; *Klassenkampf und Rassenkampf. Beitrag zur Kenntnis der deutschnationalen Arbeitnehmerbewegung*, Hamburg, 1920; *Der Wertgutgedanke und die Gewerkschaften*, Hamburg, 1920; *Was ist Klassenkampf?*, Hamburg, 1920; *Vom christlich-sozialen Gedanken zur deutsch-nationalen Arbeitnehmerbewegung*, Hamburg, 1921;

Die geistige Gliederung der Gewerkschaftsbewegung, Hamburg, 1921; *Kulturaufgaben des DHV*, Hamburg, 1921; *Die Gefahren des Syndikalismus*, Hamburg, 1921; *Von der Markgenossenschaft zur Gewerkschaft. Eine Betrachtung zur Frage: Kaufmannsberuf und Wertgutgedanke*, Hamburg, 1922.

29. See I. Hamel, *Völkischer Verband und nationale Gewerkschaft: der Deutschnationale Handlungsgehilfen-Verband 1893–1933*, Frankfurt am Main: Europäische Verlag, 1967. It is also interesting to note that Bröcker's friend F. Sckopp was co-designer with W. Vortmann of the DHV's Hamburg headquarters (designed 1913, built 1921–9).

30. D. Nicolaisen, *Studien zur Architektur in Hamburg 1910–33*, p.49. On the Chilehaus itself see H. Busch and R. Sloman, *Das Chilehaus in Hamburg. Sein Bauherr und sein Architekt*, Hamburg: Christians, 1974; also A. Kamphausen, *Der Baumeister Fritz Höger*, Neumünster: Wachholtz, 1972.

31. This view is advanced by D. Nicolaisen in *Studien zur Architektur in Hamburg 1910–33*.

32. M. Sack, 'Die neue Backsteinpracht', in *Die Zeit*, 1 July 1994, pp.45–6.

1.1 Mönckerbergstrasse development, Hamburg

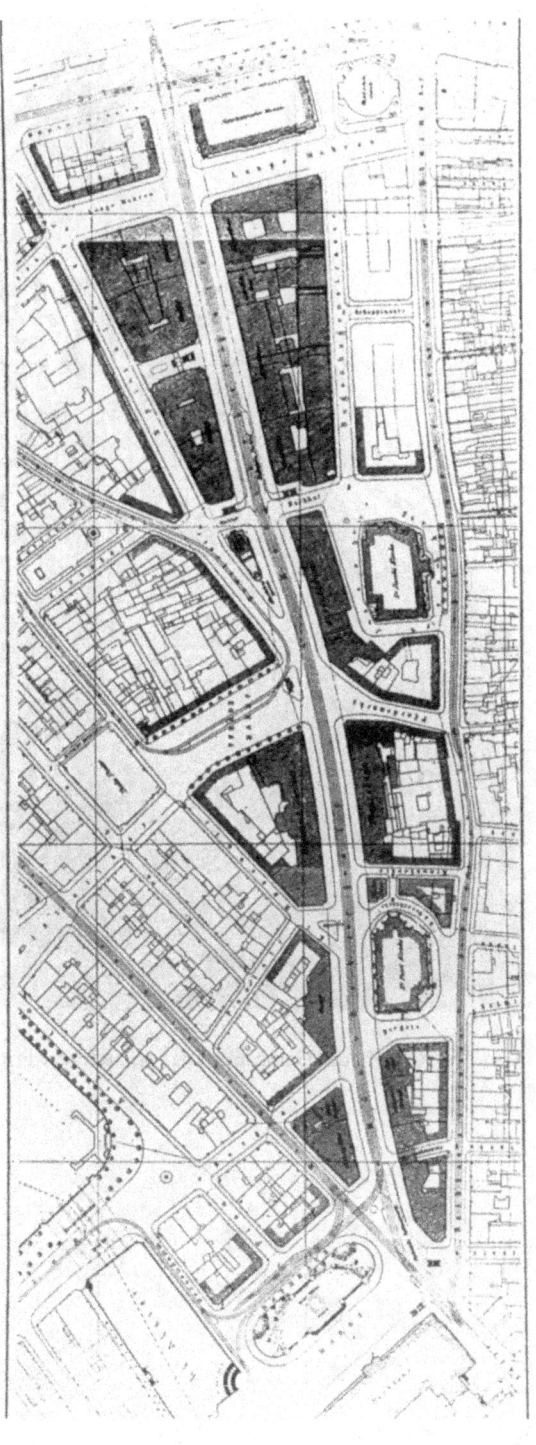

1.2 The 'Chilehaus' Hamburg (1922–4, architect Fritz Höger)

1.3 Cover by Ferdinand Sckopp to Paul Bröcker, *Über Hamburg's neue Architektur* (Hamburg, 1908)

1.4 Commercial building, 1910: design by Fritz Höger, drawing by Ferdinand Sckopp from Paul Bröcker, *Die Architektur des Hamburgischen Geschäftshauses*

1.5 Commercial building, 1910: Design by Fritz Höger, drawing by Ferdinand Sckopp from Paul Bröcker, *Die Architektur des Hamburgischen Geschäftshauses*. Built as the Niemannhaus (1909–10)

From the garden to the factory: urban visions in Czechoslovakia between the wars

Jane Pavitt

The activities of the Modern Movement in Czechoslovakia between the wars have been regarded, with some justification, as an 'heroic' period in Czech history. As a new and progressive nation, declared in 1917 by T.G. Masaryk whilst in exile in Paris, Czechoslovakia was an appropriate hothouse for avant-garde attitudes. Cut short by the Nazi annexation of the Czech lands in 1938, the artistic character of this period has acquired a particular poignancy. Kenneth Frampton, in his essay 'A Modernity Worthy of the Name,' describes the situation thus:

When one looks back over half a century to the country's modern movement, one cannot avoid being impressed by the way in which Czech modern architecture especially, together with a modern modus vivendi, became an expression that was seemingly embraced by the whole society. It was as if the spirit of modernity sustained by this culture embodied the very essence and identity of the new republic which had been created out of the ashes of the First World War and the ruined Hapsburg Empire.[1]

The 'rediscovery' of this period of Czech culture in western Europe and in America, through publications and exhibitions (particularly since the 'Velvet Revolution' of 1989) has celebrated the nation's liberalism and progressivism in the arts.[2] Such valuable studies have often concentrated on placing the Czech avant-garde within the context of the international trend towards Modernism, stressing its relations with, for example, the Bauhaus, Constructivism and Surrealism. During the 1920s and '30s great faith was placed in the international nature of Modernism, as a way of counteracting the perceived limitations of nationalist sentiment.

The urban experience was, of course, central to what might be described as the Modernist project during these years. Various avant-garde groups provided the forum for the discussion of ideas concerning the modern metropolis. The main protagonist of the 'Devětsil' group, the poet and critic

Karel Teige, saw the work of the artist as interwoven with the drama of modern street life – the café, the boulevard, nightlife and the modern industrial cityscape. Architects utilized the iconography of modernity (the ocean liner, the aeroplane, advertising and the cinema) to create a new urban architecture. By the 1930s the politicized avant-garde were investing their energies in radical social projects, such as plans for collective housing. In terms of built projects, urban areas – particularly Prague and Brno – gained a considerable number of notable Modern Movement buildings; department stores, industrial and commercial centres, buildings for leisure, private houses and apartment blocks.[3] This was supplemented by numerous publications in which architecture, urbanism and the arts were hotly debated. A number of key architectural journals publicized international developments, amongst them *Stavba, Stavitel* and *Styl*.

However, these debates should not merely be seen in the context of the international Modern Movement. This essay will examine the ways in which the development of modern urban planning was shaped by social and political circumstances within the new nation before 1917, and by business interest and state intervention after that date. It will concentrate on those urban (and suburban) visions that have received less attention in the discussion of this period, by putting debates about community planning alongside grand urban visions. It traces certain threads of influence from late-nineteenth-century social reform, via state planning legislation, to the investment in modern architecture by business in the 1930s. In particular the impact of the garden city movement is considered here not as an 'alternative' to modernity, but as an alternative form of the modern.[4]

In February 1920 the Czech government announced the establishment of the State Planning Commission for Prague and its Environs (under the Ministry of Public Works). The commission produced the Greater Prague Act a year later, which essentially extended the jurisdiction of the city planners to cover the regions surrounding the city and bring them under a single administration. The act covered transportation, public health and social amenities, and designated various areas for specific industrial or residential development, as well as legislating for the protection of the city's historic core and its green areas. The final plan was published in 1928 and this affected all future development until the war.

Masaryk's new government was a broad church: a centre-left coalition of the five main parties was elected to power in 1920, which bolstered the President's social-democratic approach. The participation of all but the most extreme of political parties meant that most social groups – Slovak, Czech, and German-speaking – were represented in parliament. Popular support for Masaryk's social agenda helped to create a culture in which Modernism could find acceptance, and was in keeping with the creation of a new, forward-looking national identity. The State Planning Commission prioritized the social and political development of the city. The first priority was to establish Prague as the seat of the presidency, which meant providing new civic and government buildings, usually commissioned through architectural competition. The social programme for architecture was also a concern from the start – even before the establishment of the Commission, in 1919, the Construction Act in Prague laid down guidelines for the development of economical tenement housing.

As the historian Rostislav Švácha has pointed out, there were three dominant theories of urban planning enshrined in the Greater Prague Act.[5] In the central business and civic areas, a monumental plan was devised which shows the influence of Otto Wagner and the model of Vienna, with wide boulevards radiating out from central squares (as seen in the development of the district of Dejvice by Antonín Engel in the late 1920s). In the suburbs, a garden-city model was advised along the lines of the new communities which had been developed in other countries – although the aim in Prague was to create green and pleasant villa communities in the suburbs rather than to initiate the radical social changes advocated by the English pioneer of this type of urban reform, Ebenezer Howard. The third approach was the reform of the concept of the apartment block.

The development of an idea

The international garden-city movement was well known in Prague by the First World War. The utopian vision of a community created as an alternative to the sprawling, laissez-faire nineteenth-century city was outlined by Ebenezer Howard in his 1898 publication *Tomorrow: A Peaceful Path to Real Reform* (later republished as *Garden Cities of Tomorrow*). Howard envisaged the garden city as a collectively owned, self-contained satellite to the city, surrounded by green belt land. His first attempt came with the purchase of land at Letchworth near London in 1902, where he engaged the architects Barry Parker and Raymond Unwin to realize his vision. Howard's book was not published in Czech until 1924, but by this point his ideas were known in the Czech lands, mainly through the work of Unwin.

The garden-city tradition in central Europe emerged from two directions – from Vienna and the work of Camillo Sitte, and from England, via Ebenezer Howard and Unwin. As Peter Hall has pointed out, most European countries had a 'home-grown garden-city advocate' who produced a diluted ('traduced') version of Howard's philosophy in the early years of the twentieth century. The 'elementary confusion between garden city and garden suburb'[6] occurs in most built projects of the period, and Prague was no exception. The Prague-based architect Jan Kotěra had been interested in the garden-city movement since around 1905, and others followed suit in the few years before the war.[7] Czech architects with a political agenda were aware of the implications of the 'collective' model of ownership and management. But the garden city ideal was equally popular with both the state and commercial investors who saw benefits in the ideal of a stable community based around family and healthy pursuits, such as gardening. Germany also provides an interesting model for Czechoslovakia in the period up to 1933.[8] German industrialists had taken to Howard's ideas in the first few years of the twentieth century – Peter Hall points out the enthusiastic response of those who thought that 'the garden-city movement helped explain good British labour relations'[9] – and the German Garden City Association, (*Deutsche Gartenstadtbewegung*) had created a model garden city at Hellerau in 1908, which was known to Czech architects.[10] The Garden City Society of Karlsruhe in Germany (Karlsruher Gartenstadtgesellschaft), sent their travelling exhibition to the Czech lands in 1911.[11]

Ideas from England and Germany had filtered through the architectural journals and had been imported by architects travelling abroad. The journal *Styl* was at the forefront of this promotion. *Styl* was the journal of the Prague Architects Association (*Společnost Architektů*) which had been founded by Jan Kotěra, Josef Gočár, Josip Plečnik and others in 1911 in order to oppose architectural academicism. The journal promoted modern tendencies in the applied arts such as Czech Cubism, and featured a range of articles on foreign architects, among them Henri Berlage, Willem Dudok, Louis Sullivan and Frank Lloyd Wright. Its publisher and contributor, Vilém Dvorák, was largely responsible for introducing English figures of the garden-city movement, such as Raymond Unwin, to the architectural community in Prague.[12] Reciprocal visits were arranged between London and Prague, with Dvorák visiting Welwyn Garden City[13] and Unwin coming to address the Prague Architects Association.[14] In 1925, *Styl* published Unwin's address on decentralised planning to the New York Congress of the International Garden City and Town Planning Federation.[15]

The garden city (or, more properly in these cases, the garden suburb) was appropriate to the situation in Prague for a number of reasons. First, it was a progression from the interest in the design of garden villas, which had resulted in a number of significant bespoke commissions around the turn of the century. Secondly, the garden-city model, as elsewhere, represented a proposed alternative for worker housing that was a far cry from the city's cramped nineteenth-century tenement blocks. In its considerations of Modern Movement planning theories in the later 1920s, *Styl* tended to take England as a starting point for these ideas. In a series of articles entitled 'Contributions to Town Planning' in 1926–7 Pavel Janák considered two influential English models: the Georgian town square and the informal planning of Welwyn Garden City.[16] Several years later, the architect Bohumil Hübschmann pointed out the influence of Letchworth and Hampstead Garden Suburb upon the planning of Hilversum in Holland, and model housing in The Hague.[17] Janák himself cited the English influence upon the planning of villa colonies in Prague in the 1920s.

In the Czech lands, there are a number of instances of the planning of experimental workers' colonies in the period leading up to the First World War which were not necessarily based on a knowledge of Ebenezer Howard or his German counterparts. For example, in the 1880s, in the iron-working town of Vítkovice in northern Moravia, the factory owner Paul Kupelweiser built a workers' colony, incorporating schools, municipal buildings and cultural and religious institutions.[18] Kupelweiser's project, in spirit if not in design, is closest to the philanthropic and commercially astute planning activities of nineteenth-century British industrialists like Sir Titus Salt, Cadbury and Lever, and a tradition that can be traced back to Robert Owen.

In the years 1909–1912, Jan Kotěra designed a colony that was close to the social ideals of the international garden city movement (see Figure 2.1). In the industrial town of Louny in Western Bohemia, he designed a colony for railway workers and their families as a satellite district away from the town centre. The colony was largely funded by the railway company. It is a mixture of informally planned housing, from small terraces to larger detached residences and some three-storey apartment blocks. The designs were published in Kotěra's influential pamphlet *Delnicke Kolonie* (originally printed in the journal *Stavitel*), which also discussed the English, German and Dutch influences on his planning philosophies.

Kotěra was, without doubt, the most influential Czech architect and theorist of his generation. He trained in Vienna under Wagner, returning to Prague as professor in the School of Applied Arts at the end of the century. He preached a doctrine of architectural 'honesty', influenced by the principles of the *Wagnerschule*. He travelled extensively in Germany, Holland and England. His influence is probably best seen in the area of domestic design. Kotěra's designs for family villas at the beginning of this century show the influence of Voysey, Bailie-Scott and Mackintosh. He orchestrated a break from the romantic tendencies of the folk revival (of which he himself had been a part) to a more progressive and rational redesign of domestic space and services.

For Kotěra, Louny was his first opportunity to apply his ideas of the healthy and functional house to the design of communities. The design of the middle-class villa is clearly important for the development of Modernism in Czechoslovakia, as it was one of the primary opportunities for architects to experiment with the reorganization of interior space. The development of urban housing projects (apartment and tenement blocks) was largely a case of designing the façade, the interior planning being left to the developer. Bespoke villa design allowed architects a freer approach to the integration of design and ground plan. In the 1890s, the artist's villa – set in the suburbs, with garden surrounds, a studio and furnished to a high aesthetic taste – was a popular ideal for the wealthy middle classes. The fashion for folk style and anti-urban allusion set the standard for a large number of garden villas built around Prague at the turn of the century.[19] The development of the 'aesthetic interior' utilizing the signifiers of romantic national identity and folkish domesticity (the inglenook, the wooden settle) was a statement about utility and 'honesty' in design as well as comfort and tradition. These garden villas also demonstrated a more informal attitude towards interior planning, with a relaxation of the traditional division between 'private' and 'public' parts of the house.

Kotěra developed this model into a more rationalized approach, and in so doing created a blueprint for the modern villa type. He felt that this vision of simple and artistic living could be tailored to the requirements of housing for all, not just for the wealthy few. Of course, this concept then had to suit the collective as opposed to the individual, but the architectural vocabulary is clearly there in his designs for Louny – brick-built homes with steeply-pitched roofs, dormer windows, simple brick and wooden decorative details. The houses are grouped around curved roads and all have ample gardens.

Kotěra's second urban experiment came in 1909, in the Bohemian town of Hradec Králové. Kotěra was invited by the municipality to draw up plans for a New Town (*Nové Město*), linking the station to the old town, as well as to provide several new buildings for the existing town – including its museum built in 1911. Kotěra completed the plan, but work did not start on the new town until after the war. The character of Hradec Králové differs considerably from the planning strategies employed at Louny. It is more monumental and formal, it shows the influence of the *Wagnerschule* and also of Czech Cubism, and owes much to Kotěra's collaborator and former pupil, the Cubist Josef Gočár, who completed the new town after Kotěra's death in 1923.

The first garden suburb in Prague was not begun until after the war, and clearly showed the influence of Kotěra. In 1919 a competition was organized by the Building Cooperative of Public Servants to design a garden community in the north-west sector of the city (see Figure 2.2). The suburb of Ořechovka was the Bedford Park or Hampstead Garden Suburb of Prague, and acquired a similar reputation for its liberal and intellectual middle-class community. It was a garden city in style rather than in philosophy. The competition resulted in the selection of Jaroslav Vondrák and Josef Šenkýř as designers for the new suburb, although a wide range of architects, including Pavel Janak and Bohumil Hübschmann, took part. Vondrák and Šenkýř's plan was based on a central garden square, with a cultural and commercial complex of buildings. The residential streets radiate out from the centre, and the grid structure softened by some curved roads and housing blocks placed at corner angles to the street plan. Most of the suburb is made up of semi-detached houses and short terraces built to standardized domestic plans, but there are also some bespoke villas, including Vondrák's own family villa. The houses display a familiar vocabulary of suburban and domestic 'comfort' – pitched roofs, dormer windows and half-timbering. The intention of Ořechovka was to be an idyllic alternative to the modern city.

Ořechovka's anti-urban and romantic character is in sharp contrast to another well-known Prague villa colony for the wealthy middle classes. Further to the north, on a steep hillside overlooking the city is the colony of Na Baba. The site of a housing exhibition planned in 1929 (although work did not begin until 1932) by the Czech equivalent to the Werkbund, the Czechoslovak Decorative Arts Association (*Svaz československého díla*), the Baba Colony took as its model the German Werkbund's Weissenhof colony of 1927, and a number of public exhibitions of new housing solutions of the later 1920s and early 1930s. In 1928, for example, the *Svaz* had organized an exhibition of new housing in Brno. Although the Prague exhibition was originally conceived as an experiment in standardized housing, its brief gradually shifted in the delay before construction began to a colony of individual luxury villas. Pavel Janák was selected to produce a plan for the site, and a wide range of Modernist architects were commissioned to design the thirty or so individual family villas. Janák justified the focus of the colony as an attempt to 'stabilize' one of the most common housing types in the country – the villa. Despite the assertively Modernist idiom in which the villas were designed – white walls, sun terraces and flat roofs – Baba is at heart a garden suburb. It provided for a broad artistic and literary clientele, as well as for bankers, professors and publishers. Standardization and minimum cost were not of paramount concern to such an audience. Despite debate in the architectural press, the popular image of Modernism was one of leisure and commerce (the department store, the cinema and the villa) rather than one of state provision for the poor.

Once the Greater Prague Act of 1921 had legislated for the development of garden suburbs in the city, two plans were begun for state-subsidized worker colonies. The colonies of Spořilov, known as the 'clerks town', and Zahradní Město (literally 'Garden Town') were built to house city workers and their families in the later 1920s. Both of these also benefitted from commercial investment. In the case of Spořilov this investment came from the Vinohrady Savings Bank. Construction began in 1925 on a site to the south-east of the city to a plan by Josef Barek. Barek, together with the architects

Vlastimil Brožek and Karel Polívka, planned this community of around one thousand family dwellings using eight variations of house design. Most of this is terraced housing, all with private gardens and grouped around 'village' squares. For the construction, which took four years, many prefabricated elements were manufactured on site.

The suburb of Zahradní Město in Záběhlice, planned in 1928, was also designed to meet the needs of a large worker community. The plan was the responsibility of Alex Hanuš, who designed a central grid plan – the main square flanked by three- to four-storey commercial and apartment blocks – with curved residential roads which fanned out from the sides. The housing (about 740 dwellings) ranged from garden terraced houses to some individual detached villas.

Such projects provided a workable and economically viable solution to problems of sanitation and mass construction. However, as they lacked a didactically Modernist image they received scant attention from the press and later, from historians. They were popular with both the state and with commerce as they stressed a traditional social structure, with much-vaunted characteristics of domesticity and 'family values'. As construction continued on both these sites in the late 1920s and early 1930s, it is possible to see the 'Unwinesque' style of the cottages give way to a Modernist language, as flat roofs, sun terraces with steel railings and porthole windows are incorporated.

In the late 1920s debate shifted towards the design of mass housing and collective living. The Czech contribution to the 1930 Brussels Congrès International d'Architecture Moderne (C.I.A.M) was the preparation of the report on Minimum-Existence Housing by the 'Leva Fronta' (Left Front) group, consisting of Karel Teige and others. The work of the Leva Fronta indicated a dramatic ideological shift, based upon criticisms of the social situation. Yet the compromises over the Baba Housing Exhibition show that the acceptance of Modernism in the Czech lands at this point was tempered by the strength of interest in the individual family villa,[20] and by the cultural investment in traditional modes of living.

The factory in the garden

Such is the background to the social philosophy of what was probably Czechoslovakia's most successful industrial enterprise of the pre-1945 period: the shoe company Bata, based in the town of Zlín, Moravia. As a case study, Bata provides a lesson in the enduring influence of the garden-city movement and the tradition of model factory towns from Robert Owen's 'New Lanark' onwards. The ideological apparatus behind Bata was patriarchal, conservative, and Victorian in its morality. Yet its use of architecture was daring and dynamic, and it promoted a progressive cosmopolitanism to the outside world.

The Bata Shoe Company was set up by Tomáš Bata and his brother at the end of the nineteenth century. The business grew from a small shoemaker's business to a factory-owning company in a few years. The transformation of the company had essentially taken place by the end of the First World War. Influenced by his experiences travelling to industrial regions in Germany and America (in 1900 and 1904 respectively) Bata returned to Zlín to set up a centralized factory system. A further visit to Ford's River Rouge plant in Detroit (and several other factory communities) in 1919 led to the complete 'Fordizing' of his own production system.[21] Until his death in a plane crash in 1933, the standardization and rationalization of the production system were principles which Bata extended to the planning of his factory community. After his death, this project was continued by his half-brother until the nationalization of the business in 1946. The company weathered difficult economic times in the early 1920s through a policy of aggressive expansion. Several other satellite factory communities were set up in Czechoslovakia, and a number abroad.[22] Bata established its own retail outlets in most Czech towns and cities, which were later upgraded to distinctive modern department stores designed by the company's in-house architecture department. Tomáš Bata's forays into local politics secured further control over Zlín: he effectively supplied the town's power and communication systems, as well as employing most of its inhabitants. By 1923, the planning of company housing was already in hand, and it is worth referring to Bata's own words from a published speech of 1931:

It would not be difficult to create a town with 50 000 people huddled in the barracks or tenement houses without caring as to how their wives and children are living and what opportunities for earning they have in the town. Our aim is to build a garden town, full of sunshine, water and green grass – a clean town with the highest of wages, prosperous crafts and business, a town with the best of schools. It is our endeavour to free our women from the last traces of physical labour and help them to arrange their homes in which they may take pride.[23]

The underlying principles of Bata's vision of an ideal industrial community can be traced to a number of sources. Mention has already been made of the influence of Fordist principles on both industrial and social relations. Bata's picture of a stable and productive community was based on an ideal of hard work and company loyalty, sharpened by competitiveness and motivation on the part of the individual worker. Family duty and pride were central to this stability, marked by his (one of many) company slogan: 'work as a collective, live as an individual'.[24]

Bata's personal domestic ideal is clearly demonstrated in the design of his family home in Zlín. It was initially under construction by a local building firm, but Bata's first meeting with Jan Kotěra led to the architect taking over the project in 1911. The house is characteristic of Kotěra's villa designs from some years earlier, although somewhat subdued in character – an informally planned arts and crafts family house, with vernacular detailing and a simple interior. After the house was completed, Kotěra was retained as architectural adviser to the Bata company until his death in 1923. It can be assumed that Kotěra's own interest in the planning of worker colonies in garden city principles had an effect upon the Bata community. As the First World War began, Kotěra was asked to draw up plans for the town centre of Zlín and the first phase of residential development. Work began on the construction of this after the war, but the economic difficulties of the early 1920s meant that little was completed. The planning of Bata's vision of a 'garden factory' was continued by Kotěra's pupil František Lydie Gahura, who was appointed chief architect of Zlín in 1923. A couple of years later Bata established its own architecture department, which was to become the third centre of modern architectural development in Czechoslovakia (after Prague and Brno).

There is a clear demarcation between the innovations in industrial and public architecture at Zlín, and the domestic vision. The worker housing conformed to a simple model: first two, and later three-bedroom houses, with a living area, kitchen and bathroom, built to a principle of 'modest simplicity in design, construction and materials'[25] (see Figure 2.4). The houses were provided with substantial allotment gardens. Usually they were arranged on a 'chequerboard' pattern, placing houses to the front or back of the plot alternately. This gave maximum privacy and surrounding green space, and had been used on other garden-city plans of the 1920s. Even the factory quarter of the town was – according to Gahura's 1924 plan – to be arranged around green spaces and leafy avenues: this he called *továrna v zahradách* or 'the factory in the garden': 'Ever since the beginning we have tried to build up the town in such a way as to grow organically out of the industrial architecture forms and with the new conception of life and work of an industrial city'.[26]

This 'new conception of life and work' was, of course, directed towards the highest possible output and profit for the company, whose employees found their social life and leisure time bound tightly to the company structure.[27] Undoubtedly, the public profile of the company and its pride in its innovative methods meant that material conditions for workers were most probably better than elsewhere. But, with Bata being both employer and landlord to the huge majority of his workers, Zlín depended upon the company's good fortunes, right down to its basic amenities.

Bata was fast becoming a national icon by the 1930s, and a symbol of the country's phenomenal industrialization. Up until his death, Tomáš pioneered a kind of evangelizing entrepreneurialism – he lectured, campaigned and published, he set up trade schools in Zlín and promoted new forms of divisional management.[28] In short, departments were made more competitive, employees were given a share in their department's successes – and of course, had to account for any failures. When the company went through periods of difficulty, workers would take a 'voluntary' pay cut to compensate for Bata's reduction in the national average cost of the company's goods, in return for cheaper rents for a limited period – and, naturally, free shoes. The company philosophy was extended to his workers' moral and educational welfare, and that of their families. The much promoted deal for married women workers offered them a shorter working day for a lower wage – so they could start later, finish earlier, and have a longer lunch break at home to prepare for their children and husband. Family obligations had to be met, particularly when they coincided with the company's financial interests. This all formed part of what has been referred to as Bata's 'moral testament'.

This philosophy was reflected in the planning of the city. Only after Tomáš's death did the Bata architects get the opportunity to experiment with forms of collective housing, and to build large-scale multistorey dwellings. Before this, Bata declared itself vehemently against anything which interfered with the 'traditional' family structure. The social collective was never seen as an alternative. In fact, Bata's community planning philosophy has all the hallmarks of the 'philanthropic' health and hygiene campaigns of the late nineteenth century in Britain: 'every man, every family, not living in the city, should have a house which gives him healthy living according to the demands of modern life.'[29]

By the late 1920s the company had developed a standardized construction system, based upon one employed in American factories. This consisted of a concrete skeleton in modules of 6.15 square metres and was used to construct all manner of buildings – factories, department stores, the Zlín hotel, hostels and civic amenities and so on. Most buildings used brick infill; others, like Tomáš Bata's memorial building in Zlín,[30] were given a glass 'skin'. It was a flexible and economic system, which allowed for multistorey, multipurpose buildings (such as the seventeen-storey Zlín administration building, designed by Vladimír Karfík). It was not, however, utilized in the first phase of construction for housing, as Bata's philosophy still favoured an image of conventional family life: 'For the right feeling of family life is required a dwelling, separated from the neighbours, in the free space of a green garden, air and sun – about the same as were built in our colony.'[31]

For Bata in the 1930s, the use of modern architecture was expedient rather than visionary. Although the corporate image presented through Bata's stores was luxurious and cosmopolitan and in design terms innovative for its time, the company took a more puritan attitude to its control over its employees' environment. This is evident when we consider the dealings between the company and Le Corbusier in the mid 1930s. Clearly regarding Bata as a corporation which might allow him to put into practice his dynamic city plans (at that point the concept of the 'linear' city), Le Corbusier prepared a number of projects for it.[32] These included two city complexes (one in Zlín and one in Hellocourt, France), as well as designs for a Bata pavilion for the 1937 Paris Exposition. None were used. The company evidently rejected Le Corbusier's proposal for multistorey apartment blocks, and the collaboration ended acrimoniously.

However, Le Corbusier's shortlived contact with Zlín had left an impression on the architects' department, which incorporated some of his ideas many years later. In the later 1930s, the department produced many plans for the high-density development of the city, beginning with three-four-storey blocks before the war and moving towards system-built standard developments in the 1940s and 50s, once the company had been nationalized. The architects' department proved to be a vital training ground for many young modern architects in the 1930s. It is doubtful that many of them were there because they shared in the Bata social vision. A number of them who worked there in the later 1930s and stayed after the war were associated with the radical left. Working for Bata put architects in touch with the leading figures of Czech Modernism, a number of whom had considerable experience abroad. Vladimír Karfík, enticed back from the United States by Jan Bata shortly after the Wall Street Crash, had worked for a short time with Le Corbusier in Paris, and then for a longer period with Frank Lloyd Wright at Taliesin. After 1927–8, Brno was becoming a recognized centre of architectural innovation, and there were close links between its societies, exhibitions and publications and the Bata architects.

If we compare Bata's vision to that of Unwin in his declarations on community cooperation, we can see the extent to which they differ. The provision of community amenities by local manufacturers, such as power and communication systems, as recommended by Ebenezer Howard, has clearly been achieved. The integration of planning and architecture has also taken place, allowing the community to develop according to a single, rather than competing, vision. The symbolic and physical centre of the town was not the green or the community hall, but the factory; with the city's amenities, and the Bata Memorial itself, all oriented towards the factory complex. Zlín in some ways was an embodiment of Unwin's vision of a town as 'the outward expression of an orderly community of people'.[33] Yet fundamentally, Bata's vision entailed the *separation* of the individual and the family unit from society. In creating an industry based on individual and interdepartmental competitiveness (and financial reward) he undermined any idea of worker-collectives.[34] His enthusiasm for a garden-city model of community planning came from a desire to impose social stability and exercise paternalistic concern. In a different political context after the war, the Bata philosophy became an exemplar of selfish individualism. The leftist architect Karel Honzik predicted a 'modern flood' of homes and cars as the result of such demands (see Figure 2.5).

There is no doubt that two main factors contributed to the success of the Modern Movement in Czechoslovakia between the wars: firstly, a strong middle class which embraced the 'democratic' and progressive image of Modernism; and secondly, the industrial and economic successes of the new nation, which gave Modernist architects the ability to realize their ideas. However, as I hope I have shown, these factors were further determined by two other considerations: firstly, that Modernist urban visions were greatly affected by the widespread acceptance of garden-city ideas in the Czech lands; and secondly, that this was based on a broadly reactionary social interest, rather than on a radical desire for change.

Notes

1. In Jaroslav Anděl (ed.), *The Art of the Avant-Garde in Czechoslovakia 1918–38*, Valencia: IVAM Centre Julio Gonzalez, 1993.

2. For example, exhibitions such as *Tschechische Kunst der 20er and 30er Jahre: Avant Garde & Tradition*, Darmstadt, 1988; Alexander vou Vegesack (ed.), *Czech Cubism*, co-organized by Vitra Design Museum and the Prague Museum of Decorative Arts, 1992; and *The Art of the Avant-Garde in Czechoslovakia*.

3. There is a danger of seeing Prague as representative of the whole of Czechoslovakia. To take the case of Slovakia, for example, the interwar period was an extremely productive time of architectural activity, particularly in the areas of health and leisure. For further detail, see *Moderná Architektura na Slovensku 20 a 30 Roky*, exhibition catalogue, Spolok Architektov Slovenska, 1991, and L. Foltyn, *Slowakische Architektur und die Tschechische Avantgarde 1918–39*, Dresden: Verlag der Kunst, 1991.

4. The premise for looking at urban visions and modernity in this way comes from influential studies such as Marshall Berman, *All that is Solid Melts into Air*, London: Verso, 1985, and Peter Hall, *Cities of Tomorrow*, Oxford: Blackwell, 1988.

5. R. Švacha, *The Architecture of the New Prague 1895–1945*, Boston: MIT Press, 1995, pp.141–51.

6. P. Hall, *Cities of Tomorrow*, Oxford: Blackwell, 1988, pp.113–14.

7. The garden-city principle was also applied to areas of Brno and Bratislava at around the same time. See Foltyn, pp.39–44.

8. England and Germany provided the most influential models for domestic planning before the war, as pointed out by the architect Jaromir Krejcar, in his publication *L'architecture Contemporaine en Tchechoslovaquie*, Prague, 1928.

9. Hall, p.115.

10. V. Šlapeta, J. Musil, and J. Novak, 'Czech Mate for Letchworth', *Town & Country Planning*, November 1984, pp.314–15.

11. V. Šlapeta, in W. Leśnikowski (ed.), *East European Modernism, Architecture in Czechoslovakia, Hungary and Poland between the Wars*, London: Thames & Hudson, 1996, p.40.

12. Unwin apparently received an honorary degree from the University: F. Jackson, *Sir Raymond Unwin: Architect, Planner & Visionary*, London: Zwemmer, 1985, p.159.

13. *Styl* contained frequent references to Welwyn. See V. Dvorák, 'Zahradní Město Welwyn u Londýna', *Styl*, V, 1924-5, p.101-8.
14. Unwin's address to the Prague Architects Association of May 1923 is published in *Styl*, IV, 1923-4, pp.79-84.
15. First published in the *Transactions of the International Garden City and Town Planning Federation Congress*, New York, 1925.
16. P. Janák, 'Příspěvky ku stavbě měst I', *Styl*, XII, 1926-7, pp.61-72.
17. B. Hübschmann, 'Anglická Cesta' (The English Way), *Styl*, XIV, 1928-9, pp.149-52.
18. See M. Matěj, I. Korbelářová, and P. Levá, *Nové Vítkovice 1876-1914*, Památkový ústrav v. Ostráve, Ostrava, 1992. I am grateful to Dr Peter Krajci of the National Technical Museum, Prague, for this information.
19. The fashion for vernacular was largely the result of the 1895 Prague Czecho-Slav Ethnographic Exhibition. Petr Wittlich quotes the artist-critic Milos Jiránek, who said in 1909 that the exhibition gave rise to a fashionable folkishness: ' "national costumes" that came straight from the Prague dressmakers, and "folk art" from patrician households, with painted embroidery in varnished frames'. P. Wittlich, *Prague Fin de Siècle*, Paris: Flammarion, 1992.
20. Vladimír Šlapeta has pointed out that, after Baba, 'the single-family house became a typological category in which all the nuances of the functionalist style were applied'. In Leśnikowski, *East European Modernism*, p.88.
21. For a more detailed account of the Bata Company and its architectural philosophy, see J. Pavitt, 'The Bata Project', *Twentieth Century Architecture, The Journal of the Twentieth Century Society*, no.1, 1994, pp.32-44. Also *Bata, Architektúra a Urbanismus 1910-50*, exhibition catalogue, Zlín, 1991. For a more personalized account of the company's history, see T. Bata, Jun. and S. Sinclair, *Bata: Shoemaker to the World*, Toronto: Stoddart, 1990.
22. Factory towns were built in Poland, Hungary, France, Germany, Switzerland, Yugoslavia and England. There were factories also in South Africa, India, Egypt, Singapore, and a failed attempt in the USA. All were designed on similar principles, ulitizing the same construction techniques and similar residential plans, produced by the Architects' Department in Zlín. See Pavitt, 1994.
23. T. Bata (translated by J. Baros), *How I Began*, Batanagar, India, 1941, p.204.
24. Vladimir Karfik, chief architect for Bata, recalled Bata's belief that '... the man who has a flat in a building with a garden is more stable, and instead of following politics would rather potter about in the garden or sit out on the lawn, so he doesn't go to the pub or political meetings' From *Bata, Architektura a Urbanismus 1910-1950*, Zlín, 1991, p.106.
25. Slapeta *et al.*, 'Czech Mate for Letchworth', p.315.
26. F. Gahura, in J. Setnićka, 'Urbanismus Architektura závodů Bata a.s. ve Zlíné', *Stavitel* (undated), p.6.
27. It is interesting to note that the Bata philosophy came under attack in England in the 1950s, when local trade unions and the *Daily Worker* attacked them for the outdated system of 'tied cottages' still operating in their community at East Tilbury, Essex.
28. According to V. Karfik, Bata had the slogan 'There are 86 400 seconds in a day' emblazoned on the factory's perimeter fence. *Bata*, 1991, p.106.
29. Tomáš Bata in a speech of 1931. T. Bata, 1941, p.60.
30. Designed in 1932 by Gahura and Zdeněk Rossmann. The glass gallery contained a Bata plane, as a sign of how Tomáš had died. The plane has since been removed, and the building is now the town art gallery.
31. T. Bata, 1941, p.201.
32. K. Frampton, *Le Corbusier, Architect of the Century*, London: Arts Council, 1987, p.29.
33. Unwin, 1909, quoted in LeGates & Stout, *The City Reader*, London: Routledge, 1996, p.357.
34. The company was initially supportive of a workers' union, hoping it would encourage good management-worker communication. But after strikes in the early 1920s, Bata fought hard against unionization. See T. Bata and S. Sinclair, 1990.

2.1 Jan Kotěra, workers' colony at Louny

2.4 Family house in Zlín, 1930s

2.2 (opposite top) Ořechovka Garden Suburb, Prague

2.3 (opposite bottom) Spořilov Garden Suburb, Prague, 1920s

2.5 'The Modern Flood': from K. Honzík, *Tvorba Životního Slohu*. Karel Honzík's criticism of modern individualism and consumption uses an image of Zlín with an image of Fordism. The top photo shows the first stage of residential development in Zlín from the 1920s (those houses with pitched roofs are among the earliest)

3

Networks and boundaries: German art centres and their satellites, 1815–1914

Robin Lenman

Against the background of immense political, social and economic changes in the century after the end of the Napoleonic Wars, the structure of the German art world was also transformed. Artistic styles – and eventually also media – proliferated. There was a large increase in the number of artists, and a major expansion of what might be described as the 'art scene', measured by the volume of art criticism in the press, the number of societies devoted to art, of visitors to museums and exhibitions, of books on aesthetics and art history and of amateur painters and children studying art in school. The art market also grew and changed, bursting its originally local and regional boundaries to become national and international in scope. This last development was all the more striking in Germany, since the country's cultural geography was (and to a certain extent remains today) for historical reasons essentially polycentric, with individual centres retaining their own distinct identities. By 1914, however, Berlin was assuming the status of a national capital in cultural as well as in political terms.

As far as the visual arts were concerned, Berlin's increasing dominance was the culmination of a century of shifting relationships between several major art-production centres. Prominent in the Romantic era, when its art community included names such as Carus, Dahl, Friedrich and Richter, was the Saxon capital, Dresden. This heroic period was followed by several decades of semi-stagnation. But in the 1890s and 1900s the city's fortunes revived: partly because of the reorganization of its exhibition system; partly because of the presence of a new generation of younger *plein-airiste* painters (and, for a while, the Expressionist 'Brücke' group); but mainly because of Dresden's association with the modern applied arts movement.

Düsseldorf's trajectory was rather different. Its heyday lasted from the 1820s until the 1850s, when its academy and its schools of landscape and narrative painting enjoyed an international reputation. Indeed, it was widely regarded as the German art centre *par excellence*, and so attracted numerous American and other foreign artists. Subsequently, at least in relative terms, Düsseldorf's position declined, partly because of changes in artistic fashion, but also because its originally idyllic character disappeared: in 1910 a French visitor wrote disparagingly of a steel town with a few resident picture-makers.[1] The chief beneficiary of Düsseldorf's eclipse was Munich, which in the second half of the nineteenth century was central Europe's leading art-production and market centre. Its assets included a celebrated academy, huge royal collections and August Voit's spacious Glaspalast, which from 1858 onwards provided the venue for a succession of ambitious national and international salons. Especially between the 1860s and the late 1880s, moreover, the city profited from the kind of artistic and commercial links with the United States previously enjoyed by Düsseldorf. Competition from Berlin intensified from the mid 1880s onwards, but Munich remained lively and prosperous, and in 1914 still had the empire's largest share of art exports.

Nevertheless it was almost inevitable that, after 1871, Berlin's importance would grow. During the Wilhelmine period in particular, and intensified by concerns about 'Americanism' and other foreign influences, debates raged about the quality of the city's culture – indeed, about whether it had a culture at all.[2] However, Berlin's vast increase in size and wealth, coupled with state efforts to create the cultural infrastructure appropriate to an imperial capital, proved increasingly attractive to artistic talent. And there was also the unique atmosphere of a great metropolis. Like Dickens' London and the Paris of Hugo and Balzac, imperial Berlin offered extreme contrasts between opulence and misery and opportunities for spine-tingling forays into a wilderness of industrial slums and suburbs. This vision of modernity in the raw drew Expressionists like Kirchner and Pechstein from Dresden and other places, and led the poet Jakob von Hoddis and Ludwig Meidner, painter of apocalyptic cityscapes, to wander night-long through the streets. Daybreak over the city's tenements, recalled Meidner later, seemed to them 'beautiful, magnificent, unique, yes, sublime and inexpressibly alluring'.[3]

A significant element in the appeal of most art centres, and equally important as a stimulus to both artists and art-lovers (themselves often art-buyers), was the existence of major art galleries. The nineteenth century was the predominant age both of museum-building and of the de-privatization of Europe's vast dynastic collections, in many countries (though not Britain) secured as part of a national, inalienable and publicly accessible cultural heritage. Particularly outstanding in Germany were the Dresden Royal Gallery, which contained treasures like Raphael's *Sistine Madonna*, and the Alte Pinakothek in Munich, housing the best of the ruling Wittelsbach family's pre-1800 acquisitions plus the Boisserée and Wallerstein collections of early German paintings bought by King Ludwig I. Both these royal institutions and new privately-founded galleries like the Wallraff-Richartz Museum in Cologne and the Städel Institute in Frankfurt am Main were rich in seventeenth-century Dutch pictures which had an important influence on contemporary genre and landscape painting. From the middle decades of the century onwards modern galleries (or sections of galleries) also proliferated, initially often regional but then increasingly national and international in scope. In Berlin the programme of cultural investment already mentioned included heavy spending on museums and the recruitment of curatorial talent from all over Germany. By 1914 state spending, the fund-raising talents of Wilhelm von Bode (Director General of the Prussian Museums) and the generosity – despite his notorious aversion to modern art – of Wilhelm II had raised the main collections to world-class stature. (Düsseldorf was the principal exception here since, partly by way of inheritance, its electoral gallery had been permanently removed to Munich at the turn of the eighteenth and nineteenth centuries; however, modern communications placed the city within reach of the galleries in Antwerp and Holland.)

As important as art collections, and functionally linked to them, were training facilities. The Dresden Academy attracted students from all over central and northern Europe in the early nineteenth century and, under the banner of *plein-airisme*, was important again by the 1900s. The refounding of the moribund Düsseldorf Academy in 1819 was (like the creation of a new university in Bonn) part of Prussian integration policy in its recently acquired Rhine province. Its international reputation by the mid century owed much to its second director, Wilhelm von Schadow from Berlin, whose pedagogical emphasis, in his best years, on colour and naturalism matched the middle-class public's taste for realistic narrative paintings. The Munich Academy's fame also owed much to a particular individual, in this case Karl Theodor Piloty. Although he specialized in large-scale salon historicism, the techniques needed to create the wall-to-wall pathos and melodrama of vast canvases like *Thusnelda in the Triumph of Germanicus* (1869–73) were readily adaptable to small genre pieces suitable for the ordinary home. Younger teachers like Franz Defregger and Wilhelm Diez trained hundreds of practitioners in this field and, especially in their own more private work, verged on the Realism associated with non-academic artists like Wilhelm Leibl and Frank Duveneck. In the 1890s the appointment of the young prodigy Franz Stuck kept the Academy abreast of emerging Symbolism and *Jugendstil*.

In Berlin the historical specialist Anton von Werner, effectively Wilhelm II's court painter, shared the Emperor's hostility to modern *plein-airisme* and Impressionism. But, as long-serving (1875–1914) director of the Berlin Academy's art school, he presided over important curriculum reforms and a substantial increase in student numbers. In an increasingly competitive atmosphere, the academies' perceived contribution to the reputation of art centres was demonstrated by the large sums spent on new buildings, the inducements offered to star teachers, and the early age – inconceivable for equivalent posts in the army or civil service – at which some directors were appointed: von Werner, for example, at thirty-two and Friedrich Kaulbach in Munich (in 1886) at thirty-six. Other selling points, such as entry requirements and the funding of grants and prizes, received careful consideration, and public criticism from within faculties, as in Munich in the late 1880s, was rigorously suppressed.

As in Paris, the presence of state institutions encouraged the proliferation of other training opportunities. Many of the Americans in mid-nineteenth-century Düsseldorf, for example, were not studying at the Academy but either working independently or taking more or less formal tuition from German masters like Andreas Achenbach or 'senior' compatriots like Emanuel Leutze.[4] Munich during the regency of Prince Luitpold (1886–1912) had many private schools; some of them, like the establishments run by Heinrich Knirr and Anton Azbé, providing preparatory training for the Academy, while others, such as the art and craft workshops run by Wilhelm von Debschitz and Hermann Obrist, offered more flexible alternative curricula. Much of the demand for private-sector teaching came from female artists, whose numbers increased considerably from the 1870s onwards, but who were barred from the leading state academies before 1918. Many academy professors – Emil Neide in Königsberg, for example, an early teacher of Käthe Kollwitz, and the Munich portraitist Hugo von Habermann – had lucrative private practices, while other artists, such as Lovis Corinth after he settled in Berlin in 1902, supplemented their earnings by running classes which seem mainly to have attracted women. (In Berlin, Munich and other cities there were also publicly subsidized 'ladies' academies' at which artists like Kollwitz, Gabriele Münter and Paula Modersohn-Becker did some of their training.)

The quality and range of these facilities largely explains the appeal of German centres to foreigners, many of them from countries where art schools were either wholly lacking or perceived as inferior to those abroad. Vassily Kandinsky, Alexei von Jawlensky and Marianne von Werefkin, for example, who arrived in Munich in the late 1890s, were the latest of a stream of Russians, and the city's art community also included numerous Scandinavians, Poles, Hungarians and Greeks. (The identification of nineteenth-century academies with nationalistic history-painting explains the authorities' refusal to permit one in Warsaw until 1903, and probably also the slow or non-emergence of comparable institutions in countries like Hungary, Finland and the Baltic states.) Particularly notable was the American colony in Düsseldorf, where a whole generation of major artists trained between the 1840s and the 1860s, motivated both by the absence of adequate facilities at home and by the linguistic and family links that many of them had with Germany. Most prominent was the Württemberg-born Leutze, who completed the first two versions of his famous *Washington Crossing the Delaware* in Düsseldorf in 1850–51, was a founder of the *Malkasten* (Paint-Box), one of Germany's liveliest and initially most radical artists' clubs – another American, Alfred Bierstadt, later nostalgically named his studio-mansion by the Hudson River after it[5] – and helped to establish the commercially important Düsseldorf Gallery in New York. Other Americans included Eastman Johnson, Worthington Whittredge, Carl Wimar and John Caton Woodville. The colony dwindled after Leutze returned home in 1859, and American interest subsequently shifted to Munich, which in the 1870s harboured an important Realist group centred around Duveneck and William Merritt Chase. Although they eventually left, other Americans settled permanently in Bavaria, and Carl Marr from Milwaukee ultimately became director of the Munich Academy.

The influence, via expatriates, of German training and artistic trends abroad was considerable: especially in the United States, but probably even more so (though as yet less well documented) in eastern Europe. But the presence of foreigners also added spice and variety to the German art scene. In late-nineteenth-century Munich salons, Puszta landscapes, Jewish festivals in Poland, and sleigh-borne travellers pursued by wolves mingled with such standard local fare as alpine sunsets and Bavarian peasant weddings. Earlier, the impact of the Düsseldorf Americans had been even greater. Leutze, like a previous generation of Americans in England, contributed to the 'revolution in history painting'[6] away from stylized depictions of mythic heroes towards realistic-seeming historical reportage inspired – like *Washington* by the aftermath of 1848 – by contemporary political events. Leutze's protégé Wimar, from St Louis, offered equally gripping but more exotic subjects such as *The Abduction of Daniel Boone's Daughter by the Indians* and *Attack on an Emigrant Train* which (at a time of large-scale emigration) impressed a public already captivated by literary accounts of the American wilderness.[7]

Although few Frenchmen came to study or work in Germany, and despite the political and cultural francophobia prevalent in imperial Germany, probably the single most potent foreign influence on German art came from France. An early example was the historical colourism of the 1840s and 1850s, which owed a considerable debt not only to Belgian history painting but also to Paul Delaroche in Paris, internationally celebrated for such macabre costume melodramas as *The Execution of Lady Jane Grey* and *Cromwell Contemplating the Corpse of Charles I*. Still more influential, later, was the Barbizon landscape school, to which Germans were extensively exposed at major shows like the Munich international salon of 1869, through the galleries of leading private collectors, for whom a sprinkling of Barbizon pictures became practically *de rigueur*, and via the quality reproductions available by the late nineteenth century. German Realism was also indebted to the French; especially to Courbet, who spent time in Frankfurt and Munich in the early 1850s,[8] and to Manet, who (like Courbet) showed at the 1869 Munich exhibition. Subsequently, France's rapid recovery after the Franco-Prussian War and the reform of the state training system inevitably – and despite cries of disapproval at home – attracted increasing numbers of Germans to Paris, described by the British *Magazine of Art* in 1881 as 'the centre of the world, . . . the art school of the world . . . and the art market of the world'.[9] (The French capital's increasingly powerful appeal to both Europeans and Americans partly accounted for the declining numbers of foreign students in German art centres from the 1880s onwards.)

Enormously influential, in Germany as elsewhere, was the Naturalism of Jules Bastien-Lepage, whose images of poor country people, painted (on the whole) *en plein air*, had an unmistakable impact on the controversial 'poverty-painting' of proto-Secessionist figures like Carl Bantzer, Gotthard Kuehl, Max Liebermann and Fritz von Uhde in the 1880s and 1890s. By the turn of the century, finally, there was the influence of French Impressionism, exerting itself through the dealing and publishing activities of Paul and Bruno Cassirer, the writings of Richard Muther and Julius Meier-Graefe, and the activities of wealthy private collectors in Berlin and elsewhere. At least ten of the Monets and Manets in the important Faure collection in Paris, for example, eventually ended in German hands.[10] Private generosity also enabled museums such as the Berlin National Gallery, the Munich Neue Pinakothek and the Mannheim Gallery to acquire expensive French masterpieces, often in the teeth of opposition from supervisory committees and, in Berlin, the Emperor. In 1906 Hugo von Tschudi, successively director of the Berlin National Gallery and the Bavarian State Galleries, wrote: 'For the painting of the nineteenth century France is the classic soil, like Italy for the Renaissance and Holland for the painting of the seventeenth century. There is scarcely a problem of modern art that was not addressed and brought to its ultimate solution in France'.[11] Such views, and von Tschudi's francophile acquisition programmes, were bitterly opposed in Parliament, by right-wing critics and by artist-politicians such as Anton von Werner and Carl Vinnen, author of the notorious *German Artists' Protest* (against French art-imports) of 1911. Their polemics anticipated a much fiercer nationalist backlash during and after the First World War. In 1914, however, the cosmopolitanism of the German art world, and especially its openness to modern French art, was probably rivalled only by that of the eastern United States.

Another aspect of the cosmopolitanism of German art centres was their role as points of access to an increasingly integrated and far-flung market. The fact that for much of the nineteenth century Scandinavia, eastern Europe and most of the United States offered only limited commercial opportunities was another reason for ambitious artists to seek their fortunes abroad. In Munich between 1869 and the early 1870s, for example, the Pole Aleksander Gierymski and the Hungarian Pál Szinyei-Merse, both young men at the start of their careers, were wooed by both local and foreign dealers;[12] while the Norwegian Edvard Munch owed much of his fame and prosperity by 1914 to German sales and patronage.[13] Market outlets were of various kinds. The longest-established were the academy salons started in the eighteenth century and by the end of the nineteenth run wholly or partly by artists' own organizations. As in other countries, they became increasingly large and problem-ridden, with a tendency by the late 1880s to spawn smaller, 'Secessionist' exhibiting societies (Germany's earliest formal Secession, in Munich, held its first exhibition in 1893; its Berlin counterpart was founded in 1898). For all their defects, however, the big salons had a massive financial turnover, attracted thousands of visitors and offered significant career advantages in the form of prizes and publicity. Their perceived contribution to the prestige of the art centres was reflected in the amounts of public money devoted to them – both for exhibition buildings and picture-acquisitions for state galleries – and the pageantry surrounding their openings.

Another vital outlet was the *Kunstverein* (art union) network, which developed rapidly after the Napoleonic Wars and eventually became international in scope: the Hamburg *Kunstverein*'s spring exhibition in 1846, for example, included items from Austria, Switzerland, France and the Low Countries as well as from all over Germany.[14] Especially in the pre-unification period German art unions were strongly committed to the creation of nationalist monumental art; and the Rhenish-Westphalian society in particular contributed large sums to such projects in places as far apart as Aachen (Alfred Rethel's frescoes in the Imperial Hall) and Memel.[15] But *Kunstvereine* also played a vital pump-priming role in the development of a middle-class picture market. By the early 1840s the Dresden-based Saxon art union had branches throughout central Germany and members as far afield as London and St Petersburg,[16] while its Rhenish-Westphalian counterpart had similar links with American cities. Although by 1900 some older societies were stagnating, new and in some cases very progressive ones were still being founded, and the movement as a whole continued to channel considerable funds to artists up until and through the First World War.

A third and, from the 1850s onwards, increasingly important component of the market was the art trade. Although some dealers were crooked or incompetent, the leading firms were playing a vital regulatory role in the marketplace by 1914 and, with their elegant city-centre galleries and contacts with museums, were respected members of the business community. Major growth points were the established art centres: Dresden, Düsseldorf and

Munich; Berlin with its gigantic sales potential; and the industrial cities along the Rhine and the Ruhr. New talent was snapped up as soon as it appeared. Within less than a year of their breakthrough in Munich in 1895, for example, the first-generation Worpswede painters were on show in the Schulte Gallery in Cologne.[17] And trade rivalries created opportunities even for the avant-garde, so that in prewar Munich several new firms competed to show the work of the 'Blaue Reiter' group.[18] By founding branches in promising locations in Germany and abroad – Cassirer in Cologne; the Munich firm of Heinemann on the Riviera – and allying with other firms – Cassirer, again, with Durand-Ruel and Bernheim *jeune* for the Faure and Pellerin sales in 1906 and 1909;[19] Herwarth Walden with galleries all over north and central Europe for his avant-garde touring exhibitions[20] – dealers increased the overall integration of the market and eroded regional and national boundaries.

Another aspect of integration was the relationship between country painting colonies and the main centres. Given the popularity of landscape and rustic genre-painting throughout the hundred years from 1815 to 1914, most artists spent weeks or months every year sketching and gathering material for pictures to be worked up during the winter in their urban studios. At the same time industrialization was transforming the character of the German *Kunststädte*; in early-twentieth-century Dresden, for example, the 'Brücke' artists depicted a bleak expanse of factories, gasometers and railway shunting-yards spreading outwards from the old city.[21] But Dresden, Düsseldorf and Munich all had superb scenic hinterlands, and neighbouring village communities were still fairly unspoiled in 1914; indeed, even the Berlin Kurfürstendamm was only a short distance away from the beauties of rural Brandenburg. As communications improved many artists travelled much further afield, to the Bavarian and Tyrolean Alps, the coasts of France, Belgium and Holland, and the fishing villages of northern Denmark and west Cornwall. Some actually settled in the country: by the 1890s, for example, the Realists Wilhelm Leibl and Johann Sperl had retreated permanently to the hamlet of Kutterling in the alpine foothills. In the prewar period Kandinsky and Gabriele Münter owned a house in Murnau near the Staffelsee, and Franz Marc lived successively in the villages of Sindelsdorf and Ried. By this time local bus and train services brought visitors from far and wide, and daily or twice-daily bundles of mail; telegrams (when the postmaster remembered) could be sent from Sindelsdorf,[22] and by 1914 Marc in Ried even had a telephone.[23] Disruptive though these links sometimes proved to be, they were increasingly necessary for the business of art production, and symbolized the artists' membership of an international avant-garde community.

In addition to micro-settlements like Murnau there were also regular country colonies that, in some cases over decades, harboured large numbers of artists. Some of these places, like the Chiemsee island of Frauenwörth and Dachau for Munich, and Willingshausen in Hesse for Düsseldorf, began as satellites of a particular centre but later attracted artists from much further afield. The north German colony of Worpswede, by contrast, although several of its founders were students or ex-students from Düsseldorf, functioned semi-autonomously, all the more so as its core members, at least in the early years, lived there all the year round.

As in other countries, artists had various reasons for living permanently or temporarily out of town. Obviously important was the desire to escape from the pollution, overcrowding and commercialization of the big centres, and the cliquishness of their art communities. Secondly, at least until the tourists came, living expenses were lower – especially the cost of models – and conditions by no means necessarily primitive. Admittedly the thatched *Katen* that housed the peat-cutters of the Teufelsmoor around Worpswede were rural slums in which tuberculosis and other diseases were rife. (Some of the human débris of this scattered community was depicted, in the Worpswede poorhouse, by the young Paula Becker.) But in the main settlement on the Weyersberg, even in the mid 1880s when Fritz Mackensen first arrived, there were comfortable farmhouses and no fewer than four inns, and it was here that the Worpswede painters lived until – as in other colonies such as Dachau, or Ahrenshoop on the Mecklenburg coast – the successful ones built or converted houses of their own.

A third reason for withdrawing to the country was a rebellion against academic orthodoxy. In 1849, for example, the nineteen-year-old Ludwig Knaus had decamped from the Düsseldorf Academy and its studio-bound conventions to paint real peasants in Willingshausen.[24] Otto Modersohn, repelled by the teaching in both Düsseldorf and Karlsruhe, wrote in August 1889, after he and Mackensen had decided to stay on in Worpswede through the winter: 'We are all aflame, away with the academies, down with the professors and teachers. Nature is our teacher and we must act according to her'.[25] The combination of *plein-airisme à la* Bastien-Lepage in the 1880s, and a monumentally stylized *Heimatkunst* in the next two decades, also led artists to abandon the cluttered horizons, sooty atmosphere and costumed waitress-models of the cities for the rural communities of Germany's moors and coasts.

Ties between art centres and colonies nevertheless remained strong. Although places like Ahrenshoop, Dachau and Worpswede all sooner or later acquired galleries of their own, their links with the larger network of art unions, artists' exhibiting-societies and dealers were indispensable to their prosperity. (This was not just a German phenomenon; the Newlyn colony in Cornwall, for instance, dispatched a freight-van full of paintings to the Royal Academy every summer and had numerous sales outlets in the English Midlands, whence many of its early members came.)[26] The classic example was Worpswede. After its unsuccessful début in Bremen in April 1895, the group's contacts with the Munich art establishment brought them a room to themselves at the Glaspalast exhibition a few months later. This appearance – which probably served the political purpose, for their hosts, of upstaging the Secession[27] – was a triumph, bringing a gold medal for Mackensen, the purchase of Modersohn's *Storm on the Teufelsmoor* by the Bavarian state, and many column-inches of enthusiastic reviews. It also had important commercial consequences in addition to the association with Schulte already mentioned. In the first two years of its existence (1897–9) the Worpswede Artists' Association exhibited in an impressive number of places: Dresden and Hamburg in late 1897; Frankfurt, Krefeld, Elberfeld, Stettin and Vienna in 1898; and the following year in Göttingen, Frankfurt, Vienna, Wiesbaden, Liegnitz, Darmstadt, Berlin – at the Secession's first show – and Dresden.[28] In fact the resulting pressures led Modersohn, followed by Heinrich Vogeler and Fritz Overbeck, to leave the Association in July 1899 because 'through all the obligations connected with it towards the [outside] world and exhibitions and, especially, towards each other, it is becoming seriously too much for us. It threatens our peace, which one needs above all for artistic creation'.[29] But the problems of success persisted, not least a disruptive (though lucrative) influx of would-be artists: 'much riff-raff, many little painting females [*Malweiblein*]' as the recently-settled Paula Becker told her family in September 1899.[30] (In Ahrenshoop, numbers increased so much that the most popular painting locations had to be rationed).[31] Later, artists' links with the wider art world continued to develop. Mackensen eventually became director of the Weimar Art School, and Vogeler became both a prolific illustrator for publishers such as the Insel-Verlag and a successful interior designer.

A key element in the expansion of the market and a bridge between centres and colonies was tourism. An early beneficiary was Düsseldorf, as English visitors explored the Rhine valley by steamer in the first half of the nineteenth century. (As one guide-book noted: 'SIGHT: Annual summer exhibition of paintings by living artists'.[32]) Later, the completion of the main rail networks brought floods of tourists to cities like Dresden and Munich, and by 1914 whole regions, including southern Bavaria, 'Saxon Switzerland' and the Tyrol, were being carved up into conveniently marketable packages by British travel agents such as Cook and Lunn. But well before this Munich's development strategy had been shaped to maximize its cultural assets, so as to attract both 'quality' tourists and permanent new residents for its villa suburbs.[33] The sales figures of the major exhibitions and dealers' records show that outside buyers – including many Americans – made a vital contribution to the art community's earnings; and artists for their part, through their pictures, their social activities, and by designing postcards and travel posters, boosted the city's distinctive 'fun-plus-culture' image. 'During the season,' wrote a French journalist in 1911, 'a whole cosmopolitan world inhabits the hotels, creating an atmosphere of elegance and luxury. Munich has organized itself to receive them well, to give them beautiful artistic emotions, to facilitate their excursions to the wonderful locations in the surrounding mountains'.[34]

As they grew more accessible, artists' colonies also became popular with tourists. Pre-1914 Ahrenshoop eventually accommodated four times as many summer visitors as permanent residents, causing overcrowding and inflation.[35] Worpswede had appeared in a guide-book as early as 1878, but the arrival of the painters undoubtedly enhanced its appeal. As the local *Wümme-Zeitung* commented in September 1895, 'The presence of this cheery little band of artists naturally brings a good deal of sustenance to our locality, quite apart from the fame that, because of the artists' successes, naturally also attaches itself to the name of Worpswede.'[36] Visitors were drawn both by the magical light and atmosphere of the Teufelsmoor, captured in the best of the paintings and seductively described by writers like Richard Muther; but also, from the mid 1890s – a time of unprecedented urban growth and concern about big-city problems – by the Nordic 'soil romanticism' of rightwing culture-critics like Julius Langbehn, whose bestselling *Rembrandt as Educator* had first appeared in 1890. Other influences included the self-consciously lyrical and *heimatkünstlerisch* works of some of the artists, Rainer Maria Rilke's 1903 Worpswede monograph in the popular Velhagen & Klasing art series, and a stream of regional ruralist fiction.

At all events, Worpswede's popularity continued to grow, especially after the arrival of the first train, on Christmas Eve 1910, at the elegant station designed by Vogeler. The following year, the art and craft showroom run by Vogeler and his brother was visited by some eight thousand people.[37] The effect, inevitably, was a perceptible change of atmosphere; higher living costs; and tension between conservationists and those local inhabitants who resented interference from improvement associations and planning committees. (The symbiosis between culture and leisure already apparent before 1914 is still more in evidence today. Despite Worpswede's designation in the Third Reich as a cradle of Nordic art, the original colony's reputation revived after 1945 and has become the focus of a whole industry. By the beginning of the 1970s, when Vogeler's famous Barkenhoff was rescued from demolition, Worpswede was attracting between two and twelve thousand visitors a day; in 1989 it boasted ten art or craft schools, several tour organizations, eight hotels and twenty-nine galleries, workshops and museums.[38])

Between the old big-city art centres (and the new metropolitan one, Berlin) at one extreme and the colonies at the other, a third kind of centre was emerging between 1900 and 1914, stimulated by the desire of certain minor rulers and states to turn the increasing demand for luxury goods to the advantage of their own capitals and industries. This development was closely linked to the rise of the modern applied arts movement which, influenced by trends in countries like Great Britain and Belgium, had begun to supplant the murk and clutter of late-nineteenth-century historicism. The older art centres, especially Munich and Dresden, naturally played a major role in this, thanks to their mature infrastructures and general attractiveness to creative people. The first two national *Kunstgewerbe* (applied art) exhibitions – both historicist – were held in the Bavarian capital in 1876 and 1888; and the turn away from historicism also owed much to Munich events such as the founding of the Secession and the appearance (in 1896) of Georg Hirth's journal *Jugend*. But the young Belgian designer Henry van de Velde made his German début in Dresden in 1897, with much greater success than in Paris the previous year;[39] and in 1906 the Saxon capital hosted the Third National Applied Arts Exhibition, a vastly ambitious enterprise incorporating more than 140 fully furnished rooms and several complete buildings.

Such shows, which attracted hordes of visitors and were exhaustively discussed in Germany's proliferating design journals, served both as showcases for new ideas and as talent-pools for governments to fish in. Thus, for example, the success in Dresden of Bruno Paul, a founder-member of the Munich United Workshops, led to his selection by Wilhelm von Bode as director of the Berlin Kunstgewerbemuseum's training school. Particularly interesting, however, was the recruitment of rising stars by rulers of minor states who hoped to enhance their capitals' standing without competing with the larger art centres across the whole range of artistic activity. Three notable cases were Stuttgart, Weimar and Darmstadt. Stuttgart, where there was a long-standing tradition of state encouragement of the applied arts, succeeded in 1902 in attracting Bernhard Pankok, who developed new experimental workshops, created links with local industry and eventually headed the reorganized State Design School. (Conditions were rather different at the Academy, where the important proto-abstract painter Adolf Hoelzel, appointed in 1905, found himself constantly at loggerheads with conservative colleagues.[40]) In Weimar, which for a century had basked sleepily in the glories of its past, the plan for a modern cultural renaissance launched by the millionaire aesthete Count Harry Kessler was thwarted by conservatism and court intrigues. However, Kessler's friend and ally van de Velde, who had been appointed to lead an 'Arts and Crafts Seminar' in 1901, survived to become director of the new State Design School which in 1919, under van de Velde's collaborator Walter Gropius, became the Weimar Bauhaus.[41]

But the most interesting prewar experiment was the famous artists' colony established at Darmstadt-Mathildenhöhe in 1899.[42] Until then, the capital of the grand duchy of Hesse-Darmstadt had been a pleasant but provincial minor *Residenz* that in the nineteenth century had lost most of its artistic talent to other places. Muther described it in 1901 as 'still the town with the wide streets devoid of people, with the frostily high-class houses; the town where, guarded by their landlady, the little boarding-school misses walk in crocodiles to the park'.[43] The colony's concept, proposed by the local wallpaper manufacturer and editor of the journal *Deutsche Kunst und Dekoration*, Alexander Koch, and enthusiastically espoused by the young Grand Duke Ernst Ludwig, involved inviting a group of outstanding designers to create their own workshops and model residences in parkland not far from the city centre. Unburdened by formal commitments, they would then proceed, in collaboration with local industry, to transform Darmstadt into a showcase of the modern design aesthetic. As the first colonists included the young Peter Behrens and the architect of the Vienna Secession building, Josef Maria Olbrich, these hopes were understandable, and in the summer of 1901 style cognoscenti from all over the empire flocked to the colony's spectacular manifesto-exhibition, 'A Document of German Art'. But unfortunately this was a financial disaster, not least because of the difficulty – already experienced by William Morris – of creating artist-designed objects at an affordable price; indeed, Behrens' house and its fittings cost 200 000 marks.[44] Longer-term problems included limited local patronage, a stoppage of public money, and the presence of an established group of architects at the Darmstadt Polytechnic determined to defend its own turf. The whole Mathildenhöhe project would probably have foundered but for dogged efforts by Koch and Ernst Ludwig and heavy subsidies from grand-ducal funds. Eventually support was again forthcoming from the city and Parliament; but another ambitious exhibition, which opened in May 1914, was cut short by the outbreak of war. The initial momentum was never regained, and in the 1920s Darmstadt once again became a backwater (see Figure 3.1).

Clearly many of the aspirations initially attached to the Mathildenhöhe scheme were ridiculously over-blown, while Ernst Ludwig has been described as over-temperamental, prone to dilettantism and incapable of choosing suitable artistic advisers.[45] However, the episode reveals what conditions were needed for the creation of large-scale cultural projects by the beginning of the twentieth century. In the first place, royal patronage was no longer enough. Although a single dedicated and wealthy (princely) individual could create or take up a vision and realize it up to a point, permanent success required political consensus and the commitment of taxpayer's money. Secondly, the tactics of Koch, like those of another talented publicist, Hirth in Munich, reflected the vital importance of the press and public relations in the promotion of any major initiative, whether it involved an artists' colony, an exhibition or a new festival opera-house. Finally, projects stood or fell within a framework which transcended local and regional boundaries. As Koch implied in a 1905 essay on 'Darmstadt and the economic significance of applied art', the ultimate touchstone of success would be the ability of 'the Sleeping Beauty among towns' to tap into the big market and lure some of the international tourist-shoppers thronging the Kurfürstendamm and the Munich Lenbachplatz in its own direction.[46]

Two at first sight contradictory conclusions suggest themselves from this survey. On the one hand, despite political unification, Germany's polycentric cultural geography was accentuated as the governments of the smaller states sought to offset Prussia's overwhelming economic and political preponderance by building up their capitals' cultural assets. Moreover, despite the growing weight of Berlin there was little sign that older centres such as Dresden or Munich were fading into insignificance by 1914. And the prestige and economic benefits of hosting and creating other cultural attractions for the German and international travelling elite meant that by this time other towns and cities up and down the Reich were seeking to profit from fashionable new movements in art and design. At a different level, on the other hand, all the various centres and their satellites were becoming more and more closely interlinked. Demand was growing more mobile, and more internationalized, and even before 1900 ambitious artists could feasibly aim for sales well beyond the bounds of Germany or even Europe. This became especially important for artists outside the mainstream, the members of the avant-gardes, who by 1914 could hope to make up for meagre interest at home by trawling a market that extended from Odessa to San Francisco – in March of that year, pictures by Kandinsky were even exhibited in Tokyo.[47] Not only as a marketplace, but as a forum for ideas and an arena for the making of reputations, the art world was larger and more integrated than at any previous time. Bursting upon this scene, therefore, the war and its aftermath were enormously disruptive. Indeed, it was not until 1989 that progress towards a truly global environment for the visual arts could be resumed.

Notes

1. J. Huret, *En Allemagne. La Bavière et la Saxe*, Paris: Fasquelle, 1911, p.67.
2. See J.H. Zammito, 'Der Streit um die Berliner Kultur 1870 bis 1930', *Jahrbuch für die Geschichte Mittel- und Ostdeutschlands*, 35 (1986), pp.234–68.
3. *Ibid.*, p. 253.
4. J.D. Ketner, 'The Indian painter in Düsseldorf', in R. Stewart, J.D. Ketner and A.L. Miller, *Carl Wimar. Chronicler of the Missouri River Frontier*, New York: Abrams, 1991, p.43.

5. N.K. Anderson and L.S. Ferber (eds), *Albert Bierstadt, Art and Enterprise*, New York: Hudson Hills Press, 1990, p.36.
6. See especially E. Wind, 'The revolution of history painting', *Journal of the Warburg Institute*, 2 (1938/39), pp.116–27.
7. See Ketner, 'The Indian painter in Düsseldorf'.
8. See *Courbet und Deutschland*, W. Hofmann (ed.), Cologne: DuMont, 1978.
9. T. Cross, *The Shining Sands. Artists in Newlyn and St Ives 1880–1930*, Cambridge and Tiverton: Westcountry Books/The Lutterworth Press, 1994, p.15.
10. H. v. Tschudi, 'Die Sammlung Arnhold', *Kunst und Künstler*, 7 (1909), p.57.
11. 'Ausstellung deutscher Kunst aus der Zeit von 1775–1875', in H. v. Tschudi, *Gesammelte Schriften zur neueren Kunst*, ed. E. Schwedeler-Meyer, Munich: Bruckmann, 1912, p.174.
12. S. Jeszensky, ' "Le déjeuner sur l'herbe" de Szinyei', *Bulletin de la Galerie Nationale Hongroise*, 11 (1960), p.24; J. Starzynski, *Aleksander Gierymski*, Warsaw: Auriga, 1971, p.9.
13. See especially *Munch und Deutschland* (exhibition catalogue), Hamburg, Kunsthalle, 1994.
14. Warburg Institute, London, CPE 574: Kunst-Kataloge 1815–46.
15. K.K. Eberlein, 'Geschichte des Kunstvereins für die Rheinländer und Westfalen, 1829–1929', *Schriften des städtischen Kunstmuseums Düsseldorf*, Vol. 3, Düsseldorf, 1929, pp.40–41, 53–63.
16. See *Verzeichnis der Mitglieder des Sächsischen Kunstvereins im Jahre 1842*, Dresden, 1842.
17. S. Weltge-Wortmann, *Die ersten Maler in Worpswede*, Worpswede: Worpsweder Verlag, 1979, p.36.
18. See R. Lenman, *Artists and Society in Germany 1850–1914*, Manchester and New York: Manchester University Press, 1997, pp.176–7.
19. *Ibid.*, p.171.
20. *Ibid.*, pp.178–81.
21. B. Hünlich, 'Dresdener Motive in Werken der Künstlergemeinschaft "Brücke"', *Jahrbuch der Staatlichen Kunstsammlungen Dresden*, 13 (1981), pp.67–100.
22. Preussische Staatsbibliothek, Berlin, Handschriftenabteilung, *Sturm* Archive: Marc to Walden, 16 June 1913 (postcard).
23. Preussische Staatsbibliothek, Berlin, Handschriftenabteilung, *Sturm* Archive: Marc to Walden, 3 [?] June 1914. The number was Benediktbeuern 20.
24. *Die Düsseldorfer Malerschule*, exhibition catalogue, Mainz: Philipp von Zabern, 1979, p.369.
25. H.K. Kirsch, *Worpswede. Die Geschichte einer deutschen Künstlerkolonie*, Munich: Bertelsmann, (undated), p.36.
26. See Cross, *The Shining Sands*, ch.2.
27. G. Boulboulé and M. Zeiss, *Worpswede. Kulturgeschichte eines Künstlerdorfes*, Cologne: DuMont, 1989, p.49.
28. M. Hausmann et al., *Worpswede. Eine deutsche Künstlerkolonie um 1900*, Fischerhude: Galerie Verlag, 1986, pp.28–31.
29. *Ibid.*, p.34.
30. S.D. Gallwitz (ed.), *Briefe und Tagebuchblätter von Paula Modersohn-Becker*, Munich: Wolff, 1922, p.83.
31. H. Glander and E. Venzmer, *Ahrenshoop*, Schwerin: Petermännchen Verlag, 1963, p.30.
32. *A practical Rhine Guide, with the leading routes through France, Belgium, Holland in full detail ... By an Englishman*, London, 1857, p.41.
33. Lenman, *Artists and Society*, pp.111–12, 156–7.
34. Huret, *En Allemagne*, pp.22–3.
35. Glander and Venzmer, *Ahrenshoop*, p.30.
36. Boulboulé and Zeiss, *Worpswede*, p.48.
37. *Ibid.*, p.95
38. *Ibid.*, pp.180–85.

39. H. van de Velde, *Geschichte meines Lebens*, ed. H. Curjel, Munich: Piper, 1962, ch. 15.
40. W. Venzmer, *Adolf Hölzel, Leben und Werk*, Stuttgart: Deutsche Verlags-Anstalt, 1982, pp.20–28.
41. Lenman, *Artists and Society*, pp.117–18.
42. *Ibid.*, pp.118–20; and, especially, *Ein Dokument deutscher Kunst: Darmstadt 1901–1976* (6 vols.), Darmstadt: Roether, 1976–7.
43. 'Darmstadt', in R. Muther, *Aufsätze über bildende Kunst*, 2 (undated), Berlin: Ladyschnikow, p.69.
44. A. Windsor, *Peter Behrens: Architect and Designer 1868–1940*, London: Architectural Press, 1981, p.18.
45. H. Uhde-Bernays, *Im Lichte der Freiheit. Erinnerungen aus den Jahren 1880 bis 1914*, Frankfurt am Main: Insel, 1947, pp.513–14.
46. A. Koch, *Darmstadt. Eine Stätte moderner Kunstbestrebungen*, Darmstadt: Koch, 1905, p.i.
47. D. E. Gordon, *Modern Art Exhibitions*, 1, Munich: Prestel, 1974, p.339.

3.1 Darmstadt: Mathildenhöhe artists' houses, c. 1905

4

The Berlin art world, 1918–1933

Malcolm Gee

Berlin – a highly questionable entity but at any rate a monstrous one. Maybe Berlin is just a perfect mechanism, a faultlessly operating force, going who knows where. On that basis Munich is a badly functioning mechanism with old fashioned parts. Or if as they say all Europe, and Germany in particular, is ill, then Berlin is a hot fantastic fever and Munich a case of sleeping sickness (with, of course, outbreaks of utter folly). So, in for a penny, in for a pound, one resigns oneself and settles for Berlin.[1]

By the later part of the Wilhelmine era, as Robin Lenman points out in his contribution to this book, Berlin was assuming the role of national capital of the German art world, despite continuing competition from traditional art centres such as Dresden, Düsseldorf, and Munich. This position was reinforced in the postwar years. Although, aided by the integration that Lenman discusses, other cities sustained a high level of artistic activity during the Weimar period, Berlin was seen as the urban centre most in tune with the epoch, which offered artists the greatest opportunities for critical and commercial success, and where the key trends in modern art in Germany were being established. This essay will examine the character and history of key parts of the Berlin art world of this time; those engaged with the promotion, display, validation and sale of contemporary art. This was a small and relatively elite 'world', but it played a significant role in the cultural life of the capital and reflected in a distinctive way many of the broad currents affecting German society in the Weimar Republic.

Berlin, notoriously, was transformed in the course of the nineteenth century from a quiet garrison town to a huge metropolis, combining the role of administrative and ceremonial capital of the new German Reich with that of a dynamic financial and industrial centre thriving on the wealth of the post-unification economy. This dramatic and savage transformation had a number of important consequences for the visual arts. The state developed an ambitious museums policy, as it sought to enhance the cultural prestige of the new national capital. As wealth increased in the city, art collecting became more extensive and the infrastructure of exhibiting organizations and private galleries developed accordingly. Berlin now began to be seen as a major international art centre: it became an exciting, and promising, place to live as an artist. Max Liebermann's return to his native city in 1884, after fifteen years in Munich, was symptomatic of this development, as was, later, the decision of the Dresden-based members of the 'Brücke' group to move to the metropolis, in 1910–11. As George Grosz put it, recalling his own return from Dresden in 1912: 'Berlin was "where it was at" '[2] (see Figures 4.1, 4.2).

Liebermann was a key figure in a network whose goal since the 1880s had been the modernization of the Berlin art scene through exposure to international trends and the development of new forms of exhibition and commercialization of art. In the Berlin Secession, founded in 1898, he and his colleagues had established a forum for the selective display of 'advanced' contemporary painting and sculpture, including work from elsewhere in Europe, that had been instantly successful with a significant sector of the Berlin public. The Secession's positions were reinforced by the activities of the Cassirer Gallery, also founded in 1898, which promoted Liebermann and other leaders of the association alongside the work of Manet and the French Impressionists, and by the critical writing in the journal *Kunst und Künstler*, owned by Paul Cassirer's cousin Bruno. Hugo von Tschudi, who became director of the National Gallery in 1896, was closely linked to the Liebermann circle, and the policy he pursued at the gallery reflected this. Partly by purchase and partly through solicited gifts from members of the industrial and financial elites – a policy pioneered in respect of earlier art by Wilhelm von Bode – von Tschudi acquired a range of modern French art that made the Berlin collection one of the most up-to-date in Europe. This approach, which was widely admired in progressive cultural circles, was also highly controversial.

Von Tschudi's departure from his post in 1909, engineered by his conservative opponents with the backing of the Kaiser, demonstrated the limits of the modernist camp's influence in the Berlin art world, and the extent to which cultural politics were affected by the power structures and ideological tensions of the Wilhelmine state. Nevertheless, by this time it was evident that Berlin had acquired the elements, in terms of demand, production and infrastructure, of a modern art system of the kind developed in France, supportive of diversity and innovation and opposed to the corporative attitudes of official bodies. The splits which took place in the Secession itself in 1910–12 were evidence of this: a new 'Expressionist' avant-garde emerged that challenged the aesthetic credo of Liebermann's generation and that demanded, successfully, space in which to exhibit and sell its work. Liebermann, who remained attached to the 'Freie Sezession' group, favourable to new art, was nicknamed the 'Kaiser of Pariser Platz' at this time. He was the figurehead of an alternative Berlin art culture, disapproved of by the court and partly excluded from official patronage, but which had extensive support throughout the art community.[3] One of the issues that emerged in the Republican period was the extent to which the new situation would allow this disjuncture between 'official' and 'unofficial' elements of the art world to be overcome. In the event, new sets of tensions and rivalries developed, partially mirroring the old ones, although within a framework that was broadly supportive of 'new art'.

In January 1919 Paul Westheim argued that his journal *Das Kunstblatt* would not change as a result of current events, as art had achieved its revolution years before.[4] *Das Kunstblatt* was founded in 1917 and it was the case that some of the features that characterized the art scene in the early Weimar years emerged at that time, after the hiatus of the first years of the war. Expressionism dominated contemporary art; inflation combined with a shortage of consumer goods led to a fragile boom on the art market; new buyers and dealers of contemporary art were emerging. The November revolution itself triggered an outburst of idealistic zeal among many young artists, while causing anxiety to some established supporters of modern art. Paul Cassirer was linked to the Independent Socialist Party (USPD), but as Karl Scheffler pointed out in *Kunst und Künstler*, socialist ideology threatened the commercial basis on which modern art had thrived.[5] His fears were not realized in the event, although the new regime did aggravate the trade through the introduction of a 'luxury' tax on art sales. The Cassirer Gallery was one of those that suspended its exhibition programme in 1920 in protest at this measure, which was amended after a sustained Press and parliamentary campaign. Although it probably did have an ideological gloss, the tax was mainly motivated by the chronic penury of the new government. It was, indeed, the changing and often severe economic conditions of the period, rather than institutional or ideological obstacles, that generated the greatest challenge to the modern art trade throughout the 1920s. While the first years of the inflation generated a, partly false, sense of feverish prosperity among the art community, the extreme inflationary spiral of 1922–3 brought business to a virtual halt. The initial years of currency stability were also difficult: it was only in around 1926–7 that the situation really seemed healthy again. Then, as Berlin reasserted itself as the 'fastest city on earth', modern art and its supporters enjoyed a short period of relative prosperity.

The art world in the urban space of Berlin

Lovis asked me this morning whether I would like to go with him to the Crown Prince's palace, where the modern collection of the National Gallery was based. I said I would love to. As it was fine, we walked along Klopstockstrasse to the Hansaplatz and took a horsedrawn cab there... We went along the Altonaer Strasse and Brückenallee to the Great Column, then along Charlottenburger Chaussee and through the Brandenburg Gate next door to the Academy. We took a detour from Unter den Linden to the Mauer Strasse, because we had business in the Deutsche Bank... Finally we arrived in Mr Counsellor Ludwig Justi's Crown Prince Palace office... From there we carried on our way to the National Gallery itself. When Corinth had seen what he wished to he took the electric tram to take him to the Secession on the Kurfürstendamm.[6]

In the museum complex on the Spree at the east end of Unter den Linden, the Wilhelmine state had established a grandiose site for high culture that linked it to the monuments of royal prestige and authority in the city. In the 1880s the art trade was based in the districts to the south-west of this area, where the financial and commercial powers of the city were concentrated. As Berlin expanded, the area to the west of this traditional centre developed as a distinctive centre of commercial and leisure activity – the rapid growth in east-west traffic that this generated was one of the problems addressed by planners envisaging the future of the city in 1910.

Although Berlin, unlike Munich or Paris, did not have an established artists' district, by the turn of the century the 'West End' had become the focal point of contemporary artistic and intellectual life. The legendary Café des Westens and the Romanische Café, both situated in the area just south of the zoo, were meeting places for the avant-gardes in literature, theatre and art – the bohemian counterpoint to the stilted world of official culture. The first exhibition building of the Berlin Secession was on Kantstrasse in Charlottenburg. In 1905 it moved to the Kurfürstendamm, at the heart of the West End. A reviewer contrasted the cosmopolitan, 'new Berlin' character of visitors to exhibitions in the Kurfürstendamm, with the petit-bourgeois, conservative profile of the crowds who frequented the annual shows at the Lehrter Bahnhof in Alt-Moabit.[7] The status of the district as a commercial and entertainment centre was reinforced in the postwar period. In a mid-1920s guide to 'vicious' Berlin, Curt Moreck described how the centre of gravity of the city's night life had shifted. Friedrichstrasse, which had been the essence of the 'Weltstadt Berlin' now suffered from its proximity to the relics of imperial power, he claimed: 'the "democratic West" where the new men live has sucked the vital life out of it... Tauentzienstrasse-Kurfürstendamm. Two sides of an obtuse angle, colliding at the memorial church. This is Berlin's boulevard. All the needs and pleasures of twentieth-century man are catered for along these streets.'[8] Characteristically it was in this area that the new picture palaces, quintessential products of the modern age, were built in the latter part of the decade. Walter Benjamin recalled that the stabilization of the political and economic situation in the 1920s was visible in the pattern of frequentation of the Romanische Café. The 'revolutionary' bohemians moved from centre stage and were replaced by the new bourgeois elites from the stock exchange, film and theatre, for whom it was an amusing, exotic, place of relaxation.[9]

These groups were, of course, potential clients for contemporary art. Some modern galleries were situated in the immediate area of the Tauentzienstrasse-Kurfürstendamm angle, but the biggest concentration of dealers was to be found somewhat to the east in the Tiergarten district. The Cassirer Gallery had opened there, in Viktoriastrasse, at the turn of the century, inaugurating a shift away from the old commercial districts further to the east. In the 1920s a series of modern galleries – Flechtheim, Neumann/Nierendorf, Goldschmidt and Wallerstein, Möller – established themselves around the Lützow Ufer, on the southern edge of the quarter to the west of the major artery of Potsdamer Strasse. This area of Berlin was particularly well suited to the art trade: it was close to the brash, rich and 'modern' West End, but also near to the traditional financial district around the Leipziger Strasse. And the Tiergarten quarter itself was a haven of discrete luxury, redolent of the confidence, and opulence, of the prewar metropolis[10] (see Figure 4.3).

The development of the Lützow Ufer area as a pivotal centre of the art trade constituted a major shift of gravity in the cultural geography of the city. However, as Lovis Corinth's 1923 itinerary demonstrates, the older foci of the Berlin art world were not abandoned in the democratic era. Artists seeking recognition and sales, besides engaging with the Secession or one of the other exhibiting associations in the city, and seeking commercial support from dealers, still acknowledged the importance of the official institutions of the capital – the Academy on Pariser Platz and the National Gallery, at the other end of the Unter den Linden – in the validation and valorization of their work. It was, indeed, the development and interaction of all these elements, in a hierarchy headed, uneasily, by Justi's National Gallery (1909–33), that constituted the structural history of the Berlin art world in the period.

Artists and their organizations

As he crossed the Pariser Platz in 1923, Corinth no doubt gave a thought to Liebermann, who lived and worked there. For ten years the two men had been enemies, since the acrimonious split in the Berlin Secession of 1913, when Corinth had sided with the minority who attacked Paul Cassirer's hold on and policy at the organization. Now he was President of the Secession and Liebermann (since 1920) President of the Prussian Academy of Arts, to which Corinth himself had been elected in January 1919. Their prestige and power represented the triumph of modern art in the Republic, but, symptomatically, just as neither of them were entirely comfortable with the new Germany, they now stood for relatively conservative values in art.

'Art is lawfulness, not licence. The artist is free and only answerable to his Demon. But his Demon is the law that he subscribes to.'[11] Liebermann was committed to the principle of total individual freedom in art, both on pragmatic and philosophical grounds. As he said in his first address as President of the Academy, a man who had suffered in his youth from the rejection of Impressionism was not going to condemn out of hand a new art movement that he did not understand.[12] His artistic credo, buttressed by references to Kant, was that aesthetic quality was realized intuitively in response to nature and to the materials of art: it was in essence a free individual statement. However, while these beliefs led him to adopt a very liberal position on certain aspects of artistic policy, in relation, notably, to state interference and to academic notions of aesthetic rules, they also led him to be highly sceptical of much new art, particularly that which spurned the discipline engendered by the artist's effort to engage with and translate his perception of the world. Another factor played an important role in the line he adopted as President of the Academy: his inherent elitism, that had been a central feature of the exhibition policy of the Secession. He believed in the democratic freedom to create, but his concept of actual artistic quality was aristocratic.

Liebermann sought to reassert the prestige of the Academy and its role in the Berlin art world by combining a judicious recognition of 'new forces' in art with the maintenance of high standards in the selection and display of work. In 1920 he issued specific invitations to members of the art community in order to increase the representative character of the Academy exhibition. Established members of the Expressionist generation, like Max Pechstein and Karl Schmidt-Rottluff, now became regular exhibitors. Pechstein was one of several new academicians, including Hans Purrmann and Käthe Kollwitz, elected in the early years of Liebermann's presidency. This policy met with some resistance from conservatives, and new elections to the fine arts section of the Academy were blocked from 1924 onwards. It also caused friction in the modern art community: to some observers it seemed as though the old Secession, with its selective policies and ties to a small art-world network, had resurfaced with the backing of the state. Liebermann clashed with Justi over the relationship between the Academy and the National Gallery, and he suggested that other selective exhibitions were superfluous. In his 1923 address to the Academy he argued that as art was now free from external interference only two types of public exhibitions were justified: a single jury-free show for all comers, and that of the Academy, whose role was to maintain standards and ideals in art practice.[13]

From this perspective the Secession no longer had a *raison d'être*, and Corinth apparently wrote to Liebermann in protest at the suggestion. 1923 was a very difficult moment for his group: they had been forced to reduce their exhibition space and had not held an autumn show in Berlin the previous year. Corinth had invited Friedrich Ebert, the President of the Republic, to the spring opening, as a way of emphasizing the role of the Secession in the cultural life of the capital. In his speech for the event he asked the President to recognize this by providing State support 'in this fearful time.'[14] The Secession survived: it represented a solid, if rather conservative, constituency in the art community whose needs were not fully met elsewhere. This was not the case with the 'Free Secession', the group that Liebermann himself had helped to set up in 1913. The Free Secession had retained the exhibition building at 208 Kurfürstendamm but moved out of it in 1920 because they could not afford the upkeep. The association appears to have led a nomadic existence over the following few years, finally being wound up in 1925. As Liebermann pointed out in a note to Corinth, he was himself affected by his conclusion that organizations of the Secession type were unnecessary – he had resigned from the Free Secession, of which he was honorary President.[15] The inflation crisis dealt a final blow to a grouping that was already weakened by a lack of backing and a diminished sense of purpose in the conditions of the postwar era.

Liebermann's vision of an art world regulated by a single institution reflected, ironically, a conservative desire for a well-ordered, hierarchical art system that the aesthetic revolution of the previous fifty years had rendered unrealizable. On the other hand, the demise of the Free Secession suggested that Berlin could not sustain an overly fragmented system of public exhibitions. In a situation characterized by a broad public acceptance of modern art trends, general economic uncertainty and fragility, and an artistic community with a constant need to exhibit, the artists' associations opted for cooperative exhibition strategies. The Free Secession itself had participated in the 1921 summer exhibition at the Lehrter Bahnhof, which had three distinct fine art sections for the Berlin Artists' Association, the Free Secession, and the November Group. The latter, founded in the heady days of the revolution, quickly evolved into an eclectic interest group for advanced art. Although it held a few separate shows, the November Group took part regularly in the annual summer Berlin art exhibitions throughout the 1920s. For its tenth anniversary in 1929 it combined with the Jury-free art show; an event initiated in 1921 with the intention of bringing art closer to the people that, according to Karl Scheffler, rapidly developed into a coalition of artistic tendencies.[16]

The art trade

Although few of them apart from Scheffler shared Liebermann's extreme position on the matter, critics tended to agree that there were too many general art exhibitions in Berlin, showing too much second-rate work, without a sense of coherence or direction. 'What we need is audits, summings up of the Sonderbund type,' Walter Ley complained in 1920, 'and what we get is not even a useful market, now that the market has become so grotesque that it needs sellers rather than buyers.'[17] The function of qualitative selection that observers called on the associations to perform was carried out by dealers as a normal feature of their commercial policy. Dealers did not, however, satisfy the demand for comprehensive evaluative surveys of the state of German art. Particularly in the immediate postwar years, their activities were seen as part of the unhealthy art 'machine' that had developed in the city, emphasizing novelty over quality, and encouraging young artists to entertain unrealistic career expectations. 'Hurry up, hurry up – if you still want to acquire some eternal values, quickly get on the phone and call the nearest dealer to get yourself everything from Simone Martini to George Grosz', Hans Werner Woerzerich ironized, in his contribution to a polemic over prices in 1922.[18] Dealers were central to the phenomenon of commercial speculation in contemporary art: for a time it seemed that the triumph of material over spiritual values that cultural critics of all persuasions feared had actually occurred. Berlin was not a *Kunststadt*, Lothar Brieger claimed in 1919: ' . . . Berlin has art dealers with enormous capital, like Hamburg has coffee dealers. For them art is a commodity and conjuncture, spiritual dregs for snobs.'[19]

In the mid 1920s there were approximately eighty established art galleries in Berlin, of which around a quarter dealt in contemporary art. Compared to Paris, this was relatively few, but the trade in Berlin was far more extensive than in other German cities.[20] The basis of this position had been established before 1914. The war and its aftermath destroyed the economic confidence that had underpinned the growth of the art trade, but also created economic and cultural circumstances that in some respects favoured modern art. The mood of democratic renewal that characterized the postwar atmosphere in Berlin suited the promotion of a modern aesthetic, particularly, in the fraught circumstances of 1918–1920, one that emphasized subjective 'inner' values; inflation encouraged a flight to luxury goods on the part of those who had funds; the collapsing exchange rate meant that older, established art was being snapped up at high prices by foreign buyers. Commentators like Brieger were exaggerating in their depictions of the wave of speculation in art that took place but certainly there was a high level of activity between 1918 and 1922 involving both established and new dealers. However, as inflation got out of control at the end of 1922 and in 1923 after the French invasion of the Ruhr, the art trade entered a crisis. Few collectors had disposable funds, particularly in dollars or Swiss francs, the only money worth having, and foreign interest in contemporary German art was minimal. The views of dealers canvassed by *Das Kunstblatt* in September 1923 were almost uniformly pessimistic: one gallery pointed out that as things stood they would have to sell forty watercolours a month by a young artist just to pay their heating bill – a level of turnover that would have been impossible even when the market was flourishing.[21] The stabilization of the currency at the end of the year reintroduced some order into the market but the harsh financial and economic conditions of the next two years made selling difficult. Then, from 1926 to 1929, the Berlin art trade entered a period of relatively stable prosperity.

The policy and success of dealers confronted by these rapidly changing circumstances were conditioned by two key factors: their attitude to new German art and the resources – in terms of stock, reserves and clients – that they disposed of. The Paul Cassirer Gallery, in keeping with the ideas of its leading artists, had always presented contemporary German art in the context of European Modernism, stemming from Paris. Cassirer's principal prewar competitor, the Fritz Gurlitt Gallery, on the other hand, had sought to emphasize a distinctive German strain of modern art. Both these galleries – particularly Cassirer – had built up significant stocks of recognized art and established a network of wealthy clients by 1914. Importing French art was more difficult after 1918 – Cassirer indeed faced severe financial difficulties for a time as a result of a dispute with Parisian dealers over ownership of stock.[22] However, while supporting some Expressionists, notably Kokoschka – from before the war – and Kirchner, who was given a major exhibition at the gallery in early 1924, the Paul Cassirer Gallery maintained its previous aesthetic policy in this period. It was the principal holder of modern French art in Germany – as a major Cézanne exhibition in 1921 emphasized – and the commercial agent for the modern 'establishment', that included Liebermann, Kollwitz and Barlach. Wolfgang Gurlitt, in 1918, set out to position his gallery firmly as the leading outlet for the best in contemporary German art. A luxurious new set of rooms on the Potsdamer Strasse was inaugurated with a Max Pechstein exhibition, and Pechstein became the modern star of the Gurlitt Gallery's exhibition programme and graphics output, a counterpart to the senior figure of Corinth (whom Gurlitt had represented since 1913). Pechstein was linked to the radical artists' movements that were briefly active in the aftermath of the November Revolution, and a representative of the 'historic' Expressionist movement in Germany. Gurlitt's postwar promotion of his art marked a high point in his career, and signalled the gallery's alignment with the consensual view of Expressionism as the dominant style of the new era. The policy was commercially successful until hyper-inflation hit, when, faced by the problems this caused, Gurlitt withdrew his backing of Pechstein. The gallery, like Cassirer's, had the resources to survive but pursued a less distinctive pro-modern stance in the latter years of the decade.[23]

The inflation period virtually put an end to the Der Sturm Gallery as a significant player on the Berlin scene. The financial basis of Herwarth Walden's business had always been precarious, and he suffered in the postwar years from defections to other dealers – whom he accused of opportunism. Another long-standing supporter of Expressionism, I. B. Neumann, travelled to New York in 1923 in the hope of developing a market for the work of Beckmann there. He was disappointed, and in the somewhat precarious circumstances, did not return to Germany for two years (and then only briefly). Ferdinand Möller also went to the United States in 1923 in the hope of achieving some precious dollar sales. He found that demand for contemporary German art was slight, and that his artists' expectations were unrealistic. When he returned to Berlin early in 1924 the conditions had become so difficult that he closed his gallery in the city, trading only from home in Potsdam.

In the summer of 1927 Möller felt confident enough to reopen in Berlin, in new premises on the Schönberger Ufer. One of his neighbours in this zone on the edge of the Tiergarten district was Alfred Flechtheim, who had opened a branch of his Düsseldorf business at Lutzow Ufer 13 in 1921. Flechtheim moved his home to Berlin at the end of 1923. In 1927 he too responded to the better conditions on the market by refurbishing his gallery space. Between 1927 and 1930 both these dealers enjoyed considerable success as specialists in the modern field. Within it, however, they occupied significantly different positions, that partially mirrored those of Cassirer and Gurlitt in their sector of the market. Flechtheim had opened his first gallery in Düsseldorf in 1913, with the support and advice of Paul Cassirer. His contacts in Paris included Wilhelm Uhde and Daniel-Henry Kahnweiler, the German dealers in contemporary French art. After the war he collaborated closely with Kahnweiler's gallery, the Galerie Simon, to import art from Paris into Germany. Although in 1919 Flechtheim had flirted with the vogue for Expressionism, renewed contact with Paris, by his own account, put paid to this.[24] He shared Kahnweiler and Carl Einstein's scorn for art that laid claim to emotional power while lacking the formal discipline and complexity of Parisian art. French art is the model for a modern European art, a 1919 gallery note stated: 'There is no point in protesting or cursing: it is not unpatriotic to acknowledge the fact unreservedly.'[25] Throughout the 1920s the Flechtheim galleries were the most important suppliers of work by Braque, Derain, Gris, Léger, Picasso and Vlaminck to German collectors and museums. However, although it was sometimes perceived as such, Flechtheim's was not just an outlet for French art. He had long-standing arrangements with some German artists, notably Rudolf Levy and Hans Purrmann, who had, like himself, formed their aesthetic convictions in Paris before the war. And in the 1920s he also promoted artists outside this tradition. In 1928 he organized a major Berlin exhibition of Max Beckmann that confirmed the artist's exceptional status on the German art scene.

From late 1925 onwards Grosz was attached to the gallery. This development coincided with the artist's disillusionment with Communism and his desire to reassert his personal artistic identity. (In fact he used the financial independence it provided to decamp to France for an extended visit.) But it also demonstrated the breadth of Flechtheim's taste, his commercial acumen, and a maverick streak that led him to relish a certain degree of provocation: 'In the old days Alfred always brought the air of Paris with him to the Rhine ... Now it doesn't waft round him any more, or only rarely, when he comes here. These days it is the sharper, but also somewhat cooler, air of Berlin', commented Eulenberg in 1928.[26] The gallery, and its owner, occupied an important and distinctive place on the Berlin cultural scene of the mid to late 1920s: it stood not just for French influenced taste, but for a cosmopolitan awareness, intelligence and sense of style that was in tune with an important sector of Berlin society and contributed to the specific character of life in the city. Fernand Léger, in Berlin in 1928 for an exhibition of his work at the Galerie Flechtheim, was struck by the difference in atmosphere from Paris: 'Berlin doesn't sleep,' he reported to readers of the Parisian newspaper L'Intransigeant. 'Flechtheim tells me, astonished: "I sell pictures at three in the morning." You need special nerves to live at this level of activity.'[27] (See Figure 4.4.)

Fundamentally, Grosz recalled on hearing of Flechtheim's death in 1937, '... his art dealer's heart only warmed for France.'[28] Writing to Kirchner in 1929 about a possible sale to the collector Hermann Lange, Ferdinand Möller commented that he had 'stupidly' become a major buyer of French art under Flechtheim's influence.[29] While Flechtheim maintained, in his distinctive way, the francophile tradition that sought to merge German culture into a European matrix, Möller was a modernist who sympathized with the long-standing resentment of some German artists against the importers of contemporary art from Paris. 'We have a German art! But if the Germans carry on stupidly covering their walls with the left overs from French studios, the next generation will be left speechless at this folly', he stated in a manifesto article that appeared shortly after he reopened his Berlin gallery.[30] Möller's aesthetic position and commercial policy remained virtually unchanged throughout the 1920s. It was based on the core values represented by the prewar founders of German Expressionism, above all Erich Heckel, Otto Mueller and Karl Schmidt-Rottluff. He supplemented their work with that of younger artists such as Max Kraus, that could be clearly linked to the movement. The opening exhibition in the new gallery in 1927 included nine paintings by Heckel and Mueller, seventeen by Schmidt-Rottluff, and twenty-two by Kraus, with a sprinkling of works by other established figures, including Kirchner, Pechstein and Rohlfs.[31] At the end of the decade Möller also promoted artists from the Munich Expressionist school, and recognized the Constructivist branch of the contemporary Modernist movement. In the 1930 exhibition *Vision und Baugesetz* he contrasted the 'formal' and the 'expressive' tendencies in contemporary art, while seeking to demonstrate their underlying commonality. It was characteristic of his approach that he sought (unsuccessfully) to persuade Kirchner to contribute a selection of recent paintings to this show, both as a demonstration of the link between 'construction' and 'expression' and to bestow the prestige of an Expressionist master on the work of the younger generation.[32]

Ludwig Justi and the National Gallery

Möller's concern that German collectors remained in thrall to the prestige of French art had some justification. Certainly, the Galerie Flechtheim was a meeting point for a cross-section of Berlin society, from the world of high finance to that of sport and entertainment, in a way that Möller's own gallery was not. There did exist, however, in the latter years of the republic, a fairly broad base of collecting support for contemporary German art, including that associated with the Galerie Möller. This was demonstrated, *inter alia*, by two exhibitions held at the National Gallery in the spring and summer of 1928 of modern German art from Berlin collections. The first of these focused on work by the established figures of the Modern Movement, from Barlach to Pechstein. The second covered an eclectic range of contemporary artists, including Kraus, Beckmann, Dix and Grosz. According to one of the young museum staff who had researched the shows, they had been surprised by the volume of response to the initiative, that ended up drawing on well over a hundred local collections.[33] In his preface to the first exhibition the director of the National Gallery, Ludwig Justi, praised those collectors who acted from disinterested motives and acquired new German art that took its value 'from itself', and not the international art market.[34] Putting the gallery in the position of validating (and benefiting from) this activity, thereby actively engaging in the modern art scene in the city, was symptomatic of the policy that Justi had pursued at the National Gallery since 1918, courting controversy in the process.

Justi became director of the National Gallery in 1909 at the age of 33, as a result of von Tschudi's departure for Munich.[35] The job was both a promotion and something of a poisoned chalice, given the state of art politics in Berlin at the time. He adopted a prudent but relatively 'modern' policy – in 1912 he succeeded, for example, in obtaining the Kaiser's approval of the purchase of a major painting by Max Slevogt. He was an astute operator in the Prussian bureaucracy, and managed to negotiate a relatively independent position in the museum service and the replacement of the problematic 'Landeskunstkommission' by a smaller advisory committee. He was, however, viewed with suspicion by the modern art establishment around Liebermann, who saw him as 'the Kaiser's man' and he apparently made little effort to overcome this prejudice. He himself saw the Liebermann circle as a clique with powerful commercial interests that it was his duty to avoid. This difficult relationship turned into open conflict in the changed circumstances after 1918. Because he was a civil servant Justi could not be sacked, although he believed that there were intrigues to have him removed from his post at the National Gallery.[36] In fact he acted quickly to demonstrate his commitment to change: he submitted a paper to his superior in the Prussian Ministry of Culture in December 1918 in which he argued that the National Gallery should open a special section concerned with contemporary art. He proposed that the newly vacant Crown Prince's Palace (on Unter den Linden, near the Museum island) should be taken over for this purpose. In June 1919 the Finance and Culture Ministries agreed to this plan and in August the exhibition rooms in the palace were opened to the public. Originally announced as the 'Gallery of Living Art', they were now more neutrally identified as the 'New Section of the National Gallery.'[37]

The displays in the palace were frequently disrupted by temporary exhibitions, which were a key feature of the policy that Justi and his team pursued in the *Neue Abteilung*. However, the conceptual organization of the galleries appears to have remained fundamentally the same until the very end of the Weimar period. The ground floor was mainly occupied by the work of established but second-rank Berlin artists. The main rooms on the first floor presented the National Gallery's collection of modern French art and its German equivalent. The top floor was given over to contemporary 'advanced' art. The gallery hosted some exhibitions from abroad but the principal orientation of the exhibition programme was towards German art.[38] Survey shows were devoted to senior figures such as Christian Rohlfs (1920), Curt Herrmann (1924) and Lovis Corinth (1923)[39]; memorial exhibitions were held in honour of Franz Marc (1922), Paula Modersohn-Becker (1922) and

Otto Mueller (1930). A major retrospective of the work of Edvard Munch was organized in 1927 – although he was Norwegian, Munch's reputation had largely been made in Germany and he was widely acknowledged as a key figure in the emergence of a distinctive 'German' form of modern art. The Crown Prince's Palace also put on small exhibitions of work by the current generation – Kirchner, Pechstein, Heckel and Klee, for example, in 1921–23. When the palace finally became state property in 1927, thereby allowing some proper refurbishment to take place, the top floor rooms were laid out on the model of small one-man shows, with a whole room or an entire wall devoted to, *inter alia*, Heckel, Nolde, Kirchner and Beckmann.[40]

In extending the National Gallery's activities into an engaged presentation of recent and contemporary German art, Justi was applying ideas about the role of the museum in society and the art world that had been developed in Germany before the war, and that were also applied energetically in other German art centres during the Weimar years. His achievement at the Gallery was widely admired – including by Alfred Barr, who visited Berlin on several occasions after 1927.[41] This support for Modernism was, naturally, contested by conservative critics. However, the most damaging criticisms of his policies came from 'progressive' circles in the Berlin art world, above all from Karl Scheffler and Max Liebermann, who conducted a sometimes virulent campaign against him throughout the period.

The antipathy towards Justi was partly a matter of personality. There were, however, substantive issues at stake, that concerned power and artistic policy at the National Gallery. Liebermann challenged Justi directly over the constitution of the purchasing committee at the Gallery. He, Scheffler and others, including Paul Westheim, repeatedly criticized aspects of the hanging and exhibition policies Justi pursued. The arguments over the committee, which reached a peak in 1924, arose from an inherent tension (evident in the days of von Tschudi and Anton von Werner) between the Academy and the director of the National Gallery. Justi initially proposed that he should operate without a committee. If there had to be one, he argued that it should represent art 'consumers' as well as practitioners. Liebermann demanded that the Academy control appointments. The acrimonious dispute was only resolved in 1927 through a compromise imposed by the ministry, whereby each party put forward a list of candidates and the Minister chose from them.[42] In this conflict, Liebermann was defending the corporate interests of Academicians. However, his attitude was coloured by his fundamental disapproval of Justi's overall approach at the gallery, and this was shared to some extent by many other observers. The main accusations made against him were that his backing for contemporary art was suspect and ill-judged, that his reliance on loans and exhibitions was misplaced, and that the presentation of modern art at the National Gallery was lacking in coherence and overly nationalistic.[43]

These disputes were, in fact, generated more by the structural problems of the institution than by the character of its director. Some of these were common to all museums of the period that engaged with contemporary art, but the specific conditions in Berlin rendered them particularly acute. Once the National Gallery opted to show the work of contemporaries, arguments over selection and exclusion were inevitable. It was a Berlin, Prussian, national institution with international standing, that relied heavily on loans because its own budget was extremely small. After 1918 the notions of 'the modern', the social role of art, and its relation to national identity had been central to debates over art practice, reproducing the tensions between revolutionary fervour, liberal compromise and nostalgia for the Wilhelmine era that were general features of the Weimar experience. In this context a 'National Gallery' that pleased all its constituencies was no doubt impossible. Justi exposed himself to general criticism precisely because he tried to adopt a balanced policy. He was particularly aggrieved that Liebermann maintained his 'Old Testament' hatred of him, despite the fact that he had purchased several of his paintings and moved his work to the main building in 1932. Liebermann, however, considered his support for contemporary Modernism uncritical and opportunistic. Paul Westheim, who also accused him of playing 'art politics', on the other hand, criticized the Gallery for its conservatism in relation to contemporary art. Meanwhile, although he had rarely dealt with their galleries, he was accused by nationalist critics of collaborating with 'Cassirer-Flechtheim & Co.' against the interests of German artists[44] (see Figures 4.5, 4.6).

In fact, although some foreign art was shown in the Crown Prince's Palace, and the association he founded in 1929 with the help of the collector Eduard von der Heydt had the express purpose of increasing holdings in this area,[45] Justi had always interpreted the National Gallery's mission primarily as the validation and promotion of German art. His defence of contemporary art included an explicit condemnation of French influence and the notion of 'European' culture: 'Our best young artists have not been to Paris,' he wrote in 1923, 'they carve from their own wood.'[46] He apparently believed that his record in this respect would stand him in good stead as power in Prussia shifted to the right after 1931. When the Nazis came to power, however, he was quickly removed from the directorship of the National Gallery. Liebermann had stood down from the presidency of the Academy in 1932 in the face of politicized disputes, and resigned from the institution itself in 1933. The art trade had been in great difficulties since the beginning of the depression. With the advent of the Nazis most prominent Jewish dealers, including the directors of the Cassirer Gallery and Alfred Flechtheim, left Germany. Looking back bitterly some years later, Justi described himself as an outsider in the Berlin art world of the Weimar era: 'from a gothic town, an old German family, son of a romantic father: an intruder in Liebermann and Cassirer's sphere, where they had previously held complete sway.'[47] The polarity this remark establishes between metropolitan culture and traditional German values, with its implicit anti-semitism, had certainly played a role in shaping attitudes towards contemporary art in Berlin in the 1920s. It was true that within the art world of the time there existed a powerful network of dealers, critics and collectors many of whom were Jews. They had made a key contribution to the development in Berlin of an infrastructure for the support of the visual arts that was stronger and more responsive to innovation than anywhere else in Germany. However, despite the polemic it attracted, the National Gallery with its 'New Section' was an important element in this whole. Events in the 1930s destroyed the balance of forces shaping modern culture in the city. Until this politically determined tragedy they had, in fact, interacted effectively to sustain art activity in Berlin in a period of rapid change and extreme economic fragility.

Notes

1. Hans Kauden, 'München 1922', *Der Querschnitt durch 1922*, Düsseldorf, Frankfurt a Main, Berlin: Verlag der Galerie, Flechtheim, 1922, pp.248–9.
2. George Grosz, *Ein kleines Ja und ein grosses Nein*, Hamburg: Rowohlt, 1955, p.94.
3. The extensive literature on Berlin art and cultural politics in this period includes Peter Paret, *The Berlin Secession. Modernism and Its Enemies in Imperial Germany*, Cambridge, Mass., and London: Harvard University Press, 1980; N. Teeuwisse, *Vom Salon zur Secession*, Berlin: Deutscher Verlag für Kunstwissenschaft, 1986; B. Paul, *Hugo von Tschudi und die moderne französische Kunst im Deutschen Kaiserreich*, Mainz: von Zabern, 1993; G. and W. Braun (eds), *Mäzenatentum in Berlin*, Berlin and New York: Walter de Gruyter, 1993.
4. 'Jenseits der Graben weiter', *Das Kunstblatt*, 1919, 1, p.1.
5. 'Die Zukunft der deutschen Kunst', *Kunst und Künstler*, XVII, pp.309–28. On events in the Berlin art world in 1918–19 see Joan Weinstein, *The End of Expressionism. Art and the November Revolution in Germany 1918–19*, Chicago and London: The University of Chicago Press, 1989, ch. 2.
6. Thomas Corinth (the artist's son), personal recollection of 26 March 1923, in *Lovis Corinth. Eine Dokumentation*, Tübingen: Verlag Ernst Wasmuth, 1979, p.303.
7. Julius Bab, 'Vom Berliner Bildermarkt', *Pester Lloyd*, 7 September 1911: cited in Paret, *The Berlin Secession*, p.81.
8. Curt Moreck, *Führer durch das 'Lasterhafte' Berlin*, Leipzig: Verlag moderner Stadtführer, c.1925.
9. 'A Berlin Chronicle', in W. Benjamin, *One-Way Street and Other Writings*, London: New Left Books, 1979, pp.311–12.
10. Benjamin, recalling Klopstockstrasse specifically (on the northern edge of the Tiergarten quarter), declared 'this point of space ... is for me the strictest pictorial expression of the point in history occupied by the last true élite of bourgeois Berlin.' 'A Berlin Chronicle', *One-Way Street*, p.307. See also N. Teeuwisse, 'Bilder einer verschollenen Welt. Aufstieg und Niedergang der Berliner Privatsammlungen 1871–1933', in *Der Unverbrauchte Blick*, Berlin: Martin Gropius Bau, 1987, pp.13–39.

11. Max Liebermann, opening address at the 1923 Academy exhibition, reproduced in Max Liebermann, *Vision der Wirklichkeit*, Frankfurt am Main: Fischer, 1993, p.146.
12. *Ibid.*, p.139.
13. *Ibid.*, p.145. For an assessment of Liebermann's time at the Academy see Peter Paret, 'The enemy within – Max Liebermann as President of the Prussian Academy of Arts,' The Leo Baeck Memorial Lecture 28, The Leo Baeck Institute New York, 1989.
14. Reproduced in T. Corinth, *Lovis Corinth. Eine Dokumentation*, p.302 (Ebert was unable to come in the end).
15. Liebermann to Corinth, 30 September 1923: in T. Corinth, *Lovis Corinth. Eine Dokumentation*, p.307.
16. Helga Kliemann, *Die Novembergruppe*, Berlin: Deutsche Gesellschaft für Bildende Kunst, 1969; Scheffler, note on Berlin exhibitions, *Kunst und Künstler*, 1922–3, p.102.
17. *Das Kunstblatt*, 1920, 6, pp.178–82.
18. *Der Sammler*, 1922, 17, pp.257–61. The original article by Eugen Quandt, 'Preispolitik-Kulturpolitik', appeared in issue 14.
19. *Der Sammler*, 1919, 46, p.5.
20. *Handbuch des Kunstmarktes: Kunstadressbuch für das deutsche Reich, Danzig und Deutsch-Österreich*, Berlin: Antique Verlaggesellschaft Hermann Kalkoff, 1926. For the development of the German art market before the war, see Robert Lenman, *Artists and Society in Germany 1850–1914*, Manchester and New York: Manchester University Press, 1997, ch. 4.
21. 'Wirtschaftslage und Aussichten des Kunstmarktes', *Das Kunstblatt*, 1923, pp.294–301.
22. He had purchased the Pellerin collection of work by Manet before the war in a consortium with Durand-Ruel and Bernheim-Jeune.
23. On the early years of the Fritz Gurlitt Gallery, see Teeuwisse, *Vom Salon zur Secession*, pp.104–26. The new rooms were described enthusiastically by Biermann in *Der Cicerone*, 1918 no. 13/14, pp.215–16; Pechstein recalled the break caused by inflation in *Erinnerungen*, Munich, 1963 (reprinted 1993), p.107.
24. 'Zehn Jahre Kunsthändler', in *Der Querschnitt*, 1923. On Flechtheim's career in general, see *Alfred Flechtheim. Sammler. Kunsthädler Verleger* (exhibition catalogue), Kunstmuseum, Düsseldorf, 1987; Alex Vömel, 'Alfred Flechtheim, Kunsthändler und Verleger', *Neue Folge (Frankfurt)*, V, 1967, pp.90–113.
25. *Auf dem Weg zur Kunst unserer Zeit*, Düsseldorf, July/August 1919.
26. 'Flechtheim und Düsseldorf', in *Der Querschnitt durch Alfred Flechtheim* (special issue to celebrate his fiftieth birthday), 1928, p.5.
27. Fernand Léger, 'Berlin 1928', in *L'Intransigeant* (Paris), 16 April 1928.
28. George Grosz, *Briefe*, p.256. Letter of 18 February 1937 to Herbert and Amrei Fiedler.
29. Letter of 30 March 1929. Reproduced in Eberhard Roters, *Galerie Ferdinand Möllers: die Geschichte einer Galerie für moderne Kunst in Deutschland 1917–1956*, Berlin: Berlinische Galerie, 1984, p.243.
30. 'Wer trägt die Verantwortung', *Deutsche Allgemeine Zeitung*, 7 November 1927, cited in Roters, pp.94–5.
31. *Verzeichnis der Eröffnungsausstellung in den neuen Räumen Schöneberger Ufer 38*, July – September 1927.
32. See letter of Möller to Kirchner of 11 June 1930, reproduced in Roters, pp.254–6.
33. Alfred Hentzen, 'Die Neue Abteilung der National-Galerie im ehemaligen Kronprinzenpalais', *Jahrbuch Preussischer Kulturbesitz*, X, 1972, pp.9–75, here p.55. The senior assistant for these exhibitions, Ludwig Thormaehlen, presented them in *Das Kunstblatt*, 1928, pp.131–6, 284–6.
34. *Ausstellung deutscher Kunst aus Berliner Privatbesitz*, April 1928, pp.7–8.
35. Kurt Winkler, 'Ludwig Justi – Der Konservative Revolutionär', in Heinrike Junge (ed.), *AvantGarde und Publikum*, Cologne/Weimar/Vienna: Bohlau Verlag, 1992, pp.173–86. For his work with the modern collection in particular, see Hentzen, 'Die Neue Abteilung...' Both texts draw on Justi's unpublished memoirs in the Zentralarchiv der Staatlichen Museen zu Berlin, Preussischer Kulturbesitz.
36. *Memoirs*, p.159.

37. Noted by Paul Westheim in his review of the opening, *Das Kunstblatt*, 1919, pp.285–6.
38. There were exhibitions of 'Valori Plastici' and 'Modern Dutch Art' in 1920 and 1921. Political considerations may have played a part. Justi and his political masters were interested in using culture to build bridges in the postwar years. He also claimed that exhibitions of the 'Section d'Or' (Paris) and of modern Russian art were vetoed by his political masters: contribution to 'Fünf Jahre "Kronprinzen-Palais"', *Das Kunstblatt*, 1924, p.241.
39. In keeping with his status, the large Corinth exhibition put on in 1926 after his death was held in the main National Gallery building.
40. Hentzen, 'Die Neue Abteilung'; also, Jörn Grabowski, 'Die Neue Abteilung der National-Galerie im ehemaligen Kronprinzenpalais. Raumansichten aus den Jahren 1932–3', *Jahrbuch Preussischer Kulturbesitz*, XXVIII, 1991, pp.341–56.
41. Anette Gruszynski (ed.), *Museum der Gegenwart – Kunst in öffentlichen Sammlungen bis 1937*, Düsseldorf: Kunstsammlung Nordrhein-Westfalen, 1987; Vernon L. Lidtke, 'Museen und die zeitgenössische Kunst in der Weimarer Republik', in E. Mai and P. Paret (eds), *Sammler, Stifter, und Museen*, 1993, pp.215–34. Justi asserted Berlin's primacy in this movement through the establishment of the periodical *Museum der Gegenwart* in 1930. On Alfred Barr, see Christopher Grunenberg, *The Politics of Presentation: Museums, Galleries and Exhibitions in New York 1929–1947*, PhD thesis, The Courtauld Institute of Art, University of London, 1994, ch. 2, 4.
42. Hentzen, pp.32–6; Justi, *Memoirs*, pp.551–62.
43. The principal texts are summarized in Hentzen, pp.22–6, 32–9, 68–71.
44. Justi recalled this bitterly in his memoirs, p.304. The remark on Liebermann is made on p.564.
45. See Jörn Grabowski, 'Der Verein "Freunde der National-Galerie" 1929–1945', *Verein der Freunde der Nationalgalerie*, 7, pp.6–23.
46. 'Von deutscher Kunst der Gegenwart' (1923), in A. Hentzen, P. O. Rave, L. Thormaehlen (eds), *Ludwig Justi: Im Dienst der Kunst*, Breslau, 1936, pp.170–72.
47. *Memoirs*, pp.305–6.

4.1 (top) National Gallery Berlin, 1866–76 (Arch. August Stüler, Heinrich Strack)

4.2 (bottom) National Gallery Berlin, Impressionist Room (3rd floor, room 6, 1908)

4.3 (top) Viktoriastrasse (Tiergarten), c. 1935

4.4 (bottom) Interior of Alfred Flechtheim's house, c. 1925

4.5 (top) Felix Nussbaum, *Der tolle Platz*, 1931 (oil on canvas, 97 × 195.5 cm)

4.6 (bottom) New section of the National Gallery, Crown Prince's Palace, top floor, 1929–30

5

Cultural institutions as urban innovations: the Czech lands, Poland and the eastern Baltic, 1750–1900

Luďa Klusáková

The cultural function of towns in central and eastern Europe during the modern period has largely been dominated by a discussion of the role of high culture in the regional capitals of the Habsburg empire, the German states and divided Poland. Yet this was not how most people experienced urban culture. In the nineteenth century the majority of Europe's urban population lived in small or medium sized towns, and their experience of urban culture was influenced as much by the provision and availability of public amenities as by high art. The aim of this chapter is to undertake a survey of urban cultural innovations in a region where small towns predominated, and the experience of their inhabitants was provincial rather than cosmopolitan. My own focus is within a larger and more broadly-defined east-central Europe between the Baltic, Russia, Germany and the Danube, rather than a central Europe conceived as coterminous with the boundaries of the Habsburg empire. Although in many respects the experience of small-town life varied little across the region, there was a broad range of different types of urban settlement, and an examination of the ways in which cultural institutions were established, when innovations were introduced, and by whom, reveals the great diversity of urban cultural life here.

Industrialization in the region began tentatively in the first half of the nineteenth century and gathered pace from the 1850s onwards. In comparison with the more dynamic 'core' economies of the West, however, there was little truly urban industrialization here for most of the period under discussion, and most towns and cities remained relatively small. But the cultural life of the region's towns experienced a continuous stream of innovations from the later eighteenth century onwards, inspired by examples of urban development in western Europe. Indeed the introduction of something new, the transmission of new cultural values, was a witness of international contacts; a proof of the town's relationship with mainstream European thinking.[1]

Regional urban networks

Although the theme of this chapter is the cultural function of towns, it is necessary first of all to make a few general observations on the urban networks themselves, and the role of towns within this unfamiliar region.[2] Then as now, the urban networks of east-central Europe were diverse. Bohemia and Moravia, in the mountainous south-west of this region, were densely settled, and had a well-developed urban network with a small town every thirty kilometres or so. They shared a broader pattern of settlement, established in the later Middle Ages (and still discernible to the present) with neighbouring parts of south-eastern Germany and south-western Poland, from Bavaria and Saxony to Kraków and Lublin. Most of these urban centres were small: a town of 5 000 was reckoned sizeable, and exerted an important influence on its hinterland. By the end of the nineteenth century a provincial capital with some higher administrative functions and economic importance generally had a population of over 10 000.[3]

Beyond the mountains of southern Poland the landscape opens up into the north European plain. Here the medieval pattern of urban settlement was enriched during the early modern period by the establishment of numerous private towns. Great Poland (*Wielkopolska*) and Royal Prussia, the areas around Poznań and Gdańsk respectively, were relatively densely settled, while the urban population of Pomorze and Podlasie in the east, and Mazowia (the area around Warsaw) was much sparser. In addition, distances here were greater than in western Europe, the condition of roads was poorer, and each of the towns themselves served a more extensive hinterland. Furthermore, Poland's urban network had effectively been fragmented by the end of the eighteenth century as a consequence of the partitions. Different foreign administrations were introduced into the annexed territories, and regional centres such as Kraków (the medieval Polish capital), Poznań, Lublin and Lviv gained in cultural importance throughout the nineteenth century.

Latvian (formerly Livonian) and Estonian towns were part of a larger urban network which extended along the shores of the Baltic as far as the North Sea. The history and cultural tradition which they shared with coastal towns and sea-ports further to the west was reflected in their layout and architecture, and in their communal organizations;[4] and although the urban culture of the Baltic was less developed than that of north-western Europe, it was clearly far more advanced than that of the rest of the Russian empire, which absorbed these areas during the early eighteenth century.

The impact of modern demographic growth on the urban culture of the region was felt first in Bohemia and Moravia with the start of significant migration into the towns from the middle of the eighteenth century and by the towns of the north-east up to a century later. Despite the growth in the size of the towns, the basic patterns of the region's urban networks remained effectively unaltered, but changes in attitudes towards public life and the cultural functions of towns were of considerable importance.

Institutions, innovations and the cultural functions of towns

The development of urban culture can be measured in terms of the growth of social, cultural and educational institutions, and of those amenities which made life in towns safer, healthier and more comfortable: in short, more civilized. Such institutions were accessible not only to the urban public, but to the society of the hinterland as well, and were instrumental in transmitting new social and cultural values which brought about deep and fundamental changes in the societies they influenced. Their introduction followed asymmetrical patterns, however, and much depended on who promoted them, when and where, so that the relationship between innovations and the pace of modernization reveals a great deal about the uneven development of the region as a whole.

This unevenness is also reflected in the differing rates of diffusion of various types of innovation. These can be categorized according to social accessibility and function – i.e., whether they were basic amenities or luxuries – and according to the amount of investment required to provide them. High levels of initial investment were necessary for the introduction of basic technological innovations – such as water supplies and sewage systems – which proved beneficial to the whole of urban society and which reflected not merely local levels of technical progress, but changes in the social consciousness and cultural attitudes of urban elites. As such they are an index of the gradient of development not only between western Europe on the one hand, and central and eastern Europe on the other, but between internal 'cores' and 'peripheries' within the region itself.[5]

Cultural innovations proper, that is, those institutions open to the public, such as parks, theatres and so on, were also initially high-cost investments, and at first only accessible to the elites. They appeared first in the region's capital cities during the later eighteenth century, reaching smaller country towns only in the course of the next hundred years or so, and became widespread throughout the region only after the First World War. Even in small towns, however, there might be a public park, a promenade, and a hall which served for both theatrical productions and balls. The introduction of such cultural institutions in the provinces very much depended on a number of local factors, including the relative prosperity of the town and its hinterland, and the role of local individuals. Most such towns were administered by the old preindustrial elites, who generally felt responsible for questions of urban development, in so far as they participated in local government. However, much depended on what measure of local self-government the municipality or district enjoyed, and in practice there was a great deal of diversity in terms of what could be achieved by local initiatives.

In Poland, for example, it was the aristocracy that had to be convinced of the advantages of flourishing towns, and of the need to change state policies towards urban development. Decisions about the introduction of urban innovations in pre-partition Poland were generally taken by representatives of the local nobility rather than by municipal bodies. In private towns, of course, it was the owner who took decisions and controlled both local government and administration. But the crucial problem in Polish urban planning was that burghers had inferior status to the nobility, and those aristocrats who took up 'urban' professions were punished with the loss of their privileges. The Polish Estates made a last-ditch attempt to reform the constitution on the eve of the second partition, and did manage to change conditions in respect of the royal towns. But in partitioned Poland conditions altered again as the three imperial powers took control.[6]

In other parts of the region, however, the burghers themselves had a greater say in the affairs of local government. The towns of the eastern Baltic were still ruled by the old merchant elites organized in guilds, and they controlled the administration of the towns. In Livonia, for example, the central government was represented by the warden of Livonia, and he was able to exercise some influence; and in Riga the traditional elite effectively continued to rule until 1877. In Bohemia and Moravia the participation of the town-dwellers themselves in urban local government was considerable. Members were elected from among the burghers until the administrative reform of 1784. Thereafter, eligibility for election was subject to approval by the central bureaucracy. The decisions of local government institutions could be rather odd, however, where the particular interests of the body's members were at stake, as in the case of the town council of Třebíč in Moravia, which decided in 1835 that the municipal archives were not worth keeping, and sold them off as waste paper.[7]

The modernization of town centres

The drive to redevelop towns in the late eighteenth century was very much a part of the contemporary preoccupation with 'rationalizing' society, and notions of town planning reflected not only the aesthetic ideals of Enlightenment intellectuals but basic concerns about safety and amenities as well: the discourse of urban redevelopment combined the classical tastes of the elite with a desire to modernize the organization of urban space.

In Poland the impetus for the redevelopment of towns came from the enlightened aristocracy in the entourage of King Stanislav August.[8] It was the final achievement of the country's political elite during the last years of the independent Polish state. Ideas for the reform of the towns were presented to the assembly of the Polish Estates by leading representatives of the aristocracy. A. Potocki in 1744, and A. Zamoyski in 1764 both argued for a more positive attitude towards the social role of commerce.[9] The reform programme was accepted by the party of Czartoryski, one of the most powerful Polish magnates, and concentrated on the renovation of towns, on building and on 'good order'. Special attention was paid to the regulation of street networks, the completion of large-scale architectural projects and the planting of greenery in the town centres.[10]

Regulations were introduced in 1764, for example, to eliminate wooden constructions from the centre of Warsaw; and shortly afterwards the nobility were empowered to set up local institutions (the so-called *commissiones boni ordinis*) as organizations for the general improvement of towns and their economies. The work of the commissions involved only the royal towns, and its objectives were largely cosmetic, aimed at improving the aspect of towns in the hope that this would somehow enable them to function more efficiently (or at least provide a pleasant environment for the assemblies of the Estates). Until the constitution of 1791 there were no real reforms aimed at improving the condition of the towns or enhancing the status of their inhabitants, and town-dwellers themselves, whether merchants or artisans, were not generally involved in the movement for urban reform. The programme of urban modernization was very much a project launched by the nobility, and organized by local members of the aristocracy.

By the end of the eighteenth century much of central and eastern Poland and the Baltic region had been annexed by Russia where the principles of urban development had been imported from the West by Peter the Great and developed by Catherine.[11] The building of towns – and their regimentation – was promoted vigorously from around the turn of the century throughout the Russian empire, including these new territories in the north-west. In Tallinn (Reval) for example, the local authorities began to take a much greater interest in the condition of the town during the last quarter of the eighteenth century. Measures were taken to improve the appearance of buildings and the condition of the streets, and to increase fire safety. New buildings were to be built with brick or stone, rather than wood, and roofs were to be rebuilt with tiles. Pavements were introduced to cope with the problem of increased traffic in the streets. Building regulations for Tallinn were established gradually, following the strengthening of administrative links between the central government and the Baltic provinces in 1784, and from 1785 new construction could take place only in accordance with the town plan. The new regulation was at first applied only in the suburbs; no new construction was undertaken in the centre, apart from the improvement of facades, and it became quite common to refer to albums of model house-fronts which were produced as guidelines especially for this purpose. At the same time topographical surveys were undertaken. In 1797, for example, engineers were asked to produce plans of all the town's public buildings and drawings of facades, a project which produced the earliest extant pictorial record of the most important buildings. The internal territorial organization of the town was regulated with the division of the centre into quarters and the fixing of boundaries between suburbs; building plots were given numbers. Finally, after 1821, a remodernization of the town centre was undertaken in accordance with the strict building regulations introduced by the imperial governor general, Marquis Palucci.[12]

In Tartu (Dorpat), Estonia's second city, and the only other urban centre in the region with a clear cultural function, the same orderly classical principles were applied during the modernization and reconstruction of the centre (See Figure 5.1). Here, however, the town was rebuilt following a massive fire in 1775, which had reduced it to ashes, but cleared the way for complete renovation. Not surprisingly, improved fire safety was a central consideration here too. As in Tallinn wooden constructions were replaced by brick and stone. Equally, however, the elimination of traditional wooden structures was symbolic of a desire on the part of the authorities not only to be modern, but also to appear modern. New houses were built in line, and streets were straight, with pavements for pedestrians.[13] Order, cleanliness and improved safety were, of course, prime objectives in the reconstruction of both towns, but the aesthetics of eighteenth-century classicism also played an important part.[14] Surprisingly, this innovative spirit at the end of the eighteenth century did not reach Riga, which was considered to be the regional metropolis with the closest contacts with remote western Europe.

'High cost' cultural innovations

The eighteenth century also witnessed the emergence of the first cultural institutions typical of a modern city, such as museums, theatres, concert halls and parks. These were high-cost innovations, which were initiated in the eighteenth century by the aristocratic elites of the day, although they had their own private art collections, gardens and the space and resources to host musical and theatrical entertainments. These were new, public institutions, open to all those who could pay for tickets,[15] and they were to be the cultural locations of a new 'bourgeois' elite whose time had not yet come. The introduction and diffusion of such cultural institutions followed similar patterns to western Europe (for example, the Netherlands) but came later and were less dynamic:[16] the merchants, bankers and businessmen of the Habsburg empire did not gain positions of economic and political importance until after 1848 and the liberalizing reforms of 1860.

The development of cultural institutions was an uneven process which continued throughout the nineteenth century, gathering pace in the years after 1860. Although research has shown that the aristocracy promoted urban redevelopment in the Czech lands during the last three decades of the eighteenth century – both in Prague and in smaller towns – the intensive diffusion of such changes came only with the Czech nationalist movement in the second half of the nineteenth century. In Poland, on the other hand, towns were in such a poor state at that time that no efforts to modernize could make good the deficiencies resulting from years of neglect. Financial resources were limited and urban enterprises were on a modest scale.[17] Polish towns had fewer buildings with public functions. Z. Bobrowski, who classified Polish towns in four categories according to a number of criteria – including the incidence of cultural institutions – found that complex urban development was more evident in private residential towns such as Białystok or Zamość – which were in the second category – than in the metropolis, Warsaw – in the first category. The cultural development of towns in the third category – provincial capitals such as Lviv, Vilnius, Poznań and Lublin – was the responsibility of their respective commissions. Towns in the fourth category, which differed little from villages, had very rudimentary public institutions – generally a church, a public house and a hospital.[18]

The government commission which regulated urban development in Poland made a functional distinction between public and private buildings. In 1791 it recorded town halls, hospitals, inns, public houses, prisons and baths as public buildings, and shops if the premises were separate from private houses. The number of such public buildings increased as urban administration expanded, hygiene became more important, and commerce flourished. The largest investments were in Warsaw: a water supply was introduced in 1767; a theatre opened in 1775 and Poland's first circus was established in 1780. The Academy of Sciences and the National Museum were also founded in Warsaw. Investment in cultural institutions in the provinces was more modest. Primary schools were established by the local aristocracy, and secondary schools and libraries by the religious orders such as the Jesuits or the Piarists. A lack of financial resources often meant that facilities were shared: theatres, for example, doubled as ballrooms. In Poland (as, indeed, in the Czech lands and the Baltic too) such cultural institutions were to become important instruments of the nationalist movement.

The partition of the Polish state transformed Poland into three separate peripheral provinces during the following century, each on the margin of a large empire. 'Internal' economic links effectively broke down as the governments of Prussia, Austria and Russia each pursued similar policies in an effort to integrate the separate Polish provinces into their respective states after the final partition of Poland in 1795. The institutional position of towns remained unchanged, but the number of towns was reduced administratively by all three imperial governments, and this was followed by government intervention in urban administration.

In the eastern Baltic the position of towns was influenced by the growth of St Petersburg. Tallinn and Pärnu developed spa facilities, but Tallinn lost some of its regional administrative functions as a result of the close vicinity of the new Russian metropolis.[19] The importance of Riga was diminished in the same way, although it remained the most important Baltic port and preserved its image as the most 'European' town in the region. A contemporary topographic journal described it as a strong, well-built Hanseatic town, similar in outlook to other major ports in the region. It had all the signs of an established town, with all the traditional institutions: self-government and local administration, guilds, schools and churches. But no mention is made of any new institutions, and it seems there was an almost total absence of innovation. A small public library functioned in the early decades of the nineteenth century, but the theatre came much later, in 1863, and the museum of ethnography and the art gallery followed in 1901 and 1905 respectively.[20] Growth and change in Tartu began with the reopening of the university in 1802 after a hundred years, which established the town as a cultural centre, and prompted considerable investment in new building.[21]

The cultural role of capital cities

None of the cities considered here were capitals of independent states during the period under discussion. East-central Europe was a region in which small countries were absorbed by neighbouring empires and lost their statehood. Nevertheless, cities such as Prague, Warsaw and Buda retained many of the cultural functions of a capital city, and others, such as Kraków, Poznań, Tallinn and Riga, exerted a great deal of regional influence. Such cities did not differ significantly from each other in the range of cultural and educational institutions they offered. The Polish historian of the eighteenth century, Emanuel Rostworowski, has commented that the age of absolutism was the period when intellectual development began to proceed symmetrically, when 'the clocks of intellectuals reached a synchronic pace'. Communities of intellectuals, he continues, were no longer isolated, but were basically at the same level.[22] They created a local intellectual environment in which urban innovations could be developed.

Central European capitals were all rather small and provincial when compared with the leading cities of Europe. Prague, with 77 000 inhabitants, was one of the more important capitals in the region at the end of the eighteenth century.[23] It was larger than most other important towns within the same region, for example Dresden, Munich, Nuremberg, Leipzig, Bratislava and Buda. It was also larger than the Polish towns of Kraków and Wrocław, but about the same size as Warsaw; and if we extend this comparison further to the north-east, it was larger than Vilnius and Riga, and about seven times larger than Tallinn.

Medieval Prague had grown out of an agglomeration of five independent towns;[24] and although the city did not resume the dynamic growth of its earlier years until the second half of the nineteenth century, it nevertheless retained important cultural functions.[25] In the country, the tradition of Prague as the royal residence and the capital of a lost state was very much kept alive, although its real administrative jurisdiction was limited to the historical region of Bohemia alone: Moravia and Austrian Silesia had their own administrations, responsible directly to the central bureaucracy in Vienna. The Church hierarchy was in Prague, however, and it remained the city of residence for the Czech aristocracy. Its position was further strengthened by the presence of the principal cultural and educational institutions, and not least by its central position. There was never any doubt of Prague's leading place in the national urban hierarchy of the Czechs.

Cultural life in Prague was strongly influenced by the mainstream European Enlightenment. The society of university scholars and intellectual bureaucrats, who met frequently in salons, masonic lodges, clubs and cafes, created a favourable environment for the exchange of ideas and social gossip.[26] Most of Prague's forty-one private libraries were open to the public, as was the university library. Music was very important to the cultural life of the city and flourished both at private concerts and at the opera and theatres. A periodical press emerged and intellectual life began to take on an institutionalized character as scholarly and scientific societies were founded which would furnish the foundations for a national museum and gallery and an academy of sciences. There were also international links with nearby German cities such as Vienna, Dresden and Leipzig, and with France. Czech historians themselves have been rather sceptical about the cultural life of eighteenth-century Prague. Their image is of a provincial, even a parochial society, *bürgerlich* in the German sense, rather than 'bourgeois' and aristocratic. Prague society at the end of the eighteenth and the beginning of the nineteenth century was composed primarily of aristocrats, their servants, priests and soldiers.

It is perhaps surprising that such a social milieu launched a successful programme for the defence and regeneration of the Czech language.[27] Social change took place gradually during the first decades of the nineteenth century and, although the old elite did not disappear, merchants, bureaucrats and businessmen became more important. Both the old and the new elite spoke German, whereas Czech was spoken by artisans, shopkeepers, workers and servants; and since there was a relatively low level of illiteracy – largely as a result of the reforms of Maria Theresa – all these people had an interest in the newspaper and periodical press, 'calendars' and the theatre. While there was considerable cultural activity in Prague, it was largely due to the efforts of a relatively small educated elite. This is documented by the early history of the Czech-language periodical press, which had so few subscribers that it suffered financial difficulties.[28] Czech society only really became interested in the Czech press at the time of the 1848 revolution, and even then there was evidently stronger demand for it in the country than in the capital.

The situation in cities of a size and political importance similar to Prague's, such as Kraków, Warsaw, Riga or Tallinn, was broadly similar. Indeed, it was not so much in the outlook of major cities – maybe provincial compared with Vienna, but nevertheless the closest symbol of European urban culture – that regional differences were apparent, but in the conditions of provincial cities, small towns and villages. Indeed, we should scarcely be able to speak of the capital's *central* role if strong urban networks had not existed: and it is within these networks, which differed widely in density and structure, and in the cultural role of the provincial towns within them, that the diversity of urban cultures in this region is most evident.

The cultural role of provincial towns in the context of modernization

The provincial towns that functioned as cultural centres and models of urban life in the sparsely populated rural lands of east central Europe were smaller than their counterparts in the west, and generally had more of an agrarian character. While regional capitals showed signs of modernization analogous to those in similar cities throughout Europe, a comparison of small towns such as these produces a much more complicated and diverse picture. Those towns with over 10 000 inhabitants represented the new and rapidly expanding provincial centres. Many established provincial centres whose position had been based on their administrative importance (such as Kouřim and Loket in Bohemia) lost their economic dynamism during the course of industrialization in the second half of the nineteenth century. New industrial centres were founded only on a limited scale in Bohemia and Moravia. In Poland, private towns (such as Białystok) had been founded even in the eighteenth century, and new towns, such as Lodž, were founded in the nineteenth century in industrial locations. In Estonia no new towns were established.

In Bohemia, those towns with regular weekly markets supplying urban communities with agricultural produce had the best chance of development. Some of these became regional commercial centres, and acquired an important cultural role with influence over an extensive rural hinterland. In addition to such regional market towns there were others whose importance depended on the long-established presence of the local authorities for the district (the *Kreisamt*), a function which had also enhanced their economic importance. Litoměřice, České Budějovice and Plzeň are all examples of this type. Others, as we have noted, lost such functions and declined in population and economic significance.

The new type of large provincial centre was typically a market town or private town which also became an important manufacturing centre. Towns such as these – textile-manufacturing Liberec, for example – gradually attracted administrative institutions as well, and attained a certain cultural importance. In Bohemia and Moravia even market towns and the larger district capitals (*Kreisstädte*) had grammar schools, and this dense network of primary and secondary schools was one of the most important factors in the dissemination and development of cultural traditions in the provinces. Eventually such towns also acquired other cultural institutions such as theatres, museums and societies founded by local people.

Under the influence of the patriotic enlightened intellectuals of the time the theatre in particular came to be seen as the institution with the greatest cultural significance, and there was a determination not only to see more theatres established, but to have performances in the native language; the development of Czech-language culture was an important task for the national movement. This took a long time. In the first half of the nineteenth century the theatre in the Czech lands was dominated by amateurs. Theatrical performances took place at least once in 121 Czech towns (nine in Moravia); permanent theatre buildings were to be found in Plzeň, Třeboň, Tábor and Polička; and in many other places there were public venues used for theatre which also served a number of other social and cultural functions.[29] In České Budějovice the theatre was opened in 1819 in a reconstructed old brewery, and in nearby Jindřichův Hradec theatre-goers shared the ballroom. In Jihlava in Moravia the first opera performance probably took place in 1740, but it was not until 1850 that a reconstructed monastery building began to serve as a permanent theatre as a result of the efforts of a local businessman: by 1856 it had been taken over by the municipal authorities. During the eighteenth and nineteenth centuries these new, 'modern' cultural institutions were often situated along the new boulevards constructed on the site of recently demolished fortifications or in buildings confiscated from the Church as a result of the Josephinian reforms. But these were districts which were swallowed up into town centres as urbanization accelerated. The best example of such a development is Plzeň, where the town walls were torn down in 1795 and replaced by a public park, a school (1805–1808) and a theatre building (1832). In most Bohemian and Moravian towns the removal of fortifications began between the 1820s and 1850s.[30]

The cultural function of the towns of the Habsburg monarchy began to grow during the eighteenth century, as the traditional elite in the empire's regional capitals promoted artistic and other social activities which were already open to the public, such as theatres, libraries, art collections and parks. The second period of intense cultural development was around 1848, but came to a halt with the repressive political backlash of 1850 and did not resume for another decade or so. The liberalization of political life in the towns was reflected by the increased activity of new local elites after 1860, the period when most cultural, social and educational institutions were founded, and the more significant cultural centres were generally those large towns, such as Plzeň or Jihlava, which already had important administrative functions and a thriving local economy. Nevertheless, in Bohemia and Moravia at least, there were some small towns without an important political role – Litomyšl and Kroměříž, for example – that did have a local significance as centres of culture. Further east, in Poland and the Baltic, only the larger towns, such as Lviv and Poznań, had a cultural role of any significance. In small agricultural towns this function was effectively non-existent.[31] Many of the smaller Polish towns had lost their administrative functions during the partitions, and retained only a residual economic importance in the context of the agricultural economy.

The cultural development of towns in the regions under discussion was dependent on the social status of urban society, which was limited by absolutist policies. The imperial powers adopted similar policies regulating urban functions.[32] On the other hand the nation-building movements in all three empires considered cultural and educational institutions important tools for gaining wider political support through the transmission of cultural values and ideology. Their distribution therefore not only reveals the range of services available to townspeople but also reflects the state of society as a whole.

Notes

1. On the concept of innovation see Bernard Lepetit and Jochen Hoock (eds), *La Ville et l'innovation en Europe 14e–19e siècles*, Paris: EHESS, 1987; and Marjatta Hietala, *Services and Urbanization at the Turn of the Century. The Diffusion of Innovations*, Helsinki: SHS, 1987. On the concept of transmission of cultural values see Anthony Grafton and Ann Blair (eds), *The Transmission of Culture in Early Modern Europe*, University of Pennsylvania Press, 1990.

2. As an introductory guide to the labyrinth of changing borders and sub-regions of central and east-central Europe see Dennis P. Hubchick and Harold E. Cox, *A Concise Historical Atlas of Eastern Europe*, London: Macmillan, 1996. On urban society in general see Ulrich im Hof, *The Enlightenment. An Historical Introduction*, Oxford: Blackwell, 1997, pp.49–62, and a monograph quoted extensively by im Hof: Jerzy Wojtowicz, *Miasto europejskie w epoce oświecenia i rewolucji francuskiej*, Warsaw: Panstwowe wydawnictwo naukowe, 1972.

3. See Maria Bogucka, 'The Network and Function of Small Towns in Poland in Early Modern Times' in A. Mączak and T. C. Smout (eds), *Gründung und Bedeutung kleinerer Städte im nördlichen Europa der frühen Neuzeit*, Wiesbaden: Harrasowitz, 1991; R. Nový, 'Městská síť v Čechách' in Josef Petráň (ed.), *Počátky českého národního obrození*, Prague: Academia, 1990, pp.33–43; L. Klusáková, 'The Asymmetry of Urban Growth. Some reflections on the peripheral character of urban development in the Czech Lands and in Central Europe during the 18th and 19th centuries,' in *Historická Demografie* 15, 1991, pp.77–97.

4. See Michel Mollat du Jourdain, *Evropa a moře*, Bratislava: Archa, 1994 (Europe and the Sea – simultaneously published in England by Blackwell: Oxford).

5. For the terms 'core', 'semiperiphery' and 'periphery' see the writings of Immanuel Wallerstein, *The Modern World System. I–III*, New York, 1974–88. For 'internal periphery' see Hans-Heinrich Nolte, 'The Position of Eastern Europe in the International System in Early Modern Times', *Review*, IV, 1, Summer 1982, pp.25–84; H.-H. Nolte (ed.), *Internal Peripheries in European History, Zur Kritik der Geschichtsschreibung*, vol. 6, Göttingen, 1991, pp.5–28; and *European Internal Peripheries in the Twentieth Century*, Wiesbaden: Franz Steiner Verlag, 1997.

6. See Elzbieta Kaczynska, 'Bürgertum und städtische Eliten in Kongreßpolen, Rußland und Deutschland im Vergleich' in Jürgen Kocka, *Bürgertum im 19. Jahrhundert. Deutschland im europäischen Vergleich*, Munich: Deutscher Taschenbuch Verlag, 1988, p.467 ff.

7. Jan Janák, *Třebíč. Dějiny města.* II, Brno: Blok, 1981, p.43.

8. Maria Bogucka and Henryk Samsonowicz, *Dzieje miast i mieszczanstwa w Polsce przedrozbiorowej*, Wrocław: Ossolineum, 1986, pp.566 ff.

9. Tadeusz Wróbel, *Zarys historii budowy miast*, Wrocław: Ossolineum, 1971.

10. Wojciech Trzebiński, 'Nadzor budowlany i przepisy policyjno-budowlane w Polsce oświecenia jako środki naprawy miast królewskich', in A. Gieysztor and T. Roslanowski (eds), *Miasta doby Feudalnej w Europie środkowo-wschdnieij, Przemiany społeczne a układy przestrzenne*, Warsaw, Poznań, Toruń: Państwowe Wydawnictwo Naukowe, 1976, pp.255, 268.

11. V. V. Kirillov, 'Russkoye gradostroitelstvo na perechode ot srednievekovia k novomu vremeni', in *Russkyi gorod*, 8, Moscow, 1986, pp.3–30; 'Russkyi gorod epokhi barokko (kulturnyi i esteticheskyi aspekt)', in *Russkyi gorod*, 6, Moscow, 1983, pp.127–62.

12. Helmi Üprus, *Tallinn aastal 1825*, Tallinn: Kirjastus Kunst, 1965, pp.27–9, 34. This includes drawings of house-fronts from 1820–25.

13. V.V. Kirillov, 'Russkyi gorod epokhi barokko', p.160.

14. Raimo Pullat and Tarvel Enn, *Istoria goroda Tartu*, Tallinn: Eesti Raamat, 1980, p.108.

15. Robert van Engelsdorp Gastelaars, Michael Wagenaar and Martin Dijst, 'The Diffusion of Public Leisure Facilities over the Dutch Urban System in the 19th Century', in Lepetit and Hoock (eds), *La Ville et l'innovation en Europe*, pp.113 f.

16. Ibid.

17. M. Borowiejska-Birkenmajerowa and J. Demel, 'Działałność urbanistyczna i architektonyczna senatu wołnego miasta Krakowa w latach 1815–1846', in *Studia i Materiały do teorii i historii architektury i urbanistyki*, IV, Warsaw, 1963, p.5; W. Kalinowski and S.Trawkowski, 'Uwagi o urbanistyce i architekturze miejskiej królewstwa kongresowego w pierwszej pol.XIX w.' in *Studia i Materiały do teorii i historii architektury i urbanistyki*, I, Warsaw, 1956, pp.55–152.

18. Z. Bobrowski, 'Budynki użyteczności publicznej w Polsce wieku oświecenia' in *Studia i Materiały*

do teorii i historii architektury i urbanistyki, III, 1961, pp.8–138. See also Jan Wąsicki, *Ziemie polskie pod zaborem pruskim. Prusy Nowowschodnie 1795–1806*, Poznań, 1963, and *Miasta zachodniego pogranicza Wielkopolski, 1793–1815*, Poznań, 1960, and other works by the same author. Bohdan Baranowski: *Życie codzienne małego miasteczka w XVII i XVIII wieku*, Warsaw, 1975.

19. William Blackwell, 'Modernization and Urbanization in Russia: a Comparative View', in Michael Hamm (ed.), *The City in Russian History*, University of Kentucky Press, 1976, pp.299–305.

20. August Wilhelm Hupel (ed.), *Topographische Nachrichten von Lief-und Ehstland*, 3 vols, Riga, 1774, 1777 and 1782. Here vol. 1, pp.135–41. See also Anders Henriksson, 'Riga. Growth, Conflict, and the Limitations of Good Government, 1850–1914', in Michael F. Hamm (ed.), *The City in Late Imperial Russia*, Bloomington: Indiana UP, 1986, p.178.

21. This tradition was started by the Jesuit college, founded in 1583. The college became the Swedish *gymnasium* (grammar school) in 1630, and a university by 1632. After 1699 the Academia Gustaviana was moved to Pärnu and functioned till 1710. Then the town surrendered to Russian armies, and that was also the end of the university for nearly a hundred years. The institution's language of instruction was German and it exerted an enormous influence throughout the Russian empire.

22. Emanuel Rostworowski, 'Polska w Europie oświeconych', in *Kwartalnik Historyczny*, 1980, 1, pp.3–15.

23. J. Petráň,' Pražská metropole', in J. Petráň (ed.), *Počátky českého národního obrození*, Prague: Academia, 1990, p.83; Paul Bairoch, Jean Batou and Pierre Chèvre, *The Population of European Cities. Data Bank and Short Summary of Results*, Geneva: Droz, 1988. The data on capitals and large towns in the region is reliable, but the enumeration of towns is incomplete and in some cases incorrect.

24. This was much the same pattern of development as that of Kraków, Buda and Pest, and Tallinn. Each of the five districts of Prague had its own local government, and only in 1784 were four of them united (the old town, the new town, Hradcany and Malá Strana). Even in the late nineteenth century the large industrial suburbs still had the status of separate towns.

25. According to Palacký, *Popis království českého*, Prague, 1848, Prague had 67 906 inhabitants in 1843 and by 1890 the population had reached 182 530.

26. J. Petráň, 'Pražská metropole', pp.83 ff.

27. On the character of the Czech national revival see Miroslav Hroch, *Social Preconditions of National Revival in Europe*, Cambridge, 1985, esp. pp.8–12, 44–61.

28. Karel Bezděk, 'Noviny', in J. Petráň (ed.), *Počátky českého národního obrození*, pp.248–50.

29. On the role of the theatre in Czech towns see František Černy, 'Místo divadla v životě českých měst v 19. století' in *Studie a materiály* I, Národní Galerie, Prague, 1983, pp.52f.

30. See F. L. Rieger (ed.), *Slovník naučný* (Riegrův), Prague 1860–74; Vceňovací operát stabilního katastru, Ústřední archiv geodézie a kartografie, fond Stabilní katastr.

31. See Maria Bogucka, 'The Network and Functions of Small Towns in Poland in Early Modern Times', in Mączak and Smout, *Gründung und Bedeutung kleinerer Städte*, pp.222 f., 228. There is a very useful general survey in M. Bogucka and H. Samsonowicz, *Dzieje miast i mieszczaństwa w Polsce przedrozbiorowej*; Gilbert Rozman, 'Comparative approaches to urbanization: Russia, 1750–1800' in Hamm (ed.), *The City in Russian History*; R. Pullat, *Gorodskoje naselenije Estonii s konca XVIII veka do 1940 goda*, Tallinn, 1976.

32. See Helena Madurowicz-Urbańska, 'Struktura miast i osiedli typu miejskiego w wielkim Księstwie Poznańskim, Królewstwie Polskim i Galicji w drugiej połowie XIX wieku (do 1910 roku)' in *Badania nad historią gospodarczo-społeczną w Polsce*, Warsaw, 1978, pp.171 ff.

5.1 Wilhelm Stavenhagen, *View of Dorpat (Tartu)*

6

Castles, cabarets and cartoons: claims on Polishness in Kraków around 1905

David Crowley

Polish culture in the nineteenth and early twentieth centuries was notoriously hermetic. It has been self-obsessed to a degree that most foreign observers find difficult to comprehend. Their difficulty derives from the fact that the majority of Polish writers, artists and even architects during this period have taken 'the national condition' as their dominating theme. The tri-partition of Poland in the late eighteenth century denied the Poles political sovereignty. Although the subsequent rule over the ancient lands of Poland by Russia, Prussia and Austria had quite distinct and different local effects, the loss of political sovereignty and the depression of Polish institutions through explicit policies of repression and assimilation – most notable in Russian Poland – or of indifference – characteristic of Austrian rule – placed a particular responsibility on artists and designers: they were expected to take on the national voice. Artists took the opportunities afforded to them by their craft to affirm, or at least to express and to reflect upon, the state of Polishness. Nationality, in the face of active campaigns to at first repress and then later in the century to assimilate the Poles, was a matter of affirmation. Ernest Renan might have had the Poles – or at least the large gentry class – in mind when he formulated his famous dictum that 'The nation is a daily plebiscite.'[1] Consequently, worth and significance in the arts were measured on a scale of patriotic affirmation: good art was that which stressed 'Polishness.' Visiting a Polish museum with a collection of art from this period, it is rare to find works that depart from this standard. Art took on a didactic role as educator of the nation in lessons of Polishness and national history.

Nevertheless, it is possible to find works which repudiate the patriotic mission of Polish art. The subject of this essay, a series of drawings made in 1905 of a single view of a group of buildings on Wawel Hill in Kraków, offers such a rare example.[2] In fact, the drawings offer a wry commentary on the claims of various political constituencies as well as differing languages of art and architectural design to speak for the nation. That these works are relatively unknown and are rarely exhibited testifies to their marginal place in the nationalized canon of Polish art history. Whilst not landmarks in this history, these highly coded and sometimes malicious drawings, produced for the amusement of a small coterie of Cracovian intellectuals, offer a valuable commentary on the meanings of Polishness current in the early years of the new century.

'Kraków – the National Work of Art'

Kraków in 1900 was a provincial city of around 85 000 inhabitants in the poor and overcrowded Austrian crownland of Galicia-Lodomeria. An old and dilapidated city, it was in a state of relative decline in comparison to the rapidly expanding and modernizing urban centres of the Dual Monarchy.[3] Modern industrial invention and modish architectural expression were only belatedly affecting the life of the city. In fact, in Viennese eyes, Kraków was regarded as a parochial backwater: officers in the Austro-Hungarian army, for example, viewed a posting to Galicia-Lodomeria with dread.[4] Nevertheless, in the last decades of the nineteenth century Kraków was invested with emphatic national significance for Polish citizens of the Dual Monarchy (as well as those living under Russian and German rule). A number of associations and bodies were established with the explicit intention of stressing Kraków's significance in Polish history and countering a perceived threat to the city and its architectural and cultural monuments resulting from its low standing in a neglected province. The *Towarzystwo Miłośników Historii i Zabytków Krakowa* (Society of Friends of Kraków's History and Monuments) founded in 1896 was an enthusiastic conservator of the urban fabric and promoter of the city's history and culture. It commissioned a commercial photographic business owned by the Krieger family to record the state of the city in a series of hundreds of photographs. The mood of these works, in various published studies,[5] was strongly elegiac. They depicted a deeply historic city which, despite its state of disrepair, nevertheless testified to the historic vitality of Polish culture in a bygone age when Kraków had been the seat of Polish kings. This concern with the heritage of the city was, in effect, an expression of nationalist sentiment: a form of economic and emotional investment in the face of Austrian negligence.

Organizations like the Society of Friends can be characterized accurately as a conservative force in city culture, antagonistic to proponents of modernization and new urban development. In contrast, others working as artists and writers, who could not be described as either politically or culturally conservative, also contributed to the invention of Kraków as the centre of Polish national heritage. Most famously, the symbolist playwright-painter Stanisław Wyspiański treated the city and its history as a reservoir of themes for his major works in the literary, decorative and fine arts. The history of Kraków offered a compendium through which Wyspiański could express his complex and often critical relationship with Polish history and national identity. So, in effect, a coalition of interests united (to some extent inadvertently) in promoting a special place for the city in the national consciousness. It might even be said that the culture of 'heritage' that they fostered acted as a kind of curious brake on the currents of Modernism which then coursed through the other major urban centres of the Dual Monarchy. For whilst the Cracovian intelligentsia were in no sense isolated from events and debates in Vienna with, for example, artists such as Józef Mehoffer and Julian Fałat showing their work at the first Vienna Secession in 1898 or the city architect, Jan Zawiejski, establishing a practice in the imperial capital in the same year, nevertheless a prevailing commitment to the city and to registering its national valency depressed the appeal of Modernist experimentation.

The veneration of historic Kraków, like any construction of heritage, required audiences. Poles were encouraged to visit the city on 'national pilgrimages' (*pątnictwem narodowym*) organized by the *Towarzystwo Szkoły Ludowej* (Society of People's Schools). This association, established in 1891, arranged guided tours of the city which were designed to heighten patriotic sensibilities. The Society was particularly keen to proselytize Poles from Eastern Galicia who were regarded as the national constituency at greatest risk. Coming from the fringes of the crownland and constituting a minority population in a demographic mix dominated by Ukrainians, these pilgrims were most likely to benefit from the national elixir available in Kraków.[6] Typically, these tourists' route took them along the ancient royal way, the traditional course of the Polish kings on entering the capital – then also the only tram line in the city, newly electrified in 1901. This route through the city was a journey through Polish history marked by predominately aristocratic, romantic and religious foci with occasional detours to acknowledge particular modern additions to the city. After leaving the railway station they would pass the new *Teatr miejski* (Municipal Theatre, 1893). Cracovians were very proud of this new feature of their city which, though in part modelled on the Vienna Opera and technically inventive,[7] was cloaked in a vocabulary of forms and motifs which made conscious reference to Kraków's major architectural monuments. As if to make his intention explicit, the architect, Jan Zawiejski, had the legend '*Kraków Narodowej Sztuce*' (Kraków – the National Work of Art) inscribed across the building's facade.

The pilgrims' way then took them, on passing through the medieval

Florian Gate marking the entrance to the ancient heart of the city, to the *Rynek główny* (Main Square). The Rynek was the site of many of the city's historic buildings as well as more recent monuments: the Gothic Marian Church which, in the late 1880s, had been restored by artists associated with the Academy of Fine Arts; and Tadeusz Rygier's statue of Adam Mickiewicz, the romantic soldier-poet and Polish nationalist, which had been erected in 1898. At the centre of the square, the *Sukiennice* (Cloth Hall), until recently disfigured by a decaying sprawl of shacks, had been carefully restored in the late 1870s to accentuate its sixteenth-century Renaissance-style attic with its grotesque masks and a rippling 'Polish parapet'. The interior of the first floor of this building had been opened to the public as a gallery in October 1883 (on the bicentenary of the 'Relief of Vienna' led by Jan Sobieski) and was used to display the National Gallery's collection of nineteenth-century art. These works were dominated by the romantic, messianic canon exemplified by the paintings of Jan Matejko. Leaving the Rynek along Grodska Street, a thoroughfare flanked by some of the most ancient churches and town houses in the city, these pilgrims would end their promenade at Wawel Hill, a complex of buildings which includes the city cathedral and the royal residence.

Wawel, though dating back to the eleventh century, is dominated by buildings from the Renaissance, the age when the great Jagiellonian dynasty had greatest European influence. The site of the royal palace until the capital was moved to Warsaw at the end of the sixteenth century, Wawel remained the burial place of monarchs as well as many Polish saints, heroes and poets. It was also the site of many celebrated moments and events in national history, the significance of which had been accentuated by the Romantic movement in the nineteenth century. Most famously, one of Edmund Wasilewski's poems of 1839 contains these lines – famous to the point of school text-book cliché: 'Na Wawel, na Wawel Krakowiaku żwawy, / Podumaj, potęsknij nad pomnikiem sławy' (To Wawel, to Wawel, go briskly Cracovian / Reflect longingly over moments of glory).[8] Wawel was characterized by the time of these popular pilgrimages as the *ara patriae*. This conflation of religious devotion and a spirit of sacrifice with patriotism was the characteristic mix in the construction of the city's national heritage (as well as Polish Romantic nationalism). This combination had been evident when, for instance, in 1890 the body of Mickiewicz, who had died in exile and been buried outside Paris in 1855, was reinterred in a cathedral crypt on Wawel. This event was turned into a great public spectacle; a melancholic, theatrical procession along the route followed by the 'national pilgrims.'[9] Such *pompes funèbres* as well as the legends and myths about the history of Wawel embroidered by art had the effect of consecrating this hill into the *sacrarium* of Polish history in the minds of Poles. For a people who seemed only to have a past, Wawel was made to embody the glittering moments of that history.

At the same time, however, Wawel also reminded the Poles of the present: it stood as evidence of their loss of freedom. Wawel's contemporary uses by the Austrians illustrated the extent and changing nature of Austrian suzerainty over the Poles. They had turned Wawel into a garrison fortress in 1846 and during the political conflicts which wracked central Europe two years later, bombarded the city from there. Even during the period of peaceful accommodation with Vienna after 1867, military building works on the hill defaced Wawel; notably scouring medieval frescoes from its walls. Most poignantly, for the Poles at least, Austrian additions and remodelling to the site included a military hospital. This incensed patriotic Poles who saw its peace-time role, in part that of a clinic for the treatment of venereal disease, as an affront to this venerable hill. However, in the course of the century, Austrian rule became increasingly benign as Vienna struggled to maintain control over its sprawling and politically unstable multi-ethnic empire. Austria sought to 'buy off' dissent with policies which extended greater autonomy to her dominion peoples, notably with the *Ausgleich* (Compromise) with Magyar nationalism in 1867. Although the Poles did not achieve the degree of political autonomy enjoyed by the Magyars, they were offered greater opportunities to exercise control over their lives through regional and local government, and associations established to promote Polish culture in the region (such as the aforementioned *Towarzystwo Szkoły Ludowej*). Consequently, in this atmosphere of Austrian debilitation Cracovian patriots sought to win concessions from Vienna by displays of loyalty.

Wawel offers a good illustration of this tactic in practice. In 1880 it was offered in the name of the entire nation by the Galician diet and the Marshal of the province, Ludwik Wodzicki, as a gift to Emperor Franz-Josef I as a private residence.[10] This was a kind of tactical proposition designed to rid Kraków of the garrison on the hill. The Austrian Emperor could not reject this extraordinary gift and so ordered the withdrawal of the troops. But this Polish gesture was a wily tribute: for at the same time the Emperor could not take charge of buildings in such a state of disrepair. The royal palace was destined to remain his 'future residence'. When the first major withdrawal of the troops finally occurred after much Habsburg vacillation and negotiation on 7 September 1905, it was met with great Polish celebration. A major restoration programme began – following a series of more or less *ad hoc* projects[11] – under Zygmunt Hendel, funded by a public subscription scheme called 'Wawel Bricks' which raised 800 000 crowns. This interest in the future of Wawel also extended to artists and architects who produced a number of fantastic projects.[12]

A number of young figures associated with what was described around

1900 as *Modernizm*, a local variant of Secessionism, were roused by the return of Wawel to Polish control. Whilst Polish Modernism shared the pan-European sense of departure from the confines of academicism in its fantastic imagery and stylistic invention, unlike some of the more exaggerated forms of aestheticism found elsewhere Cracovian artists such as Jacek Malczewski and Stanisław Wyspiański tended to regard their work as part of a continuing national campaign for independence. So whilst, for example, many of the painters of this period are often described as 'Symbolist,' their works tend to reject indeterminate allusion and hazy suggestiveness in favour of unambiguous images.[13] Allegory was the means by which many artists as well as architects kept the ambiguity of modern stylistic invention in check. In particular, their allegorical forms drew predominately upon historical narratives to make comment on present circumstances. Cracovian Symbolism might be described as a hybrid form of 'Modernist historicism'. In this spirit, even modern buildings like Zawiejski's scheme for the *Teatr miejski* synthesized identifiably Polish historical motifs with technical and stylistic invention, free of the constraints of historical 'veracity' required of architects a generation earlier. A number of Wawel schemes from the early years of the new century offer examples of this kind of allegorical Modernism.

Stanisław Wyspiański, for instance, produced a number of works which connected Wawel with themes of resurrection. He designed four stained glass windows around 1900 for the cathedral. These cartoons were a series of portraits of legendary figures from national history including Kazimierz Wielki, the last king of the Piast dynasty and unifier and modernizer of fourteenth-century Poland. The King's remains, crowned and dressed in his coronation cloak, had been unexpectedly discovered during restoration work on his tomb in 1869.[14] His reburial on Wawel had been cause for patriotic celebration, another great *pompe funèbre*. This Piast monarch was reclaimed in Wyspiański's image as a symbol of the power of Poland which, despite defeat, rises from the grave just like the values associated with the King. Wyspiański returned to the theme of Wawel in 1904, as the Austrian garrison's withdrawal was imminent, when he remodelled the site as the 'Polish Acropolis' in collaboration with an architect, Władysław Ekielski. By adding great public spaces including a vast amphitheatre as well as erasing the Austrian military buildings from the site,[15] the 'holy hill', temple and citadel were self-consciously evoked as symbols of continuity and duration. These young designers were concerned to sustain Wawel's prominent national role after its return to Polish control: 'We are aware,' Ekielski stressed in 1908, 'that Wawel ought to be a focus for national life, as the ideal essence of popular and intellectual culture and as its visible form in a series of buildings.'[16]

The reclamation of Wawel from the Habsburg authorities was only a minor victory for the Polish patriots and their strategy of loyalty to Vienna. Nevertheless, it was one of a number of significant events in 1905 which caused the pulse of Polish nationalism to beat faster. In particular, Russia's war with Japan and the uprisings in the Romanov empire prompted nationalist demonstrations in all three partitions. In Kraków the Poles gathering at the statue of Mickiewicz to burn images of their oppressors included the socialist leader, Ignacy Daszyński, who put a torch to a portrait of Nicholas II in February 1905, a gesture which sought to fuel Polish nationalism as well as to signal solidarity with the Russian radicals. In concert, such events served to bring Polish nationalist dreams of independence and unification to a peak around 1905.

Zielony Balonik

Tourists guided on national pilgrimages in Kraków would not have found on their itinerary an artists' cabaret which opened in the city one month after the Austrian troops withdrew from Wawel.[17] The *Zielony Balonik* (Green Balloon), modelled on French literary café-cabarets, after its inaugural evening on 7 October 1905 rapidly became home to the city's Modernist circles and, in particular, to Kraków's painters, writers, and architects.[18] This cabaret met in a café, Jama Michalikowa (Michael's Den), decorated with unflattering caricatures of local worthies, bureaucrats and politicians, as well as a *szopka*, a traditional Christmas crib, which was used as a puppet theatre. The *Zielony Balonik* was renowned for iconoclasm: anti-clerical diatribes issued from its stage; cabaret costume and dance challenged conventionally-held sexual mores; the notorious Satanist, Stanisław Przybyszewski, used this platform to shock conservative Kraków. Above all, in its pronounced disrespect for national tradition, the *Zielony Balonik* sought to puncture the solemn, reverential disposition of the city. Tadeusz Boy-Żeleński, a famous host of the cabaret, coined the word *pomnikomania* (memorial-mania) in one of his *Zielony Balonik* poems to describe Kraków's morbid obsession with the past.[19]

On its second night the *Zielony Balonik* held an 'exhibition'. Jama Michalikowa was decorated in parody of the annual salon held by *Sztuka* (Art), a local association of Modernist artists. In satire, one of the hosts of the cabaret dressed in the style of a Habsburg official wearing a tricorn announced the opening of the exhibition in pigeon Polish with a strong German accent. Works caricaturing styles of art identified with local artists (often participants in the cabaret) were mounted on the walls of the café, including cartoons depicting Wawel. They were sketched in pastel by Karol Frycz and were accompanied by rhyming captions penned by local journalist Witold Noskowski.[20] These drawings were a facetious celebration of the recovery of Wawel.[21] But these sketches, however ephemeral, were not expressions of sheer iconoclasm. The 'national question' over the status of Poland appeared to be coming closer to resolution (as the return of Wawel augured) and various groups in Polish society at this time laid claim to the responsibility of leading the nation out of oppression. Five *Zielony Balonik* views of Wawel offer sardonic commentaries on the actions and ideologies of various claims to be the stewards of Polishness in difficult times. Furthermore, in their use of coded languages they adopt and parody the allegorical mode of much Polish art of the period (and depart from the aggressively caricatural cartoons produced for the cabaret).

Each drawing took the same view of Wawel; an unmistakable massive buttress known locally as the *Kurza Noga* (Hen's Leg). Each drawing in the first instance exploited the immediate and then widely understood discourse which placed Wawel at the heart of national heritage and established it as a symbol of Polish claims to sovereignty. One of these cartoons is captioned 'Zawiejski's Wawel' and shows the buildings on the hill in an exaggerated Secessionist style (see Figure 6.1). The decoration of Wawel is described in a rhyming caption at the foot of the sketch thus:

> *Z secesyjnych ramek*
> *Secesyjny zamek*
> *Lśni bogato i pstrokato*
> *Jak lubi Zawiejski*
>
> *Przystawki i murki*
> *Na filarkach Dziurki*
> *Jak [to] umie i rozumie*
> *Architekta miejski.*[22]

Jan Zawiejski was an influential figure in Modernist architectural circles in Kraków where he had been awarded the title, as the *Zielony Balonik* rhyme acknowledged, 'city architect' in 1900. As the designer of a number of major civic projects in the 1890s and 1900s, he was identified as a harbinger of stylistic innovation – broadly paralleling the invention of the Wagnerschule in Vienna.[23] In fact, the renown that he secured for his design of the *Teatr miejski*, completed in 1893, was such that he was given licence to practise in Vienna in 1898. His success there, as Jacek Purchla has recorded, came from his fashionable Secessionist designs for spectacles such as the 1899 Vienna Opera ball.[24] Despite prospering with a fashionable clientele, Zawiejski came under attack in the imperial capital. The right-wing journal, *Vaterland*, singled out this 'stranger from Galicia' as a decadent influence in the capital and, in effect, forced his return to Kraków. So, it would seem that a malicious note is struck in the *Zielony Balonik* drawing of 'Zawiejski's Wawel' for though his reputation in Vienna was that of a Galician interloper, in Kraków he was, inescapably, viewed as an architect infected with Viennese culture.[25] Zawiejski's 'Viennese-ness' is marked both by the application of the twin-headed eagle, symbolizing the Dual Monarchy, on 'his' Wawel design and by his apparent enthusiasm for modish styles emanating from Vienna, the rich, ornamental language of Olbrich-style design. Whilst this sketch might be seen in the first instance as a snipe at a well-known local figure – who was also caricatured in the cabaret's puppet theatre – , it can be seen as a wider comment about the uneasy relationship between Vienna and Kraków. For Wawel, at that moment extricated from one form of Austrian suzerainty, was ironically dressed in the decorative language of another; that of Viennese fashion. Whilst Galician Poles enjoyed quite distinct freedoms compared to their compatriots living under Russian and Prussian rule, they nevertheless viewed rule from Vienna with a wary eye. In this way the *Zielony Balonik* cartoon offers an ironic comment about the changing effects of Austrian rule. In four more drawings Frycz and Noskowski developed this theme with more sophistication through a critique of different claims made by various Polish interests to represent the interests of the nation.

The insurrectionary tradition of Polish nationalism had always been most active in the Russian partition; the product of a climate of conspiracy, censorship and repression. Consequently, Russia's war with Japan, the 'Bloody Sunday' massacre and the crisis which ensued in 1905 were triggers for strikes, demonstrations and assassinations of figures associated with Tsarist power by Polish nationalists seizing the moment to issue a blow to an ailing empire. The war with Japan particularly encouraged Polish agitators who saw themselves as brother Davids against a common Goliath. In 1904 both the Left and the Right schemed to forge alliances with Japan by sending missions to Tokyo to secure arms. Polish politicians living under the rule of the Tsar even assumed the names of Japanese generals as pseudonyms. In popular literature Japanese achievements and culture were characterized as valiant. All things Japanese, it seemed, were adopted to advance the Polish cause. Wawel too, in a second *Zielony Balonik* cartoon, is turned into a site of Polish nationalism infected with Japanese culture (see Figure 6.2).

But the drawing of Wawel in a Japanese style, produced little more than a few months after the fall of Port Arthur, Russia's most important stronghold in the Pacific, should not be understood simply as a reference to the fashion for Japan resulting from its war with Russia: it also had strong local resonance. In Kraków, like much of Europe, *Japonisme* was a notable tendency in Polish painting in the years before the turn of the century. In particular, Feliks 'Manggha' Jasieński's private collection of Japanese prints and decorative art had been an important point of reference for many young artists including Wyspiański.[26] In his attempts to popularize Japanese and *Japoniste* art, Jasieński allied his interests in the art of the Far East to the national cause. 'I have shown you Japan', he claimed, 'to teach you to think about Poland, thus following in the footsteps of artists who have thought about Japan in a Japanese style for over two thousand years.'[27] The lesson of Japanese art was that of a coherent vision of national identity which did not 'fall into slavish imitation of Western art.' The *Zielony Balonik* cartoon seems to take Jasieński literally at his word. Parodying the style of Hiroshige's woodcuts with a characteristic inclusion of a red panel of calligraphic text, Wawel is decorated with banners, paper lanterns and dragons' heads. This Polish view (and view of Poland) is turned suitably Japanese by the inclusion of branches of cherry blossom and lotus flowers as well as a richly-plumed phoenix – a symbol of regeneration. The cartoon seems to ridicule both the incorporation of Japan into the insurrectionary culture of Polish nationalism as well as the claims of Jasieński about the lessons for Polish culture, by drawing upon the powerful symbolic valency of Wawel as the sombre locus of Polishness.

Both Jasieński and the architect Zawiejski were regular butts of humour, as well as active participants, in *Zielony Balonik* evenings. In three further drawings of Wawel the aim of the cabaret satire was less focused on its social circle and the attacks on the politics of national leadership were more concentrated. The third drawing shows Wawel in a state of accelerated, exaggerated decay, yet it is ironically captioned as a scheme for 'restoration' authored by Count Karol Lanckoroński and supported by the city council (see Figure 6.3). This drawing passes comment on the work of the city council which, on acquiring greater autonomy from Vienna and following a great fire in 1866, had initiated a series of major restoration works in the city. Although some of its earlier actions were undertaken in the spirit of social and urban improvement – notably in slum-clearance projects and promoting new building work in the city around the *Nowe Miasto* (New Town) – , the major restoration works around the turn of the century, under the influence of the city's active conservation lobby, were designed to bolster the city's national status. As I have already noted this usually meant work on major architectural monuments such as the *Sukiennice* and the Marian Church. Around 1900 Kraków, it would seem, was undergoing a process of embalming. The key subject in this *Zielony Balonik* cartoon is the stout and no doubt familiar figure of 'His Excellency Count Lanckoroński' standing with his camera. He is credited as a force behind the restoration of Wawel which, in fact, he was as a member of the *Kierownictwo Odnowienia Zamku Królewskiego* (Directorship for the Restorations of the Royal Palace) and he personally funded particular works in the cathedral.[28] Lanckoroński, the paterfamilias of a powerful aristocratic Polish dynasty, was a self-appointed representative of the Poles in the higher chamber of the *Reichsrat* in Vienna as a prominent member of the *Koła Polskiego* (Polish Circle) of conservatives. In this, Lanckoroński played out a role of national leadership which his family had assumed since the fifteenth century. Above all, he was a conservative figure both in his politics as a watertight loyalist to the emperor and in his artistic proclivities. He was a celebrated connoisseur and collector of Renaissance art, a renowned antiquarian and the patron of a number of archaeological digs in Greece and Asia Minor.[29]

Lanckoroński's conservatism was not a form of passive political inertia: he actively sought to exercise his influence and, following a long-standing tradition of the Polish aristocracy, saw himself as a guardian of Polish culture. When in 1901, for example, the treasury of the cathedral on Wawel Hill came under the attention of the restorers, proposals were made for a new decorative scheme with frescoes designed by Polish artists. Lanckoroński attacked various designs including in particular those by the Modernist painter, Józef Mehoffer. He was particularly vexed by Mehoffer's archangel Gabriel, a winged boy dressed in a blue smock and a simply-patterned sash, against a flatly-patterned vegetal motif. He was outraged by what he saw as both a desecration of venerable tradition evidenced in Mehoffer's flattened, highly aesthetic style of design and a lowering of the aristocratic character of Wawel in the 'peasantness' of the artist's imagery. He published at his own expense a brochure to propagandize his views, pillorying Mehoffer for his 'figures of innumerable peasant boys with wings on their backs'.[30]

In the light of this minor dispute, the *Zielony Balonik* cartoon of Lanckoroński's vision of Wawel is, in the first instance, an attack on a well-known figure who was occasionally antagonistic to Cracovian Modernism (and therefore to many of the artists and writers associated with the *Zielony Balonik* circle). But this image can also be understood as a more substantial criticism of the conservatism of the aristocracy in Polish culture. Lanckoroński, by his relationship with the symbol of Polishness, Wawel, is made to stand for the class which laid claim to the protection of Polish interests in Austria.

In the latter years of the nineteenth century the aristocracy and, more importantly, the dominance of traditions of aristocratic culture, long claimed as the authentic measure of Polishness, came under increasing attack from various constituencies, notably from the socialists and Darwinian Positivists. The nostalgic retrospection of the aristocracy and its much celebrated lineage back to the 'golden ages' before the partitions were now seen as forms of 'Polish obscurantism and nobiliary ignorance'[31] and had, it was claimed, left Polish culture in a state of stagnancy and necrosis. There was little evidence of any benefit brought to Galicia. By the early years of the new century there was a strong resentment of the Polish magnates in Vienna who were accused of letting the region continue 'as a sort of primitive agrarian hinterland to support the industrial growth of Bohemia and the Austrian lands'.³² This poor crownland was wracked with poverty and even famine whilst other provinces prospered. Like the effects of national leadership by the aristocracy, Wawel is depicted as stagnant and dead despite the claims of those who promise its restoration. It stands as no more than a nostalgic memory of golden ages past.

An alternative vision of Polishness offered at the time as an antidote to the aristocratic vision was also the subject of comment by the *Zielony Balonik* artists (see Figure 6.4). In the drawing, Wawel is depicted remodelled in the so-called 'Zakopane style', a regional vernacular style promoted by a group of intellectuals gathered around Stanisław Witkiewicz, a critic and painter from Warsaw. Zakopane was at this time a small town in the foothills of the Tatra Mountains, one hundred kilometres south of Kraków. Witkiewicz, as a tourist to the region in the late 1880s, 'discovered' the wooden peasant homes found there. In a series of articles he developed the persuasive but erroneous thesis that the vernacular buildings found in this distant and isolated region were the last vestiges of a style of architecture that had once been found throughout Poland. In this they ought to remind the Poles of a time before the march of modernity and before the partition of the country by her neighbours. The logic of his pseudo-scholarly and archaeological argument presented a seemingly unavoidable conclusion for those who sought an essentially Polish style of architecture. The Zakopane style was proposed by its supporters as the 'true' foundations of a new, emergent Polish style. To illustrate the potential of his discovery, Witkiewicz and his colleagues set about building a series of villas in a refined, sophisticated variant of the vernacular in the Tatra region in the 1890s. They were also active in seeking to spread the style throughout all three partitions; in other words, to 'nationalize' it. Although the architectural profession was largely resistant to the Zakopane Style, it provoked a heated discussion in the pages of Kraków's architectural press around 1900.³³ Whilst the profession rejected the work of these 'dilettantes' as overly-expensive and ill-suited to urban settings, Witkiewicz was, nevertheless, frequently applauded for reminding the Poles of an overlooked source of Polishness; the peasantry. In this light, the vernacular offered a kind of antidote to the aristocratic, courtly traditions of Polish culture; a new source of Polishness untainted with compromise and unpolluted by self-interest.

Again the *Zielony Balonik* cartoons offer a tart commentary by ridiculing Witkiewicz's claims to the Polishness of this regional style: Wawel, the seat of kings, is turned into the home of a peasant. Furthermore, Witkiewicz's pseudo-archaeological conceits are exposed as yet another form of national sentimentality, by their projection onto the altar of Polish Romanticism, Wawel. And just as Lanckoroński was made to stand for the Galician aristocracy, Witkiewicz becomes a symbol for a wider tendency of what was disparagingly known as *chłopomania* (peasant mania) found throughout Polish culture in the 1900s – both Kazimierz Sichulski's paintings of Hucul life and Władysław Reymont's four-volume novel cycle *The Peasants* (1904–9), for example, sought to sanctify the peasantry.

Such forms of vernacularism found many opponents, not least amongst them the young Polish socialist movement which looked upon such ahistorical Romanticism with scorn as an idyllic and folkloric vision, blind to the harsh conditions of life for the rural poor. These activists were fired by the great poverty, illiteracy and emigration which marked Galician life at this time.[34] Nevertheless, questions of Polishness demanded the attention of Galician socialists too. Like the enthusiasts for peasant culture, Polish socialists attacked the aristocracy for their torpor and for acting in self-interest. In 1905–6 the largest socialist party, *Polska Partia Socjalno-Demokratyczna* (Polish Social-Democratic Party / PPSD) in Galicia published seven issues of *Hrabia Wojtek* (Count Wojtek), a folio of lithographs mostly drawn by Witold Wojtkiewicz. Named after the leader of the Polish magnates in Vienna, Count Wojciech Dzieduszycki, this satirical publication reserved its venom for the actions of the Koła Polskiego (Polish Circle). Dzieduszycki was caricatured on its pages as a donkey, a symbol of intransigence and dim-wittedness, determined to obstruct the extension of the franchise in the Austrian crownlands.[35]

Whilst it was relatively easy for the socialists to attack the aristocracy for shortcomings in the exercise of their self-proclaimed role as the protectors of Polish interest, grasping the reins of 'national leadership' was, nevertheless, a thorny issue for the Left. It proved to be a vexing problem which climaxed in rifts and schisms in the movement. Polish socialism sought to combine the pursuit of social revolution with national independence. But the relatively small membership of the PPSD, the leading left-wing party in Galicia, and its failure to attract votes at election forced the issue.[36] Pragmatic, indurative voices sought to convince the party that their only chance of achieving popular support was to don the clothes of nationalism, in other words, to press the national cause, whilst for Marxist members of the anti-nationalist *Socjal-demokracja Królewstwa Polskiego i Litwy* (Social Democracy of the Kingdom of Poland and Lithuania) like Rosa Luxemburg in the Russian partition, the nationalist cause was a distraction from their primary political purpose. Increasingly compromise with popular forms of nationalism compelled the centre-left groups like the PPSD to distance its programme from that of rival groups led by Polish Jews.[37]

In the light of the recent emergence of the Left on the political scene in the last decades of the nineteenth century, the irony of a socialist Wawel is evident (see Figure 6.5). The ancient seat of kings has suffered a coup d'état and its splendid regal towers and spires have been transformed into the clichés of socialist iconography: a smoke-belching factory city and offices of the *Naprzód* ('Forward'), the PPSD newspaper. The socialists' uneasy claims on national leadership are revealed as a fraud. Romantic Poland has been delivered into the modern world of industrial progress. Amongst the signs applied to the cathedral facade are those advertising a *Rzeznia koszerna*, a kosher slaughter-house, and a *Mikwa*, a bath-house attended by menstruating Jewish women. Their presence raises a disturbing aspect of particular claims on Polishness at the turn of the century, as well as the spectre haunting Polish-Jewish relations. Anti-semitism was a potent force in the political culture of Kraków. Increasingly, conservatives were keen to play the anti-semitic card to depress support for socialism, then often crudely caricatured as a Jewish politics – a line of attack that the leader of the Socialists, Daszyński, denounced as 'bestial'. In this cartoon the sacrarium of Polish history, Wawel, shown from its cathedral side, is counterpoised with two potent folk devils of the anti-Semitic mind.[38] The *Mikwa* and the slaughter-house had long been subjects of vicious folklore and associated with 'blood myths,' the stories of the re-enactment of the crucifixion on the bodies of Christian children and ritual murder for blood to cook Passover matzah. This *Zielony Balonik* cartoon is an indiscriminate, and probably unintentioned, testimony to the extent to which ethnicity was increasingly becoming used as a gauge of Polishness. It was a feature of the mass politics of the last decades of the nineteenth century and culminated in the extension of the franchise in Austria in 1906 for which the socialists had pressed so strongly.

Whilst one might not attach great significance to these ephemeral and sometimes rather indiscriminate satirical drawings designed to ridicule all shades of political and aesthetic opinion, they nevertheless testify to the extent to which the Poles sensed the coming moment in 1905. Different interests vied to speak for the nation and to offer competing visions of Polishness. These small sketches ridicule such claims. They make a point which very few others were prepared to make in the prevailing mood of nationalism in Polish culture. Jan Baudouin de Courtenay, a professor of linguistics at Kraków and St Petersburg and a great libertarian, was at his most active and most isolated in the early years of the century. He wrote a number of essays and pamphlets on the subject of the 'autonomy' of peoples living under the rule of Vienna and St Petersburg. In these works Baudouin de Courtenay could not, as Jindřich Toman has noted, write the noun 'patriotism' without putting it in inverted commas or qualifying it with the expression 'so called'.[39] The *Zielony Balonik* cartoons of Wawel too put inverted commas around the various claims on Polishness, national leadership and patriotism made in Kraków in 1905. They sought to expose the self-interest that underpinned these claims.

Notes

1. Ernest Renan quoted in Peter Alter, *Nationalism*, London: Edward Arnold, 1989, p.12.
2. These cartoons are held in the Państwowe Zbiory Sztuki na Wawelu (State Collection of Art at Wawel).
3. Budapest, for example, was one of the most rapidly growing cities in the world in this period. See the introduction to T. Bender and C. E. Schorske (eds), *Budapest & New York*, New York: Russell Sage Foundation, 1994; and John Lukacs, *Budapest 1900*, London: Weidenfeld and Nicolson, 1988.
4. István Deák, *Beyond Nationalism. A Social and Political History of the Habsburg Officer Corps 1848–1918*, Oxford and New York: Oxford University Press, 1990, p.109.
5. These included the Society's yearbook, *Rocznik Krakowski*, published from 1898, as well as Stanisław Krzyżanowski et al, *Kraków – Jego Kultura i Sztuka*, Towarzystwo Miłośników Historii i Zabytków Krakowa, 1904, which was published with a grant from the Austrian Ministry of Public Works in a revised form and condensed as Leonard Lepszy, *Cracow. The Royal Capital of Ancient Poland. Its History and Antiquities*, London: T. F. Unwin, 1912.
6. See Janina Bienarzówna and Jan M. Małecki, *Dzieje Krakowa: Kraków w latach 1796–1918*, III, Kraków: wyd. literackie, 1979, p.261 for details of one tourist's visit to Kraków who encountered the city's historic sites along this route.
7. See Jacek Purchla, *Teatr i jego architekt*, Międzynarodowe Centrum Kultury, Kraków, 1993.
8. Edmund Wasilewski, *Poezje*, Kraków: nakładem krakowski spółki wydawniczej, 1925.
9. See Janina Bienarzówna and Jan M. Małecki, *Dzieje Krakowa*, III, 1979, pp.264–6.
10. This idea originated in a publication written by Teodor Ziemięcki entitled *Zamek na Wawelu i Muzeum Narodowe*, 1879. His scheme sought to transform Wawel into part imperial residence and part national museum.
11. It should be noted that various restoration projects had, in fact, been underway since 1880 including significant work on the Cathedral in 1903. A good recent source detailing these schemes is *Studia Waweliana*, III, Kraków, 1994 which includes material from the 1992 conference 'Wawel w wieku XIX'.
12. See Stanisław Tomkowicz, *Wawel zabudowania wawelskie i ich dzieje*, 1908.
13. See, for example, Elizabeth Clegg's consideration of the themes of nationalism and symbolism in the work of Jacek Malczewski: Elizabeth Clegg, 'The Siberian Tea Party: Jacek Malczewski and the Contradiction of Nationalist Symbolism,' in *Apollo*, April 1989, pp.254–9.
14. See Józef Buszko, *Uroczystości kazimierzowskie na wawelu w roku 1869*, Ministerstwo kultury i sztuki, Kraków, 1970.
15. See Jarosław Krawczyk, 'L'Architecture parlante de Wyspiański et son sens messianique' in *Polish Art Studies*, no. 7, 1986, p.65.
16. Władisław Ekielski quoted in Lechosław Lameński, 'Cztery "Zamachy" na wzgórze wawelskie' in *Builetin Historii Sztuki*, vol. 45, part 1, 1983, pp.109–10. See also Władisław Ekielski, *Akropolis. Projekt zabudowań wawelu na latach 1904–1906*, Kraków, 1908.
17. See Tadeusz Boy-Żeleński, 'O szopce krakowskiej "Zielonego Balonika"' originally published in 1930, reprinted in Henryk Markiewicz (ed.), *Tadeusz Boy Zeleński o Krakowie*, Wyd. Lit., Kraków, 1973, pp.483–507.
18. See H. B. Segel, *Turn of the Century Cabaret*, New York: Columbia University Press, 1987, pp.221–53.
19. Boy-Żeleński's poem '"Pomnikomania" Krakowska' is reproduced in Tadeusz Żeleński, *Boy Słówka*, Wyd. Lit., Kraków, 1954, pp.301–2.
20. Noskowski, trained as a classical singer, was a critic for *Czas* reviewing musical performances and exhibitions. He was the son of the eminent translator and journalist, Władysław Noskowski. Frycz trained as a painter in Munich, London (under Hubert Herkhomer) and at the Académie Julian in Paris, in the first years of the century. He was a prominent figure in Cracovian artistic circles as a member of *Sztuka* and as the designer of a number of interiors including that of Jama Michalikowa in 1911.
21. This theme was not entirely original. Kazimierz Sichulski, for example, produced a series of satirical drawings on this theme for *Liberum Veto*, n. 22, 1903. See Tomasz Weiss, *Legenda i Prawda Zielonego Balonika*, Wyd. Lit., Kraków, p.255.

22. 'From a secessionist frame / A secessionist castle / Sparkles rich and stippled / So loved by Zawiejski. Buttresses and walls / On the columns, dimples / How the town architect / Knows and Understands all'

23. It should be noted, however, that the direct influence of Otto Wagner, Professor of Architecture at the Academy of Fine Art in Vienna, on the architects of the city was relatively slight. Zawiejski was in fact one of a number of prominent architects in Kraków who studied under Heinrich von Ferstel at the Technische Hochschule in Vienna in the 1870s and 1880s. See Jacek Purchla, *Jak powstał nowoczesny Kraków*, Wyd. Literackie, Kraków, 1990, p.72.

24. *Ibid.*, p.74.

25. In fact his most celebrated design in Kraków, the city theatre, was realized with technology and craftsmanship provided by leading Viennese firms. See Marian Dąbrowa, 'Kultura Galicji w latach 1867–1914' in Walter Leitsch and Maria Wawrykowa (eds), *Austria-Polska*, Warsaw and Vienna: Wyd. Szkolne i Pedagogiczne / Österreichischer Bundesverlag, 1989, p.217.

26. See Feliks Jasieński, *Manggha. Promenades à travers le monde, l'art et les idées*, Warsaw, 1901; Ewa Miodońska-Brookes and Maria Cieśla-Korytowska, *Feliks Jasieński i jego Manggha*, Kraków: Universitas, 1992; and *Manggha wystawa kolekcji Feliksa Mangghi Jasieńskiego* (ex. cat.), Muzeum Narodowe w Krakowie, 1989.

27. Feliks Jasieński cited by L. Kossokowski in the catalogue to the *Inspiracje sztuka japonii w malarstwie i grafice polskich modernistów*, Kraków: Muzeum Narodowe, 1981.

28. In 1902 Lanckoroński commissioned Antonii Madeyski to sculpt a monument to Queen Jadwiga, a fourteenth-century Polish saint, on a sarcophagus of yellow marble. See Angela Sołtys, 'Pomnik Antoniego Madeyskiego na tle problemu resturacji katedry Krakowskiej' in *Studia Waweliana*, III, Kraków, 1994, pp.157–67.

29. There is some discussion of Lanckoroński's patronage of these archaeological expeditions to Greece, 1882, and Asia Minor, 1885, in Mieczysław Paszkiewicz, *Jacek Malczewski in Asia Minor and Rozdół*, London: The Lanckoroński Foundation, 1972. It should be noted that Lanckoroński, not least as Malczewski's patron, was not entirely antagonistic to Modernist art, regarding it as legitimate in its place and in fact welcoming art's 'emancipation' from historicism.

30. Karol Lanckoroński, *Nieco o nowych robotach w katedrze na Wawelu*, published by the author [n.d.], p.16. Mehoffer responded with his own polemical publication: Józef Mehoffer, *Uwagi o sztuce. Odpowiedź na list Hr. Karola Lanckorońskiego w sprawie restauracyi katedry na Wawelu*, published by the author, 1903.

    The dispute between Mehoffer and Lanckoroński is discussed in Jadwiga Puciata-Pawłowska, 'Sprawa polichromii w skarbcu katedry wawelskiej w świetle polemik i wypowiedzi artysty' in *Acta Universitatis Nicolai Copernici: Zabytkoznawstwo i konserwatorstwo*, 5, Torun, 1974.

31. Stanisław Brzozowski writing about Sienkiewicz (1906) cited in Jacek Wozniakowski, 'Myth and Normality' in *Canadian-American Slavic Studies*, vol. 21, no. 1–2, Spring 1987, p.43.

32. Edward Crankshaw, *The Fall of the House of Habsburg*, Harmondsworth: Penguin, 1983, p.35

33. W. Ekielski, 'Spór o zakopiańszczyznę i styl polski' in *Architekt*, vol. 3, no. 6, 1902, pp.57–62 and vol. 3, no. 7, 1902, pp.81–4.

34. Over 10 per cent of the population of Galicia emigrated from the region between 1891 and 1910. Franciszek Kubiczek *et al* (eds), *History of Poland in Numbers*, Warsaw, 1994, p.83.

35. See Wojtkiewicz's cartoon entitled 'Demonstracja koła polskiego (z prezesem na czele) przeciwko zaprowadzeniu powszechnego głosowania w Galicyi' in *Hrabia Wojtek*, no. 1, 1905.

36. In the 1907 elections to the Galician Diet only seven PPSD deputies were returned in the 105 seats it contested (Neal Ascherson, *The Struggles For Poland*, London: Michael Joseph, 1986, p.44.). Whilst, at this time, the socialists were relatively uninfluential in Galician political life, the liberal atmosphere of the city allowed the Left to flourish. Political parties based in Russian Poland such as the *Socjal-demokracja Królewstwa Polskiego i Litwy* published their tracts and newspapers in Kraków unhindered.

37. Ignacy Daszyński cited in Frank Golczewski, 'Rural anti-semitism in Galicia before World War 1' in Chimen Abramsky, Maciej Jachimczyk and Anthony Polonsky, *The Jews in Poland*, Oxford: Blackwell, 1986, p.100.

38. Although dealing with a somewhat later period, see Szymon Rudnicki, 'Ritual Slaughter as a political issue' in *Polin*, 7, 1992, pp.147–60.

39. See Jindřich Toman, 'Nationality as Choice: Baudouin de Courtenay's Individual Approach' in *Cross Currents*, 10, 1991, pp.47–56.

6.1 Karol Frycz, *Zawiejski's Wawel*, 1905

6.2 Karol Frycz, *Manggha's Wawel*, 1905

6.3 Karol Frycz, *Project for the restoration of the Castle by the City Council*, 1905

6.4 Karol Frycz, *Wawel in the 'Zakopane style'*, 1905

6.5 Karol Frycz, *Socialist Wawel*, 1905

7

'Gruss aus Wien': urban tourism in Austria-Hungary before the First World War

Jill Steward

Looking back to the year of 1882 Arthur Schnitzler recalled an encounter on a Viennese street:

> ... a traveller walking toward me on the outer Burgplatz, his red Baedeker in his hand, binoculars slung around his neck. Vienna was his home, yet Moni – which was the affectionate nickname we used rather than his more imposing real name, Solomon – had decided to spend his eight day vacation like a genteel stranger, conscientiously seeing all the Vienna sights. I can't recall whether he had moved to a hotel for the purpose of playing his part consistently.[1]

Solomon was not the only tourist out on the streets seeing the Viennese sights. From the beginning of the decade the number of tourists visiting the city steadily began to increase, marking the beginnings of the industry which was to make such an important contribution to the city's economy after the First World War. Before the war when Vienna was still the symbolic and administrative centre of the Austro-Hungarian empire, it was by far the largest of all its cities and the only one with a well-developed tourist culture. This chapter will examine the formative influences on the industry in its early days before the First World War and the main features of the culture associated with it.

In the early twentieth century the rise of nationalism in the Dual Monarchy meant that the location of effective political power within the empire began to shift away from its traditional centre in Vienna towards the regional capitals of Budapest, Prague, Kraków and Lvov. Not only did the the rise of nationalism indirectly influence the character of Vienna's own tourist culture but it helped to make the empire's provincial capitals into tourist centres in their own right as they became sites of regional and national pilgrimage. This essay will therefore examine briefly the way in which the two principal regional centres of the empire, Budapest and Prague, began to use tourism as a way of registering their political and cultural independence from Vienna, although neither of them could, as yet, claim to be a centre of international tourism.

The early days of the tourist industry

The foundations of urban tourism in central Europe were laid with the building of the railway networks. The spread of economic and industrial modernization across the Habsburg lands, although uneven and concentrated in Bohemia and Moravia, contributed to the rapid growth of Vienna and subsequently to that of Prague and Budapest. The latter became the fastest growing city in central Europe after Hungary was granted its independence in 1867.[2] As the empire's newly prosperous middle classes gradually began to participate in European-wide practices of bourgeois leisure they began to take holidays involving excursions and outings.[3] Many of central Europe's wealthier families developed a propensity to travel farther afield and to engage with various forms of commercialized cultural and recreational tourism. This tendency was encouraged by continual improvements in the roads, the water communications along the Danube and the growth of an integrated railway system which linked together all the major towns and cities in the empire. By 1895 it was possible to travel by express from Vienna to Budapest in four hours although not until the end of the century was the Hungarian railway network substantially completed.

Vienna was the focus of the empire's railway system. For many centuries it had been the largest and most important city in central Europe, host of pilgrims *en route* for the Holy Land and to Grand Tourists. Although by the late nineteenth century Vienna was by far the largest tourist centre in the empire, as a centre of foreign tourism it could not compete with Paris, London or Berlin. This was partly because of its geographical position, which was peripheral to the popular tourist regions of the western Alps and east of the routes leading from northern Europe to the warm South. In 1890, while 334 000 tourists visited the new imperial city of Berlin only 200 000 visited Vienna.[4] Most came from imperial Germany and Russia and the rest from America, France and England. The bulk of the city's domestic tourists were from Bohemia, Moravia and Silesia, with a relatively small number from Budapest.[5]

Vienna's role as the administrative and symbolic centre of the empire meant that its visitors were characterized by their social diversity, since many were there on diplomatic, military and commercial business. German tourists often included the city on their itinerary because of its past association with the Grand Tour, while others were attracted by the fame of its social and cultural life and its luxurious shopping facilities. Many visitors from within the empire travelled there for domestic business, often staying with friends or family, while yet others were attracted to the city's medical and educational facilities. Mark Twain, one of the better known foreign visitors, stayed there for the benefit of his daughter's musical education while his wife was treated at one of the spas which sprang up on the periphery of the city.

The beginnings of Vienna's tourist industry were marked by attempts to improve the accommodation provided for visitors.[6] In the early nineteenth century the city's resources had been severely strained by the Congress of Vienna and it was not until Vienna hosted the World Exhibition in 1873 that the first modern hotels appeared along the new Ringstrasse, the boulevard enclosing the inner city.[7] This grand exhibition was intended to reinstate the Dual Monarchy's claims to inclusion amongst the leading European powers after its military defeat by Germany and the emergence of the new and powerful Wilhelmine empire in the north. Foreign visitors soon reported that Vienna's facilities were far inferior to those of Paris. Emily Birchall, wife of one of the exhibitors, arriving on a late train found 'no omnibus, no cab, nothing but a dainty little pair-horse brougham quite unfitted for luggage.... What a benighted way this seems of receiving hordes of visitors in a great city like Vienna.'[8] High prices, the unfinished state of the exhibition and hotels, and the untrained nature of their staff led to more unfavourable comments. However Birchall found much to enjoy, including the new trams linking the exhibition site in the Prater to the city centre.[9] The city's relationship to the modern tourist industry was confirmed when the travel agent Thomas Cook used the opportunity provided by the exhibition to incorporate the Austrian and German railways into his system when he secured exclusive concessions from the railway companies for the transport of guests and exhibitors.

The agency's high hopes for the exhibition failed to be realized as *Cooks' Excursionist* reported that 'The Exhibition opened in a muddle, there is panic on the Bourse, and our "own correspondent" of the *Daily News*' could not get 'relief to his stomach's cravings' for 'love nor money.'[10] A cholera epidemic and bad reports of the actual exhibition compounded its problems. The *Art Journal* declared:

such was the intention, such the boast, to concentrate in the greatest hall the world ever saw, the most glorious collection that the imagination of man ever compassed. and how has this promise been kept? 'If you seek an answer, look around', look on every side, and then in some distant corner ruminate over the gap between the promise and the performance.[11]

Self-interest and the magistrates brought prices down to a reasonable level but foreign visitors stayed away and the overall attendance of around 5 million visitors fell far short of the 16 million who attended the Paris exhibition. This resulted in a spectacular loss for the exhibition. It nearly bankrupted the city, and two of the three new luxury hotels were commercial failures.[12]

During the following decades, however, the number of visitors to Vienna grew steadily and although foreign tourists were still drawn mainly from the elite classes the appearance of *Pensionen,* and of guidebooks targeting a more popular audience indicated the emergence of a wider and more highly differentiated market generated by the growth in domestic tourism. Pocket guidebooks such as Hartleben's *Wien* (1893), Grieben's *Reiseführer: Budapest und Umgebung* (1905-6), Meurer's *Handy Illustrated Guide to Vienna* (1906) and Bermann's *Ilustrierter Führer durch Wien* (1908) were highly illustrated and less austere than the famous Baedeker.[13] As working conditions gradually improved domestic tourism also included the day trippers ('passing trade') from an ever-widening range of social groups who made excursions to places like the Prater. Tourists with their guidebooks became an increasingly common sight in the areas between the new Ringstrasse and the outer ringroad of the *Gürtel* and the older central core of the city. Elite visitors stayed at the luxurious Imperial or Bristol hotels, both located on the socially prestigious Kärntner Ring. Less wealthy tourists were catered for by the *Pensionen* in the neighbourhoods around the new university, the General Hospital and the numerous clinics between Alserstrasse and Währingerstrasse. The inner city, which was still lived in by aristocracy, and the newly built Ringstrasse with its open spaces and its impressive public monuments and private apartments, formed a natural and self-contained arena for touristic activities, a process reinforced by the high-class shopping facilities of the Graben, the Kohlmarkt and the Kärntnerstrasse.

The growth of a tourist culture

Vienna was the first of the empire's principal cities to experience the emergence of a commercialized tourist culture, a phenomenon which only began to appear in Budapest just before the First World War and was still barely apparent in Prague. The emergence of Vienna's tourist culture was marked not only by its new hotels and restaurants but by the publication of popular guidebooks and souvenirs, and entertainments put on specifically for tourists.[14] Guidebooks were important components of the systems of verbal and visual representation which made tourist cities intelligible to their visitors. As such they were instrumental in the formation of tourist culture as they mapped out the places relevant to tourists geographically and socially and indicated where the appropriate forms of leisure and entertainment were to be found. Highly structured by the devices and conventions of the genre, guidebooks identified lines of passage through the sights, suggesting itineraries and routes and directing visitors to places where their requirements could be met.[15]

Sightseeing was an activity in which all tourists participated. The standard itineraries suggested for Vienna invariably included the Imperial Palace in the inner city and the civic and state buildings along the Ringstrasse. By the early twentieth century other sights of interest to tourists included the city parks and gardens and the new *Stadtbahn* and the electric trams which were still a novelty to some visitors from the less developed parts of the empire. Many central-European visitors were attracted by the museums, opera house and *Burgtheater* which were cultural monuments in their own right and contributed to the city's image as a major cultural centre, the home of Mozart, Beethoven and Brahms and an aristocratic way of life in which the cultivation of art and music was central. The omission of certain areas from the guidebooks and the verbal and visual framing of the main sights of tourist interest contributed to the way in which visitors were encouraged to see the city as a series of picturesque and imposing urban landscapes, turning them into assets of value to the new commercialized tourist culture.[16]

The evolution of an urban tourist culture was assisted by the efforts of the authorities and entrepreneurs to provide the kind of facilities which their visitors considered essential. By the early twentieth century these included features which became ever-more prominent in Vienna's tourist publicity. By 1911 the authorities could boast of the city's modern utilities: hygiene, fresh drinking water and a new transport system.[17] Visitors brought with them not only considerable amounts of money but their expectations of what a place had to offer. In the case of Vienna this invariably included a belief in the pleasure-loving behaviour of its inhabitants. From the end of the eighteenth century travel memoirs testify to the Viennese love of pleasure, the exuberant social life of its elite circles and the liveliness of its popular culture. The correspondent of the London *Times*, Henry Wickham Steed, believed that the city's foreign reputation for 'gaiety' really began with the Congress of Vienna in 1815, when special efforts were made to entertain the diplomatic visitors and their retinues with dancing, masked balls and other forms of pleasurable pastimes.[18]

The city's patterns of leisure and entertainment were ideally suited to tourism. Condemned by the puritanical Thomas Cook as 'a carnival of folly and vice' the Viennese Sunday was traditionally associated with outings and excursions to traditional places of entertainment such as the *Gasthäuser* (pubs) and the *Heurigen* (wine taverns) in the formerly outlying wine villages on the edge of the *Wienerwald*.[19] The coming of the railways meant that the Viennese themselves often preferred to go further out to Mödling or Baden.

Many of their traditional places of entertainment were being swallowed up by the new suburbs, which now stretched as far as Dornbach and Neuwaldegg. In the picturesque villages of Nussdorf and Grinzing, easily accessible by tram from the tourist zone of the centre, the largest of the remaining *Heurigen* began catering specifically for foreign tourists with hot buffets, entertainments, flower and toy sellers and taxis.[20] Beyond them the rural countryside was turned into a protected zone, popular with tourists and residents alike as the *Verschönerungsverein* (association for the protection of rural beauty) conserved the woods and controlled and signposted the paths and walkways.

The Prater, on the opposite side of the city, was the other principal amusement centre for tourists. Once a royal park, it contained lawns, paths and sporting facilities including a race course. A legacy of the 1873 exhibition, the Rotunda housed a steady stream of conferences and congresses. While the Prater catered for all the social classes, in practice they did not mix. Baedeker described the *Nobel Prater* of the *Hauptallee* as a 'fashionable resort in spring, when many fine horses, elegant toilettes, and handsome faces will be observed.'[21] By the early twentieth century the upper classes usually appeared only for special events such as the formal spectacle of the Flower Corso, a traditional staged ritual of aristocratic display contrasting sharply with the workers' May Day parade. Events of a musical and theatrical nature put on to entertain tourists were kept exclusive by the nets sealing off the grounds while admission by ticket placed the events beyond the means of the humbler visitors.[22]

The latter were catered for by the 'Wurstelprater' containing *Gasthäuser*, snack bars and an amusement park. By the early twentieth century the amusements of former days – the panoramas, stereoscopes and other traditional entertainments such as the calf with six legs, the giant lady, and the hairy man – were superseded by mechanical flip-flops and the *Kinos*, the moving picture shows, of which there were around one hundred and fifty in the city by 1914.[23] A huge *Riesenrad*, or Ferris wheel, built to commemorate Franz Josef's Jubilee in 1898, rapidly became to Vienna what the Eiffel Tower was to Paris: its postcard image almost rivalling that of St Stephan's Cathedral in its popularity. In the English Garden a British company set up an early version of a theme park, 'Venice in Vienna' (*Venedig in Wien*), in 1895 and it attracted two million people including many day trippers, foreign tourists and members of the *mondaine* world of Vienna.[24] The imitation canals, gondoliers, palazzi, restaurants and theatres were particularly popular with young officers who found the imitations of French culture represented by the 'Parisiana' including a version of the 'Moulin Rouge' particularly appealing.[25] The associations which these conjured up were not entirely coincidental, since prostitution was a well-established feature of this particular corner of the Prater. To maintain the interest of the public, much of 'Venice' was replaced by an 'international city' while a new Olympia arena claimed to be the largest open air theatre in Europe, able to contain four thousand people.

Another indication of the new tourist culture was the proliferation of images aimed at the tourist market. The most picturesque and photogenic areas of Vienna belonged to its inner core and these, together with the monuments of the Ringstrasse, were put to a new commercial use as the subject of souvenirs aimed at tourists (see Figure 7.1).[26] Postcards were invented in Austria in 1869 and were sold everywhere: they were produced and retailed by many of the Viennese publishing houses such as Phillip and Kramer and the Brüder Kohn.[27] The work of watercolour artists such as Erwin Pendl, Ernst Graner and Francis Witt and Vienna's many commercial and amateur photographers was endlessly reproduced in postcard form.[28] The very presence of the postcard seller with his tray marked out a place as a tourist sight while hotels, restaurants and shops all used postcards to advertise their services. The Hotel Wimberger in the fifteenth district, conscious of the way that tourists brought into the city not only considerable amounts of income but their own social and cultural patterns, promised a 'Münchener Bierhalle' (see Figure 7.2). Even the *Wiener Werkstätte*, the purveyor of high art for a social elite, produced several thousand cards as a source of income and as a way of promoting its products. These were clearly aimed at tourists since they represented most of the sights on the standard itinerary such as the Belvedere, the Hofburg and Franziskanerplatz. The artists of the *Werkstätte* hoped that wealthy visitors might bring commissions for their luxurious art and design products. Carl Moll, the entrepreneurial force among the Secession artists, also had connections with the Gallery Mietke, which advertised in Cook's *Welt-Reise Zeitung*, the Viennese edition of the *Excursionist*, and the artist himself frequently turned out pretty images of tourist spots.

As the suburbs crept outwards and the new tenement blocks altered the appearance of familiar cityscapes, greater emphasis was placed on the more picturesque corners of the city such as Beethoven's home in Heilingenstadt. This was a version of a *Pawlatschenhaus*, a form of domestic building originating in village architecture and found only in the old village cores in the suburbs.[29] Sights of this kind matched the modern urban tourist's desire to escape from the more unpleasant aspects of city life visible in the industrial districts outside the tourist zones and present in the increase in noise, traffic and pollution. The more picturesque of the city's inhabitants were often included in watercolours of the urban landscape in order to create a sense of scale and to provide local colour. At the same time they became self-conscious objects of interest in their own right as various forms of the city's social and cultural life were exploited for touristic purposes. Traditional events such as the famous *Fiakerball* of the carnival season provided visitors with examples of the 'authentic' culture of 'gay Vienna'.[30] Yet the character of such balls had changed. Originating in the spontaneous gatherings based upon the participants' occupations, they had become increasingly commercialized since the 1860s under the auspices of the enterprising Fiaker-Milli, a well-known prostitute.[31] By 1905, under the heading of 'Popular Festivals', the Baedeker guide to the city felt the need to point our that the 'Redout' balls were now 'select' assemblies to which admission was 'invitation-card' only, a device by which the city's elites could protect their social life from intrusion by the socially undesirable, including the new type of tourist who travelled without the appropriate letters of introduction.[32]

Urban guidebooks now often included sections on 'city life',[33] and the category of 'Viennese types' was a popular genre of the postcard trade covered by reproductions of picturesque watercolours as well as documentary style photographs. Many of these images were derived from repertoires of urban stereotypes well established in the Viennese Press. Hans Schliessman, for example, produced enormously popular pictures of Viennese characters and scenes from everyday life for humorous magazines like *Humoristische Blätter*, *Kikeriki* and *Fliegende Blätter*.[34] Encountered by tourists in postcard form, the meaning of these images lost the sharp satirical edge they acquired in the work of writers such as Eduard Pötzl, the popular feuilletonist of the *Neue Freie Presse*.[35] Instead, in the pages of the *Wiener Cicerone* (1907), they offered reassuring tokens of the legibility of a socially unfamiliar environment, as 'Viennese types' such as the *Pratershreiber* were helpfully identified, accompanied by little illustrations.[36] This particular guidebook also made use of collaged photographs, originally produced for the postcard trade, which used pictures of popular actors posing as 'Viennese types' superimposed onto background images of the city. The staged effect transformed the city into an extension of its own theatrical space (see Figure 7.3).[37]

The impression of the theatrical nature of Viennese life was facilitated not just by the life of its coffee houses but also by the traditional rituals of self-display which were an important feature of the social life of Viennese high society.[38] The wealthy visitor who was fortunate enough to have a room in one of the luxury hotels overlooking the Kärntnerstrasse could observe the daily *corso*, or promenade, which took place between the hours of three and five and where other social groups; the upper-middle classes, the *demi-monde* and the leaders of artistic society, emulated the rituals of seeing and being seen. (A similar ritual was observable in Budapest.) Other formal social spectacles such as the Flower *corso* in the Prater, while expressive of a rigidly hierarchical society where the recognition and maintenance of social distinctions still counted for so much, helped to generate the kind of social events which foreign tourists could enjoy in the belief that they were witnessing yet another authentic expression of the local culture. These events were significant not only for 'sightseers' from outside the city but also for day trippers from the suburbs. As Peter Fritzsche has pointed out in his study of Berlin, the growth in newspaper readership and the contents of the Press encouraged metropolitan dwellers to position themselves as tourists and observers of themselves.[39] In many cities with large immigrant populations like Vienna or Budapest excursions to see spectacles of this kind, to view new monuments, visit the Prater or the City Park, or to witness big religious processions for events no longer generally celebrated as local festivals like Corpus Christi in Vienna or the Feast of St Stephen in Budapest, could be understood as a way of becoming incorporated into the culture of the place in which they now lived.

A particularly important feature of Vienna's tourist culture was generated by its unique imperial role. As the traditional imperial *Residenzstadt* the city retained a glamour which was an important feature of its attractiveness to both foreign and domestic tourists. Performances of the palace band (*die Burgmusik*) provided a popular and much satirized form of entertainment for tourists and for locals and were the subject of one of Schliessman's most popular paintings.[40] Many of the city's monumental buildings such as the Votivkirche and the Hofburg were testaments to the Habsburgs' attempts to instil dynastic loyalty into their subjects. The gardens of Schönbrunn, the summer home of the emperor, were easily accessible by electric tram or the new *Stadtbahn*. As a place for excursions it was popular with everyone, especially with its grand menagerie and the rare spectacle of baby elephants.[41] The axes and allées of the formal garden, designed in the Baroque manner, expressed the idea of imperial power as visitors looked out over the city from the decorative folly temple of the Gloriette. This mandatory bird's-eye view theatrically extended out beyond the palace and its grounds. The panoramic view of the outstretched city became a backdrop to the imperial residence while, at the same time, linking it to other important landmarks evocative of the Habsburgs' dominant presence.[42]

Cultural tourism and the rise of nationalism

Throughout the empire there were buildings and monuments named in honour of various members of the imperial family. By the time the Emperor had cut the ribbon on Prague's new Franz-Josef bridge in 1901 tourism within the empire had acquired a new significance. The rise of nationalism made it increasingly evident that the empire was formally held together only by its relationship to the Habsburg dynasty. The growth of national and cultural self-consciousness amongst its diverse ethnic populations meant that tourists viewed its urban monuments in ways which were mediated by their class, ethnic, linguistic, and religious affiliations.[43] Bohemian Czechs visiting Vienna, fighting for the recognition of their own cultural and linguistic identity, viewed the city's monuments to the heroes of German culture such as Goethe and Schiller in a very different light from the way that they were seen by the Bohemian Germans whose sense of identity, bound up with an allegiance to the Habsburgs and to German language and culture, was symbolized by the numerous monuments they erected in Bohemia to Joseph II.[44] Ethnic tensions between Czechs and Germans were not confined to Bohemia. A party of tourists from Prague visiting the Hunting Exhibition in Vienna in 1910 found themselves set upon by a group of radical German nationalists with bricks, broken bottles and bad eggs. The *Reichspost* lamented the incident as *eine Schädigung des Fremdenverkehrs* (a blow for tourism).[45]

This expression of xenophobia originated in the hostility felt by many native Viennese to the economic, social and political changes which were taking place in their city where by 1890 65.5 per cent of the inhabitants had been born elsewhere – in Bohemia, Moravia and Polish Galicia. By 1910 immigration into the city had increased the population to over two million. While foreign visitors invariably commented on the cultural diversity of the city's population, the tensions between the different ethnic groups were manifested in the hostility felt towards the immigrant communities by many of the indigenous Germans and an increasing emphasis in the local Viennese Press on the distinctively *gemütlich* nature of Viennese life.[46] *Gemütlichkeit* was the quality which the local press ascribed to 'true' Viennese as opposed to 'foreigners' like the immigrant Czechs or Magyars, thereby invoking stereotypical images of 'charming old Vienna' and nostalgia for a time before the building of the Ringstrasse, an era of 'characters' in beer houses, of old wine gardens, cafés and villages all now overtaken by the new suburbs.[47] Deeply rooted among the small tradesmen and lower-middle class of the suburbs, the sentimentalized 'culture of nostalgia' came to form a central element in touristic representations of Vienna. Depictions of an 'authentic' Viennese culture, in which the peculiarities of the *Wienerisch* dialect invariably played a part, also had the effect of marking out and reinforcing awareness of the cultural differences and 'imported' ways of life of the immigrant communities of the industrial suburbs, many of whom recognized a language other than German as their primary tongue.[48] Even the gastronomic pleasures of the restaurant became culturally significant as advertisements for *'alte Wiener Küche'* or *'alte Deutschstube Cuisine'* aligned menus with a more culturally homogenous past than the culinary diverse present exemplified by the foodstuffs available in the *Naschmarkt*.

By contrast with Vienna, Budapest only acquired the status of a capital city in 1872 when it was formally constituted out of its three parts, Buda, Óbuda and Pest. However, as Hungary benefited from the *Ausgleich* of 1867 the city rapidly became the fastest growing urban centre in central Europe. The new constitution of the Dual Monarchy gave Hungary its political independence and initiated the country's rapid economic growth, stimulating the mobility of the population to the extent that by 1895 Budapest registered a total of 130 000 visitors. Prague, also a *Residenzstadt*, grew less rapidly and remained much smaller although it continued to expand. Czech nationalists felt that the Austrian government denied Prague practical recognition of its role as the historic capital of Bohemia and as the centre of the most highly industrially advanced part of the empire. Nationalists in both cities were anxious to establish their distinctive cultural identities. In Budapest this was bound up with the government's programme of Magyarization, the promulgation of measures intended to assimilate Hungary's non-Magyar populations into the culture of the dominant Magyars. In Prague the Czech nationalists actively supported and promoted Czech culture as the industrialization of the city encouraged immigration from the surrounding Czech lands, turning its German inhabitants into a minority. In both cities ethnographic and trade exhibitions played a role in establishing cultural identity through the display of national achievements.

In Budapest the Millenary Exhibition of 1896 and its accompanying festivities were intended to celebrate the occupation of the Carpathian basin by the Magyar people and were heavily bound up with the policy of Magyarization. Anxious to compete with Vienna, the government had previously set up an International Ticket Office for the State Railways with branches in Vienna and Constantinople (1884). This body was subsequently to combine the functions of tourist promotion and the role of the government's national public relations agency, all without involving any substantial funding.[49] However, for the exhibition substantial funding and promotional support was forthcoming since the government wanted to use the opportunity to divert the sympathy of foreigners from the causes of Hungary's suppressed ethnic groups. Pamphlets were published for this purpose which provoked replies in kind from oppositional groups and aggressive counter-demonstrations in Belgrade.[50] The celebrations left their mark upon the city in the form of monuments to Magyar culture, most notably public buildings, museums, bridges, the first underground railway, the Millenary Monument on Heroes Square and an exhibition hall, while Vajdahunyad Castle in the City Park, originally designed as a temporary structure for the exhibition, was rebuilt in 1907 because of its popularity.[51] The disappointing attendance at the exhibition, two-thirds of which was Hungarian, made the government reluctant to provide further financial support for tourism. Nevertheless by

1900 there were about fifty hotels in Budapest near the eastern railway station and along the quaysides, the most luxurious situtated in the fourth district along the Danube Corso and in the centre of the remodelled Pest although there were no modern pensions until two years later.[52]

In Prague the growth of Czech nationalism played a key role in turning the city into a centre of regional tourism. The founder of the Bohemian Industrial Museum, the Czech patriot Vojta Náprstek, firmly believed in the role that travel and visits to significant places could play in the cultivation of a sense of history.[53] The most important national monument intended for this purpose was the Bohemian Museum, the outcome of the museum company founded in 1818 for the collection of works of art and other objects of Bohemian origin. A similar organization promoting Czech language and literature generated the Bohemian theatre which, when it burnt down in 1881, was immediately rebuilt by public subscription. Like the 'Czechish-Slavonic' Ethnographical Museum housed in the old Kinsky villa, the aim of the Bohemian Museum was to give the Czech community an awareness of its own cultural heritage. The museum was completed in 1891, the year that Prague was host to a trade and ethnographic exhibition which, despite some cooperation in the planning stages between the Czech and German trade associations, turned into a celebration of Czech achievements and was therefore boycotted by the Bohemian Germans.[54] The exhibition attracted over a million Czechs and Slavs from all over the empire and beyond and contributed to the growth of mass Czech national self-consciousness. Legacies of the exhibition included a scaled-down version of the Eiffel Tower, a maze and a funicular railway on Petřín Hill.

Although Vienna's tourist industry continued to expand, by the beginning of the twentieth century the city was beginning to find itself competing with the new regional tourism while the empire's rural resorts and spas were increasingly attractive to urban dwellers seeking mental and physical health in natural surroundings.[55] Partly as a response to this trend, health settlements such as Kaltenleutgeben sprang up on the outskirts of the city. In Budapest, the 'city of spas', health tourism won official support as the Hungarian government followed up earlier initiatives and began to develop the country's spas by setting up a separate Tourism and Travel Company (1902) for this purpose and an office for tourism in Budapest.[56] The latter benefited from the growth of domestic passenger traffic on the expanded and nationalized railways as newly prosperous Hungarians took advantage of the modern facilities of their own capital rather than travelling to Vienna, from which they felt increasingly alienated politically. By the early twentieth century many of Budapest's spas had been redeveloped, either privately or by the municipal authorities which now owned them. The Lukásbad spa, for example, was redeveloped by a public company which built a new hotel and modernized its facilities.⁵⁷ One of the best known of the city's health and pleasure resorts was Margaret Island in the middle of the Danube. This park, with its gardens, spa and cafeteria, was enormously popular with the elite classes who could afford the price of admission. Its owner, the Archduke Joseph, had developed it in the 1870s, equipping it with modern baths and a hotel. In 1900 the Ministry of Commerce helped to fund the building of a bridge linking the island to the river bank, making it easily accessible. In 1908 the city authorities bought the island for further development although the price of admission continued to exclude the poor.⁵⁸ The city authorities were also responsible for the building and development of the new Gellért bath with its attached hotel specifically for tourists.

Throughout the more highly developed parts of the empire, the regulatory and promotional roles assumed by its trade and tourist associations indicated that they understood the commercial potential of tourism and the importance of publicity. This was particularly true in Vienna where these organizations were extremely active. Such financial support as there was for tourism in Austria and Hungary came, not from the governments, but from municipal and regional authorities and the railway companies. In Austria the Ministry of Railways (founded in 1896), which was responsible for publicity and timetables, provided the only direct state support for tourism, setting up information and travel bureaux including one in London (1902), followed by others in New York, Paris and Berlin.⁵⁹ Approached by exhibition organizers from London with a view to setting up a big Austrian trade and tourism exhibition in 1906, the Viennese associations eagerly agreed to participate and to contribute the bulk of their own costs.⁶⁰

A similar attitude was adopted by Prague City Council which helped to sponsor the Bohemian section of the exhibition. This was organized by Count Franz Lützow, a fervent Czech nationalist who was eager to attract influential and sympathetic visitors to Prague. Formerly an attaché to the Austrian embassy in London, Lützow had previously written an English guidebook to Prague, a history of the city and its principal monuments.⁶¹ The exhibition handbook extolled the picturesqueness of 'Old Prague', its castles, views and quaint old streets like Golden Lane, whilst clearly setting out Bohemia's claims to a separate historical and cultural identity. The authors complained that under Austrian rule the life of Prague as 'a residential town has vanished and with it the influx of foreign guests'. They criticized the traditional western habit of associating Bohemia with the 'uncivilized' Slavonian tribes of the east while emphasizing the region's links with the Hussites, evidently hoping that the sympathy of Protestant tourists might prove politically helpful.⁶²

In 1908 a similar exhibition was put on in Hungary. Initial difficulties were caused by the passive opposition of the Minister of Commerce, despite the fact that Britain was one of Hungary's main trading partners. Unfortunately, although the exhibition attracted 1 293 989 visitors, Hungary was not yet included in Cook's system, so that most western tourists continued to think of Budapest as remote and inaccessible.[63] By 1912 the situation was improving as the beauties of Hungary were heavily promoted in the Viennese version of the *Excursionist*, and the number of visitors to Budapest had doubled to around 250 000, although only 15–35 000 of these were foreign.[64]

Within the empire, as the rationale underpinning the union of the different linguistic and ethnic communities became increasingly anachronistic, tourism became a useful vehicle for Habsburg myth-making. The presence of domestic and foreign spectators was essential to the success of the carefully staged events which constituted the various Jubilee celebrations punctuating the Emperor's lengthy reign. These displays presented Franz Joseph as a kind of folk hero, father of the Habsburg 'family of nations'.[65] The broad new streets of Pest and the wide boulevards of the Viennese Ringstrasse provided perfect settings for theatrical displays of imperial splendour, one of the most spectacular of which was undoubtedly the hugely expensive and lengthy Viennese pageant celebrating the Emperor's silver wedding in 1879. Designed by Makart, the history painter, 10 000 or so participants dressed in the costumes of Habsburg Flanders depicted the benign effects of the Habsburg reign on art and industry.[66] By the 1908 Jubilee the rise of nationalism led to a change of theme as deputations from each province trooped along the Ringstrasse. Dressed in their own national costume, they represented the complete range of ethnic communities while the indefatigable Emperor saluted for three hours. The Habsburgs had long used printed images for propaganda purposes and they now found a new outlet in the tourist souvenirs produced for these events.[67] One of the most popular was the Jubilee postcard, designed by Koloman Moser for the *Staatsdruckerei* in 1908.

By the end of the decade Vienna had developed all the features of a modern tourist culture and events such as the civic visit from the Lord Màyor of London promoted Vienna as a 'model city, a hive of industry and a place of pleasure', with nearby winter sports, and luxurious shopping.[68] New attractions such as a Viennese Music Week raised the total of foreign visitors to over 100 000, 20 per cent of all visitors.[69] However, the numbers of foreign tourists still fell short of the numbers attracted to Berlin or Paris. Wickham Steed commented that, 'for forty years the Viennese have been studying how to draw a stream of foreign visitors to their city and for forty years have been astounded at their failure.'[70] Yet before the First World War the industry was making a substantial contribution to the city's economy. Foreign tourists spent around ten crowns on board and lodging and twelve crowns on other forms of spending, including pleasure, so that the 500 000 foreigners who visited the city for an average of three days contributed to a total of around 20–25 million crowns per annum. In addition to this there was the income from domestic tourism.[71]

Ilsa Barea writes that the 'local colour' of the popular songs which told the Viennese that they and their city were 'unique, marvellous and extremely lovable was as truthful as the chromo-lithographs of that time.'[72] Before the First World War Vienna's tourist culture came to depend heavily on the naturalized and indigenous myth of 'old Vienna' which masked the tensions of modern Viennese life and which reduced the city's cultural identity to the elements of nostalgia, royal glamour, gaiety and *Gemütlichkeit*, a 'fairytale' as one work of romantic fiction set in the city described it.[73] Wickham Steed described the air of unreality which pervaded Vienna, which he attributed partly to the success of the old Habsburg stratagem of 'diversion' by amusement.[74] Of the Viennese he said:

> They enumerate the attractions of Vienna, the multiplicity of its pleasures, the beauty of its monuments and the charm of its natural surroundings; but they forget that for a capital to act as a magnet upon strangers it must have a soul of its own with which the stranger can secretly commune. Both Vienna and 'the Viennese' are soulless or, at least, their 'souls' are so much in abeyance that neither thrills the thoughtful stranger with that inward satisfaction that moves the heart.[75]

It was not surprising therefore that foreign visitors who penetrated beyond the staged myth of 'old Vienna' were bound to find something disturbing in the back regions, making unfavourable associations between the pleasure-seeking ways of its inhabitants, the signs of imperial decay and ethnic nationalism. For as Vienna's imperial power slipped away to the peripheral regions of the empire, to the regional and national centres like Prague and Budapest where many of the principal tourist sights were associated with national hopes for the future, their Viennese equivalents appeared to be associated only with the past. In a city whose public monuments constantly reminded viewers that cultural identity was a controversial and contested issue the demand for a 'Viennese soul' was itself a demand for the realization of a tourist myth.

Notes

1. Arthur Schnitzler, *My Youth in Vienna*, London: Weidenfeld and Nicolson, 1968, p.102.
2. For the relative rates of growth of Prague, Budapest and Vienna see Gary Cohen, 'The social structure of Prague, Vienna and Budapest', in Gy. Ránki (ed.), *Hungary and European Civilization*, Budapest: Akamémiai Kiadó, pp.182–3.
3. See Wolfgang Kaschuba, 'German Bürgerlichkeit after 1800: Culture as Symbolic Practice,' in Jürgen Kocka and Adrian Mitchell (eds), *Bourgeois Society in Nineteenth-Century Europe*, Oxford: Berg, 1993, pp.392–422.
4. The founding of the German empire in 1871 increased its attraction to German visitors while the restructuring of Austria-Hungary in 1867 reduced the catchment area for immigration into Austria

and stimulated the growth of Prague and Budapest. See Elisabeth Lichtenberger, *Vienna: Bridge Between Two Cultures*, trans. Dietlinde Mühlgassner and Craig Reisser, London and New York: Belhaven, 1993, p.5.

5. For a discussion of tourist statistics and the problems of calculating 'foreign' tourist flows in central Europe see Peter Jordan, 'Die Entwicklung der Fremdensverkehrsströme in Mitteleuropa (1910–1990) als Ausdruck Politischer und Wirtschaftlicher Veränderungen', in *Mitteilungen der Österreichischen Geographischen Gesellschaft*, 132, Vienna, 1990, pp.144–71. See also Françoise Knopper, 'Berlin et Vienne dans les relations de voyage 1900–1930', *Cahiers d'études germaniques*, 1993, 24, pp.253–66; Franz Baltzarek, 'Fremdenverkehr und Sport' in *Das Zeitalter Kaiser Franz Josephs 1880–1916*, 2. Teil, Schloss Grafenegg: NÖ Landesmuseum, 1987, p.167, and Karl Pauschenwein, 'Die Entwicklung des Fremdenverkehrs in Wien und Niederdonau', PhD thesis, Hochschule für Welthandel, Vienna, 1941, pp.75–6.

6. Helmut Kretschmer, 'Hotelboom – gestern und heute', *Wiener Geschichtsblätter*, 1988–9, pp.71–9.

7. Karlheinz Roschitz, *Wiener Weltausstellung, 1873*, Vienna: Jugend und Volk, 1989.

8. Emily Birchall, *Wedding Tour – January to June 1873 and Visit to the Vienna Exhibition*, David Verey and Alan Sutton (eds), Gloucester and New York: St Martins Press, 1985, p.125.

9. Peter Capuzzo, 'Transportation system and urban space: Vienna 1865–1938', precirculated paper, Cities in Eastern and Western Europe, Third International Conference of Urban History, Central European University, Budapest, August 1996, 1–15, p.2.

10. *Cook's Excursionist and Tourist Advertiser* (London), 21 May 1873, p.5. I am indebted to the Thomas Cook Archive, London, for this material.

11. *Art Journal* (London), July 1873, p.219.

12. Kenneth Luckhurst, *The Story of Exhibitions*, London and New York: Studio, 1951, p.220.

13. Julius Meurer, *A Handy Illustrated Guide to Vienna and its Environs*, Vienna and Leipzig: Hartleben, 1906; Moritz Bermann, *Illustrierter Führer durch Wien und Umgebungen*, Vienna: Hartleben, 1908; Fritz Hollrigl, *Wiener Cicerone, Illustrierter Fremden-Führer durch Wien und Umgebungen*, 16th edn, Vienna, 1907.

14. *Das Etablissement Ronacher im Wort und Bild: nebst einem ausführlichen Fremdenführer*, Vienna: Anton Ronacher, 1888, repub. Vienna: Archiv, 1992.

15. See Michel De Certeau, *The Practice of Everyday Life*, trans. Steven Randall, Berkeley, University of California Press, pp.119–28 on 'tours' and 'boundaries'.

16. For 'imaging' the city see Neil Harris, 'Urban Tourism and the Commercial City,' in W. Taylor (ed.), *Inventing Times Square: Commerce and Culture at the Crossroads of the World*, New York: Russell Sage Foundation, 1991, pp.66–82.

17. See 'Vienna the Beautiful', *The London Illustrated News*, 9 December 1911, p.962. This contrasted with Prague where conflicts between Czechs and Germans delayed the installation of a clean water supply.

18. Henry Wickham Steed, *The Habsburg Monarchy*, 4th edn, London: Constable, 1919, p.202.

19. *Cook's Excursionist*, 15 August 1868.

20. Felix Czeike, 'Landpartien und Sommeraufenthalte; Die Entwicklung vom ausgehenden 17 bis zur Mitte des 19. Jahrhunderts', *Wiener Geschichtsblätter*, 1988–9, pp.41–79. Heinrich Gruber, *Red Vienna: Experiment in Working Class Culture 1919–1934*, New York and Oxford: Oxford University Press, 1991, pp.117–18, and Robert Rotenberg, 'Viennese wine gardens and their magic', *East European Quarterly*, 4, 1984, pp.447–60.

21. Karl Baedeker, *Austria-Hungary: Handbook for Travellers*, Leipzig: Baedeker, 1905, p.65.

22. Robert Rotenberg, *Landscape and Power in Vienna*, Baltimore: Johns Hopkins University Press, 1995, pp.55–8.

23. Ulrich Storch, *Das Pratermuseum*, Vienna: Museum der Stadt Wien, 1993, pp.116–18. L. Kellner, P. Arnold and A. L. Delisle, *Austria of the Austrians and Hungary of the Hungarians*, London, 1914, pp.131–4.

24. See Norbert Rubey and Peter Schoenwald (eds), *Venedig in Wien; Theater- und Vergnügungsstadt der Jahrhundertwende*, Vienna: Ueberreuter, 1996.

25. Hollrigl, *Wiener Cicerone*, p.70.

26. For example, typical photograph albums aimed at tourists were *Neustes Monumental Album von*

Wien: Sechzig der schönsten Ansichten, 3rd edn, Vienna: Halm and Goldberg, 1908; Paul Wilhelm, Wanderings Through Vienna, Vienna: R. Lechner, c. 1908.

27. Felix Czeike 'Wiener Kunstpostkarten,' Wiener Geschichtsblätter, 38, 4: 1983, pp.167–9.

28. See for example the exhibition catalogue, Das Zeitalter Kaiser Franz Josephs 1880–1916: 2. Teil, Schloss Grafenegg, 1985, cat. nos, 1, 11, 3, 26, 1, 4.

29. Renata Kassal-Mikula, 'Architecture from 1815–1848', in Robert Waissenberger, Wien 1815–1848: Zeit des Biedermeier, London: Alpine Fine Arts Collection (UK), 1986, pp.151–3.

30. For a discussion of the complexities of tourist cultures and the interaction between visitors and inhabitants see Tom Selwyn, 'Postlude', in Jeremy Boissevain (ed.), Coping with Tourists, pp.247–54 and Jeremy Boissevain, 'Ritual, Tourism and Cultural Commoditization in Malta: Culture by the Pound?' in Tom Selwyn (ed.), The Tourist Image: Myths and Myth Making in Tourism, Chichester and New York: John Wiley, 1996, pp.109–10.

31. Ilsa Barea, Vienna: Legend and Reality, London: Pimlico, repub. 1992, p.319.

32. Karl Baedeker, Austria-Hungary, Leipzig; Baedeker, 1905, p.8.

33. Bermann, Wien, pp.136–52.

34. Walter Kloschatzky, Viennese Watercolours of the Nineteenth Century, New York: Harry Abrams, 1988, p.226.

35. Eduard Pötzl, Wiener Skizzen aus dem Gerichts-Saal, Vienna: Rosner, 1884.

36. Hollrigl, Wiener Cicerone, pp.9–15.

37. For a discussion of 'staged authenticity' see Dean MacCanell, The Tourist: a New Theory of the Leisure Class, New York: Schocken, 1976; and Tom Selwyn, 'The anthropology of tourism: reflections on the state of the art', in Anthony V. Seaton et al (eds), Tourism: the State of the Art, Chichester and London: John Wiley, 1994, pp.730–71.

38. See Donald Olsen, The City as a Work of Art, London, Paris and Vienna, New Haven: Yale University Press, 1986, pp.235–48 for a discussion of Vienna as a setting for Selbstdarstellung (the presentation of the self in a role).

39. Peter Fritzsche, Reading Berlin 1900, Cambridge, Mass: Harvard University Press, 1996, pp.161–5.

40. Kloschatzky, p.226, f.n. 259.

41. Kellner et al, Austria of the Austrians, p.40.

42. Rotenberg, pp.57–8.

43. Robert Berman, Modern Culture and Critical theory: Art, Politics and the Legacy of the Frankfurt School, Wisconsin and London: University of Wisconsin Press, 1989, p.165.

44. Nancy Meriwether Wingfield, 'Conflicting Constructions of Memory: attacks on Statues of Joseph II in the Bohemian Lands after the Great War', Austrian History Yearbook, 28, 1997, pp.151–3.

45. Monika Gletter, 'Urbanisierung und Nationalitätenproblem' in Peter Berner, Emil Brix and Wolfgang Mantl (eds), Wien um 1900: Aufbruch in die Moderne, Munich: R. Oldenbourg, 1986, p.186.

46. Lichtenberger, Vienna, p.5; Eda Sagarra, 'Vienna and its Population in the Late Nineteenth Century: Social and Demographic Change 1870–1910' in Gilbert. J. Carr and Eda Sagarra (eds), Fin de Siècle Vienna, Dublin: University of Dublin Press, 1985, pp.187–203.

47. Barea, Vienna, pp.318–23.

48. See Michael John and Albert Lichtblau, Schmelztiegel Wien einst und jetzt. Zur Geschichte und Gegenwart von Zuwanderung und Minderheiten, Vienna: Böhlau, 1993.

49. Joseph Böröcz, Leisure Migration under Capitalism and State Socialism: an Austro-Hungarian Comparison, PhD thesis, Baltimore, 1992, p.65.

50. Scotus Viator (R. W. Seton-Watson), Racial Problems in Hungary, London: Constable, 1908, p.184.

51. Katalin Sinkó, 'Die Millenniumsfeier Ungarns', Das Zeitalter Kaiser Franz Josephs 2, pp.295–300.

52. John Lukacs, Budapest 1900: an Historical Portrait of a City and its Culture, London: Weidenfeld and Nicolson, 1988, p.57.

53. Will. S. Monroe, Bohemia and the Čechs; The History of the People, Institutions, and the Geography of the Kingdom, together with accounts of Moravia and Silesia, London: G. Bell, 1910; and Walter White, A July Holiday in Saxony, Bohemia and Silesia, London: Chapman and Hall, 1857, pp.146–50. For an account of the relationship between museums, language and the construction of national identity

see Benedict Anderson, *Imagined Communities, Reflections on the Origin and Spread of Nationalism*, 2nd edn, London and New York: Verso, 1983.
54. Milan Hlavačka and František Kolář, 'Tschechen, Deutsche und die Jubiläumsaustellung 1891', *Bohemia* (1991), 32, 2, pp.380–411.
55. See Robin Lenman in Chapter 3 of this volume, on tourism in the adjoining regions of southern Germany.
56. Mária Vida, *The Spas of Hungary*, trans. Éva Vámos, Budapest: Franklin Nyomda, 1992, p.29; Böröcz, pp.64–5.
57. Vida, p.26.
58. Anon, 'Therapeutic Bath: Margaret Island, Budapest', 1908. By 1906 the number of 'passing guests' was over 100 000 annually with 11–12 000 longstay guests.
59. Bernecker, 'Die Entwicklung des Fremdenverkehrs in Österreich,' pp.237, 326.
60. Catalogue of the Imperial Royal Austrian Exhibition, Vienna, 1906. *Bericht über die Österreische Austellung, London, 1906*, Vienna: Staatsdruckerei, 1907.
61. See Franz Lützow, *The Story of Prague*, Medieval Towns Series, London: J. M. Dent, 1902.
62. *A Guide to the Bohemian section and the Kingdom of Bohemia: a Memento*, Prague: Alois Wiesner, 1906, p.17. This was subsequently published as a guidebook in 1911. See J. V. Polišensky, *Britain and Czechoslakia*, Prague: Orbis, 1968, pp.64–5.
63. Figures from the *Report on the Hungarian Exhibition*, London, 1908, cited by Harold Hartley, *Eighty-five Not Out: a Record of Happy Memories*, London: Frederick Muller, 1939, p.210. *The Queen 'Newspaper' Book of Travel* considered that letters of introduction were still necessary for foreigners visiting Budapest. M. Hornsby, *The Queen 'Newspaper' Book of Travel: a Guide to Home and Foreign Resorts*, London: Cox, 1909, p.311.
64. Lukacs, p.57; Böröcz, pp.108, 142.
65. For a discussion of the Habsburg mission, its construction and presentation, see James Shedel, 'Emperor, Church, and People; Religion and Dynastic Loyalty during the Golden Jubilee of Franz Joseph', *Catholic History Review*, 76, 1990, pp.71–93.
66. Werner Telesko, 'Die Wiener historischen Festzüge von 1879 und 1908: Zum Problem der dynasticshen Identitätsfindung des Hauses Österreich,' *Wiener Geschichtsblätter*, 51, 3, 1996, pp.133–46.
67. Andrew Wheatcroft, *The Habsburgs: Embodying Empire*, London and New York: Viking, 1995, pp.27–84.
68. *Illustrated London News*, 9 December 1911, pp.962–74.
69. Baltarek, p.163.
70. Henry Wickham Steed, *The Habsburg Monarchy*, London: Constable, 1919, pp.202–6.
71. For the economics of the empire see David F. Good, *The Economic Rise of the Habsburg Empire, 1750–1914*, Berkeley: University of California Press, 1984, pp.273–4. Good states that, of net foreign income from 1911 to 1913, Friedrich Fellner calculated that 50.6 million crowns were from tourism out of an inflow of 596.7 m crowns. These figures are disputed. Good has reworked them to arrive at a net income of 300.3 million crowns. He calculates a total GNP of 16.301 billion crowns. See also Paul Bernecker, 'Die Entwicklung des Fremdenvehrkehrs in Österreich', *Österreich-50 Jahre Republik 1918–1968*, Vienna: Institut fur Österreichkunde Verlag, 1968, pp.94–114.
72. Barea, p.320.
73. Dorothea Gerard, *The City of Enticement*, London: Stanley Paul, 1911. See Harro Kühnelt, 'Dorothea Gerards Romane aus dem alten Österreich', in Sylvia M. Patsch (ed.), *Österreich: England/Amerika: Abhandlungen zur Literatur-Geschichte*, Vienna and Munich: Christian Brandstätter, 1986, pp.94–114; Jill Steward, 'The "travel romance" and the emergence of the female tourist', *Studies in Travel Writing*, 1998, 2.
74. Henry Wickham Steed, *Through Thirty Years, 1892–1922: A Personal Narrative*, Vol. 1, London, 1924, p.196.
75. Wickham Steed, 1919, p.202.

7.1 *Führer durch Wien*, c. 1908

7.2   Vienna, 1904. Advertisement for the Hotel Wimberger in Fünfhaus

7.3   (opposite) 'Gruss aus Wien', 1905, collaged photograph with drawing of 'Viennese Types' by Ch. Scolik

7.4 (top) Souvenir of the 1891 Prague exhibition

7.5 (bottom) The Lukásbad, Budapest, c. 1900

Big-city Jews: Jewish big city – the dialectics of Jewish assimilation in Vienna c. 1900

Steven Beller

It would be straightforward to discuss the history of the Jews in Vienna at the turn of the century in terms of 'cultural boundaries'. Jews were, after all, the most obvious example of ethnic and religious difference in central Europe in the nineteenth and twentieth centuries, the central European's 'other' of choice. There will indeed be much made of this ascribed otherness in the following pages; yet to talk only of boundaries when it comes to the Jewish role in the urban world of central Europe is not enough. The city, and the modern Jewish experience, are also very much about connections; bridging the boundaries, laying down paths of communication.

'Central Europe' is a case in point. Much ink has been spilled about where central Europe is; in other words, how it is to be geographically defined. Yet the lines which are drawn around territories are not as important in this instance as the lines which link cities. The easiest way of defining the cultural world of central Europe around 1900 is as the set of connections which linked Vienna, Prague, Budapest, Brno, Trieste, Kraków, Berlin, Breslau, Lemberg and Czernowitz, among others. Urban culture is thus as much about networks as it is about boundaries.

Similarly, talking of the relation between ethnicity and the urban centre only in terms of boundaries risks missing the remarkable process of osmosis which goes on between ethnic groups and the city, whoever and wherever the ethnic group and city might be. The complex and often messy process of interaction which occurs between ethnic tradition and urban culture is precisely that: inter-action. While ethnic groups radically change their attitudes and cultural assumptions, indeed their identities, in the new urban environment, there can also be substantial continuities, with the old particular identity replaced – but by a new particular identity related to the old. Moreover, this is a dialectical, two-way process, so that, in assimilating the particular ethnic group, the city also takes on, accepts, assimilates in another sense of the word, traditions, customs, forms of expression – cultural material in general – which originated in the heritage of the particular ethnic group. As in all dialectical processes, the end result is neither urban culture as it was, nor ethnic tradition as it was, but rather a new synthesis which contains elements of both. A good example in the United States might be the emergence of jazz. In central Europe, a good example is the subject of this essay: the role played by the assimilation of Jews in the making of 'Vienna 1900' into a capital of twentieth century culture and thought.

Vienna was one of the great capitals of Jewish assimilation in the nineteenth century.[1] Jews from all over the Habsburg monarchy, especially from Bohemia, Moravia, Hungary and Galicia, came to the city and integrated into the economic, social and cultural life, and the lifestyle, of the Austrian capital.[2] To talk of 'assimilation' for a group which by 1914 comprised nearing 200 000 people covers a multitude of complexities and differentiations. The processes were indeed so complex that it has become fashionable in retrospect to talk not so much of 'assimilation', but of 'acculturation' or 'integration'.[3] As the word used historically has always been the former, I shall stick to that term, but keeping in mind that it describes a process which was anything but straightforward. Assimilating into a new, urban culture is just not a simple thing to do, and it is made even more complicated if one's religious identity and tradition is not that of the bulk of the urban population. Moreover, as highlighted above, the process is not a one-way, but rather a two-way street. As Jews assimilated into Vienna, or at least the Vienna of their experience, they also strongly influenced the character and image of that Vienna.

If the assimilation of Jews in Vienna created *Grossstadtjuden*, clumsily translated as 'big-city Jews', this process of Jewish assimilation and integration also had a very large part to play in making Vienna itself into a *Grossstadt*. In other words, so I will claim, the consequence of Jews becoming Viennese was that Vienna became a 'Jewish big city' – in its image especially, but also to a great extent in reality.

Vienna, it is true, had for a long time been a large city, indeed one of the largest in Europe, but for all that it had not really had the qualities one expects from a 'big city' in the sense of *Grossstadt*. This is not all that surprising since Vienna's primary purpose was to serve as the *Haupt- und Residenzstadt*, that is to say, the capital of an empire – whether Holy Roman or Austrian – and the home of that empire's dynasty; the Habsburgs. Due to that family's tradition and standing, Vienna was a centre of Roman Catholicism. It was also, again largely due to the Habsburgs and their Baroque relationship to the arts, a major centre of aristocratic cultural patronage, and hence of culture, especially in music and theatre. However, westerners such as Madame de Staël tended to see it as fusty and provincial.[4] Under Joseph

II it had begun to transcend these more Court-bound cultural spheres to take shape as a major intellectual and cultural centre of the German-speaking world in general, but this development was effectively halted by the revolutionary wars, relative economic stagnation, and Metternich. It was only in the second half of the nineteenth century that Vienna, partly supplanting its role as a dynastic centre, *became* a *Grossstadt* in the sense both of being a major centre for commerce, finance and industry, and also of being a major intellectual and cultural centre, with its own 'big-city', urban culture.

In speaking of a 'big-city' culture, I mean a culture in which one is not dominated by agrarian or rural values; one has a *modern* education, in other words, one has broken at least somewhat with tradition; one sees oneself as part of a new, trans-regional, indeed international economic and cultural world. 'Metropolis' is at all times tied up with 'cosmopolis'. The *Grossstadt*, in order to be true to itself, must also at the same time be, at least in spirit, a *Weltstadt*.[5] The wider the horizon the better. Vienna had effected the transition to this sort of culture by 1914, and that it did so as well as it did was in great part due to the role played in its cultural and intellectual life by Viennese Jewry.

One simple aspect of this was that by the late nineteenth century Jews provided a far greater number of adherents to the new, 'big-city' culture than their proportion in the populace as a whole would have led one to expect. The reasons for this disparity in following the norms of the new, modern, urban culture are many and varied, having to do with the Jews' social and economic position within society in general, but also with cultural and intellectual factors which were independent of merely 'social' factors.

There were, to put it another way, pre-existing factors which worked to the 'advantage' of Jews in this process of cultural urbanization, before they came to Vienna. Socio-economically, Jews were already concentrated in the sectors of pre-modern central European society and economy – trade and finance – which became the engines of the emerging modern, capitalist economy. This functional status, whether as moneylenders or traders, had been forced on Jews in pre-modern Europe by a combination of the religious and cultural traditions and economic and financial exigencies of Christian society. The net result in terms of modernization was, however, that the vast majority of Jews were not peasants and thus not tied – legally, culturally or emotionally – to the land, to the pre-modern, subsistence economy, or to the set of attitudes that went with it. As traders and financiers, however lowly their status might be in practice, Jews had also, perforce, much more contact with other centres of commerce and finance, providing the basis for that wider horizon spoken of above.

There were also factors which cannot simply be explained by the Jews' prescribed social position. Their own religious tradition meant that they put far more emphasis on learning than other central European groups did, including Catholic Austrian Germans. The content of that learning was, of course, solely religious, and the stress put on it in many traditional communities was almost equalled by the stress put on avoiding secular study as a distraction from the study of God's Word. However, the value placed on learning was clearly something which would eventually be of great power when applied to the new, education-oriented world of the big city.[6] Similarly, while traditional Jewish life could look desperately backward and 'Oriental' to commentators then and now, there were aspects to its structure – or lack of structure – which would also find ready adaptation to the new, modernizing world. The lack of ordained priests within the religious world, and the lack of the sort of sophisticated and powerful religious hierarchy found in the Catholic system, meant that the Jewish religious and indeed social world was far 'flatter' in terms of status than its Catholic counterpart in central Europe, while also having less effective controls over individual members. It was this sort of circumstance which could enable later, modernizing commentators, to comment on the 'liberal' and indeed 'democratic' nature of Jewish community life – with partial justification.[7]

Such traditional factors would in themselves have given Jews coming to Vienna attitudes different from their fellow, non-Jewish central Europeans, yet any such difference was already greatly amended for most of these incoming Jews by their exposure to, and adoption of, the ideology of emancipation. It is this ideology which was the most powerful vehicle for realizing the modernizing potential of those factors in traditional Jewish life outlined above, and making the new Jewish identity one that was tailor-made for the new, modern world.

Emancipation meant on one level the obvious: liberation from the discriminatory and oppressive measures against Jews which had been the pre-modern, religiously-based, European method of managing the presence of Jews within a Christian community. Emancipation also meant, not quite as obviously, the freedom to be equal, to be recognized as a human being, and not a (pejoratively understood) 'Jew'. The way in which the fight for Jewish freedom from persecution developed meant that emancipation came to be seen in terms of a *quid pro quo*, a deal in which the Jew's right to be regarded as a *Mensch*, a human being, and not as a 'Jew' depended on his having *merited* this change of status. As David Sorkin has shown, the movement for emancipation assumed Jewish self-improvement, so that Jews would earn the right to be viewed as fellow citizens.[8]

This self-improvement was seen to include a certain amount of assimilation and willingness to give up those 'disturbing' differences, those aspects of the old, traditional identity which particularly marked one off from one's fellow citizens. In theory, however, this did not mean joining traditional non-Jewish society, with its ancient anti-Jewish hostilities and customs and traditions which in turn were regarded as barbaric in the traditional Jewish world; rather the purpose of this casting-off of old Jewish forms of identity was in order to join and *act* in the new world of 'pure humanity', of enlightened modernity.[9]

Many Jewish individuals no doubt cast off their former Jewish identity and were only too happy to *think* themselves free of any association with their former fellow Jews. Yet it is far from clear that complete apostasy and self-denial of this order was what the vast majority of central European Jews, even in Vienna, intended.[10] The number of conversions is too small to warrant such a claim, and evidence even from prominent converts of a continuing Jewish identity further casts such a simplistic claim into question.[11] Instead, reading liberal Jewish periodicals of the time such as *Neuzeit*, we can see that Jews assumed that the new world of 'pure humanity' was not only one which treated Jews as equal, but also, beyond all the externalities of religion such as dress and custom, was in essential accord with Jewish values.

If the old Jewish identity was cast aside in the spirit of emancipation and assimilation, its core remained. The old identity was not so much destroyed as 'taken up', *aufgehoben* in the Hegelian sense, transformed into a new Jewish identity. This new version saw a strong emphasis on education, albeit now secular. It also laid great weight on the ethical side of life and art, which had much in common with the *Aufklärung* or German Enlightenment, with Lessing, Kant, Beethoven and Schiller.[12] In the rest of the German-speaking world this Jewish understanding of German heritage produced its own subtle variations from the German norm. But in Austria and particularly in Vienna, with Austrian culture's emphasis on aesthetics as an expression of the power of the Baroque, Habsburg, Catholic state, the affinity and identification of the majority of Austrian Jewry with the values of the *Aufklärung* made for much clearer, indeed crasser, differences between what Jews understood as modern society on the one hand and Austrian reality on the other.

Even before most Jews set foot in Vienna, therefore, there existed the makings of a new, modern Jewish identity, with many continuities with the old, traditional identity, and many stark differences from the prevalent Viennese or Austrian one. This new identity was closely linked to the emancipating influence of German liberalism, and the Jews who came to Vienna with this identity carried with them goals familiar to students of that political movement: *Besitz* (property); *Bildung* (education); and *Freiheit* (freedom).

Property was in all likelihood the largest incentive, and is the best explanation for the flocking of Jews to Vienna as soon as they were allowed in 1848. Until then Jews had officially been prohibited from living in the city. There were, it is true, a significant number of families, the *Tolerierten*, who had gained exceptional permission of residence, and other Jews, without such permission, who either circumvented or flouted the law in order to take part in the lucrative cloth trade within the city. This created a situation where the actual number of Jews in the city was far in excess of the official figures.¹³ Nevertheless, the prohibition clearly acted as a drag on Jewish immigration, and the relaxation of the ban in the wake of the revolution of 1848 saw a large number of economically motivated Jewish immigrants come to the city to make their fortune in the growing textile and commodities markets. Under neo-absolutism in the 1850s some restrictions on Jewish rights in Vienna were reimposed, but once these were finally lifted in 1860 a second wave of economically motivated Jewish immigrants followed.¹⁴

The journal *Neuzeit*, the unofficial organ of the liberal Jewish establishment in Vienna, complained in the 1860s of the way in which *Provinzjuden* were coming to Vienna with only hope in their pockets, and no immediate prospect of gainful employment.¹⁵ Nevertheless Jewish immigration to Vienna continued to be very high, and remained so into the early twentieth century.¹⁶ Some of the Jewish immigrants, especially from the earlier immigration waves, were fabulously successful economically and financially, rivalling the old established *Tolerierten* families in wealth if not always in prestige. Most were not, and there is much evidence suggesting that many Jews in Vienna were poor.¹⁷ Structurally, however, the large majority of Viennese Jews had by 1900 become bourgeois. That is to say, as Ivar Oxaal has pointed out, that roughly two thirds of Jewish money-earners were classified either as self-employed or as salaried, with only about one third in the wage-earning bracket, an earnings structure which was almost the mirror image of the rest of the city's population. Moreover, while there had clearly been a shift from careers as independent merchants and businessmen to being employees within larger firms, Jews remained largely within the commercial and financial sectors.¹⁸

The major new area of occupational interest for Jews was in the liberal professions: law, medicine and journalism, those vocations where an investment in education could be realized with a relatively large measure of independence from state intervention or state barriers to career advancement, in contrast to more traditional Austrian spheres such as the bureaucracy.¹⁹ The Jewish entry – in very large numbers – into the liberal professions in Vienna was a result of the second goal which Jews brought with them to the city; education. Jews made use of the educational opportunities available in Vienna in numbers quite disproportionate to their percentage of the population. If Jews accounted for around 10 per cent of the population in the late nineteenth century, they comprised 30 per cent of all students at Vienna University in the 1880s and, despite an increasingly hostile environment at the premier Austrian seat of higher learning, they still made up 25 per cent of the student body in 1905.²⁰ Moreover, at the level of elite secondary education, Jews comprised 35 per cent of all male pupils at the city's central *Gymnasien* (roughly translated as grammar schools), and 39 per cent if one excludes the anomalous, largely aristocratic Theresianum.[21]

This very high over-representation in the higher levels of the educational system is all the more remarkable as Jews could not in practice expect to get the jobs for which such an education was supposed to qualify one; namely a post in the higher echelons of the Habsburg bureaucracy. The unofficial bar on Jews from the better jobs within officialdom was not absolute, and conversion was often the entry ticket, if not to European culture, then at least to a good bureaucratic career.[22] Yet the anti-Jewish pressure that prevailed meant that Jewish individuals with ambition tended not to waste their careers on lowly positions within the bureaucracy but rather to take their chances as lawyers, doctors, journalists, or as qualified, salaried office workers in the private sector. If, under the old dispensation, most Jews had been pedlars, with an elite of Talmudic scholars and wealthier 'money-Jews', now, under the new circumstances, Jews were merchants and traders, office clerks and salesmen, with an elite of industrialists, bankers and liberal professionals; people with a doctorate. Education, now secular rather than religious, remained a major criterion of status discrimination within the Jewish community.

Freedom, the third goal of immigrating Jews, was clearly something which the city, by reputation at least, provided in abundance. Traditionally the city, especially the big city, has been associated with opportunity and fortune, and Vienna clearly was able to provide such chances at material self-betterment, most obviously through the stock exchange, which was, all anti-Semitic prejudices notwithstanding, heavily populated by Jews.[23] This freedom to better oneself materially was matched – as the above figures from the educational system already suggest – by a large freedom for intellectual and spiritual improvement, and many Jews took such opportunities to their logical conclusion, becoming writers, artists and thinkers, as the very large Jewish presence attests in the culture of Vienna in 1900.

The city also provided an environment where there were not quite the rigidities of rural or provincial life. This gave Jewish individuals more freedom to cross the boundaries which had previously kept them from the rest of society, so that they were now free to join fully in that society, whether this took the form of involvement in cultural life – as members of the public or as patrons; in social life – as hostesses of salons; or in consumerism – represented perhaps most effectively in Vienna by the leisurely world of the coffee house. Such positive freedom to cross boundaries and enter other, previously cordoned-off spheres of society, went hand in hand with more negative freedoms. There was, for instance, the freedom not to be seen primarily as a Jew – the other side of emancipation – and there was also the freedom from previous social constraints. To enter the free realm of the city could mean leaving behind the prohibitions and inhibitions of pre-modern, provincial Austrian society, which had traditionally kept Jews in a separate and lowly status. It could also mean, however, leaving behind the prohibitions and inhibitions of pre-modern, provincial and rural Jewish society, which, whatever the liberal Jewish establishment in Vienna might claim, had itself imposed strict cultural, religious and social codes of behaviour on its members, whether in ghettos such as Pressburg and Prague, the *Gassen*, (streets) of provincial Bohemia, or the *shtetls* of rural Galicia.

In this respect Vienna provided more freedom than other cities in central Europe, having the reputation among more conservative Jewish circles in the provinces of being a 'godless city'.[24] This reputation was not entirely deserved, but there was a grain of truth to it, at least relatively speaking. The Viennese Jewish religious community was, due to the previous prohibition against Jews in the city, brand new, with little if anything in the way of old traditions to which to appeal. This newness, which it shared with the rapidly increasing community in Budapest, sharply differentiated it from old centres of Jewish life and learning such as Prague. The consequence was that there tended to be far less corporate cohesion, with newcomers finding a concomitant lax observance of the ritual laws. This left individuals free from what could be seen as the burdens of tradition, which led in turn to more rapid secularization and indeed atomization of Jewish society.[25] The Viennese Jewish Press was full of articles complaining about the pressures to assimilate and the prevalence in the city of mixed marriages and conversions.[26] While anti-Semitism was seen as the main threat to the Jews in Vienna from the 1880s onward, the disintegration of Jewish religious life internally was also bewailed, as the title of an article from August 1895 in *Neuzeit* indicates; 'The axe from without, the worm from within'.[27]

Other articles complained of similar spiritual maladies: the replacement of idealism by a base materialism;[28] belief by unbelief;[29] the loss of Jewish independence and pride in favour of supine conformism.[30] The big city was seen in the pages of such journals as *Neuzeit* and the *Österreichische Wochenschrift* as the destroyer of Judaism;[31] it was also seen as the breeding ground of anti-Semitism. One of the more convincing explanations for why this might be so was given by the eminent geologist and Liberal, Eduard Suess – himself of partially Jewish descent – who attributed the animosity against Jews in Vienna to the Darwinian struggle to succeed amongst the various immigrant groups in Vienna, with the Jews having the misfortune of being singled out as the 'others'.[32] Already, in 1895, commentators on Viennese anti-Semitism had hit on the idea of 'negative integration' in explaining anti-Jewish attitudes as a result of the dynamics of ethnic competition within the big city.

Thus the big city was often seen in very negative terms even by the liberal Jewish Press – among Jews the image of *Grossstadtjuden* could be a very negative one. This is exemplified by Adolf Dessauer's novel of the same name, published in 1910, where the big-city Jews of the title display, in formulaic fashion, all the bad characteristics listed above, and then some. The hero figure in the book, one might have guessed, turns out to be an idealistic Christian.[33]

Yet the pejorative understanding of this urban Jewish experience is all a matter of perspective. In the 1890s such developments and problems could appear to augur very badly for Viennese Jewry. From today's perspective, however, they could also be viewed positively. For they were all very modern, urban problems; the problems, in other words, of a group of individuals who were thinking, writing and acting as big-city people, as citizens of the modern, urban world. Moreover, they were doing so not merely as big-city people, but as big-city Jews, for their Jewish background meant that, on average, they were far more liberal, educated, and cosmopolitan, than their fellow Viennese.

Jewish assimilation was not merely the process of fitting into an existing urban culture; it was also about having a large impact on, indeed largely shaping, that urban culture as it developed in the second half of the nineteenth century. The high culture and urban style which made Vienna 1900 so significant as a metropolitan, big-city centre of modern thought and culture is, frankly, unthinkable without the Jewish contribution to it. In so many aspects and in so many fields of cultural and intellectual endeavour, Jewish individuals played a crucial, often predominant role.

Just to what extent the city's Jewish population helped shape the modern high culture of *fin-de-siècle* Vienna is suggested by looking at the supposed social basis of that culture. The conventional wisdom of current historiography, as exemplified in the work of Carl E. Schorske, is that it was the educated elite of the liberal, bourgeois sector of Viennese society which was the social reservoir of the city's modern culture.[34] Yet, once one begins to analyze this educated elite in ethnic terms, then it turns out to have been in large majority a Jewish group. We have already seen the significant overrepresentation of Jews in the city's educational institutions, and in the more 'liberal' occupational sectors, and these are striking in themselves. Once one combines these tendencies, however, and looks for the Jewish presence at the point where higher educational qualification and liberal, bourgeois background met in turn-of-the-century Vienna; in the set of *Maturanten* (graduates) from the city's *Gymnasien* with fathers in liberal bourgeois occupations, then one finds a clear predominance of Jews. Almost two thirds of all male graduates in this group were Jewish,[35] and the equivalent figure for female *Lyzeen* graduates would appear to be even higher.[36]

This largely explains the well-known phenomenon that Jews predominated in many groups in Viennese modern culture, especially in literary and intellectual pursuits. Freud's circle of psychoanalytic disciples was almost exclusively Jewish in its early years, and remained predominantly so later. Most of the Austrian Marxist thinkers were of Jewish descent, as were a majority of the members of the Vienna Circle of Logical Positivists, and the two greatest thinkers associated with, but not of, the group: Ludwig Wittgenstein and Karl Popper. The group 'Young Vienna' was the literary heart of 'fin-de-siècle Vienna'. Over two thirds of its members were Jewish by descent. In other fields, such as music, the Jewish presence was, if not quite so dominant, still very large and influential, as the names of Gustav Mahler and Arnold Schoenberg suggest. There were not many prominent Jews in the fine arts – there were very few Jewish members of the Secession, for instance, and none of the prominent architects were Jewish. Even here, though, Jewish individuals played very substantial roles as patrons and propagandists of the new, modern art. It was largely families of Jewish descent who subsidized the art of the Secession and the architecture of Adolf Loos. The Secession's building, still to be seen with its 'golden cabbage head' on the Naschmarkt, was financed by none other than Ludwig Wittgenstein's father, Karl.[37]

It is in this context that the following 'prize game' from the November 1900 issue of Karl Kraus's *Die Fackel* becomes understandable, if still, for today's taste, rather off-colour. Ostensibly sent in by a contributor, it read:

'Dear Fackel!
Prize game: A lady
Sits on a chair by Olbrich – Darmstadt,
Wears a dress by Van de Velde – Brussels,
Earrings by Lalique – Paris,
A brooch by Ashbee – London,
Drinks from a glass by Kolo Moser – Vienna,
Reads a book from the publishers Insel – Munich, printed with letters by Otto Eckmann – Berlin, written by Hofmannsthal – Vienna.
To which confession does the lady belong?'[38]

No answer is given, and the irony lies in the fact that the obvious answer to the question – that the lady is Jewish – is very likely not the correct one. Given the high rate of conversion among the extremely wealthy industrialists' and bankers' families who were the chief sponsors of Jugendstil in Vienna, the answer could just as well be Catholic or even Protestant. The 'joke', if you can call it that, was that 'confession' was not the real point; rather descent was what counted when it came to the question of Jewish patronage of modern art, and here the appellation of *le gout juif*, once we ignore its pejorative connotations, was objectively fairly accurate. Even where

Jews did not lead as creators, they often had a large influence as consumers and supporters.

To take an overall view, it was Jewish individuals, as creators and as consumers, who played the leading role in creating the high culture of turn-of-the-century Vienna. As we should expect, these individuals brought their own ideas and assumptions with them from their particular central-European Jewish experience. Themselves products of the dialectic between Jewish tradition and Jewish modernization, they thus brought a Jewish aspect to bear on Viennese Modernism, whether intentional or not, and whether they were aware of it or not.

The impact of this dialectic made itself felt in the special qualities which characterized the high culture of Vienna at this time. There was a strong emphasis on individualism, even among Marxist thinkers. There was a great stress on the ethical responsibility of art and the artist, which was perhaps clearest, ironically, in the work of Karl Kraus and his 'Krausian' followers, such as Arnold Schoenberg and Ludwig Wittgenstein, and which led to a critical approach best summed up by the term 'critical modernism'.[39] Such attitudes illustrated not only a big-city character, but also the strong traces of the central-European Jewish experience outlined above.

By 1900, Vienna had acquired a big-city culture which did not have all that much to do with its usual traditions and values – as the Counter-Reformation *Haupt- und Residenzstadt* of the Habsburgs – but which was greatly influenced by the experiences and values of its big-city Jews. Karl Kraus, writing with an acid pen about the evils of the *Neue Freie Presse* and the financial interests which backed it, wrote in March 1901:

'The end result must be, that the remaining differences in custom and attitude separating the two neighbouring groups will disappear, and when, thanks to the corrosive influence of a powerful jobber-journalism, the desired assimilation *of* the population *to* the subscribers of the *Neue Freie Presse* will have been achieved, then the *other* assimilation is no longer necessary.'

Just to make his point crystal clear, Kraus added that the chief editor of the *Neue Freie Presse*, Moritz Benedikt, wanted the 'assimilation – of the Christians'. To complete the message, Kraus commented: 'It is no idle coincidence, that the man who wants to achieve the expulsion of the subscribers of the *Neue Freie Presse* by all means is also the Sunday humorist of the same paper.'[40]

With this sideswipe at Theodor Herzl and his Zionist movement, Kraus made it doubly clear that he was not only identifying the *Neue Freie Presse* and its readership as principally Jewish, but accusing them of trying to convert the Viennese populace to their Jewish value system. Even if we give Kraus satiric licence, it was a mean-spirited, nasty attack; the hint at conspiracy was fallacious and irresponsible, and the whole claim about the *Neue Freie Presse*, its readership, Viennese Jewry and the Viennese generally exaggerated. Yet Kraus's perception was based on a sort of reality, if not the one which he himself depicted.

Benedikt and the many other Jews who were part of Vienna's cultural elite, including Kraus himself, were deeply influenced by their experience of emancipation and assimilation. Many, such as Sigmund Freud or Arthur Schnitzler, recognized at least partially the role their Jewish background played in their lives and work. Many others would have preferred to have escaped completely their Jewish heritage and their existential Jewish situation. But any such attempts to escape, as in the case of Otto Weininger or indeed Karl Kraus himself, simply ended up by illustrating how entrenched was the Jewish aspect in Viennese culture and society.[41] Willy-nilly, the Jewish experience of so many members of Vienna's cultural elite had a strong impact on those individuals' views and hence on their work, and also, one might add, on the views and work of their non-Jewish colleagues.

In the attempt to participate in the life of the big city, Vienna's Jews, in effect, largely created the cultural world of Vienna around 1900. What Vienna's big-city culture would have been like without the large Jewish presence is an extremely interesting question, but not one which, as a historian, professionally averse to dealing in counter-factuals, I feel comfortable in answering. Suffice it to say, however, that when Hugo Bettauer wrote his novel *The city without Jews* in 1922, about what would happen if Viennese Jewry were to be expelled from Austria, he not only predicted twenty years in advance the expulsion and destruction of Austrian Jewry, but he also identified what so many commentators subsequently noted of Vienna for decades after 1945, almost until today: namely its character as the largest provincial town in Europe.[42]

The problem was that Kraus had only been about half right (or less) in his claim about the assimilation of the Viennese populace to a Jewish culture. The influence of the Jewish experience might have been crucial in determining the Viennese 'big city' high culture, which we now look back on with a mixture of admiration and nostalgia. It might also be said to have been a very significant factor in the creation of mass, commercial culture, whether it be the operetta or the film industry – even some of the most famous and popular *Wiener Lieder*, Viennese popular folksongs, were written by Jews. Yet, obviously, there were other cultural influences on the Viennese populace, other effects inherent to a big city, which meant that the sort of metropolitan-cosmopolitan, liberal, open-minded and sophisticated big-city culture of the central-European ideal, and which Viennese Jewry did so much to bring about in the first decades of this century, never did manage to penetrate too far beyond the confines of the Jewish bourgeoisie and become the dominant culture of the rest of the city's inhabitants.[43] If the thought of Freud and Wittgenstein, the work of Schnitzler, Canetti and Broch, the music of Mahler and Schoenberg, the biting satire of Karl Kraus, point to one expression of the central-European urban experience, the dreary, desperate and deluded world of Hitler's Vienna points to another.[44]

How little the one Vienna, of sophisticated urbanity, was able truly to influence and change the other big city, the world of desperate economic struggle and petit-bourgeois, anti-Semitic prejudice is illustrated by the depraved and traumatic events of March 1938 and after. Those Jews who were able to escape the Holocaust often found other 'big cities', or their functional equivalents, in the English-speaking world, to which to donate their immense intellectual and cultural gifts. Meanwhile Vienna, after many decades, is once again showing some signs of a 'big-city' culture. One thing is fairly clear, however: after the events of 1938–1945 the history of Vienna as a *Jewish* big city is over.

Notes

1. On the history of Viennese Jewry, see Ivar Oxaal et al. (eds), *Jews, Antisemitism and Culture in Vienna*, London: Routledge, 1987; Steven Beller, *Vienna and the Jews, 1867–1938: A Cultural History*, Cambridge University Press, 1989; Marsha L. Rozenblit, *The Jews of Vienna, 1867–1914: Assimilation and Identity*, Albany: SUNY, 1983; Robert S. Wistrich, *The Jews of Vienna in the Age of Franz Joseph*, Oxford: Oxford University Press, 1988.
2. By 1910 there were 175 318 Jews in the city, which constituted 8.6 per cent of greater Vienna, and roughly 12 per cent of the population living within the old, pre-1890 urban boundaries. Such percentages were not as high as in Budapest, for example, where Jews accounted for 23 per cent of the population, but much higher than in other cities with prominent Jewish communities, such as Berlin, where Jews made up around 5 per cent.
3. Cf. Rozenblit, *The Jews of Vienna*, pp.3–11.
4. Madame de Staël, *De l'Allemagne*, Paris, 1958 [orig. 1813], vol. 1, pp.98–135. On Vienna's history, see Ilsa Barea, *Vienna*, New York: Knopf, 1966.
5. See György Konrad, 'Die Herausforderung der Grossstadt', in P. Berner, E. Brix and W. Mantl (eds), *Wien um 1900: Aufbruch in die Moderne*, Vienna: Geschichte und Politik, 1986, pp.259–75.
6. Beller, *Vienna and the Jews*, pp.88–105.
7. Ibid., pp.106–13.
8. David Sorkin, *The Transformation of German Jewry, 1780–1840*, Oxford: Oxford University Press, 1987, pp.13–40.
9. Beller, *Vienna and the Jews*, pp.137–43.
10. Rozenblit, *The Jews of Vienna*, pp.127–46.
11. Beller, *Vienna and the Jews*, pp.226–9.
12. Ibid., pp.144–55.
13. Nikolaus Vielmetti, 'Zur Geschichte der Wiener Juden im Vormärz', in Klaus Lohrmann (ed.), *1000 Jahre österreichisches Judentum*, Vienna: Roetzer, 1982, pp.93–111; Sigmund Mayer, *Die Wiener Juden: Kommerz, Kultur, Politik 1700–1900*, Vienna: Löwit, 1918, p.243–7.
14. Mayer, *Wiener Juden*, pp.326–35.
15. *Neuzeit* [Nz.] 21 November 1862, no. 47, p.553.
16. Beller, *Vienna and the Jews*, p.44.

17. Peter Pulzer, *The Rise of Political Antisemitism in Germany and Austria*, London: Halban, 1988, pp.13–14.
18. Ivar Oxaal, 'The Jews of young Hitler's Vienna', in Oxaal, *Jews, Antisemitism and Culture in Vienna*, pp.33–8; Ivar Oxaal and Walter R. Weitzmann, 'The Jews of Pre-1914 Vienna', in *Leo Baeck Institute Yearbook*, XXX, 1985, pp.420–32; see also Rozenblit, *The Jews of Vienna*, pp.47–70.
19. Beller, *Vienna and the Jews*, pp.37–40, 59–69.
20. Ibid, p.34.
21. Ibid, p.52.
22. Ibid, p.188–90.
23. William O. McCagg, 'Jewish Wealth in Vienna, 1670–1918', in Michael K. Silber (ed.), *Jews in the Hungarian Economy, 1760–1945*, Jerusalem: Magnes, 1992, p.74.
24. Mayer, *Die Wiener Juden*, pp.298–300.
25. Ibid, pp.203–15, 273–5; Vielmetti, 'Juden im Vormärz', p.99.
26. *Nz.*, 31 May 1895, no. 22, p.233. Although the Press spoke of mixed marriages, technically there could be none, as civil marriage between Jews and Christians was not legal. One of the main reasons for the relatively high rate of conversion of Viennese Jewry was that, under Austrian law, a Jew and a Christian wishing to marry had a choice of one partner – usually, but not always, the Jew – converting to the religion of the other, or both leaving their religions and becoming *konfessionslos*.
27. *Nz.*, 16 August 1895, p.361.
28. *Nz.*, 4 May 1866, no. 18, p.199; *Nz.*, 3 April 1896, no. 14, p.139.
29. *Nz.*, 6 January 1899, no. 1, p.5.
30. *Nz.*, 9 March 1900, no. 10, pp.95–6.
31. For instance, Joseph Bloch, 'Wie gebieten wir Einhalt dem rapiden Verfall des religiösen Geistes?', *Österreichische Wochenschrift*, 15 October 1884, no.1, pp.3–4.
32. *Nz.*, 5 April 1895, no. 14, pp.144–5.
33. Adolph Dessauer, *Grossstadtjuden*, Vienna: Braumüller, 1910.
34. Carl E. Schorske, *Fin-de-siècle Vienna: Politics and Culture*, London: Weidenfeld, 1980, pp.5–10, 302–11.
35. Beller, *Vienna and the Jews*, pp.49–55.
36. Rozenblit, *The Jews of Vienna*, pp.121–2.
37. Beller, *Vienna and the Jews*, pp.14–32.
38. *Die Fackel*, mid November 1900, no. 59, p.28.
39. Beller, *Vienna and the Jews*, pp.207–37; see also Allan Janik, 'Vienna 1900 Revisited: Paradigms and Problems', in *Austrian History Yearbook* 1997, XXVIII, p.20.
40. *Die Fackel*, mid March 1901, no. 71, pp.1–2.
41. Beller, *Vienna and the Jews*, pp.221–9.
42. Hugo Bettauer, *Die Stadt ohne Juden*, Salzburg: Hanibal, 1980 [1922].
43. Steven Beller, 'The City as Integrator: Immigration, Education and Popular Culture in Vienna, 1880–1938,' in *German Politics and Society*, vol. 15, no. 1, Spring 1997, pp.117–31.
44. See Brigitte Hamann, *Hitlers Wien*, Munich: Piper, 1996; Steven Beller, 'Geschichte zweier Städte: Hitlers Wien, Herzls Wien', in *Transit*, vol. 10, autumn 1995, pp.79–94.

9

Popular culture and politics in imperial Vienna

Tim Kirk

Austria's defeat at the Battle of Königgrätz (Sadova) in 1866 marked a turning point in the country's history, the consequences of which were the passing of political supremacy in central Europe to Prussia and far-reaching constitutional change at home. From the perspective of Wilhelm Ellenbogen, however, a leading Social Democrat, the establishment of a workers' educational association in the Vienna suburb of Gumpendorf a year later was a more important event.[1] It marked the beginning of an educational and cultural project undertaken by the emergent Austrian labour movement which was to reach its most complete fulfilment in Vienna during the 1920s, when – arguably – the cultural dimension of Vienna's socialism set it apart from other socialist municipalities.

The foundations for the cultural policies of 'Red Vienna', however, were very firmly laid in the years before the First World War. Intellectuals in the Austrian Social Democratic Workers' Party (*Sozialdemokratische Arbeiterpartei*, SDAP) recognized the importance of culture in reinforcing the hegemony of the ruling classes. Culture was a commodity like others to which workers should have equal access: 'In every nation the modern proletariat finds itself excluded not only from the enjoyment of the material goods of this world;' wrote a party commentator in 1907, 'the more [it] develops, the more strongly and more painfully it senses that the elevated existence which comes to us from art is also a privilege of the propertied.' The ruling classes, he argued, were as indifferent to the intellectual development of the ruled, as they were to their material well-being.[2] The SDAP set out to make up for the educational deficit of the working class through its own educational work. At the same time, culture as a commodity could provide a focus for workers' leisure time as well as giving access to the privilege and power available to the educated. Here, too, the SDAP were acutely aware how workers were excluded from cultural enjoyment: 'After all,' argued Stefan Grossman, 'the worker too has a right to enjoy his hard-earned leisure!'[3]

The problem for the SDAP, however, was that the cultural education which would enable workers to make their social and political challenges on equal terms also had to be earned, and meant further hours of self-improvement after a long day of exhausting manual work, whereas less demanding opportunities for relaxation and enjoyment were afforded by the expanding commercial 'leisure' industries of the turn of the century. From the outset Social-Democratic cultural policy was caught between challenging the workers' exclusion from high culture and steering them away from the temptations of passive consumption. More than this, a policy which promoted 'high culture' in preference to light entertainment also had to make discriminating value judgements on the classical and contemporary canons; and that might mean making value judgements that were at odds with prevailing cultural fashions. Should the party's caste of educational mentors approve Modernist works, for example (whether in art, literature, drama, music or architecture); or should they only promote the classics? Cultural politics in *fin de siècle* Vienna was something of a minefield.

The turn of the century was critical to the development of popular culture, just as it was to the development of popular politics. It was not only the SDAP which engaged in the arena of cultural politics, but the parties of the populist Right as well, and especially the Christian Social Party, which controlled the city council and promoted its cultural ideology both in the schools and in the city's public culture. Ideas about the role of culture in society, and about the role of the state or the party in culture which were to have momentous effect after 1918 were developed in the last decades before the First World War.

Perhaps understandably, historians of working-class culture in Vienna have concentrated primarily on the inter-war years, when the SDAP was in power.[4] The focus of this essay will be the formative years of Social-Democratic cultural and educational work before the war, when the party's policy was oppositional. It will seek to locate the party's programmes within the context of a more general popular culture by looking at the ways in which the working people of Vienna spent such free time as they had at their disposal and the development of leisure and commercial entertainment in the city. It will seek to assess the responses popular culture elicited from politicians, journalists and the educated middle classes; and will examine in particular the ways in which the leaders and functionaries of the Social Democratic Workers' Party sought to harness and direct the – often intermittent – aspirations of a small section of the organized working class towards cultural and political self-improvement.

Popular culture in Vienna

The origins of Vienna's modern popular culture are to be found in the late eighteenth century. The city was the seat of the Holy Roman Emperors, and as such the foremost *Residenzstadt* in central Europe. The aristocrats who had flocked to Vienna to be near the court had displaced the city's burghers and rebuilt the old quarters of the city with their palaces.[5] Fashionable high culture, and above all tastes in music and serious theatre were determined at court and in the aristocratic salon. But the social and economic changes that were transforming the culture of all major European cities were also making their impact on Vienna, albeit a little later and on a smaller scale. In the *Vorstädte* and *Vororte* (suburbs) outside the city walls there was already a substantial class of labouring poor, many of whom had recently arrived from outside the city, attracted by work in the service sector, attending to the needs of the wealthier classes; or as artisans or labourers in the small manufactories of the urban periphery.[6] Boundaries between work and free time were still fluid in the proto-industrial society of the plebeian suburbs and the disciplines of industrial society were often resisted by a defiant insistence on observing 'traditional' customs.[7] Much of the free time of the emergent working class was spent drinking and gambling, so much so that one Vienna suburb was called the 'biggest tavern in the Holy Roman Empire';[8] and the culture of heavy drinking on Sundays followed by absenteeism on 'blue Mondays' frustrated the aspirations of market-orientated employers to an orderly division of work and free time sufficiently to prompt attempts to regulate workers' leisure activities.[9] A preoccupation with the effects of excessive drinking was to be a leitmotif in commentaries on working-class culture up to the Second World War and beyond.[10]

Between the two extremes of the court and the suburban tavern there was already an emergent bourgeois culture, not so self-confident as to unsteady the political order of the empire during the revolutionary and Napoleonic wars, but assertive enough to prompt the aristocracy to rethink their own tastes and redefine the exclusivity of their own culture. Thus, it has been argued, the preference for the undemanding Italian salon music of the eighteenth century was devalued once it could be heard in bourgeois houses, and those aristocrats who sought to display their more refined tastes turned (rather belatedly) to the complexities of the music of Mozart and, perhaps ironically, of Beethoven.[11] For the most part, however, the culture and leisure of the middle classes at the onset of industrialization was characterized on the one hand by a concern, during the Biedermeier period, with domesticity, privacy and the family but also by new forms of public culture situated in clubs, theatres and restaurants.

In addition there were shared spaces within the city where the different social classes to some extent came together. Chief among these was the Prater, Vienna's most important pleasure garden, but other open spaces, such as the city park and the Vienna woods, would acquire a similar importance.[12] The Prater had once been an old imperial hunting ground and had been opened to the public by Joseph II in 1766. Coffee houses and restaurants had quickly been established, balloons were launched there, and fireworks displays were also held. But despite the semblance of social mixing, the different classes tended to keep to their own territory, and the grandest spectacles were seldom within the reach of those with more modest incomes.[13] More accessible for many of the lower classes were the entertainments of the 'böhmischer Prater' in the suburbs.[14] In 1776, another of Joseph's reforms established the freedom of any individual to entertain the public, clearing the way for the establishment of private theatres and touring troops of players in Lower Austria, and the latter flourished in the Vienna *Vorstädte* in particular, where three new theatres had been founded by the end of the eighteenth century.[15]

During the nineteenth century Vienna grew very rapidly in size and population, largely as a result of industrialization, immigration and the incorporation of the outer suburban districts: the city had fewer than a quarter of a million inhabitants in 1800, and more than two million by 1914. Its social structure was increasingly dominated by the industrial working class, along with a lower middle class of public and private white-collar employees and small business people. The appearance of the city was transformed by the demolition of the city walls, the building of the Ringstrasse, the consolidation of bourgeois suburbia between the ring and the outer *Gürtel*, and the expansion of the more proletarian suburbs beyond: Vienna's class hierarchy was arranged in concentric circles.

The culture of the city was also transformed. By the end of the nineteenth century reductions in work time and higher wages, along with the disciplines imposed by an urban industrial society, had led to a clearer separation of work and leisure,[16] and although class remained an important determinant of taste, two developments in particular ensured that the consumption of modern popular culture transcended class boundaries: the spread of literacy and the development of commercial leisure. In the later eighteenth century, as in other parts of German-speaking Europe, the state had begun to regulate basic schooling, and Joseph II had been insistent on the necessity of rudimentary primary school education for all children between six and twelve – albeit for utilitarian reasons – and compulsory education had been introduced in 1869.[17] Rates of literacy in central Europe rose from 15 to 90 per cent between 1800 and 1900.[18] By 1902 there were 188 educational societies of one kind or another in the city. Popular libraries were founded in the inner suburbs in the late 1870s, and Catholic educational associations, like their Social Democratic counterparts, also kept small libraries. As in other parts of Europe, philanthropic liberal businessmen and professionals also sought to provide free and 'unpolitical' public libraries for all classes in the city, such as that of the *Allgemeiner Nieder-österreichische Volksbildungsverein*, which was established in 1877.

Not only did more people read, but they read a far greater variety of material.[19] Where masters and servants had often read the same – largely religious – literature up to the eighteenth century, literary tastes now diverged, although not clearly along lines of class or educational level. Novels of all kinds became very popular among the educated middle classes, and the taste for such literature was often shared by 'senior' members of the domestic staff in bourgeois households, who took light novels home from lending libraries and passed them on to their masters.[20] And although people read more books they were often looking for familiar contents, recognizable characters and predictable plots. Genre fiction became a lucrative industry, and mass-produced light fiction was often sold from door to door in serialized parts by book pedlars, or *Kolporteurs*.[21]

Although 'classical' literature was also serialized in this way, and the pedlars occasionally sold religious material, *Kolportage* or 'back stairs' novels (*Hintertreppenromane*) were more often than not sensationalistic genre fiction – Gothic horror, crime, ghost stories and so on – and each weekly part was a cliff-hanger in order to persuade the subscriber to part with the money for the next instalment. The Social Democrats and others interested in the improvement of the lower classes disapproved strongly of such literature, and not least on account of the commercial exploitation of the poor. Serialized novels, they pointed out, seemed cheaper than editions of the classics because they cost, typically, fourteen hellers a week, whereas an edition of a classical work might require an immediate outlay of four or five crowns. In reality, however, the cost of such a *Kolportageroman* over the seventy or eighty weeks of its serialization might amount to much more. Max Winter, an undercover investigative journalist for the Social Democratic *Arbeiterzeitung*, accompanied two salesmen on their rounds in the spring of 1905. One of their customers, a master joiner, had already paid some eight crowns for the fifty-seven parts of *Die Königstochter im Irrenhaus* ('The King's Daughter in the Madhouse'); and a Czech servant girl with more literary aspirations had been subscribing to a serialized version of a work by Schiller, and would have paid twenty-four crowns for the eighty instalments by the time she had finished collecting them. Nobody had told her, Winter commented, that she could probably buy the works of Schiller, Goethe and Lessing together for the same price.[22] Although Winter's investigations also revealed that the readership of the *Kolportageroman* was more diverse than might have been expected – customers included an officer's widow and a language teacher –

the principal market was among the petit bourgeois of inner suburbia and domestic servants: 'How many thousands from the servant classes', asked the *Österreichische Hauspersonalzeitung* in 1911, 'spend what little free time they have reading such trashy literature, i.e. love stories, crime novels and other such books of this kind...?'[23]

Similar tastes were catered for by the expanding popular newspaper press. Then as now the *Kronenzeitung*, which dealt in sensationalism as much as in 'hard' news, was the mass-circulation daily which was perhaps most popular with the working class, to the despair of party intellectuals.[24] The themes familiar from *Kolportageromane*, however, were more clearly reflected in more 'specialist' publications than in daily newspapers. One such publication was the *Österreichische Kriminal-Zeitung*, whose first issue appeared in April 1907 and which carried articles on suicide, prostitution and pederasty, and advertisements for private detectives and breast-enlargement creams.[25] Its prurient readers were offered titillating accounts of life in a nether-world of criminality and sexual licence, laced with enough moralizing indignation to preserve the pretext of 'investigative' journalism.

As in other European cities, however, by far the most dramatic popular cultural innovation at the turn of the century was the cinema. The first picture house opened in the Kärntnerstrasse in 1896, showing Lumière brothers' films that had been seen in the first demonstrations in Paris and elsewhere. The shows were considered an unpretentious novelty in a popular entertainments business whose repertoire encompassed light theatre and novelty mechanical attractions, and the cinema seemed at first to be very much in the established tradition of the panorama and the magic lantern; many of Vienna's cinemas were concentrated in the Prater alongside other such side-shows. But it quickly proved itself to be a cultural industry of a qualitatively new order. It expanded rapidly when film rental companies were set up after the turn of the century. By the eve of the First World War both Austria and Hungary had their own film production companies, and there were over 600 picture houses in Austria and 270 in Hungary, 113 of which were in Vienna and 92 in Budapest.[26] Despite the persistence for several years of itinerant cinemas in tents and country inns, the picture house was very much an urban phenomenon, and rapidly established itself as the most popular form of commercial entertainment in towns and cities. Moreover, cinema epitomized the 'classlessness' of popular culture even more than commercial publishing. It was immensely popular among all social groups, from members of the imperial family to industrial workers and their families for whom it might be an occasional treat. The cinema audience was an early microcosm of the modern 'mass' consumer society, which was to be so much the target of commercial marketing strategy and the object of government policy in the twentieth century.[27]

The politics of culture

Except in so far as popular participation in culture was the consequence of government educational and social policy, the governments of the late nineteenth century did not yet have cultural or arts policies as such. Government intervention on a large scale through ministries of 'popular enlightenment' and state agencies were not to come until the popular and plebiscitary politics of the inter-war years. And whereas other states, including Hungary, might actively promote the celebration of nationhood or empire with the enthusiastic support of the middle classes, even this was problematic for the government of multinational Austria, which was compelled to take into account the divergent national sympathies of urban intellectuals in Vienna, Prague, Trieste and Ljubljana. Only the dynasty, explicitly represented as supra-national, could be celebrated, and then not without provoking scepticism.[28] The coordination of policy for the regulation of culture was strictly a pragmatic business. The commercialization of leisure demanded the licensing of venues, the review of safety regulations, police supervision of censorship and so on.

Not surprisingly, the cinema in particular, on account of its popularity and economic importance, provided the impetus for precisely such a coordination of policy between a number of government departments. The first steps towards the evolution of a state policy for a leisure industry are discernible in the agenda of an investigation into the cinema organized by the government on the eve of the First World War.[29] A questionnaire was sent out to local authorities, representatives of the business community and other interested parties and discussions were subsequently held in the Ministry of the Interior over a number of days in April 1912. Much of the business was mundane, and dealt with practical everyday problems, from the training of projectionists to the revision of fire regulations. But it was also clear from the material that had been gathered by the ministry, and in the contributions from many of those present, that no threat to cultural standards was more reviled by the guardians of public taste and decency than the cinema. Its intoxicating and addictive effects were compared to those of alcohol, and its global ubiquitousness to that of diseases carried by European empire builders to the farthest corners of the earth.[30] It became a vehicle for any number of social and cultural anxieties: the poor would steal to pay for tickets, it was asserted;[31] it kept people away from church, and would render smaller and provincial theatres economically unviable – and theatre, once suspect but now increasingly respectable, was a cultural form whose superiority was taken for granted, however lacklustre the company and its performances or mediocre the work it performed. Furthermore, the darkened auditoria were a positive invitation to immorality among the young.

Little wonder, then, that cinema quickly attracted the hostility of conservative pressure groups. In April 1910, for example, the Lower Austrian Catholic Women's Organization had made representation to the Ministry of Culture and Education, seeking measures to protect schoolchildren from the dangers of visiting cinemas. And in the opinion of a number of Catholic and educational organizations who submitted a petition to the Minister of the Interior in 1912, the cinema was the latest of a whole range of hidden dangers in the city which constituted a threat to the spiritual and moral development of young people. The content of cinema films, it was argued, had a much more damaging effect than was generally accepted. Scenes of criminal life were common and immoral films not only excited instincts which ought to be inhibited, but also had a debilitating effect on the nerves. Children left the cinema, it was asserted, with feelings of fear, anxiety, nervousness and sleeplessness. Furthermore, their education was damaged, and their sense of reality impaired by the presentation of a fictitious world full of untruths and impossibilities, which were rendered credible by moving pictures.[32] Such views reflected a more widespread concern about the manipulative effects of cinematographic realism.[33]

In the event the prewar state was disinclined to interfere in the business more than was absolutely necessary and was circumspect in its approach to some of the more strident claims of cultural conservatives. But the cinema business itself took such criticisms seriously for the most part, and responded in public in the columns of a growing specialist press, where even articles that were critical of the cinema were reprinted in the (vain) hope of encouraging a fairer and more reasoned debate.[34] Despite the carping, however, its enthusiasts were determined to celebrate the cinema as a popular symbol of modernity, and its opponents were caricatured in the same specialist magazines as old-fashioned and reactionary, while composite fictional cinema 'types' from all walks of life, but generally well situated – the officer, the privy councillor's wife, the governess – were described in detail to lend cinema-going respectability[35]

If the state was reluctant to intervene in cultural politics with general policies, the importance of culture was much more clearly recognized at municipal level. Both major parties in Vienna recognized the importance of guiding, and indeed shaping, popular taste. The governing Christian Social Party was conscious that it had inherited the city from a liberal bourgeoisie whose grandiose projects, particularly the Ringstrasse, had made the capital what it now was. Nevertheless, culture had to be a part of a broader programme of public works and such developments as there were rapidly revealed the difficulties of evolving a municipal cultural policy which had to reconcile the aesthetic sensibilities of the city's cultural elites with the tastes of party members and voters, while keeping an eye on the costs to ensure that extravagance and ostentation did not unbalance the books. The public culture of the Christian Social era sought to suggest a dynamic and technically progressive city, and functionalism was the architectural order of the day, but the problems involved in achieving all these objectives at once quickly became clear – the city council's rejection of Otto Wagner's design for a municipal museum was an instructive case in point. The city remained on firmer ground when sponsoring projects which enhanced the quality of the broader cultural experience of its supporters, such as extensions to the city's cemetery and suburban parks.[36] In the ideology of the Christian Social reform era green spaces in and around the city not only afforded its inhabitants open spaces for the pursuit of leisure, but had an additional and perhaps more important utilitarian purpose in their function of improving public health.[37]

In addition, the Christian Social, as the party of municipal government, were responsible for the provision of primary education, probably the single most important element in the development of the cultural life of the majority of citizens. However, although new schools were built in an effort to keep pace with the rapid growth of the city's population, the curriculum, which largely consisted of basic literacy and a 'moral' education intended to instil respect for the naturally hierarchical order of society, provoked criticism from the Social Democrats and the anti-clerical *Jungen*, a group of disaffected teachers organized in the *Zentralverein der Wiener Lehrerschaft*.[38] The disagreement was essentially over access to *Bildung* – the cultural education transmitted to upper-middle-class children by the humanistic *Gymnasium* and the university. The possession of *Bildung*, it was felt, was the quality which gave the *Bildungsbürgertum*, the 'educated middle class', its social status and sense of authority. The reading, writing and religious instruction of the municipal school system was, in the view of the dissident teachers, a denial not only of access to culture, but also of opportunity to challenge the middle classes on their own terms, and thus a denial of access to any social mobility.

The importance of *Bildung* for the Social Democrats came, then, not from any pious conservative respect for 'high' culture, but from a recognition of the social value and political importance of that culture, and its role in reinforcing the hegemony of the *Bildungsbürgertum*. It is in the light of these political considerations that the Social Democratic commitment to providing an alternative to the basic educational provision of the state should be seen. The SDAP's approach to workers' education and culture was focused and systematic. Social Democratic educational associations had existed since the 1860s, initially as a substitute for more explicit forms of political organization, but the party's cultural and educational work really took off in the decade or so before the First World War. It comprised not only lecture series and evening courses, but libraries, concerts, and the organization of an alternative calendar of celebratory festivals, at the centre of which was May Day. 'The proper disposition of a worker's free time is no small thing and no small concern' wrote Stefan Grossmann in 1908. 'Of course, we want to fill the free time of the proletarian above all with serious work, work for the political and economic struggle. We want to fill it with educational endeavours but because we know that the bacilli of petit bourgeois philistinism [*Spiessbürgerei*] are picked up most easily through "entertainment" we should also be concerned about workers' holiday celebrations.' Workers' festivals, Grossmann went on to add, would be a lot better if they were organized through a central office in every town.[39] The Social Democrats, no less than their Christian Socialist adversaries, recognized the need to determine the nature of popular culture in the age of popular politics, and it was in this sense that the foundations for the Red Vienna of the 1920s were already being laid, in opposition, before 1914.[40]

There was, then, a clear political reasoning behind the party provision of workers' education from the outset. It was seen as a prerequisite for the long-term integration of new members into the labour movement: popular courses offered by the university and the *Volksheim* (municipal adult education) were increasingly considered inadequate because the essential basics were missing: an understanding of the capitalist system and the worker's own class position within it. (Indeed, those who promoted private forms of popular education had always hoped that they would soothe social tensions and help to reconcile class differences.[41]) So it had long been a tradition for local party and union branches to hold popular lectures at their weekly or fortnightly meetings. In addition, the various Social Democratic organizations in each district of Vienna would get together to provide longer educational courses, and there was an unsuccessful attempt in the 1890s to centralize all these activities for the whole city and beyond in a Lower Austrian Organization for Education and Instruction. The drive towards the provision of centralized city-wide resources and activities was revived in the first decade of the twentieth century with the founding in 1903 of the educational association *Zukunft* (Future), whose purpose was the provision of lecture series for the Social Democratic and trade union organizations of Vienna and Lower Austria. A further step in this direction came with the establishment in 1904 of the *Wiener Arbeiterschule* (Vienna Workers' School). The school's syllabus, which consisted of politics and sociology, economics, law and the history of socialism, was clearly intended for committed political activists – who could, in addition, contribute something to the cost of the courses – rather than the majority of the rank and file. In 1908 the school had 177 students. Of these two-thirds were under the age of 30 and all but four of them were men.[42] The provision of more popular courses followed a few years later with the establishment of a party education committee. Between the beginning of November 1908 and the end of June 1909 the committee was responsible for organizing 1216 lectures. Of these almost half (569) were for trade unions, and just over a quarter (338) for educational associations, but some were specifically for women's organizations, young people's organizations, sports associations and other audiences. Above all, the party was anxious to get its political message across to a rank-and-file membership which read very little, and accordingly the majority of lectures were about socialism, the party and its programme, employment law, and other social questions; but there were also series on first aid, child-rearing, women's health, the history of the theatre, literature and biology.[43]

The necessity of providing workers with culture that was ideologically reliable was reiterated in the rhetorical leading article of the party's new journal, *Bildungsarbeit*, in September of the same year. The children of artisans, peasants and the lower middle classes had become proletarian wage-earners; but, it was argued, they retained their narrow perspectives and, without class consciousness, were susceptible to the 'thousand voices' of the bourgeois world.[44] The party set out to advise workers, or at least the functionaries and activists who read the Social Democratic periodical press, on cultural and educational matters.

The chief concern was with what workers read.[45] The Social Democratic establishment was aware of the difficulty workers had in gaining access to the best books, and *Bildungsarbeit* regularly featured lists of recommended books for those building up their libraries. However, these generally comprised very worthy educational or political titles which might complement rather than replace more popular tastes for the better off among the working class.[46] There were also more specialized lists on particular issues, such as alcohol and the 'women's question', and special lists of recommended books for children and young people.[47] But the party was also aware that, despite its best efforts, the attempt to educate popular literary taste could only be partially successful. Library statistics were carefully monitored, and they clearly demonstrated that the taste for contemporary light fiction far exceeded that for explicitly political or educational works.[48] Jules Verne was consistently popular, as were a handful of other authors whose work has proved less enduring. Writers such as Zola, who were approved of by the party and were apparently popular as well, were the exception rather than the rule.

The party's concern with the establishment of a socialist aesthetic was not restricted to literature. *Bildungsarbeit* also published lists of recommended pictures by approved artists which were available as cheap prints, among them Delacroix's *Liberty Leading the People*, scenes depicting ordinary working people and landscapes by such artists as Courbet, Millet, Max Liebermann,

Meunier, Segantini, and a number of lesser-known contemporary German artists.[49] A free exhibition of reproductions of paintings (*Wandschmuck*), with an accompanying explanatory lecture series, was organized in Vienna in October 1909. It attracted 3 500 visitors in a fortnight, some 80 per cent of whom, it was claimed, were workers and their families. The exhibition then went on to tour the suburbs and the provinces.[50]

The Social Democrats paid similar attention to music and the theatre. The cultural reputation of the city had been made by music, and the party was determined that the workers should share in it. Workers' symphony concerts were organized from 1905 and continued during the First Republic. The repertoire consisted largely of conventional classical works by well-known composers. Music by Beethoven, Berlioz, Brahms, Schubert, Schumann and Hugo Wolf made up the programme for 1912–13. But the party was also proud to put on more 'modern' work by Richard Strauss and even Richard Wagner. The popular musical culture of the city proved to be more appealing, however. Most Viennese were less familiar with Richard than with Johann Strauss, whose waltzes were more often performed at the workers' concerts than *Till Eulenspiegel*. There were also special 'Viennese evenings' with more popular music, and significantly, it was one of these which was the only event to be sold out.[51]

Socialist critics were disparaging about the theatre in Vienna. Josef Luitpold Stern commented despairingly in 1912 that workers' tastes in theatre were 'petit bourgeois' and went on to recommend a number of plays, adding that those which were not mentioned in his review might just as well not have been performed.[52] An alternative was provided by the *Verein Wiener Freie Volksbühne*, an association presided over by Engelbert Pernerstorfer, whose artistic director was Stefan Grossmann, editor of the *Arbeiterzeitung*. It started out in 1906 with some 3 500 members and had 14 299 by 1911, almost half of whom were workers (and 40 per cent were women). It rented private theatres for its performances, eventually settling in a house on the Neubaugasse. More ambitious plans for the construction of a new theatre were thwarted by objections on the part of the authorities, and eventually the *Freie Volksbühne* ceased performances after the outbreak of the war.[53]

The Social Democrats were not the only political party to undertake educational work. Quite apart from their influence on the cultural activities of the city council, clerical activists were active in Christian-Socialist organizations such as the Commission for Christian Youth Education and the *Volksbund der Katholiken Österreichs*, which operated throughout German-speaking Austria. Although much smaller in scale than the SDAP's own network of organizations, such groups, along with those of the German nationalists, were taken seriously as potential rivals by the Social Democrats.[54] Both of these rivals operated more successfully outside the capital, however. In fact most German nationalist cultural activity was concentrated in a very few ethnically mixed provinces such as Bohemia and the South Tyrol, where the movement already had political organizations and could exploit the disaffection of local German workers. In Vienna itself, however, it was the educational organizations of the Social Democrats that made the greatest impact.

The culture of Vienna at the turn of the century was caught between a number of competing claims. The established 'high culture' of the traditional elites was being challenged on every front by the new artistic avant-garde. Both faced competition from the products of the new cultural industries which attracted customers from all sections of society – albeit without supplanting more traditional plebeian entertainments. The state itself did not yet have a coherent approach to cultural policy, and relied on existing censorship laws to oversee the arts, and action on the part of the appropriate ministries to regulate the leisure sector. The political importance of culture was recognized more clearly by the new popular political parties than by the imperial authorities or the liberal establishment, and while the governing Christian Socialist Party in Vienna used the municipality to promote its own cultural identity, the Social Democrats worked in opposition to prepare the ground for a radical counter-culture which would emancipate the working class and give them access to the broader cultural heritage of German humanism, without which, they believed, workers would remain impotently excluded from avenues to power and social advancement. The combined perceived threats of artistic experimentation, cultural populism and 'revolutionary' workers were understood by cultural and political conservatives as so many facets of the same doom that was undermining the old order, and the themes of conservative critiques of popular culture throughout the twentieth century were all present in its first decade. Young people, it was repeatedly asserted, were at risk of corruption; 'decadence' and 'degeneracy' threatened to eclipse a nobler cultural heritage; and standards would be eroded by the passive consumption of undemanding forms of leisure. When the old order finally collapsed in 1918, attitudes to culture were polarized further by the acute awareness of political defeat on the part of the elites.[55] Cultural policy, moreover, became too important to be left to *ad hoc* decision-making by an uncoordinated range of authorities. In the Vienna of the 1920s the cultural policies of the city council constituted a natural application, by the party in office, of the cultural ideology and practices it had developed during decades of opposition. The politicization of culture in the years between the wars was of a different order to the initiatives of the turn of the century but the foundations for those developments were laid before 1914.

Notes

1. Friedrich Slezak, *Ottakringer Arbeiterkultur an zwei Beispielen*, Vienna: Slezak, 1982, p.4.
2. E. Pernerstorfer, 'Die Kunst und die Arbeiter', *Der Kampf*, 1, 1907–8, pp.38–41. Here, p.39.
3. Stefan Grossmann, 'Die Feste der Arbeiter', *Der Kampf*, 1, 1907–8, 182–4.
4. See above all Dieter Langewiesche, *Zur Freizeit des Arbeiters. Bildungsbestrebungen und Freizeitgestaltung österreichischer Arbeiter im Kaiserreich und in der ersten Republik*, Stuttgart: Klett-Cotta, 1979; and Helmut Gruber, *Red Vienna. Experiment in Working Class Culture 1918–1934*, Oxford: Oxford University Press, 1991.
5. See Ilsa Barea, *Vienna*, London: Pimlico, 1992, pp.58–110: 'The Legacy of the Baroque'.
6. See Markus Cerman, 'Proto-industrialization in an urban environment: Vienna, 1750–1857', in *Continuity and Change*, 8 (2), 1993, 281–320. Appendix B lists occupations in the Vienna suburbs.
7. See E. P. Thompson, *Customs in Common*, London: Penguin, 1991, p.51.
8. See Karl Ziak, *Des Heiligen Römischen Reiches größtes Wirtshaus*, Munich and Vienna: Jugend und Volk,1979.
9. See Michael Hann, 'Die Unterschichten Wiens im Vormärz. Soziale Kategorien im Umbruch von der ständischen zur Industriegesellschaft', PhD thesis, Vienna, 1984; and Stefan Greif, 'Plebejische Kultur im Wiener Vormärz. Zur Bedingung und Erscheinungsform von Alltagskultur und Freizeit großstädtischer Unterschichten im Übergang zur Industrialisierung', MA thesis, Vienna University, 1988, and also by Greif: 'Wider die gefährlichen Klassen. Zum zeitgenössischen Blick auf die plebejische Kultur im Wiener Vormärz', in *Österreichische Zeitschrift für Geschichtswissenschaften*, 2, 1991, pp.59–80.
10. See for example Michael Schacherl, 'Ein viermonatlicher Bierboykott und seine Wirkung auf die Arbeiter', *Der Kampf*, 2, 1909, pp.273–7; Gruber, *Red Vienna*, pp.116–17.
11. See Tia DeNora, 'Musical Patronage and Social Change in Beethoven's Vienna', *American Journal of Sociology*, 97 (2), 1991, 310–46.
12. On parks see Robert Rotenberg, *Landscape and Power in Vienna*, Baltimore: Johns Hopkins University Press, 1995.
13. See Hans Pemmer and Nini Lackner, *Der Prater. Von den Anfängen bis zur Gegenwart. Neu bearbeitet von Günter Düriegl and Ludwig Sackmauer*, Vienna: Jugend und Volk, 1974; Gerhard Tanzer, *Spectacle müssen seyn: Die Freizeit der Wiener im 18 Jahrhundert*, Vienna: Böhlau, 1992, pp.141 f.
14. Wolfgang Slapansky, 'Der böhmische Prater: zur Kulturgeschichte einer Wiener Vergnügungsstätte an der Peripherie', PhD thesis, Vienna, 1991.
15. Franz Hadamowsky, *Wien. Theatergeschichte*, Vienna: Jugend und Volk, 1988, pp.255–6.
16. See Arnold Sywottek, 'Freizeit und Freizeitgestaltung – ein Problem der Gesellschaftsgeschichte' in *Archiv für Sozialgeschichte*, 33 (1993), pp.1–20. See also Lynn Abrams, *Workers' culture in Imperial Germany: leisure and recreation in the Rheinland and Westphalia*, London: Routledge, 1992; and 'Leisure and Society in Europe, 1871–1945' in Martin Pugh (ed.), *A Companion to Modern European History 1871–1945*, Oxford: Blackwell, 1997, pp.70–88. Here p.71.
17. Seven thousand out of 17 000 school-age children in Vienna attended school. See T. C. W. Blanning, *Joseph II*, London: Longman, 1994, p.68.
18. Rudolf Schenda, *Volk ohne Buch. Studien zur Sozialgeschichte der populären Lesestoffe 1770–1910*, Munich, 1977, pp.444 f. Cited in Marina Tichy, *Alltag und Traum. Leben und Lektüre der Dienstmädchen im Wien der Jahrhundertwende*, Graz and Vienna: Böhlau, 1984, p.60.
19. See Rolf Engelsing, *Zur Sozialgeschichte deutscher Mittel und Unterschichten*, Göttingen: Vandenhoeck & Ruprecht, 1978, pp.112–54: 'Die Perioden der Lesergeschichte in der Neuzeit'.
20. Tichy, *Alltag und Traum*, p.61.
21. *Ibid.*, pp.64–9. See also Roland A. Fullerton, 'Creating a Mass Book Market in Germany: The Story of the "Colporteur Novel" 1870–1890', *Journal of Social History*, 10 (1977); Robin Lenman, 'Mass Culture and the State in Germany' in R. J. Bullen, H. Pogge von Strandmann and A.B. Polonsky (eds), *Ideas into Politics. Aspects of European History 1880–1950*, London, Croom Helm, 1984, pp.51–9. Here pp.51–2.
22. Max Winter, 'Wer liest die Schundromane? Ein Tag Kolporteur und Expeditor', *Arbeiterzeitung*, 7 May 1905, p.7.

23. Cited in Tichy, *Alltag und Traum*, p.65.
24. Winter, 'Wer liest die Schundromane?'
25. *Österreichische Kriminal-Zeitung*, 1/1, 1 April 1907, and 1/16, 5 August 1907.
26. Austrian State Archives, Allgemeines Verwaltungsarchiv (AVA), K.K. Ministerium des Innern. Allgemein (MI) 20/6a. 2172, 1912; Patrick Brantlinger, 'Mass media and culture in *fin-de-siècle* Europe' in Mikuláš Teich and Roy Porter (eds), *Fin-de-siècle Europe and its Legacy*, Cambridge, 1990, pp.98–114. Here p.99.
27. There seem to be no comprehensive extant data on the cinema audience in Austria to compare with those for Germany. See Emilie Altenloh, *Zur Soziologie des Kino. Die Kino-Unternehmung und die sozialen Schichten ihrer Besucher*, Jena, 1914; but see also Peter Mänz, 'Frühes Kino im Arbeiterbezirk. Ein neues "Volksvergnügen" im Spannungsfeld von Kulturindustrie, Arbeiteralltag und Arbeiterbewegung' in *Österreichische Zeitschrift für Geschichtswissenschaften* 2, 1991, pp.81–101.
28. See for example Robert Musil, *The Man without Qualities*, 1, London: Picador, pp.99–102.
29. AVA, MI 20/6a. 2172, 1912. Representatives of six ministries and all the provincial governments of Cisleithania were present, along with representatives of various interested parties.
30. See Richard Guttmann, *Die Kinomenschheit: Versuch einer prinzipiellen Analyse*, Vienna and Leipzig: Anzengruber Verlag, Brüder Suschitzky, 1916.
31. AVA, MI 20/6a. 2172, 1912, Enquête über das Kinematographenwesen. Stenographisches Protokoll, p.54.
32. AVA, MI 20/6a 2172, Sozialpädagogische Gesellschaft and others to Ministry of the Interior, 22 March 1912.
33. Stark, 'Cinema, Society and the State', pp.128–9, in Gary D. Stark and Bede Karl Lackner (eds), *Essays on culture and society in modern Germany*, College Station Arlington: Texas A&M University Press, c.1982.
34. See *Anzeiger für die gesamte Kinematographenindustrie*, 1/1 September 1907.
35. See the series of 'Kino-Typen' and 'Kino-Karikaturen' in *Das Welttheater. Zeitung für die Besucher der Kinematographentheater*, which was published in Vienna from February 1912.
36. John Boyer, *Culture and Political Crisis in Vienna. Christian Socialism in Power, 1897–1918*, Chicago and London: University of Chicago Press, 1995, pp.10–12.
37. See Robert Rotenberg, 'Gardens of Reform' in *idem, Landscape and Power in Vienna*, Baltimore and London, 1995, pp.148–87.
38. Boyer, *Culture*, pp.46–50.
39. See Stefan Grossmann, 'Die Feste der Arbeiter' in *Der Kampf*, I, 182–4.
40. On the much more visible socialist culture of republican Vienna in the 1920s see Helmut Gruber, *Red Vienna*.
41. See Langewiesche, *Zur Freizeit des Arbeiters*, 46 ff. The university and *Volksheim* courses nevertheless remained very popular. *Ibid.*, p.52.
42. Leopold Winarsky, 'Die Bildungsanstrebungen der organisierten Wiener Arbeiterschaft' in *Der Kampf*, 2 December 1908, pp.110–34. Here, pp.111–12; Robert Danneberg, 'Sozialdemokratische Erziehungsarbeit' in *Der Kampf*, 2 July 1909, pp.453–62. Here p.459.
43. Danneberg, 'Sozialdemokratische Erziehungsarbeit', p.455.
44. 'Unsere Aufgabe', *Bildungsarbeit. Blätter für das Bildungswesen der deutschen Sozialdemokratie in Oesterreich*, 1, 1909, p.1.
45. Rudolf Neuhaus, 'Was liest der Wiener Arbeiter?', *Bildungsarbeit*, 1, January 1910. pp.4–6.
46. See, for example, 'Eine Bibliothek um 100 Kronen', *Bildungsarbeit*, 1, November 1909, p.9.
47. See *Bildungsarbeit*, 1, January 1910, p.6, 4/7 April 1913, p.63.
48. Neuhaus, 'Was liest der Wiener Arbeiter?'; Robert Danneberg, 'Die Wiener Arbeiterbibliotheken. Beilage zur Aprilnummer 1911 der "Bildungsarbeit". See also 'Wie können unsere guten Bücher einen zahlreichen Leserkreis finden?', *Bildungsarbeit*, 3/7, May 1912, pp.67 f.
49. *Bildungsarbeit*, 1/3, November 1909, pp.5 f.
50. *Ibid.*, p.6.

51. *Bildungsarbeit*, 4/9, August 1913, pp.8–9.
52. *Bildungsarbeit*, 4/1–2, September 1912, p.6. On Stern's taste, intellectual formation and aspirations for the working class see also Gruber, *Red Vienna*, pp.85–6.
53. Hadamowsky, *Theatergeschichte*, pp.779–87.
54. *Bildungsarbeit*, 2, November 1910, pp.18–19; *ibid.*, 3, October 1911, p.18. On the Volksbund see Boyer, *Culture and Political Crisis*, pp.298–321.
55. See Adelheid von Saldern, 'Massenfreizeitkultur im Visier. Ein Beitrag zu den Deutungs- und Einwirkungsversuchen während der Weimarer Republik', in *Archiv für Sozialgeschichte*, 33, 1993, pp.21–58.

'Making a living from disgrace':[1] the politics of prostitution, female poverty and urban gender codes in Budapest and Vienna, 1860–1920[2]

Susan Zimmermann

At the turn of the century the Habsburg monarchy's two capitals, like other central European cities, faced problems of mass poverty and indigence. Only a small proportion of the poor could claim support from the community. The rest were often reduced to begging on the streets or to vagrancy. Such a way of life was strictly forbidden and was punishable by arrest, detention and occasionally with forcible return to the town or village of origin. For women, however, the metropolis of the turn of the century offered a third means of survival: prostitution. This was not expressly forbidden; rather, it was regulated. 'Registered' prostitutes could operate on the streets so long as they kept to the prescribed rules; those who were not registered were subject to the same set of punishments as male and female beggars and vagabonds. From the 1890s onwards, there were various attempts by the municipal authorities to come to grips with the problem of poverty and social 'deviation' and their outward manifestations. However, these efforts took a markedly different form according to whether their object was prostitution or begging and vagrancy.

In the great cities at the turn of the century, poverty, or the effects of class division as transferred to the streets, was a highly gender-specific phenomenon. The culture of poverty was made manifest in a way that was determined by the sex of those who were its victims. A thorough analysis of municipal policy towards the lower classes must be careful to include those policy elements that were directed at prostitution, even if contemporaries regarded these as having to do with hygiene and morals rather than with poverty as such. Seen from this perspective, both the policies concerned with poverty and those concerned with welfare may be regarded as highly gender-specific. Why and to what extent did female and male poverty take different forms and why was poverty in the two cities as a whole perceived by the authorities in a gender-specific way? Why was begging forbidden, but prostitution merely regulated? Finally, why did the official reforms aimed at both phenomena proceed in markedly different ways? None of this can be explained without an understanding of the ways in which prostitution and the discourse surrounding it represented the problem of female poverty. By the same token, it is also inexplicable without an understanding of how prostitution became both a symbolic and an actual expression of the problem of gender in its political and personal dimensions.

There has so far been no systematic research into municipal policy towards prostitution which considers its implications on the politics of both gender and poverty. For the new women's history, prostitution has been a topic of major significance. Studies of early feminism inevitably have to deal with the question. The morality campaigns and the abolitionist movement constituted an important part of the activities of the early women's movement. Through analysis of the policies of regulation and of the broader context of the debates about sexuality and sexual reform at the turn of the century, the new women's history has arrived at diverse lines of interpretation.[3]

But women's history has also paid scant attention to prostitution policy as the legislative expression of attitudes in the realm of gender. The history of the striking relationship, not only between prostitution and the sexual order of bourgeois society in general, but also between sexuality, prostitution, and the political treatment of female poverty, still awaits investigation.[4]

The historiographical situation is different with regard to what has been defined as 'gender-neutral' research into the policies on poverty and welfare politics of the big conurbations. It has been well established that poverty politics used both a repressive strategy designed to punish and – where possible – eliminate begging and vagrancy, and a persuasive one based on institutional care and outdoor relief available only to certain groups. Nevertheless, this research has tended simply to accept hidden assumptions about poverty on the one hand ('deserving' and 'undeserving', male and female), and 'immorality', or female sexuality, on the other. Thus, the contemporaneous distinction between control of prostitutes, and the regulation of other manifestations of problems related to poverty and marginalization, rests on distorted underlying premises.[5] Poverty and the politics of poverty are very often described as phenomena without any gender dimension worth taking into consideration.[6] Whereas begging and vagrancy are treated as something apparently gender-neutral, prostitution, as well as other specifically 'female' and erotically associated manifestations of the poverty of women, remains beyond analysis.

Using the examples of Budapest and Vienna, I will attempt to explore the way in which questions of gender and problems of poverty were interwoven in the period of the Dual Monarchy and even after the First World War. The approach of the authorities and reformers to the problem of prostitution and an analysis of how the politics of prostitution relate to other areas of urban poverty policy will serve as the major focus of this study.

Urban poverty and gender codes

That the prostitutes in the big cities at the turn of the century were poor is neither the discovery of women's history, nor even of the abolitionists or of other pressure groups for morality. Even the reports of the police, who were primarily responsible for combatting and controlling prostitution, candidly admitted as much. 'Most' of the prostitutes, according to these reports, turned out to be 'servant girls without employment, working women without jobs [or] waitresses'.[7] In short, as it was expressed by a contemporary observer, 'poverty is the fatal factor which so often leads astray the morals of the young women from the lower strata'.[8] The ups and downs of the business cycles, for instance during the years 1913 and 1914 in Budapest, clearly exerted a direct influence on the market of prostitutes: 'Since the time of the devastating economic crisis, Budapest is depressed by such a frightening poverty *that the flesh of girls has become disgustingly cheap.... Along Andrássy Street and the Danube Promenade the detectives used to catch numerous girls* who sell their bodies for some fillers.'[9]

On the other hand, the extent to which female poverty was related to, or perceived to be related to, specifically female forms of 'indecency', 'immorality' and 'loose ways of living',[10] in other words by offering and using erotics – the body and sexuality – for the purpose of survival, is far less common.[11] Yet a careful reading of the sources demonstrates that this was the case. Not only were those women who, under the regulation system, were picked up in the streets and pubs under suspicion of being prostitutes treated by the authorities as transgressing the social norm of female decency; the majority of those women whose poverty and social 'deviation' appeared in 'indecent' forms were basically denounced because they were assumed to be prostitutes. The practice, after the introduction of the system of regulations in Vienna in 1873, was to issue a 'bill of health' (a document pertaining to the registration of prostitutes) to all those women who were handled by the police authorities for any reason.[12] Women suspected of trying to find support from the authorities by using false personal data were uniformly considered – if they were not married – to be immoral. The journal of the authorities for aid to the poor noted, for instance, that:

cases are more and more numerous of women with children who claim to have been left without financial support and accommodation, and therefore or because of other reasons apply for aid often stating that their husband or pimp has played them false.... These kind of claims have often nothing to do with reality. The pimp not infrequently waits nearby, hoping for a positive result to the baseless application.[13]

One of the most striking cases illustrating the different ways people perceived and handled 'undeserving' poverty, vagrancy and 'destitution'[14] in the metropolis comes from the well-known chronicler of Prague's Lesser Quarter, Jan Neruda. In his extensive report on 'A Typical Day at the Headquarters of the Prague Police', Neruda describes how every woman who had been picked up was automatically suspected of prostitution; every single one of those imprisoned or interrogated is presented as if she were in one way or another an example of specifically female immorality. He describes, for instance, the case of a girl who, on her very first day in Prague, had gone to sell her services; despite a police ban, she returned repeatedly to the city. While being interrogated at the police station she began to unbutton her clothes' in order to prove that without a chemise she would be unable to find even a maidservant's job.[15] By contrast, the sexuality of male vagrants is apparently deemed to be non-existent, their bodies simply being described as repositories of vermin and sources of stench.

The social significance of the gender code as manifested above repeatedly transcended the proper domains of poverty and prostitution politics. The ideological foundations of this code appeared with special palpability in the various struggles of the police against women suspected of so-called 'covert' prostitution. The persecution of women's immorality and its literary description in the media – by means of social reportage, articles and police reports – daily conveyed the message connected with this code to women and men of all the different social strata. This persecution and suspicion of women who ignored the established bourgeois norms of behaviour was part and parcel of the thoroughly practical gender politics of the metropolis, targeted mainly towards women of the unpropertied classes. The notion of 'covert' prostitution – and the politics based upon this stigmatizing concept – was in fact an umbrella concept for very different patterns of female behaviour:

> Most young women and men are unable to settle the sexual question by simply entering into marriage. On the other hand, not all women can go out to the streets, but they do not want to become vestal virgins either. As a consequence of this, a female type begins to appear more and more frequently, whose search for sexual intercourse is motivated by passion and love and not by the wish for financial gain, but as these women have found satisfaction they do accept – a woman's body having a special value – with real or pretended modesty, its equivalent. In the meantime they consider themselves to be 'decent' women and in the majority of the cases they manage to mislead the authorities.
>
> These women are persecuted by the police sometimes with special rigour. If they are once or twice surprised in the very act, they begin to be considered as women practically engaged in the ancient profession.... In Pest one sees a whole army of housemaids, needlewomen, and female teachers roaming about, always eager to

have this or that kind of adventure. They accompany you where you wish for some money, perhaps a supper, a week-end excursion or even a couple of warm words. Some of them begin to deal directly in prostitution; the majority however looks at these adventures as a source of entertainment and satisfaction only.[16]

All those women whose relationships with the other sex could not be reduced to the patterns of either the virgin or the faithful wife and mother were suspected of 'covert' prostitution. To put it another way, all those who, *within* the existing circumstances and pressures were ready to maintain sexual or erotically motivated relationships with men, outside of conjugal or *de facto* conjugal ties, became suspect. Within the norms of the established morality of bourgeois society, there was no place for such behaviour by women.

The functions and roles of this rigid bourgeois sexual code for the society of the nineteenth and early twentieth century may be interpreted in different ways. It is uncertain for instance whether these phenomena indicated a real suppression of 'immoral' behaviour or only its stigmatization. Talk about the 'attractive furies with charming faces' who flooded the streets of Budapest in bevies[17] can possibly be interpreted – along psychological and historical lines – first of all as an expression of bourgeois fears, as a discourse generated in the realm of the 'other side' of bourgeois sexual culture. The relationship between social reality and this moral code, with its corresponding gender politics, is no less ambiguous. Was bourgeois society really as puritanical as it wished to think? Was discourse on moral problems and the handling of sex so overwhelmingly present in the different social domains because the bourgeois sublimation and control of sex was already in its advanced phase? Or is it possible that the whole discourse on moral issues and gender politics simply had not much to do with reality? And finally – at the time of the emergence of the 'mass society' of the twentieth century – what was the nature of the authorities' attempts to transmit bourgeois moral norms and adequate behaviour patterns to the lower strata?

An analysis of the politics of prostitution in Vienna and Budapest around the turn of the century can of course contribute only in a limited way to the elucidation of these problems. It is obvious, however, that it was by no means only talk when the policy of the time dealt with the behaviour of women in sexual or erotic terms. The moral police definitely dealt with such public manifestations in a concrete way; they identified, stigmatized and punished these phenomena, and these measures were not limited to symbolic activity but had legal consequences – which probably again comprised a symbolic dimension and generated deterrent effects. Thus, for instance, in 1896 the Vienna court confirmed the sentence of a district court (Mariahilf) in a decision which makes palpable how narrow the acceptable lines of female behaviour were:

The accused person admits that she had financial support from persons A and B. With A she had a normal sexual life, and she offered satisfaction for the bodily wishes of B in other ways, through his talking to her. Already this acknowledgement proves that the accused used her body for immoral business, as by offering her body she induced *both* to give her financial means.[18]

Sanctions resulted not only from 'evidence' of prostitution; from 1895, for example, local police stations in Vienna regularly monitored and documented women reported pursuing 'covert' prostitution, even when these did not confess and the police lacked any evidence.[19]

The gender politics behind the regulation of prostitution and the prosecution of 'covert prostitution' were without doubt intended to transmit bourgeois moral codes to the non-bourgeois strata. Even if the *moral* claim of these policies was broader and more general, it was basically limited to the monitoring and 'keeping clean' of public places. It is true that in Vienna in the period of neo-absolutism, measures were sometimes taken by the police which clearly encroached upon the private sphere of ordinary people. In the suburbs, the police intended to separate 'people who lived together without marriage documents. In many flats even garments and pieces of furniture had to be rearranged accordingly.'[20] But the Court of Justice in Public Administration had already ruled in an 1879 sentence that a woman could not be banned from public places solely for the reason that 'she lives in an illegal and immoral relationship with someone else' so long as this fact does not 'disturb the life of the community because of people's disapproval or the non-observance of public morality'.[21]

The focus upon public space and upon the disturbance of public order was fully in harmony with the politics against vagrancy and beggary. These principles were – in Vienna from the last decade of the nineteenth century, more than in Budapest – paralleled in poor relief and welfare policies by new interventions directed towards prevention. These measures penetrated directly and indirectly deeper than before into the private sphere, with the goal of preventing the emergence of public and 'undeserving' poverty. A transformation of this type took place in the domain of moral politics (in other words, relating to prostitution) to a significantly lesser degree. While the entire bourgeois moral discourse relating to women was very intensive, those measures of welfare policy which had more ambitious aims than a simple control and 'cleaning' of public places remained very limited in scope. This limitation was the consequence of two interrelated factors. On the one hand, the social reforms before the war – carried out mainly in Vienna – were unambiguously concentrated around the welfare support for families of the lower strata. The family had to be limited in its relations with outsiders, and to embody petty bourgeois moral values. On the other hand, the social spread of bourgeois moral codes and norms of sexuality actually encouraged a so-called 'double morality'; the spread of bourgeois norms meant that prostitutes, or at least unattached women, were ever more necessary. The social predicament of women who were not anchored in the bourgeois or the aspiring proletarian family remained essentially the same. Sexual relationships condemned as 'prostitution' did not cease to exist. The spread of a respected small-family model throughout society was connected with the regulation of sexual life in marriage or exclusive long-term relationships. Less respected or undeserving forms of sexuality were driven out of the near-bourgeois sphere of the lower classes.

Social policies aiming to inculcate the lower strata with the lifestyle of the bourgeoisie reproduced and sharpened the contrast between 'moral' and 'immoral' women. Women's 'immorality', on the other hand, was perceived as an eternal and unchanging element of the social order as such. For this reason, when the reform of welfare policy began, little changed in the spheres of prostitution and the social integration of 'immoral' woman. This ambivalence and ambiguity was also expressed in the movement for the protection of children, in so far as it dealt with the 'neglect of boys' and the 'immorality' of girls who 'flirted for financial reward'.[22]

In the theories and ideologies of the regulationists, and in the corresponding persecution of 'covert' prostitution and registered prostitutes' violation of the regulations, none of these circumstances was taken into account. But even the most progressive opponents of these phenomena did not always perceive the significant social foundations and functions of official policy. While regulationists mostly emphasized the need for a health policy to offer medical control for the greatest possible number of women concerned,[23] the latter generally criticized and denounced the mishandling of perfectly innocent women by the police.[24]

The spectrum of alternatives demanded was broad and contradictory, ranging from purely moralising demands to end sexual double standards for men, to positions advocating the complete abolition of regulations. Supporters of sexual reform awaited the decline of prostitution due to a system of new and free norms for all men and women; both genders, they argued, should integrate their sexuality into a 'more developed' personality, to direct and form it in a voluntary way under the control of a new Self. The repression of the 'instincts' of women and the 'vulgar gratification of urges' of men should be superseded by a controlled integration of 'instincts' in freely chosen ties of love. On the basis of such patterns, the external and socially repressive norms moulding sexual relationships and sexuality and the supervision of such norms by the police would be unnecessary – as reformers of sexual norms and conduct maintained.[25]

Therefore, even the most radical opponents of this system of regulations did not abandon the contempt they felt for women who were unable to acquire such a new bourgeois subjectivity. Sexual patterns of behaviour outside the norm of monogamy, or which violated the traditional female code, remained taboo. This was characteristic even of abolitionist women in the left-liberal wing of the women's movement in Vienna.[26] It was also true of those 'radical' feminists in Budapest whose political activities were far more reserved in questions relating to sexual life.[27] Rosa Mayreder, the most radical female advocate of sexual reform in German-speaking Austria, maintained that those women who accepted their 'reified' position 'objectified themselves' and were 'of a lower nature', provoking thereby the lower instincts of men. Instead, Mayreder argued, a woman 'should do nothing which denies her personality'.[28] The abolitionism of the time reproduced in a new form, therefore, the discrepancy between bourgeois and non-bourgeois gender codes for women.

The most important difference between regulationists and abolitionists – apart from the general criticism by the abolitionists that regulationism deprives women of their basic rights as a matter of course – was that abolitionists approached questions of welfare policy concerning 'immoral' women and girls in a different way. The regulationists rejected the idea that integrative social policy measures could handle 'immoral' forms of female poverty. The abolitionists, on the other hand, demanded an increase in welfare institutions, including welfare institutions designed along the lines of prevention; these institutions were to be moulded – in accordance with the abolitionist stand-point – in the spirit of new moral norms and sexual reforms.

The regulation of prostitution and the politics of poverty

Gender-specific discrepancies thoroughly determined not only the authorities' perception of, but also their concrete administrative practice directed towards public manifestations of male and female poverty. The same discriminatory approach was apparent in their policy on 'lewd' forms of behaviour in both men and women. While beggars, both male and female, were considered simply a blot on the social body that had to be removed, prostitutes were regarded as an inevitable component in the moral and administrative framework of social life. 'Immorality' as a natural 'product of communal living' in principle should not (it was argued in Budapest) be 'a matter for police intervention'.[29] While the authorities wanted to ban male and female beggars alike from the social landscape, prostitution was handled by a system of toleration and regulation on the one hand, and was subjected to prosecution in cases of lapses in correct behaviour on the other.

A system of regulation already existed in Pest before the unification of

Budapest as capital of Hungary in 1873, and in the first Statute on Brothels, put into effect in 1885, the regulations of 1867 were essentially adopted.[30] In Vienna, as contemporary commentators reported, the idea of regulation was contested fiercely in ruling circles, that is in the government and among the clergy. The institutions charged with managing prostitution continuously postponed the introduction of any system of regulation.[31] Fear of accepting 'the authorization of whores' caused delays in formal introduction until 1873 in Vienna. The actual registration and supervision of prostitutes, however, had already begun in earlier decades.[32]

The administration of this whole system of regulation was undertaken by the so-called 'morality police', who constituted a separate sphere of administration in both capital cities.[33] In the statutes concerned with the poor, prostitution was not even mentioned. Regulations which intended the general suppression of prostitution, and which would thus have been similar to those that framed strategies for police harassment of the poor, barely existed. Nonetheless, all those who did not keep to the rules laid down for prostitution ran a permanent risk, like the beggars and vagrants, of winding up in prison, in the work-house or of being sent home under compulsion.

The regulation of prostitution in both capitals was concerned basically with ensuring regular health checks for registered prostitutes by police doctors on the one hand, and the prevention of 'public scandal' on the other. Health checks, to which only women were subject, were argued to be the most effective measure in combating the spread of venereal disease. In this way, according to the classical argument of Liberalism as put into practice by the Budapest administration, the risks to the health of other people should be reduced. In Budapest, prostitution could be carried on by registered *filles de joie* in officially licensed brothels and also in private dwellings when such premises had been approved for the purpose by the police. The requisite bills of health were issued automatically by the police authorities to both private and brothel prostitutes, so long as the latter had been certified as free from sexual disease. From the time of their registration onwards, the women were obliged to submit to a twice-weekly examination by the police doctor, for which a regular fee had to be paid.[34] In Vienna there were officially no brothels; the system was, however, similar to that of Budapest, except that the possible police measures were definitely more stringent.[35] For instance, the Vienna police authorities had the right, up until 1909, to force arrested women to submit to an internal examination for venereal diseases.[36] Women who were considered to belong to the 'immoral industry' were even forcibly registered by the Vienna police.[37] No similar powers existed in Budapest.

With all these official procedural patterns, prostitution policy was, in fact, a specific area of the politics of the municipal and police authorities, distinct from those policies pertaining to poverty in general. In spite of this, all poor women whose behaviour contradicted the specific norms of female behaviour or the rules regulating these norms were subject to serious police persecution. This persecution was of the same 'logic' and in part had the same consequences as the usual repressive measures directed towards the poor. Just as with begging and vagrancy, the principle behind this policy was that of the maintenance of public order. However, while begging and vagrancy were considered a threat to order, and therefore subject to police repression on the grounds that they were forbidden, the procedure for dealing with prostitution was different. For prostitution was, within certain limits, officially tolerated and regulated, so the policies aimed at maintaining public order and morality could not simply consist of practices of persecution and oppression. In order to 'prevent scandal', the permitted prostitutes were instead liable to investigation if their behaviour violated accepted public norms. 'Covert prostitutes', on the other hand, were persecuted as a matter of official policy, for they operated without official permission and sometimes clashed with the norms of public morality.

In Budapest registered prostitutes were thus forbidden from 'roaming the streets' and 'wandering about', as well as from disturbing 'public order and morality'. Sexually marked patterns of hairstyle and dress were forbidden, so 'hair worn loose' or 'the conspicuous disclosure' of busts were not permitted. 'Covert' prostitutes committing 'sexual offences' in private or in public spaces were threatened with one month in prison. The legal basis for sentencing was in both cases the 'transgression law' of the police and the Communal Act on Prostitution.[38] In Vienna the possible punishment for unacceptable behaviour by prostitutes (including 'walking about provocatively') was imprisonment for between one and eight days.[39] With the so-called 'Vagrancy Act' of 1885, a new form of punishment was introduced which was stricter than the police regulations and the rules of the old penal code. In more serious cases of transgression of the rules, 'covert' prostitutes were sentenced, according to the new act, to imprisonment of between eight days and three months and in special cases, they were sentenced to forced labour.[40] Confinement in the communal asylum and workhouse in Vienna was also standard practice, independent of the new regulation.[41]

If the person concerned had no right of permanent residence in Budapest or Vienna, after having served her prison sentence for transgression of the prostitution regulations, she could expect to be sent back to her place of origin in the provinces like any beggar or vagrant of either sex.[42] In dealing with non-local prostitutes who were not willing to comply with the usual regulations, the police of both capitals cultivated, over the decades, the practice of expulsion and banning. It was emphasized time and again that especially in cases where the convicted prostitute had no other source of income – a 'respectable trade' – vigorous action had to be taken.[43]

In cases where a woman wanted to leave the system of registration and control of prostitutes, she had to reckon with an official procedure which stemmed unambiguously from the police measures relating to the poor. To be able to leave the register and to give back the bill of health, prostitutes in Budapest had, without exception, to prove that they had appropriate income derived from an ordinary trade. In Vienna, this practice applied only to those under compulsory supervision.[44]

All in all, illegal prostitution and the 'immorality' of woman who caused a public scandal were unwelcome forms of behaviour in the lower classes. The principles and repressive methods of handling prostitutes paralleled those applied by the police departments to the poor. It is therefore no accident to find in the police statistics, together with the executive policy against beggars and vagabonds, the category of 'immorality', which, according to the rules, was not supposed to be 'the object of police intervention'. The general differences in the social manifestations, patterns of perception, and administrative and police handling of female and male poverty were definitely reflected in the police statistics. Some types of women's poverty were categorized in specific and morality-related items. In Budapest, of those imprisoned or remanded in custody prior to expulsion from the capital on account of vagrancy or begging, only some 20 per cent were women. If one includes those who were held for offences against the regulation of prostitution, practising 'covert' prostitution, or soliciting,[45] the picture changes. When this specifically 'female' manifestation of poverty is taken into account, the proportion of women rises to about 30 per cent, and from 1907 to around 40 per cent.[46] In Vienna at the beginning of the 1890s, prostitution made up between 22 and 35 per cent of complaints about the transgression of begging and vagrancy laws. In this category those simple police measures which were taken because of 'loose conduct or suspicion of loose conduct' were not included, but their number was at least equal to those complaints based on the vagrancy law.[47]

Naturally these figures do not include prostitutes registered in accordance with the law,[48] nor do they reflect the socially tolerated or accepted female strategies of survival, which never came under the spotlight of the morality police. Nevertheless, in Budapest even before 1907 about two-fifths, later well over one half, of the women held on grounds of both categories were imprisoned or interned on account of infringements of the prostitution regulations and not as beggars or vagrants.[49]

The reform of prostitution policy and the emergence of modern welfare programmes

Of course, the treatment of prostitution by the police and the authorities changed over the decades. As with the 'struggle against the nuisance of begging and vagrancy', some dominant trends are discernible in the attempts at reform. However, these basic tendencies varied, depending on whether they were aimed at prostitution or at poverty. The intentions behind the reform of prostitution were directed towards creating a deeper and clearer separation between prostitutes and 'moral' women. The authorities wanted to impose bourgeois moral norms on all female citizens. The system in Vienna was already more repressive at its very foundations than that in Budapest. The transition from police suppression of prostitution to toleration in Vienna was a process resisted by the most influential 'upper circles' and therefore slow and contradictory. Consequently, the newly introduced system of regulation was very repressive there from the outset. The statute of 1885 in Budapest, on the other hand, did not involve compulsory registration and medical examination. Compared with the Austrian circumstances, the municipal policy of Budapest at the time was in a more marked way influenced by the characteristic laissez-faire outlook of liberalism.

However, it was against this background of growing protests about the lack of female decency in public spaces that from the 1890s a process of limited restructuring of the system of regulation was set in motion. The crucial point was the struggle against 'covert prostitution'. This was seen as highly dangerous to public health, by which, of course, was meant the health of the prostitutes' male clients. As prostitution in general was regarded as a necessary evil, and therefore tolerated, this struggle could only mean, as the police report explicitly put it,[50] 'increasing the number of *filles de joie* who were subject to health checks under police supervision; and as far as possible, reducing the number of unsupervised prostitutes'. In Vienna the reforms, which gathered momentum at the same time, also stood under the aegis of this struggle against 'wild prostitution'.[51]

In each capital, the reform comprised roughly three perspectives: increased surveillance coupled with a determined effort at stamping out illicit, or 'covert' prostitution; an easing of constraints on legal, registered prostitutes; and lastly, a move toward the localization and geographic isolation of prostitution. It will be seen that gender politics, embedded in the system of regulation, directly influenced all three specific strands of the reform.

From the last decade of the nineteenth century, the police in Budapest began 'to go after persons who did not voluntarily submit to regulation ... in such a way and for so long that their trade was made impossible'.[52] In the 1890s, detectives in plain clothes were deployed to enforce the rules and the surveillance system became centralized. In due course, official surveillance was increased to cover areas that served 'as assembly points for female persons suspected of covert prostitution', that is, over certain coffee houses and nightclubs.⁵³ With these measures, the attack on suspects acquired a demonstrably new character after the turn of the century. While in 1894, the compulsory registration of unofficial prostitutes was still categorically rejected, a police ordinance of 1900 opened up the possibility of mandatory medical examination and 'strict police supervision' of 'female persons' who 'were regarded as suspects because of evidence supplied by the police or from other reliable sources', and who had further justified these suspicions on account of their 'inability to document satisfactorily their way of life, occupation and income'.⁵⁴ The new statute that came into force in 1909 gave definitive official sanction to this long-standing practice of surveillance and control. 'Covert' prostitutes who resisted registration could, from then on, be forced to undergo the regular gynaecological examinations.⁵⁵ In this way, a mechanism was introduced that bore a striking similarity to the enforced registration that had long existed in Vienna.

As a result, any woman who 'was involved in prostitution' and therefore also anyone suspected of 'covert' prostitution, was now obliged to conform to the regulations laid down in the statute.⁵⁶ The police had, in fact, acquired a legal right that, in principle, could be employed against all women. Moreover, as was the case in Vienna, ordinance after ordinance – and eventually the new statute – defined in ever more precise terms what forms of behaviour would be tolerated in public. In place of references to the 'vagrancy' of suspect women, the statute now spoke of 'attention-seeking ways of walking ... in the streets', 'loitering in groups' and behaviour 'injurious to public decency'.⁵⁷ In Vienna this differentiation process reached its climax in the 1890s. After the turn of the century, the strict rules of conduct for prostitutes and 'suspicious' women were replaced by a mandate 'to comply with the general regulations valid for everyone'. In the new statute of 1911, enforced registration and vaginal examination in cases of simple suspiciousness were formally prohibited.⁵⁸ In Budapest, from 1907 onwards, the strategy of mass surveillance and control began to show specific results. The yearly total of suspect or convicted women in police gaol was double that of the preceding years.⁵⁹

The second strand of the reform eased the constraints placed on registered prostitutes. In Budapest, the 'disadvantages' of the officially conducted trade were somewhat reduced as a consequence of the continual harassment of 'covert' prostitution, and in turn this was to increase the attractions of voluntary registration. Towards that end, the metropolitan police introduced in 1896 a new category of prostitutes, the so-called *'filles de joie* with street permits'. The idea was to relieve prostitutes of the necessity of producing evidence of a place of residence – a cripplingly expensive obstacle. This measure was specifically designed to bring the 'indigent' under medical supervision.[60] The police emphasized several times that they were not allowed to handle the registered prostitutes in a more forceful and drastic way than their 'covert' counterparts.[61] With the introduction of a category of 'women with a health certificate' (in Budapest from 1901) and the 'discreet prostitute' (in Vienna between 1900 and 1911), the process was taken a step further. This provided for police supervision to be exercised 'confidentially'.[62] Finally, in Budapest the fees for regular medical examination by the police doctor were abolished. In this way at least the financial burdens of prostitution could be made more bearable for those who registered. On the other hand, if evidence of venereal disease was found during examination, instead of issuing an order to take appropriate action as had hitherto been the practice, the person concerned was forcibly admitted to hospital – as was the case in Vienna from 1873 if the prostitute did not go to the hospital of her own free will.[63]

As previously stated, all these arrangements were not intended as welfare measures that would make resort to prostitution unnecessary: they were aimed at securing more registration and bringing about less unofficial prostitution, viewed particularly as a danger to male health. The interplay between the more severe treatment of the covert trade and an easing of the lot of the registered prostitutes resulted in an ever more comprehensive network of police surveillance of female 'indecency' and 'decency'.

In the third strand of reform in Budapest, this growing supervision, together with the need to prevent offences against 'public decency', resulted in an increased containment of permitted prostitution in small, clearly delineated and easily-policed areas within the greater public space. In order to prevent the *'filles de joie* walking the streets' wherever possible, from 1909 onwards police licences were issued to the owners of coffee houses, taverns and dance halls; by these means, the places concerned were officially recognized as 'assembly points' for registered prostitutes. These locales were under constant police surveillance and could be raided at any time. Women suspected of unofficial prostitution – and therefore potentially all unregistered women – were denied entry to licensed premises of this kind. Consequently, such places became *de facto* no longer part of the public space. The same was true for the newly introduced opportunity (which, however, remained unrealized in practice) to establish 'private colonies of *filles de joie*' and the use of apartments for the rendezvous of the prostitutes and their clients.[64]

All in all, the reforms resulted in a slight improvement in the situation of those who plied the trade of prostitution in accordance with official norms.

In Budapest, this improvement was coupled with aggressively implemented extensions of regulation. The surveillance and supervision of registered prostitutes increased, as did harassment of unofficial ones. In Vienna the intensity of this procedure diminished around the time of the First World War. Finally, in Budapest, the localization of permitted prostitution in public spaces also increased. Hence, prostitution was partly regulated and partly repressed; in both cases the reforms led to greater harshness.

All these developments were markedly different from the reforms in the policy for dealing with beggars and vagrants, whom the authorities in both capitals wanted to banish altogether from the streets. At least in Vienna, the transition to full-scale industrialization was followed by certain changes in the 'struggle against begging and vagrancy'. This new approach took into consideration the needs of the emerging industrial labour market. It foreshadowed the genesis of a kind of modern welfare policy, put into practice in Austria but not in Hungary. In the western half of the monarchy, preventive social and economic measures, together with the provision of welfare, were increasingly thought to be as important as sterner treatment of those beggars and vagabonds who were regarded simply as 'work-shy'.[65]

In Hungary and Budapest there were no such initiatives to support a social policy for reintroducing the vagrants and beggars into ordinary proletarian society. But here too, in certain respects, the tendency to relax the pressure against this sector of the population could be felt, at least until 1913, when the new act on 'labour obligation' for the 'work-shy' was passed by Parliament. The numbers of women imprisoned in police gaol or remanded in custody pending their expulsion from the city for infringement of the by-laws governing prostitution, showed no decrease whatsoever after the turn of the century. This was in clear contrast to the falling numbers of those detained under the laws against begging and vagrancy.[66] Although the authorities on their own admission knew that many women worked as prostitutes in addition to their 'respectable' job, prostitution was indiscriminately branded as being undeserving of any community action that might alleviate its causes. Only those measures against more or less professional 'white-slave traffic'[67] and against soliciting were, over the years, intensified in Hungary.[68]

Social reform movements demanded measures to restrict prostitution, but the authorities looked at the introduction of welfare policy for prostitutes and 'endangered' women with sceptical reservation. In both capital cities predominantly small, independent pressure groups – social reformers and feminists – campaigned for new ideas about public assistance and moral 'deliverance' for prostitutes or for the prevention of prostitution. In Vienna the endeavours of the reforming groups in the new act on prostitution of 1881 distinctly alleviated pressure. In the Hungarian capital, however, similar efforts (particularly those of the Association of Feminists), which were proposed with no less enthusiasm but in more moderate terms, remained without real success.[69] The Budapest police maintained their defensive, resolute posture. The office of the morality police opened its doors only reluctantly to the philanthropic work of representatives of the Society Against White Slavery, a national branch of the International Association Against White Slavery (in England, The National Vigilance Association).[70] Only on the eve of the First World War did the municipality begin to develop welfare measures for young prostitutes, under the rubric of the defence of children and adolescents.[71] In Vienna such efforts at protecting the young had already begun to influence police procedure at an earlier date.[72]

Welfare policy for prostitutes and 'endangered' women and girls remained, in both capitals, basically the concern of social reform groups. Neither in Vienna nor in Budapest was there an intensity of activity comparable with that of, for example, the movement for protecting children. Efforts to grant welfare to prostitutes and the 'endangered' played but a small role within the rich repertoire of bourgeois and social-reforming philanthropy. In Budapest it was the Society Against White Slavery – a group related to the religious moral movements – which cared for the welfare and 'preservation' of women whose morals they considered less than perfect. From 1911, its female members visited women in hospitals suffering from venereal diseases, and tried to 'persuade' them 'to remain within the pattern of behaviour of a decent and settled life'. In 1913, the society opened an asylum for 'women in moral danger'.[73] Only very sporadically and modestly, however, did the activities of the many and different associations of women in both capitals begin to coordinate their activities with the authorities' initiatives for reducing prostitution.

Endeavours to promote the acceptance of classical bourgeois moral norms among non-bourgeois female citizens were thus left both in Vienna and Budapest predominantly to the authorities; these policies remained strictly regulatory over the decades. The ideals of the radical reformers and abolitionists – to overcome prostitution as a phenomenon embedded in the structure of society by bringing about a 'new' sexual morality – did not exert any influence on the practical welfare policies of either the authorities or the philanthropists. These kinds of themes were discussed only in highbrow intellectual circles in Vienna.

All in all, prostitution policy unquestionably underwent a process of change and modernization in both capitals. Like the policy on poverty, prostitution policy was basically intended to improve control over the public sphere and to suppress and expel lifestyles not in accordance with social norms. In both fields, municipal reform policies led to more sophisticated definitions and the differentiation and constriction of these norms. Despite these parallels, however, the starting points and the aims of the modernization of prostitution policy were quite different from the reform of welfare policy in the two cities.

Of all municipal policies directed at poverty-related phenomena, prostitution policy was the one which least involved the new categories of modern welfare and social policy. The poor-law policy above all sought to eliminate the 'grey zone' between wage labour and absolute marginalization. Thus in Austria the reform of the vagrancy laws was intended to give some kind of assistance to those who were able to work but were unemployed for a limited time. In the extremely fragmented society of the Hungarian capital there was little possibility to create such integrative new welfare programs.[74]

The reform of prostitution policy was organized according to a different although related logic to that which drew a distinction between those 'willing to work' and those who were not. Here the intention was to separate 'registered' and 'covert' prostitution, with which would come a stricter supervision of the one and a more rigorous persecution of the other. The gender order of bourgeois society, with its sexual and moral double standards, vast market for prostitution and other erotic amusements, developed as a result of political and social liberalization, urbanization and rapidly spreading market relations in the growing cities. Yet simultaneously one of the basic intentions of gender politics in the metropolis was to disseminate bourgeois norms of female morality among the non-bourgeois classes, and to prevent their violation in public. This led to the intensification of the fight against the 'grey zone' between morality and immorality and to a tightening up of the regulations on prostitution in the course of the reforms. All women, including those of the underclasses, the unmarried and the divorced, were to be forced between these strict alternatives and, where some doubt over classification persisted, forced classification took place, and the woman in question became subjected to official control as a prostitute. This was accompanied, especially in Budapest, by a policy of dividing up the public space. Clearly circumscribed zones of the city were to be used only by official prostitutes. Prostitutes or 'immoral women', entering the areas used by 'moral' women, were not to be visibly recognizable as prostitutes, either in Budapest or in Vienna.

In this way, prostitution policy was primarily intended to establish and to stabilize a specific sexual code, one which – in one way or another – affected every woman. The corresponding ideology of female immorality as something timeless and natural further dominated prostitution policy. Prostitution policies remained for the most part untouchable, inaccessible to any substantial reinterpretation. Prostitution continued to be regarded as a natural, not as a social phenomenon, and municipal welfare policy carefully avoided reacting to what was defined as prostitution in a more integrative way. This also holds true for prostitution policy in Vienna, notwithstanding the relaxation of regulations on the eve of the First World War. This is because such reforms were not matched by adequate elaboration of substantial welfare measures for prostitutes.[75] The primary intention of prostitution policies remained the submission of women to a gender code set by the male bourgeois population. If poor women attempted to oppose this callous and aggressive policy, they found themselves in the same place as those poor men and women who refused or were incapable of integrating into the system of wage labour: in gaol, in the workhouse, or in their place of origin in the provinces.

Notes

1. Josef Schrank, *Die amtlichen Vorschriften betreffend die Prostitution in Wien, in ihrer administrativen, sanitären und strafgerichtlichen Anwendung*, Vienna, 1899, p.24.
2. A more detailed version of this article is also part of the *History Department Yearbook*, 1994/5, Central European University, Budapest, 1996. It was written with the support of the Hochschuljubilaeumsstiftung der Stadt Wien.
3. Important among others are: Theresa Wobbe, *Gleichheit und Differenz. Politische Strategien von Frauenrechtlerinnen um die Jahrundertwende*, New York, 1989, pp.48–54; Judith Walkowitz, 'Gefährliche Formen der Sexualität', in Georges Duby, Geneviève Fraisse and Michelle Perrot (eds), *19. Jahrhundert (Geschichte der Frauen*, vol. 4), Frankfurt and New York: Campus, 1994, pp.418, 421, 423–30; Karin Jušek, *Auf der Suche nach der Verlorenen. Die Prostitutionsdebatten im Wien der Jahrhundertwende*, Vienna: Löcker, 1994, p.167; Linda Mahood, *The Magdalenes. Prostitution in the Nineteenth Century*, London: Routledge, 1990, pp.159, 161, 163; Alain Corbin, *Women for Hire. Prostitution and Sexuality in France after 1850*, Cambridge, Mass., 1990, p.xii. The author describes the perspectives of the anti-regulationists with one expression as 'discreet prohibitionist'.
4. One important exception is the historical research of Mahood, *The Magdalenes*, 1990, on penitentiaries and the penitentiary movement for prostitutes in nineteenth-century Scotland.
5. Here I do not analyse the gender-specific procedures of politics toward poverty relating to the 'deserving' poor. See Susan Zimmermann, 'Das Geschlecht der Fürsorge. Kommunale Armen- und Wohlfahrtspolitik in Budapest und Wien 1870–1914', in *L'Homme. Zeitschrift für feministische Geschichtswissenschaft*, vol. 5, no. 2, 1994, pp.19–40.
6. An exception is Detlev J. K. Peukert, *Grenzen der Sozialdisziplinierung. Aufstieg und Krise der deutschen Jugendfürsorge von 1878 bis 1932*, Cologne, 1986. In the introduction (pp.14–16) Peukert explicitly mentions that the care for girls was an independent and in many respects autonomous corpus of laws and politics compared to that for the young males to which his study is limited.
7. *Budapest Fő- -es Székesvárosi Állami Rendőrség 1897 évi működése* [The activity of the State Police of the Capital City and Royal Residence of Budapest in the year 1897: Hereafter *Állami Rendőrség*], Budapest, 1898, p.242. Exactly the same was said about the prostitutes of Vienna, when they were conscripted for the first time in the late 1860s. See H. Montane (pseudonym for Franz Höfberger), *Die Prostitution in Wien, Ihre Geschichte und Entwicklung von den Anfängen bis zur Gegenwart*, Hamburg, Leipzig, Vienna, 1925, p.52 and p.96.
8. Franz Hügel, *Zur Geschichte, Regelung und Statistik der Prostitution*, Vienna, 1865, p.208. A Hungarian observer spoke about 'poor women, women fighting a desperate struggle with poverty'. János Cséri, *Budapest Fő- és székváros Prostitutió-ügye* [Prostitution Affairs of the Capital City and Royal Residence of Budapest] 1893, p.20.
9. *A közbiztonság almanachja 1914. évre* [Public Security Almanac 1914], Budapest, 1913, p.208.
10. The latter was the official concept in Vienna for the police punishment of arrested 'indecent' women.
11. Even among the more informed contemporaries, those 'theories' which considered prostitution the typical form of female *crime* were better known. For Austria see Hugo Herz, 'Die Vagabundage in Österreich in ihren Beziehungen zur Volkswirtschaft und zum Verbrechertum', in *Zeitschrift für Volkswirtschaft, Sozialpolitik und Verwaltung*, 14, 1905, pp.603–5.

12. See Montane, *Prostitution in Wien*, p.68.
13. *Blätter für das Armenwesen der Stadt Wien*, vol. 2, 1903, p.130.
14. The latter was an official term in the Austrian part of the monarchy.
15. Jan Neruda, *Aus dem Alltag der Prager Stadtpolizei. Eine Erzählung aus der Zeit der k. u. k. Monarchie*, Prague: Vitalis, 1993 (reprint), p.61.
16. Kornél Tábori and Vladimir Székely, *Az erkölcstelen Budapest* [Immoral Budapest], Budapest, 1908, pp.32-3.
17. Kálmán Károlyi, *Budapestnek vesznie kell!* [Budapest must perish], Budapest, 1891, p.13; *Leleplezések a polgár világából* [Revelations from the World of the Citizen], Budapest (n.d), p.5.
18. *Amtsblatt der k.k. Polizeidirektion in Wien*, 1896, p.76.
19. Schrank, *Vorschriften*, p.82; *Amtsblatt der k.k. Polizeidirektion in Wien*, p.89. In such cases the presence of venereal infection was taken as a proof.
20. Franz Hügel, *Über die Quästionierung und Lösung der Prostitutionsfrage*, Vienna, 1867, p.7.
21. Schrank, *Vorschriften*, pp.66-7.
22. See for example *Állami Rendőrség*, p.206.
23. See Cséri, *The Prostitution Affairs*, 1893.
24. *A nő és a társadalom. A feministák egyesülete . . . hivatalos közlönye* [Women and Society. The Official Review of the Association of Feminists . . .] 1, 1907, p.137. The radical and often abolitionist-directed wing of the bourgeois women's movement was also engaged in criticizing such 'scandalous' affairs. See examples in Jušek, *Auf der Suche*, pp.118-21.
25. See Susan Zimmermann, *Mutterschutz und Sexualreform. Zur Geschichte des Selbstbestimmungsrechts der Frau*. M.A., Vienna University, 1986, pp.22-49.
26. The Allgemeine Österreichische Frauenverein made the struggle againt the regulatory codification from the beginning of the 1890s a question of principle, See Jušek, *Auf der Suche*, pp.144-50.
27. In its principal statement of 1905, the Association of Feminists did not clearly formulate its position on the 'sexual question'. Later they explicitly supported abolitionism. See *Tájékoztatás a Feministák Egyesülete céljairól és munkatervéről* [Information about the Aims and the Working-Plan of the Association of Feminists], Budapest, 1905, pp.6-7; *Fővárosi Közlöny, Budapest Székesfőváros Hivatalos Lapja* [Review of the Capital. The Official Paper of the Residence and Capital City of Budapest]. Hereafter: *Fővárosi Közlöny*, vol. 18, 1907, no. 3, supplement, pp.8-9.
28. Rosa Mayreder, *Zur Kritik der Weiblichkeit. Essays* (repr.) Munich: Frauenoffensive, 1982, p.209; Harriet Anderson (ed.), Rosa Mayreder, *Tagebücher 1873-1937*, Frankfurt am Main: Insel Verlag, 1988, p.81, see also pp.72-3.
29. *Állami Rendőrség*, p.181.
30. Cf. *Szabályok a kéjelgés-, bordélyházak- és kéjhölgyekről* [Regulations on Brothels, prostitutes and filles de joie], Budapest, 1867; *Szabályrendelet a bordély-ügyről* [Statute on Brothels], Budapest, 1885. (Hereafter *Bordély-ügy*.)
31. Hügel, *Über die Quästionierung*, p.12, see also pp.21, 27-8.
32. Cf. Jušek, *Auf der Suche*, p.105; Schrank, *Vorschriften*, p.45.
33. The process of transformation leading to greater independence and centralization, in the form of a special department, an independent office or (as was the case from 1908 in Budapest's Ó-utca) even a separate building accelerated around the turn of the century. For Budapest see *Állami Rendőrség*, p.169; 1908, p.186; 1909, p.193; 1911, pp.213-14; 1913, p.281; *Public Security Almanac 1910*, p.60. For Vienna, Montane, *Geschichte der Prostitution*, pp.175-6, where the relevant regulations are enumerated for the period between 1905 and 1908.
34. *Bordély-ügy*, 1885, pp.12-13, 16.
35. Schrank, *Vorschriften*, p.17. In general see Montane, *Geschichte der Prostitution*, 1925, pp.60-103; Ernst Mischler and Josef Ulbrich (eds), *Österreichisches Staatswörterbuch. Handbuch des gesamten österreichischen öffentlichen Rechtes*, vol. IV, 2nd edn, Vienna, 1909, pp.264-6; *Amtsblatt der k.k. Polizei-Direktion in Wien*, 1900, pp.1-16.
36. See Schrank, *Vorschriften*, 1899, pp.46, 69, 82. How the dividing lines between compulsion and spontaneity were interwoven in reality is illustrated by an example published in *Women and Society*, 1, 1907, pp.136-7.

37. See the description of the 1873 Act in Montane, *Geschichte der Prostitution*, p.62; *Amtsblatt der k.k. Polizei-Direktion in Wien*, 1900, p.8. According to Mischler and Ulbrich, *Staatswörterbuch*, 1909, p.265, this possibility was introduced only with this official new regulation.
38. *Bordély-ügy*, 1885, pp.16, 25–6; *Állami Rendőrség 1894*, pp.200–201; Law no. 40/1879, section 7, §§62, 75, 81, n. 6, *Magyar Törvénytár* [Code of Hungarian Laws], 1879, pp.201–4.
39. See Montane, *Geschichte der Prostitution*, pp.67, 74–5.
40. *Reichsgesetzblatt für die im Reichsrathe vertretenen Königreiche und Länder no. 89*, 24 May 1885, §5, paragraph 1–2, 4 and §7, p.209; before this, *Reichsgesetzblatt no. 108*, 10 May 1873, §§2, 3, 13, 14, pp.385, 387. See also *Instruction für die polizeiliche Überwachung der Prostitution*, published in *Amtsblatt der k.k. Polizei-Direktion in Wien*, 1900, p.14.
41. Cf. Schrank, *Vorschriften*, p.83.
42. *Reichsgesetzblatt no. 88*, 27 July 1871, §1 (paragraph c), p.229; *Toloncz szabályzat* [Decree on forced removal], §2 (paragraph b), in *Magyarországi rendeletek tára* [Code of the Hungarian Regulations], Budapest, 1885, pp.169–70.
43. For Vienna see the new police act regulating prostitution in: *Amtsblatt der k.k. Polizei-Direktion in Wien*, 1896, p.6; also p.74; Hügel, *Über die Quästionierung*, p.14; Schrank, *Vorschriften*, pp.9, 59, 69–70, 71; for Budapest see *Szabályrendelet a prostitucióról* [Statute on Prostitution], Budapest, 1909, pp.26–7. Hereafter, *Szabályrendelet*; *Állami Rendőrség 1894*, p.187; 1910, p.213.
44. *Bordély-ügy*, 1885, p.17; *Amtsblatt der k.k. Polizei-Direktion in Wien*, 1900, p.8.
45. The number of those imprisoned for soliciting was minimal.
46. See Susan Zimmermann, *Prächtige Armut. Fürsorgepolitik, Kinderschutz und radikale Sozialreform in Budapest im Vergleich mit Wien 1870–1914*, Sigmaringen: Thorbeke, 1997, Table 4, and sources and computed quantities.
47. See *Die Polizeiverwaltung Wiens im Jahre 1890*, Vienna, 1893, pp.80, 116; 1892, pp.68, 100 (author's computation). In 1876 (before the enactment of the vagrancy law) the number of women arrested for beggary, homelessness, night walking and unemployment constituted 17.1 per cent of all arrests; with arrests for prostitution included, the proportion rises to 27 per cent. See *Die Polizeiverwaltung Wiens im Jahre 1876*, pp.139–140, 142, 144 (author's computation). The statistics for Budapest did not differentiate according to gender and reasons of ordering-off. In Vienna only women sentenced after the act of 1885 were categorized separately, but not those punished for 'provocative walking around'. See Hugo Morgenstern, *Das Schubwesen in Österreich. Special issue of Statistische Monatschrift*, NF, 12, 1901, pp.23–4.
48. In 1894 (1892) the Budapest (Vienna) police registered 1115 (1606) prostitutes. The Budapest police estimated the number of covert prostitutes to be at least three times higher; the Vienna police medical service spoke of at least ten times more 'covert' than registered prostitutes. *Állami Rendőrség 1894*, pp.193, 199; *Die Polizeiverwaltung Wiens im Jahre 1892*, p.65; Schrank, *Vorschriften*, p.48.
49. Zimmermann, *Prächtige Armut*, Table 4.
50. *Állami Rendőrség 1896*, p.272.
51. *Amtsblatt der k. k. Polizei-Direktion in Wien*, 1896, p.19; cf. also 1900, pp.3, 10–11.
52. *Állami Rendőrség 1894*, pp.186–7.
53. *Szabályrendelet*, 1909, p.27; see also *Állami Rendőrség 1896*, p.277; 1897, pp.248–50; 1900, p.212; Miklós Rédey and Imre Laky (eds), *Rendőrségi Lexicon* [Police Encyclopaedia], Budapest, 1903, pp.257–9. Hereafter, *Lexicon*; *Állami Rendőrség 1896*, p.277; 1897, pp.248–50; 1900, p.212
54. The community's council, however, annulled the legal validity of this arbitrary regulation. *Review of the Capital*, vol.12, 1901, pp.370–71, 401; see also *Állami Rendőrség 1900*, p.212.
55. *Szabályrendelet 1909*, pp.26–7.
56. *Szabályrendelet 1909*, p.3.
57. *Szabályrendelet*, 1909, pp.10–11. See also *Lexicon*, pp.257–9. *Amtsblatt der k. k. Polizei-Direktion in Wien*, 1911, pp.9–11; also 1893, pp.76, 105; Schrank, *Vorschriften*, pp.10–11, 16, 46–7, 58–9, 81–2.
58. *Amtsblatt der k. k. Polizei-Direktion in Wien*, 1911, pp.1, 9–12; cf. also 1893, pp.76, 105; 1896, p.52; Schrank, *Vorschriften*, pp.10–11, 16, 46–7, 58–9, 81–2.
59. Zimmermann, *Prächtige Armut*, Table 4.
60. *Állami Rendőrség 1896*, p.276; 1897, p.241.

61. See e.g. *Amtsblatt der k. k. Polizei-Direktion in Wien*, 1896, p.74.
62. *Közlöny*, vol. 12, 1901, 373. For Vienna see *Amtsblatt der k. k. Polizei-Direktion in Wien*, 1900, pp.9–10.
63. Cf. *Szabályrendelet*, 1909, p.21; *Bordély-ügy*, 1885, pp.14–15; *Állami Rendőrség 1897*, p.242; *1899*, p.210. Montane, *Die Prostitution in Wien*, 1925, p.64.
64. *Szabályrendelet*, 1909, pp.22–3.
65. Cf. Gerhard Melinz and Susan Zimmermann, *Über die Grenzen der Armenhilfe. Kommunale und staatliche Sozialpolitik in Wien und Budapest in der Doppelmonarchie*, Vienna and Munich: Europa Verlag, 1991, pp.117–19.
66. Cf. Zimmermann, *Prächtige Armut*, chart 4.
67. On 'white slavery' see Anna Staudacher's article based on archival material, 'Die Aktion "Girondo". Zur Geschichte des internationalen Mädchenhandels in Österreich-Ungarn um 1885', in Heide Dienst and Edith Saurer (eds), *Das Weib existiert nicht für sich*, Vienna: Verlag für Gesellschaftskritik, 1990, pp.97–138.
68. For the tightening up of the Hungarian penal code (law no. 5/1878), law no. 36/1908, §§43–7, *Code of Hungarian Laws*, 1908, pp.878–91. For the §§ 512–14 of the Austrian penal code from 1852 see Schrank, *Vorschriften*, pp.113–14; on the failure to strengthen the vagrancy law from 1885 and later: Montane, *Geschichte der Prostitution*, pp.117–20; Schrank, *Mädchenhandel*, 1904; *Jelentés a 'Magyar Egyesület a Leánykereskedés Ellen' negyedévszázados munkságáról (1909–1934)*, [Report on a Quarter of a Century of the Work of the 'Hungarian Society Against White Slavery'], Budapest (n.d.). Hereafter *Jelentés*.
69. Cf. paragraphs 33, 42, 45 and 49 of the new official regulations in Vienna in the journal of the capital's police headquarters *Amtsblatt der k.k. Polizei-Direktion in Wien*, 1911, pp.10–12. For the debates on the new regulations in Budapest at the public discussion in 1906 see *Közlöny*, vol. 18, 1907, no. 3, supplement. On the interpretation of these debates see also Mór Linka, 'A prostitució rendezése Budapesten' [The Regulation of Prostitution in Budapest], in *Huszadik Század, Társadalom-tudományi Szemle* [Twentieth Century Review of Social Sciences], vol. 8, 1907, pp.246–7. The activities of the Hungarian Women's Federation were far more reserved than those of the Association of Feminists.
70. *Jelentés*, pp.57–8. *Állami Rendőrség 1912*, p.245.
71. See *Review of the Capital*, vol. 23, 1912, pp.1.198–9; *Budapest székesfőváros árvaszékének gyermekvédelmi tevékenysége 1910–1921* [The defence of children under the aegis of the orphan's office of the capital Budapest], fol. 35–6, 46–8, 64–6.
72. Cf. *Amtsblatt der k.k. Polizei-Direktion in Wien*, 1900, p.62; 1911, pp.5–6, 12.
73. *Jelentés*, pp.58, 60.
74. Such increasingly integrative politics were going to be also highly gender-specific. Men were to act as the major breadwinner and the head of a patriarchal proletarian family, while women who accepted this structure would act as 'respectable' and 'decent' housewives and paid workers alike. See Zimmermann, *Das Geschlecht der Fürsorge*, pp.35–9.
75. In 'Red Vienna' after the war, the municipal welfare policy was characterized by an exceptional boom. But even after these developments, the regulations basically remained those of the period before the war and the welfare services remained less than moderate. With the establishment of a hospital for women suffering from venereal diseases in 1922 near Vienna, the pressures against and control of 'covert' prostitution became even more intensive. The morality police and its raids turned out to be part and parcel of the daily life of the lower classes, even if new social spaces in the every day life of these classes developed, which remained remote from its action radius. See part of an interview on the moral police in Hans Safrian and Reinhard Sieder, 'Gassenkinder – Straßenkämpfer. Zur politischen Sozialisation einer Arbeitergeneration in Wien 1900 bis 1938', in: Lutz Niethammer and Alexander von Plato (eds), *'Wir kriegen jetzt andere Zeiten'. Auf der Suche nach der Erfahrung des Volkes in nachfaschistischen Ländern*, Berlin and Bonn, 1985, p.132. See also Montane, *Die Prostitution in Wien*, 1925, pp.60, 81, 89, 100–102; Heinrich Dehmal and Oskar Dreßler, *Handbuch des Polizei- und Verwaltungsrechtes*, vol. 1, Graz, 1926, pp.194, 196; Viktor Mucha and Viktor Satke, 'Beschäftigungstherapie und Fürsorge in der Heilanstalt Klosterneuburg-Wien', in: *Blätter für das Wohlfahrtswesen*, vol. 28, 1929, no. 272, pp.108–10.

Coping with social and economic crisis: the Viennese experience, 1929–1933

Gerhard Melinz

Capitalism cannot be eliminated by decree of City Hall. But big cities are in a position to provide vigorously much-needed social services in capitalist society. New Vienna is ready, willing and able to work for the good of its citizens and for the glory of socialism![1]

This was the emphatic view of Robert Danneberg, the president of the Vienna state legislature, on the eve of the world economic crisis in 1929. In the same year we find the following description in a metal workers' union journal. It draws attention to the realities of a divided labour market:

Female servants, laundry women, seamstresses, nurses – all these women have been waiting in vain for years for the ordinance to bring them health insurance. . . . The fate of these women is closely connected with the fate of women who are working in factories. And it is evident that very often the long-term unemployed or aging female industrial workers, who can no longer find a task or a job in the firm are forced to gain a meagre living as female domestic servants or laundry women.[2]

Vienna's Social Democratic administration was determined, if it could not abolish capitalism, to mitigate its worst effects; yet Red Vienna could not act autonomously: the council was at the mercy of unclear and unforeseen developments in the labour market and in the economy generally. And the predicament of these 'displaced' working-class women is one example of the way in which social realities could be drastically altered by the uncontrollable workings of the labour market. The aim of this essay is to examine the effects on the optimistic social policies of Red Vienna of the severe economic depression of the early 1930s, and the experience of those in the city who were compelled to have recourse to the social security system as it developed to accommodate the new circumstances.

Politics and changing social structures

The world economic crisis had a fundamental impact on the crumbling social structure of Vienna, but much of its effect was to accelerate changes which had been taking place since the turn of the century and more dramatically since the end of the First World War. A clear social division between the 'respectable' skilled working class and the classic poor had begun to emerge before the war, and was reinforced by the wide-ranging social policy reforms introduced in the early years of the First Austrian Republic (between 1918 and 1920). In fact large numbers of unskilled wage-earners and casual labourers were effectively excluded from this new welfare state. Female home-workers, for example, experienced very bad social conditions. Their wages were half those of women in industry, they had no collective wage contracts, and they suffered from periodic unemployment.[3] However, the clear demarcation between skilled industrial labour and other workers began to blur and became increasingly obsolete during the 1920s as changes took place in the work place.

For the social catastrophe in Vienna at the beginning of the 1930s was not simply the product of the immediate financial crisis; it was also the outcome of a number of longer-term developments. After the dissolution of the Habsburg monarchy Austria had faced particular economic difficulties. Apart from the hyperinflation of the postwar crisis, there were both severe structural problems within the national economy, and specific difficulties arising from the country's trade relations with the successor states.[4] Moreover, the role of Vienna itself had changed. It had been at the centre of an empire of fifty million people, and was now merely the capital of a small state with about seven million inhabitants. Further restrictions on the development of the economy resulted from the prohibition, in the peace settlement of St Germain (1919), of Austria's *Anschluss* with Germany. The situation was then exacerbated by the impact of the restrictive social and economic policies introduced by the government as a result of the punitive conditions of the Geneva loan (1922) and the Lausanne loan (1932). The Austrian Republic, then, suffered from a number of long-term economic problems, and Vienna, as the country's major administrative, commercial *and* industrial centre, was affected by adverse developments in all sectors of the economy.

After the First World War Vienna had become one of the *Bundesländer* (federal States) of the new republic, and as such enjoyed considerable political and economic autonomy; in particular the local authority attained sovereignty over its own tax structure. This measure of financial independence had been an essential precondition for all the *Aufbauarbeit* (reconstruction work) carried out by the Social Democratic city administration in the 1920s. The municipal authorities took advantage of their tax-raising powers, as far as circumstances allowed, in order to undertake specific social initiatives, particularly in the fields of housing and welfare. For indeed, despite all the country's economic problems there was an axiomatic belief in the necessity and socially constructive role of welfare on the part of the authorities of Red Vienna:

> The aim of public assistance is, in the final analysis, nothing less than the effort to design and implement a whole range of relief agencies to assist, as economically and efficiently as possible, in the innumerable difficulties confronting the individual or the family, and to replace old-fashioned poor relief with modern welfare work.

Moreover, it was envisaged that those who were 'economically weak and unproductive would be prepared, by means of systematic advice and guidance, and by educational intervention in all aspects of their lives, to find their place again in the economic life [of the community]'.[5]

Since 1919, then, the administration of Red Vienna had attempted to develop and implement policies explicitly for the benefit of the majority of the population, a 'civilizing' project, that aspired to the social integration and cultural transformation of the Viennese working class into *neue Menschen* (new human beings).[6] By the end of the 1920s, however, this project was increasingly forced to confront its limitations: social reality in Vienna was determined by precarious conditions of existence for large sections of the population. As the performance of the national economy deteriorated, falling tax revenues began to undermine the city's strategy. Thus although 64 000 new dwellings had been built in Vienna during the 1920s, after 1928 the number of evictions began to rise, and homelessness became a pressing problem again.[7] Furthermore, after 1931 the economic circumstances of the city were aggravated by the punitive and politically motivated economic measures undertaken against the local authority by the country's right-wing government: what Robert Danneberg referred to as a 'financial march on Vienna'.[8]

The labour market crisis

Developments in the capital's labour market since the First World War reflected the turbulence of the national economy. Not least, 100 000 civil servants and other state employees had been dismissed in the mid 1920s as a result of the terms of international loans to resolve the postwar crisis. This was followed in the latter part of the decade by a far-reaching process of economic 'rationalization' both in the manufacturing and distribution sectors, which had a severe impact on the Viennese working class. (In particular, since Vienna was at the centre of Austria's metal industry the rationalization process had disproportionately adverse effects there.) Both 'blue-collar' workers and 'white-collar' employees (*Angestellte*) were made redundant in large numbers, were put on short-time work, or were only able to obtain jobs without social insurance protection. The effects of these changes were already under way before the onset of the depression.[9] The impact of the world economic crisis on Austrian workers was nevertheless dramatic. This is demonstrated by a whole range of economic indicators which reflect the rapid impoverishment of wage and salary earners. The level of unemployment – and of short-time working – rose sharply: while in 1928 there were some 68 000 unemployed people receiving benefit in Vienna, that number had risen to 130 000 in 1933.[10] Conversely, the number of people covered by accident and health insurance declined by about a third between 1930 and 1933.[11]

The number of unemployed persons registered for work at the employment exchanges gives us a more detailed picture of which branches and sectors of the labour market were in most distress. The worst affected were unskilled workers, most of whom were women. The rationalization process had opened up more job opportunities for women, who constituted 35.8 per cent of the insured workforce by 1931 (their employment position was very vulnerable, however, and they also made up 31.6 per cent of the registered unemployed in the same year).[12] Metal workers, clerical employees, and workers in the textile industries were also severely affected.[13] A particular illustration of the impact of the crisis is provided by conditions in the construction industry in Vienna. Under normal circumstances construction workers experienced a classic seasonal pattern of employment, but in 1933, as a result of the cessation of municipal house-building activities, there were only 3 000 jobs available compared with 35 000 the year before.[14] Employers took advantage of these circumstances to reduce wages, thereby aggravating the impoverishment of working-class households. Between 1928 and 1933 the total sum of salaries and wages declined by 36 per cent.[15]

Social distress and social policy

The depressed labour market and increasing unemployment had a wide range of negative social consequences both for individuals and for households.[16] Official statistics cannot give us a complete picture of the suffering, but they are nonetheless eloquent. The number of those who received the standard unemployment benefit increased year by year from 1928 onwards; but this was not the end of the misery. After a fixed term the right to benefit expired and the unemployed were forced to go on the dole. This process of disqualification from social insurance (*Aussteuerung*) became a mass phenomenon in Austria during the early 1930s. Between January 1932 and October 1933, 64 000 Viennese alone fell victim to *Aussteuerung*. In the most extreme cases, people were compelled to apply for emergency social security payments (*Notstandsaushilfe*). However, the preconditions for the receipt of such benefits were restrictive, and 37 per cent of the applications filed in 1932 for this type of assistance were turned down on the grounds of the absence of 'severe distress'. The unemployment benefits system had the most negative effects on women, on the young unemployed,[17] and on unemployed persons over sixty, who were entitled to a modest amount of social security benefit (*Altersfürsorgerente*).[18] The number of recipients of this benefit more or less doubled between 1929 and 1933, from 15 110 to 30 015.[19]

As unemployment rose, benefits were restricted and the level of earnings fell, new sources of household income had to be exploited in order to make ends meet. From 1931 onwards the proportion of aggregate household income in the city derived from wages, salaries and pensions declined.[20] The income of the head of the household in particular became less and less important, while the share contributed by women and young adults rose significantly.[21] This was bound to have an effect on gender and generational relationships within working-class families: women became breadwinners as more and more men lost their jobs.[22] Käthe Leichter found the male partners of some 40 per cent of female industrial workers were unemployed.[23] Wages were driven down as people were increasingly desperate to find work, and this frequently led to downward social mobility. As the sociologist Benedikt Kautsky commented in 1937, 'The female student of medicine becomes a clerk, the grammar school boy an apprentice, or the skilled worker becomes an unskilled one – so the crisis destroys all hope for social improvement.'[24] In such circumstances, despite the various reductions and restrictions of access to them, the importance of unemployment and social security benefits to household income continued to increase. They constituted one of a number of ways of supplementing income. The sub-letting of rooms also took on a renewed importance, as did cash-in-hand payments of various kinds.

Such new sources were rarely enough to make good the losses to total income incurred by many working-class households during the Depression, however, and there was simply less to spend. This meant a readjustment of priorities for household expenditure. Since levels of rent were generally fixed, and there was therefore no flexibility in accommodation costs, significant savings could only be made on spending on food. From the end of 1930 the level of food consumption started to fall, and the effect was most severe on the households of the unemployed. In 1934, for example, calorie consumption per head in Austria fell below the international minimum standard of 3 000 calories per day.[25] The general improvement in nutrition that had taken place during the second half of the 1920s, therefore, was lost during the economic crisis.

The deteriorating position of young people on the labour market has already been noted. School leavers found it more difficult than ever to find a first job; and apprentices who had just completed their training were frequently among the first to face dismissal.[26] According to contemporary estimates a quarter of all the unemployed in Vienna were young people under the age of 25.[27] Where a job had served not only to integrate young people into the world of work, but also into adult society, the high level of youth unemployment now meant that many were not only without incomes but socially excluded as well. The image of large numbers of unemployed and socially marginalized young people generated fears amongst the establishment of dangerous and anti-social consequences: criminal behaviour and political radicalization on the part of young men; and an 'escape' for young women through prostitution.[28] There were half as many apprentices in 1934 as in 1910.[29]

Feeling the pressure of massive youth unemployment and fearing the potential consequences of political radicalization, the Chamber of Labour and the trade unions, in cooperation with the city council, set up drop-in centres (*Wärmestuben*) during the winter of 1930, to offer unemployed youths the chance to spend part of the day in a heated room, and to provide them with a modest meal of soup and bread. The purpose of this exercise, labelled *Jugend in Not* (Youth in Need), was primarily to occupy the young unemployed, to organize and administer their 'leisure time', and to keep them from 'loafing around' on the streets. The intention was to reinforce social discipline as well as to relieve the effects of poverty. This campaign quickly generated a complementary project: *Jugend am Werk* (Youth at Work), which organized labour squads to perform volunteer community work in exchange for a hot meal. The *Freiwillige Arbeitsdienst* (Volunteer Labour Service), set up in 1932, finally combined these two initiatives.[30]

In the field of classic welfare the principal beneficiaries were the elderly, the sick or the physically handicapped, and benefits took the form of cash stipends. Economic crisis, an aging population and the increasing number of people with a permanent right of abode in Vienna caused a steep rise in demand for support.[31] Long-term maintenance payments had already been a casualty of drastic cuts in public expenditure since 1928 – which naturally provided rich propaganda for the Christian Social opposition in Vienna. The Social Democratic councillor Honay explained the 'new' policy priorities before the Welfare Board in 1933: 'We must not try to cut back on care costs for children, but rather on support payments for the elderly disabled. After all, youth is our future.'[32]

And indeed, there was an increase in applications for aid for dependent children. The city administration's report for the years from 1929 to 1932 remarked: 'Many parents are faced with the most extreme hardship in finding the means to raise their children. Joblessness and the expiry of unemployment benefits have their most terrible consequences among children.'[33] Under the pressure of the economic crisis, benefit recipients obviously attempted to play on the system's orientation towards children's welfare. Civil servants responsible for the administration of welfare noted with suspicion that:

> many aid applicants brought their frequently quite numerous children with them, not because leaving them unattended at home would cause difficulties, but rather because they hoped thereby to expedite the handling of their case, or believed that by threatening to abandon their children in the office, they could force a favorable outcome.'[34]

It was not only that priorities changed in respect of target groups for welfare under the impact of the depression, but that the authorities were obliged to reconsider the nature of benefits as well. The Social Democrats found the use of funds for 'one-off' acts of charity 'generally inappropriate to relieve the distress of the needy, since they easily fall prey to the temptation to spend the money for other purposes'.[35] Moreover, deepening crisis and impoverishment in the years from 1929 to 1931 resulted in about 20 per cent less funds being available for approximately 25 per cent more welfare recipients.[36] The city council was forced to reorientate its aid policy fundamentally from cash payments to the distribution of benefits in kind, such as food, heating fuel, shoes and clothing for the needy. In 1931, faced with extraordinary conditions of hunger, misery and cold, councillor Julius Tandler initiated a non-partisan campaign named *Winterhilfe* (Winter Relief), which was repeated for several years, and the target group was those among the long-term unemployed who were receiving no support at all, particularly those with large families. Applicants had to undertake a means test in order to qualify, and examination of a random sample of the documents dealing with such cases suggests that some 60 per cent of all applicants were rejected.[37] The project was financed by a combination of private contributions, state subsidies and municipal funding, and only provided material support in the form of food vouchers, grocery packets, and heating fuel as well as clothing.[38] In addition meals were dispensed in pubs, institutional dining rooms or other public eating places. Rules were laid down about the quality and quantity of the food and inspections were carried out by the authorities. In practice there were often difficulties, and some participants in the scheme were excluded for not adhering to the regulations. Inspectors reported wildly varying standards, and in some cases were left wondering whether welfare recipients were not being served little more than boiled-up leftovers. In addition the unemployed might be humiliated by being made to sit apart from paying guests 'so that their poverty [was] obvious'.[39]

The severity of the crisis and the removal of the legal rights of tenants also meant that there was an increase in homelessness, vagrancy and begging; and this was despite the much-trumpeted construction of public housing in Vienna.[40] Consequently old-fashioned ways of dealing with the homeless were revived during these years. The welfare department provided drop-in centres in addition to the existing accommodation for the homeless.[41] Two-thirds of the people using them were both homeless and unemployed. In the homeless refuge for women, unemployed domestic servants, girls who had only a job for a couple of months a year, were to be found, waiting for the next job, or sometimes for the next lover.[42]

At the height of the crisis beggars returned to the streets of Vienna, as many people were forced to resort to mendicancy in order to survive. As early as the spring of 1928, a new type of beggar had begun to make an appearance in the city. The *Arbeiter-Zeitung*, the Social Democratic daily paper, reported:

beggars... are no longer [only] old and disabled, no, they are victims of our days, very often young, homeless and unemployed, with no unemployment benefit, not married; they cannot find a job, so they ask house by house for something to survive... this generation of beggars do their job in a different way... the wealth of others does not matter for them, they do not plead or beg, they enforce their claims.[43]

The renewed importance of begging in the city was indicated by the fact that social reformers organized a conference on the subject in February 1933. The participants began by discussing the results of an inquiry among Viennese beggars carried out in the summer of 1932. Although the majority of them were unemployed workers, a quarter were found to be from lower-middle-class backgrounds. Most of those interviewed were suffering long-term unemployment for the first time; almost one third of them had never made any claim for unemployment benefit before. When asked how long they had been begging, typical answers were: 'since my father has been unemployed'; or (from a mother of three children) 'since my husband has been on seasonal work'. Half of the total had already had some contact with the police and the courts.[44]

According to the theoretical model of the market economy, the 'free' labour market should provide for the social integration of individuals. In the circumstances of the depressed world economy (and especially given Austria's particular economic problems), this model did not work in Vienna between the wars.[45] The municipal welfare programme constituted a part of a general social and family policy implemented by the city as an attempt to compensate for the shortcomings of the national social security system, while at the same time attempting to alleviate the problems and side effects of industrial capitalism. The fundamental aims of Social Democratic policy in the period 1919 to 1934 were to work towards the integration of the working class into the existing system, and to contribute to the stabilization of the traditional, patriarchal working-class family.[46] The modernization of the procreation patterns of the family was intended to meet the demands of a national economy engaged in global competition.[47] Moreover, despite the hardships of the crisis, these policies consistently gained the approval of the majority of the population of Red Vienna. The remarkable electoral victories which the party continued to win throughout the depths of the Depression provided clear democratic legitimation for the 'secondary' redistribution of wealth undertaken by the local authority.

Nevertheless, changing political and economic conditions decisively narrowed Vienna's options in policy matters. High unemployment, for instance, meant falling tax revenues, and the national government (a coalition of the Christian Social Party and German Nationalists) persistently pursued a restrictive financial policy which undermined the city council's efforts. In the 1920s the system worked to some extent. Although the emphasis was on social discipline, and the normative-disciplinary pretensions of Tandler's welfare administration were evident, nevertheless in the area of 'productive' care for the needy, this welfare system yielded visible material advantages.

However, in the early 1930s, even before the removal of the Social Democratic administration, the world economic crisis compelled the council to make massive cuts in public spending. In this context the *failure* of the integrative social policies of Red Vienna was clearly evident. Squeezed by economic and political pressure from above and increasing demands from below, classic methods of managing mass poverty were very quickly revived in Vienna. Although this brought no immediate repercussions for the party in elections, tempers flared in the welfare offices. Here the victims of the crisis pressed their demands for their individual entitlements, and often made direct reference to their membership of the party.

Finally, the 'productive' modernization of social policy in Vienna and its ultimate collapse, beset by economic problems and politically undermined by the national government, also symbolizes the geographical specificity of a crisis of social and economic modernization in a semiperipheral country such as Austria.[48] The establishment of a corporatist, authoritarian state (the so-called *Ständestaat*) following the brief civil war of February 1934, and the persistence of economic crisis and reactionary politics, created the preconditions for fascism and Nazism.[49] New and more radical projects were instituted whose social theory preached community (*Volksgemeinschaft*) and social integration, yet which implemented policies of selection (and, ultimately, 'extermination') and proved to be socially destructive in practice.

Notes

1. Robert Danneberg, *Das Neue Wien*, Vienna, 1929, p.2. For an overview regarding the politics and policies of Red Vienna, see Maren Seliger and Karl Ucakar, *Wien. Politische Geschichte 1740–1934*, vol. 2, Vienna, 1985; Gerhard Melinz and Gerhard Ungar, *Wohlfahrt und Krise. Wiener Kommunalpolitik 1929–1938 (Forschungen und Beiträge zur Wiener Stadtgeschichte*, vol. 29), Vienna: Franz Deuticke, 1996.

2. 'Die Frau in der Metallindustrie', supplement to *Der Österreichische Metallarbeiter*, 1929, 4, p.3.

3. Käthe Leichter, *Wie leben die Wiener Heimarbeiter? Eine Erhebung über die Arbeits- und Lebensverhältnisse von tausend Wiener Heimarbeitern*, Vienna, 1928.

4. Trade relations among the successor states remained very close, and Austria had the highest share of trade. But the overall volume of foreign trade was shrinking, and massive tariff walls against Austria were erected by the new successor states. For a brief summary see Jürgen Nautz, 'Between political disintegration and economic reintegration. Austrian trade relations with the successor states after World War I', in David F. Good (ed.), *Economic Transformations in East and Central Europe*, London and New York: Routledge, 1994, pp.261–76; see also the chapters concerning the interwar period by Peter Berger and Stefan Karner in John Komlos (ed.), *Economic Development in the Habsburg Monarchy and in the Successor States* (East European Monographs CCLXXX), Boulder and New York: Columbia University Press, 1990.

5. *Das Neue Wien. Städtewerk*, vol. 2, Vienna, 1927, p.351.

6. For a critical and comprehensive discourse-analysis study of Red Vienna, see Helmut Gruber, *Red Vienna. Experiment in Working Class Culture 1919–1934*, Oxford and New York: Oxford University Press, 1991. See also J. Robert Wegs, *Growing up Working Class. Continuity and Change among Viennese Youth 1890–1938*, London: Pennsylvania State University Press, 1989.

7. See Alfred Georg Frei, *Die Arbeiterbewegung und die 'Graswurzeln' am Beispiel der Wiener Wohnungspolitik 1919–1934*, Vienna: Braumüller Verlag, 1991, p.179.

8. R. Danneberg, *Der finanzielle Marsch auf Wien*, Vienna: Verlag der Organisation Wien der Sozialdemokratischen Partei, 1930.

9. See Dieter Stiefel, *Arbeitslosigkeit: soziale, politische und wirtschaftliche Auswirkungen – am Beispiel Österreichs 1918–1939*, Berlin: Duncker & Humblot, 1979, p.106. According to a trade union inquiry, 13 per cent were employed only part-time. *Ibid.*, p.108.

10. See Bundesministerium für soziale Verwaltung (ed.), *Statistiken zur Arbeitslosenversicherung*, 1932–3, no. 4, p.1. See also Käthe Leichter, *So leben wir . . . 1,320 Industriearbeiterinnen berichten über ihr Leben*, Vienna, 1932, pp.22–5.

11. The number of employees covered by accident insurance fell from 174 778 (June 1930) to 119 071 (June 1933), the number of apprentices fell in the same period from 13 750 to 8 441: *Wirtschaftsstatistisches Jahrbuch (WStatJB)*, 1931–3, 84; for the data on health insurance see *Arbeit und Wirtschaft* 1932, p.122; *WStatJb*, 1931–3, p.467.

12. See Leichter, *So leben wir. . . .* For official statistics on female employment, see Bundesministerium für soziale Verwaltung, *Statistiken*, Heft 1 (1920–29), p.25; Heft 2: pp.3, 38; Heft 4 (1932–3), p.11.

13. *Ibid.*, 1932–3, no. 4, pp.2–9, 16, 18–20.

14. See Wolfgang Hösl and Gottfried Pirhofer, *Wohnen in Wien 1848–1938. Studien zur Konstitution des Massenwohnens (Forschung und Beiträge zur Wiener Stadtgeschichte*, vol. 19), Vienna: Franz Deuticke, 1988, p.107.

15. Author's own calculation from statistics in *WStatJb*, 1933–5, p.414. See also information on working-class incomes in Stiefel, *Arbeitslosigkeit*, pp.148–9.

16. The Chambers of Labour decided in 1925 to create statistical data based on the household incomes of wage and salary earners. For historians it is the best source for assessing the standard of living. See the appropriate chapters in the annual *Wirtschaftsstatisches Jahrbuch*; for a comprehensive overview of the findings of this kind of social and economic research covering the period from 1925 to 1934, see Benedikt Kautsky, 'Die Haushaltsstatistik der Wiener Arbeiterkammer 1925–1934', *International Review for Social History*, Supplement to Volume 2, Leiden, 1937.

17. Through numerous amendments to the unemployment insurance law, the policy of the Christian Social national administration and their respective coalition partners was ultimately to 'produce' new welfare cases among the 'classic' clientele of the poor and destitute.
18. The oldest female member of the metal workers' union association, Berta Sailer, was living in 1929 with such a pension of 50 schillings. In an interview for the trade union journal she said, 'It is hard to live on this pension. I have two sub-tenants, and I cook and provide for them.' With the additional money from sub-letting she was able to survive. *Der Metallarbeiter*, 1929, p.2.
19. Bundesministerium für soziale Verwaltung, *Statistiken* no. 1, p.13; no. 4, p.7.
20. *WStatJB*, 1933-5, p.414.
21. This development was also a result of the earlier rationalization process, which replaced skilled male workers with cheaper female and adolescent labour. See above 'Die Frau in der Metallindustrie', supplement to *Der Österreichische Metallarbeiter*, 1929, 8, 17, 21; 1930, 4, 8.
22. See Elisabeth Maresch, *Ehefrau in Haushalt und Beruf. Eine statistische Darstellung für Wien auf Grund der Volkszählung von 22. März 1934*, Vienna, 1938, pp.20-24. See also *Kuckuck*, 1933, no. 33, p.8.
23. Leichter, *So leben wir* ... pp.13, 103, 107.
24. Benedikt Kautsky, 'Haushaltsstatistik', p.116.
25. Ibid, p.24.
26. For evidence of the fall in the number of jobs for apprentices during the Depression, see *Gemeindeverwaltung der Bundeshauptstadt Wien für die Jahre 1929 bis 1931*, pp.526, 528. On the situation of young women see *Zeitschrift für Kinderschutz, Familien- und Berufsfürsorge*, 1934, no. 7-9, pp.84-6.
27. See Stiefel, *Arbeitslosigkeit*, p.175
28. For examples taken from media analysis see Alexandra Ledl, 'Die Gerichtssaalberichterstattung in der Ersten Österreichischen Republik in den Parteiorganen der Christlichsozialen und Sozialdemokraten von 1918 bis 1934', PhD thesis, Vienna, 1990.
29. Author's calculation based on statistical data presented in *Zeitschrift für Kinderschutz, Familien- und Berufsfürsorge*, 1936, 7, p.77.
30. For a brief overview of social policy measures for the young unemployed, see Melinz and Ungar, *Wohlfahrt und Krise*, pp.122-8.
31. Traditional regulations governing the right to residency (*Heimatrecht*), which stemmed from the Habsburg monarchy and served as a basis for claims to communal charity, were still valid. The application for, or recognition of, the right to fixed residency – in other words the admission ticket to communal citizenship – was contingent on the payment of a fee. The Social Democratic city administration was interested in maintaining this source of revenue, though, of course, in Red Vienna the fee schedule was progressively graduated according to income. But an increase in the number of welfare recipients through the back door became a latent fear.
32. Österreichisches Staatsarchiv (ÖSTA), Archiv der Republik, Christlichsoziale Partei Wien, Korrespondenz, Zl. 420/1933.
33. *Die Gemeindeverwaltung der Stadt Wien 1929-1931*, Vienna, 1949, p.253.
34. Wiener Stadt- und Landesarchiv (WStLA), M.Abt. 208, Normalien 7/2, MA 8-19.987/31.
35. *Die Gemeindeverwaltung der Stadt Wien 1929-1931*, p.205.
36. Ibid., author's calculation.
37. See Melinz and Ungar, *Wohlfahrt und Krise*, p.65.
38. The most 'Fürsorgeblätter' (welfare documents) were distributed in the following (working-class) districts: 17., 20., 10., 21., 11; the most foodstuff vouchers in 11., 20., 17., 14. etc. See Melinz and Ungar, *Wohlfart und Krise*, pp.63-4.
39. WStLA M . Abt. 208 A6/2 (Mappe Kontrolle der Speisestellen).
40. Indeed, in 1934 only 20 per cent were living in the new *Gemeindebauten* (communal apartment complexes): Rainer Bauböck, *Wohnungspolitik im sozialdemokratischen Wien 1919-34*, Salzburg: Verlag Wolfgang Neugebauer, 1979, p.152. Käthe Leichter found that just over 10 per cent of her sample of female industrial workers lived in a council flat. Leichter, *So leben wir*, p.77.
41. There were separate centres for party members, because the Social Democrats were afraid that they would become hotbeds of opposition political agitation. See Melinz and Ungar, *Wohlfahrt und Krise*, p.78.

42. See Ledl, 'Gerichtssaalberichterstattung', p.168; *Kuckuck* 1933, Nr. 43.
43. *Arbeiter-Zeitung*, 23 April 1928, p.4.
44. See *Das Bettlerwesen in Wien und seine Bekämpfung. Bericht über die am 19. Februar 1933 von der 'Ethischen Gemeinde' veranstaltete Konferenz*, Vienna, 1933.
45. See Gerhard Melinz, 'Christlichsoziale Politik und semiperiphere Entwicklung in Österreich', in Rudolf G. Ardelt and Christian Gerbel (eds), *Österreichischer Zeitgeschichtetag 1995*, Innsbruck and Vienna: Studienverlag, 1997, pp.242–5; Dieter Stiefel, *Die grosse Krise in einem kleinen Land. Österreichische Finanz- und Wirtschaftspolitik 1929–1938 (Studien zu Politik und Verwaltung*, vol. 26), Vienna: Böhlau, 1988.
46. See Gottfried Pirhofer and Reinhard Sieder, 'Zur Konstitution der Arbeiterfamilie im Roten Wien. Familienpolitik, Kulturreform, Alltag und Ästhetik', in Michael Mitterauer and Reinhard Sieder (eds), *Historische Familienforschung*, Frankfurt am Main: Suhrkamp, 1982, pp.326–68; See also Melinz and Ungar, *Wohlfahrt und Krise*; Gruber, *Red Vienna*, pp.65–73.
47. See Melinz and Ungar, *Wohlfahrt und Krise*, pp.129–35.
48. See Gerhard Melinz and Susan Zimmermann, 'Getrennte Wege. Wohlfahrtspolitik und gesellschaftlicher Transformationsprozeß in Wien und Budapest zwischen den Weltkriegen', in *Jahrbuch des Vereins für Geschichte der Stadt Wien*, Vol. 59 (1994), p.315.
49. For a comparative evaluation of 'Red Vienna' and 'corporatist state' city-council policies see Gerhard Melinz, ' "Red" and "Catholic" Social Integration and Exclusion: Municipal Welfare Policy and Social Reality in Vienna (1918–1938)', in Susan Zimmermann (ed.), *Urban Space and Identity in the European City 1890–1930s* (Central European University History Department, Working Papers Series 3), Budapest: CEU Press, 1995, pp.55–72.

Walter Ruttmann's *Berlin: Symphony of a City*: traffic-mindedness and the city in interwar Germany

Anthony McElligott

When it was released in September 1927, Walter Ruttmann's city film, *Berlin: Sinfonie der Grossstadt* (*Berlin: Symphony of a City*), received a mixed reception among critics and the German cinema-going public. Apparently documenting twenty-four hours in the life of Berlin, Ruttmann employed the cross-section technique that was just developing, to produce a montage of *tableaux vivants* of the city experience.[1]

Latterly, there has been a renewed interest in Ruttmann's work, as cultural historians have begun to explore the period, and in particular, Berlin's modernity, in greater critical detail. The main focus of this interest has been either to concentrate on Ruttmann's contribution to the development of a Modernist city film aesthetic in general, or to dwell on the relationship between film and the city as spectacle.[2] I want both to shift and to widen the discussion by narrowing the focus on a particular aspect of Ruttmann's film. I shall argue in this chapter that Ruttmann inscribed onto the film's surface a subtler textual discourse in which the city's traffic is present both as an emblem of modernization, understood here as advances in transport technology as well as technical improvements in roads and their organization, and as a signifier of modernity, defined as the experiences deriving from and responses to modernization. The artistic style and representation of technology employed by Ruttmann was one that was frequently articulated in the New Objectivity (*Neue Sachlichkeit*) that emerged in the mid years of the republican period, and which was also present in the Third Reich.[3]

In this respect, Ruttmann's film was reflective of a much more broadly-based discourse on the city as surrogate for the nation that had already begun to place traffic at its centre before the First World War.[4] There was an even more pronounced move to situate traffic at the centre of the urban cultural experience in the 1920s, as evidenced by the filmscript *Dynamic of the City* (1921–2) of Bauhaus artist László Moholy-Nagy; or the city lithographs of Franz Masereel, *Bilder der Grossstadt* which he produced in 1926; or the quiet energy of Gustav Wunderwald's *Underpass (Spandau)* of 1927; or, famously, Alfred Döblin's novel, *Berlin Alexanderplatz*. The latter was transformed by Phil Jutzi into a cinematic experience comparable to Ruttmann's *Sinfonie* shortly after the book's publication in 1929. In all these works, as in Ruttmann's *Sinfonie*, it is the cultural and psychological experiences of the tempo and rhythm of the city *per se* that are the subject of attention, rather than the named place, Berlin.[5]

These artists sought through their work not only to comment upon but also to simulate the urban experience of modernity. In Ruttmann's case, there is a clear alignment between himself and the social engineers of early-twentieth-century Germany. For Ruttmann set out to recreate the totality of the urban experience in his film, in order to fulfil his 'desire ... to build from living material, to create from the millionfold, actually existing bustling energies of the city organism, a pictorially composed analogy of the unity between people and the immediate natural forms that surround them.'[6] This fascination with the total living dynamic of the city extended beyond the narrow artistic confines of the interwar avant-garde to include a new generation of social technocrats. As Dr R. W. Schulte, the head of the Psychological Institute at the Prussian Academy for Physical Training, noted in 1929, 'the tempo and rhythm of our times are embodied in the rapid growth of our traffic, whose regulation poses the Berlin police authorities with extraordinary tasks'.[7] In the *Sinfonie* the fast-flowing traffic of Berlin might *appear* chaotic, but it never is. Instead its constituent and apparently anarchic parts are constantly configured into a single pulsating flow of order as a result of an imperceptible traffic plan, and the regulating presence of the traffic police, who together ensure that the underlying structure of urban-based capitalism remains intact.[8]

Indeed, Schulte, and he was not alone, considered traffic to be the quintessence of the modern experience, and its regulation as the rational means necessary to cool the tempo and harmonize the rhythm of cities in order to avert a collisionary breakdown of the social and economic order that would extend to the nation as a whole. Furthermore, planning the future of traffic would enable administrators, technocrats, and engineers to order and connect individual experiences within and beyond the city according to the current vision of the national goal, thus creating an ever changing and dynamic totality; what Siegfried Kracauer has referred to as 'the mass ornament'.[9]

The first section of this chapter sketches in a brief outline of the development of Germany's traffic in the early twentieth century. The second section deals with some aspects of the reception and regulative responses to traffic. The final section looks at urban traffic's impact on the wider landscape as a cultural expression of the nation, arguing that the traffic experience of the city can be taken as a, if not *the*, paradigm of Germany's modernity during the first half of this century.

The growth in traffic

The hustle and bustle of traffic *per se* has been, of course, a phenomenon of German towns and cities through the ages. But its quality altered from the last quarter of the nineteenth century as a result of increasing urbanization and the introduction of new technology, notably the electric tram.[10] The first electric tram was developed in Germany by the Siemens company in 1879 and introduced to the public at the industry and crafts exhibition of 1881 in Lichterfelde on a stretch of line 2.5 kilometres in length. Within little more than a decade a sister line had been introduced in Hamburg (1894), and henceforth its commercial future seemed assured.

By 1907 there were 225 trams in Germany, the great majority of them electricity-powered, and this number increased more than a hundredfold to 25 000 by 1937.[11] This spectacular growth was matched by the numbers using the system throughout the Reich. From an estimated 2 854 million passengers

Table 1

TRACK AND PASSENGER TRAFFIC ON THE GERMAN TRAM SYSTEM IN 1904, SELECTED CITIES

	track in km	passenger capacity	passengers in millions	carried per km
Berlin*	331.66	100 565	389.2	4.24
Hamburg*	170.42	32 610	136.0	3.63
Dresden	129.57	28 116	79.8	2.96
Leipzig	106.82	20 558	74.7	3.31
Frankfurt/M	46.99	13 100	57.7	4.00
Cologne	71.25	16 732	55.7	3.87
Munich	54.19	21 853	48.5	4.13
Breslau	53.19	24 684	46.6	3.71
Düsseldorf	46.03	10 082	24.3	3.43

*and environs.

Note: Cities ranked by volume of traffic

Adapted from: Adolf Weber, *Die Grossstadt und ihre soziale Probleme*, Leipzig, 1908, p.65.

in 1913, the number of users grew to 3 948 million by 1930 before falling back to 2 956 million during the Depression, only to rise again in the later 1930s.

As we can see from the figures presented in Table 1, a small number of big cities accounted for just over a third of this prewar traffic. This was to change during the 1920s, when the lion's share of passenger traffic became concentrated in the cities. By 1938 approximately 80 per cent of all tram passengers in the country were to be found in the 55 large cities of the Reich (i.e., those with populations of 100 000 and above; the so-called *Grossstädte*). In Berlin, the tram system carried 43 per cent of all passenger traffic in 1933 (estimated at over two million users daily). In Hamburg the number of tram passengers grew steadily until the late 1920s. And in spite of a decline from the early 1930s, they still accounted for over 63 per cent of all passengers using the city's public transport system in 1938 (see Table 2). In Cologne between 1893 and 1904 passengers on the city's tram system increased fivefold to more than 55 million annually, and continued to rise with little interruption to reach around 181 million passengers by 1928.[12]

Table 2

TRACK AND PASSENGER TRAFFIC ON THE GERMAN TRAM SYSTEM IN 1938, SELECTED CITIES

	track in km	passengers carried, in thousands	completed journeys in km
Berlin	573.4	581 545	139 422
Hamburg	227.1	165 590	55 175
Munich	121.1	164 219	40 713
Cologne	175.5	144 064	46 306
Leipzig	144.8	135 237	41 813
Düsseldorf	174.1	128 689	33 248
Dresden	138.7	120 415	35 079
Stuttgart	122.2	120 346	33 543
Frankfurt/M	120.1	105 508	29 367
Breslau	77.5	68 357	15 088

Note: Cities ranked by volume of traffic

From: *Statistiches Jahrbuch deutscher Gemeinden* 35 (1940), pp.185–6.

Meanwhile the volume of motorized road traffic in German towns and cities also had been increasing steadily since the 1890s. However, its dramatic growth and present-day form only took shape in the years following the First World War. Between the end of the inflation period and the mid 1920s, the total number of cars, omnibuses and motorcycles nearly doubled, from around 160 000 to over 300 000. Within ten years there were nearly two million vehicles on Germany's roads.

Not surprisingly, the growth in motorized vehicles was concentrated in the big cities and towns of Germany. By the end of the 1920s, shortly after Ruttmann completed the *Sinfonie*, well over a third of all motor vehicles were to be found in the 48 *Grossstädte*. Broken down into particular types of vehicle, this meant that 42 per cent of all private cars in Germany were to be found in these cities, a third of motorbuses, 48 per cent of commercial vans, and 46 per cent of motorcycles and mopeds.[13] In Berlin at the time of Ruttmann's *Sinfonie*, there were approximately 83 134 motor vehicles, of which 39 291 were private cars, 14 476 commercial vans, and 9 129 taxis. And their number continued to rise inexorably. And although Germany lagged behind other industrialized countries, especially where the private automobile was concerned, the total number of motor vehicles continued to rise dramatically, as it did in other major cities (Table 3).[14]

Although in per capita terms, Berlin had a lower ratio of cars to population, it was none the less here that the sheer volume of road traffic was greatest. A traffic survey of Potsdamer Platz on 28 July 1928 revealed that 33 037 vehicles, more than half of them automobiles, passed the square between 8 a.m. and 8 p.m. That was the equivalent of 46 vehicles per minute (in 1924 it had been 33 vehicles per minute). Another traffic survey conducted a fortnight later at the Gedächtniskirche noted 38 998 vehicles (nearly two-thirds of them automobiles), or the equivalent of 54 vehicles per minute.[15] The volume and tempo of such traffic inspired the poet Georg Goldschlag to write:

> The traffic lights blaze mystically-without-reason.
> After 'Halt' follows 'Go' and after 'Go' 'Halt'.
> At each street corner flow hourly
> ten thousand cars over the asphalt.[16]

Developments in air transportation also quickly came to symbolize the modern city's dynamic role as part of a national and international traffic system.[17] The potential of the air as the highway of the future had already been recognized before the First World War when a number of cities began vying with each other to establish permanent aerodromes designed to develop air transport as the modern successor to the steam train.[18] And an international air race held in 1911 established for the first time the flight paths between thirteen cities in middle and north Germany that would become the routes of commercial air travel in the 1920s.[19]

Table 3

CENSUS OF MOTOR VEHICLES IN SELECTED MAJOR GERMAN CITIES, 1 JULY 1928 AND 1 JULY 1935 (LATTER IN ITALICS)

	private cars	comm. vans	motor cycles	other vehicles	total	inhabitants per vehicle
Berlin	36 215	12 120	27 605	1 719	77 659	54
	75 548	*24 657*	*52 966*	*2 830*	*156 001*	*27*
Hamburg	9 703	3 829	6 811	444	20 737	54
	19 955	*8 733*	*14 587*	*741*	*44 016*	*25*
Cologne	7 843	3 385	4 134	163	15 525	47
	13 027	*4 460*	*8 393*	*332*	*26 212*	*29*
Munich	7 362	3 092	9 258	221	19 933	35
	17 914	*5 255*	*17 914*	*678*	*41 637*	*18*
Frankfurt/M	5 955	2 140	4 589	113	12 797	43
	13 812	*3 351*	*7 601*	*285*	*25 049*	*22*
Leipzig	5 907	2 329	4 954	218	13 408	51
	13 286	*3 947*	*9 935*	*386*	*27 554*	*26*
Dresden	6 984	3 114	7 166	268	15 532	40
	12 085	*4 372*	*9 918*	*421*	*26 796*	*24*
Stuttgart	5 220	2 059	3 314	114	10 706	34
	10 720	*3 272*	*5 783*	*201*	*19 976*	*21*
Königsberg	1 985	669	1 201	81	3 936	74
	4 888	*1 413*	*2 807*	*123*	*9 231*	*35*

From: *Statistisches Jahrbuch des Deutschen Reichs* (1929), p.160, and (1935), p.175.

The potential of air flight was furthered by the war. In its aftermath there were an estimated thirty-eight air companies in existence in the state of Saxony alone, but these were mostly small and uneconomic and eventually ceased operating. In time a larger and more viable company emerged, the Mitteldeutsche Aero-Lloyd, on 10 October 1924 in Leipzig. Its aim was to ensure 'with all necessary speed, corresponding to Leipzig's economic importance, that [the city] would be connected to the existing air traffic network'.[20] As in the case of road, rail and waterway networks, a fully developed air network would bind local and regional economies together into the emerging unitary system forming the modern map of Germany.

By the end of the 1920s, there were still about a dozen regional companies, though some of these were subsidiaries of the Deutsche Lufthansa. The importance attached to air traffic in this period was reflected in the financial involvement of municipal authorities in developing air transportation. For instance, the city of Frankfurt am Main took a 37 per cent share of the

Südwestdeutsche Luftverkehrs A.G.; Dortmund was heavily involved in the Luftverkehrs A.G., Westfalen, as too was Hannover in the Luftverkehrs A.G., Niedersachsen; Augsburg in Bavaria had a majority share of 66 per cent in the Schwäbisch-Bayerische Fluggesellschaft m.b.H.[21]

The Deutsche Lufthansa A.G., created in 1926 after the merger of Deutsche Aero Lloyd A.G. and Junkers Luftverkehr A.G., arose from this context of municipal interest in an intercity air network; and the company depended to a large degree on municipal subsidies for its survival. By 1927, these totalled approximately 2 356 212 Reichsmarks. The largest financial contributors were Cologne, Frankfurt and Bremen, followed by Munich, Magdeburg, Muhlheim, Essen and Kassel, some of which also enjoyed a vigorous air traffic (Table 4). At the beginning of the Depression, when the cities began to reconsider their involvement, German local authorities had a total investment of 8.5 million marks, accounting for 35 per cent of the company's shares. The cities had thirteen of the sixty-three seats on the company's supervisory board, and the Lord Mayor of Cologne, Konrad Adenauer, was deputy chairman.[22]

By the end of the 1920s most of Germany's cities and larger towns had developed air links with one another, or with national and regional capitals abroad. Moreover, they were heavily involved in expanding aerodromes into fully-fledged and modern airports capable of meeting the needs of a flying public.[23] Between 1919 and 1928 the volume of air traffic rose dramatically from just over two thousand passengers to nearly a quarter of million, of which about half were handled by just eight major airports (See Table 4).[24]

While electric trams, underground trains, and petrol-powered motor engines for land and air use represented a technological modernization of

Table 4

AIR TRAFFIC IN SELECTED GERMAN CITIES, 1929

	flight departures	passengers: arriving	departing	total passengers
Berlin	4 961	15 628	15 823	31 451
Cologne	3 874	8 498	7 842	16 340
Frankfurt/M	3 273	7 980	7 228	15 208
Munich	2 248	7 166	7 600	14 766
Halle/Leipzig	3 734	6 927	6 550	13 477
Hamburg	2 563	6 464	6 245	12 709
Hannover	3 517	5 378	4 811	10 189
Stuttgart	2 037	4 811	5 009	9 820

From: *Statistisches Jahrbuch des Deutschen Reichs* (1929), p.164.

the urban traffic experience, they were by no means the only traffic moving around in Germany's cities. Horse-drawn vehicles were much in evidence in 1900 and were still widely used in the city of the 1920s, and even as late as 1939, as is all too evident from Ruttmann's film – and its pale copy, *Symphony der Weltstadt*, by Leo de Laforgúe. The bicycle, as a functional vehicle rather than as a leisure item, gained in popularity among the working class as a cheap and efficient means of transport in the 1920s; and Robert Walser's fictional diarist, Jakob von Gunten, noted at the turn of the century: 'The people, children, girls, men and elegant women, the aged and cripples, walk pressed close next to the wheels of carriages.' (See also p. 223.) For Germany's cities, like those elsewhere in Europe, were still largely 'walked', conforming to the ebb and flow of the rhythm of the city in the first half of this century. And in Ruttmann's film the workday commences with early morning scenes of first a trickle and then a flood of workers making their way on foot to the factories.[25]

These diverse elements of city traffic: trains, trams, omnibuses, automobiles, aeroplanes, bicycles, animal-drawn carriages and pedestrians, are drawn together in Ruttmann's *Sinfonie* into a mass urban spectacle of continuous rhythmic movement. The mélée and scale of traffic in these scenes is often overpowering, always vibrant to the eye and frequently chaotic, before ultimately subsiding into an ordered urban space. The next section looks at the experience of traffic as chaos and the search for the ordered urban space.

Ordering the chaos

For several decades after the publication in 1903 of the German sociologist Georg Simmel's seminal essay 'The Metropolis and Mental Life', contemporaries believed that the myriad impressions of street life assaulting the city dweller's sensory system heightened the nervous condition of the individual, and by extension, that of society at large.[26] The city's nervous energy bubbled and boiled until it spilled over in an uncontrollable flood, destroying all in its path, before finally exhausting itself. In *Sinfonie* this nervousness is portrayed by a number of motifs: the rollercoaster ride; newspaper headlines flashing murder and economic collapse; a woman's suicide; a sudden storm; spirals; restless and physically spent animals; dogs fighting; and an argument between two pedestrians, presumably in an intensified nervous condition. In this latter scene, in particular, the brawl threatens to engulf the whole street, until a uniformed *Schupo* (policeman) intervenes. The transition from order to disorder represented in this scene mirrors contemporary fears of what might if the crowded urban space remained unregulated. Here,

Ruttmann inverts the German *Der/Die/Das* into *Das/Die/Der: Das Volk, Die Menge, Der Pöbel* (the people, the crowd, the mob),[27] signifying a transformation of a rationally ordered society into the irrational arena of the threatening mob. In 1927, this was not too distant an analogy of the events of the revolution that had shaken Germany's cities barely ten years before.

Regulating the space of the street, therefore, might act as a conduit for instilling public order within the population. For in the absence of immediately obvious and coercive means, it befell civic authorities to organize traffic in such a way as to calm the frayed nerves of the population by imposing order upon the streets. Whether as pedestrians or motorists, people were expected to follow traffic signals and norms, keep to the right; stop and go as lights or the traffic police dictated, and if travelling by public transport, to embark and disembark in an orderly fashion. Eventually traffic etiquette would become part of their everyday cognitive processes, so that all users behaved as part of the traffic system naturally.

> The German citizen needed to find something to replace compulsory military service. For a while, our housing-offices seemed like a good bet, but they didn't quite fill the bill. The athletic-clubs were a good possibility. The army had become too small. So a few able public servants travelled to America and to London. They came, they saw, they took notes – the substitute was found. German traffic regulations now replace universal military service.[28]

Although one need not agree entirely with the Communist writer Kurt Tucholsky, who saw in Germany's traffic regulations a substitute for military service, the presence of social disciplining via a developing etiquette of the road was clearly evident at the time. And for good reason.

Left to itself, traffic in the modern city also threatened to engulf society in a different but equally dangerous anarchy of metal and flesh. By the early 1900s the number of traffic accidents was already rising at a disturbing pace, doubling between 1907 and 1913 to 11 785 incidents. But after the First World War reported accidents increased at a staggering rate, reaching over a quarter of a million by 1937 (266 394). More importantly, road fatalities during this same period took on alarming proportions: rising from a mere 145 in 1907 to 7 636 in 1937 (after peaking at 8 388 in 1936).[29]

A publication of the Reich Statistical Office revealed that in the decade between 1927 and 1936 a total of 76 000 persons had been killed on the road. Given the rise in road accidents and fatalities relative to car ownership, it is not surprising that Richard Bessel comes to the conclusion that driving habits in Germany 'left a lot to be desired'.[30] Indeed, the level of fatalities prompted Hitler himself to interject in the traffic debate commenting that road fatalities since 1933 exceeded the number of German soldiers killed in the Franco-Prussian war.[31]

Around two-thirds of all road accidents took place within urban conurbations. But while larger cities such as Berlin, Hamburg, Leipzig, Munich and Cologne inevitably took the lion's share of accidents, the big city was not the inevitable arena for the worst statistics. In 1937, for instance, more people were killed in road accidents in the countryside than in urban areas.[32] Nevertheless, road deaths became a byword for the modern urban experience, and the phenomenon was seized upon by its detractors. Attention was paid to Berlin in particular, where the number of road accidents and fatalities increased steadily after 1933.[33] Richard Korherr, a Berlin statistician, described the 218 killed and 11 755 injured on the streets of Berlin in 1930 as the audit of a 'silent civil war', moving the writer Walter Kordt to ask, 'and of the many dead, do you know their names?'[34] And nine years later the Nazi ideologue, Gottfried Feder, saw in the roads of Germany's big cities infernos that consumed the German *Volk*, especially those in the prime of life (Table 5).[35]

Table 5

PEDESTRIAN VICTIMS OF ROAD ACCIDENTS IN BERLIN ACCORDING TO AGE, 1932–33

age	1932		1933	
	No.	per cent	No.	per cent
0–6	257	6.5	220	5.9
7–14	419	10.5	367	9.9
15–60	2 452	61.8	2 286	61.7
over 60	842	21.2	833	22.5
totals	3 970	100	3 706	100

From: *Statistisches Jahrbuch der Stadt Berlin* Vol. 10 (1934), pp.150–51

In the overwhelming majority of accidents, the drivers of vehicles were to blame, though cyclists and pedestrians too might be at fault, usually for not paying enough attention to traffic. In Leipzig, for instance, the police reported in 1925 that not only drivers, but pedestrians too, displayed a shocking 'lack of discipline'.[36] The cause of accidents was frequently attributed to a lack of road education: for instance, failure to give hand signals, or to indicate if one was turning or changing one's position in the road; pedestrians oblivious to oncoming vehicles and, in particular, reckless driving.

Reckless behaviour arising from a lack of courtesy for fellow road users was not a new driving trait in interwar Germany. For example, the *Münchener Neueste Nachrichten* reported in December 1907 the death of a four-year-old boy, knocked down by a van whose driver was not paying attention and was speeding.[37] In the interwar years the fascination with tempo seemed to be producing a pathological urgency for traffic to go ever faster, as depicted here by Goldschlag:

> General Motors – Daimler – Horch – Mercedes –
> Studebaker – Chrysler – Opel – Fiat – Ford –
> with trembling flanks each waits
> for freedom and a new speed record.
>
> The light is red. Pedestrians migrate
> before the vehicles at a common trot.
>
> The traffic cop separates one from the other
> only with a gesture, like a god of old.
>
> Surrounded by the power of the flood
> alone his outline raging in the tempest.
> The light turns green. A chaos is unleashed.
> Movement lurches onto the open track.
>
> In changing rhythm the mechanism hammers.
> Pandemonium and standstill. A lull and frenzy.
> Repressed waiting. Breathless panic.
> The track closes itself off. And the road is free.[38]

In Stuttgart drivers had speeding down to a fine art with vehicles racing across the city's intersections without regard for crossing vehicles or pedestrians. This probably accounts for the fact that these locations were the scene of nearly a third of road accidents in Stuttgart until the early thirties (Table 6).

Table 6

ROAD ACCIDENTS IN STUTTGART, 1932–34

	number of accidents	at cross-roads	number of vehicles on 1 June
1932	3 062	1 191	11 714
1933	3 334	1 136	13 646
1934 (1 Oct)	2 171	696	16 268

From: Staatsarchiv Dresden, MdI 14605, Richtlinien 'Kampf den Larm' (1935).

Stuttgart's problem was endemic to many cities. Königsberg's police president, Schoene, had to request the local party chief (*Kreisleiter*) in October 1936 to ensure that his officials kept to the traffic regulations: 'Unfortunately it must be noted that precisely the vehicles of the authorities and party officials are conspicuous by their immoderately fast and inattentive driving, and for ignoring traffic regulations (especially the "give way" rule), and for *sounding car horns unnecessarily.*'[39]

Such road behaviour elicited from a *Times* correspondent the following observation: 'One sometimes wonders whether it is a fundamental German characteristic to be insensitive about anybody or anything that is in the way.'[40] In Ruttmann's *Sinfonie* cars change lane at will and at high speed, and pedestrians are seen risking their lives crossing the road. What seemed clear to all concerned was that in a period of population decline, road casualties were a worrying aspect of the city, and threatened the nation as a whole. The problem thus demanded a response from the civic authorities.

The authorities in Germany had, in fact, been making efforts to combat the problem since the turn of the century. Traffic chaos could only be countered by the all-pervasive presence of the traffic policeman who, as Ruttmann repeatedly suggests in his film, could orchestrate the flows on the ground according to some invisible score. In an era of New Objectivity, the police saw themselves as 'technicians' of modernity and 'educators' of the public, 'making driving circles aware through training and warnings of their legal obligations'.[41] One newspaper put it more succinctly: 'Where there is traffic, the police dictate.'[42]

At local level this took the form of by-laws governing road use, while at Länder and Reich level initiatives were undertaken – like the inter-Länder conference of police chiefs in Berlin during the early spring of 1925 – to devise new technologies more fitting for a modern road system. The Reich transport minister hoped that through a systematization of traffic codes and signs a much-needed nationwide regulatory matrix could be put in place that would educate the public to be better and more disciplined drivers and pedestrians.[43]

At this same meeting, August Kirchner, the police president of Altona, unsuccessfully called for a regulation whereby pedestrians would keep to the right of the pavement, instead of using any part of it at will. Such a measure had already been tried in Munich at the turn of the century, but had made little headway among the public. As one of the city's local newspapers reported in 1911: 'In general, the *Münchner* walks along the pavement where the fancy takes him at that moment, without any concern for his fellow citizen or himself.'[44] Judging from anecdotal evidence, there was little change in the habits of pedestrians over the following decades. Drivers in Königsberg also seemed stubbornly inured to all attempts at traffic education, as the following comments from that city's police president indicate:

The dangers that continuing motorization brings to Königsberg with its difficult road conditions, can only be reduced to a bearable level through a stern road discipline and mutual consideration of all road users. For months I have been trying, with all the means to hand, to influence the population, especially van drivers, educationally.[45]

Indeed, it is debatable if there was any marked improvement among road users in general until the 1950s (and even if then), in spite of regulative attempts.[46]

But in spite of this, the all-pervasive presence of the traffic policeman as educator and disciplinarian was clearly entering into public consciousness by the end of the 1920s. Commenting on a series of lectures on traffic safety by Berlin's police president, Dr Weiss, the psychologist Dr Schulte noted how 'The regulation of Berlin's traffic has sought from the beginning to bring the administrative regulation of traffic through psychological laws into harmony with the mental condition of the city population as far as possible.'[47] It may be that there the authorities were having better results than elsewhere, especially among children, for

Stage and film, radio and school, press and exhibitions have embedded the activity of the traffic police in the new Germany, and especially in the new Berlin, so strongly, that the child's playfight between cops and robbers already has today become our smallest official act: the friendly arm movement of the traffic police.[48]

The same simple arm movement recurs regularly in Ruttmann's film.[49]

In *Sinfonie*, as in *Berlin Alexanderplatz* and Gerhard Lamprecht's film version of Erich Kaestner's *Emil und die Detektive* (1931), the cacophonous sounds of the city, including the sound of a car horn, are important for the daily structuring and mapping of the urban experience. For Ruttmann, in a literal sense, 'sounds become images' (*Geräusche werden Bilder*). Thus Edmund Meisel's musical score represents the 'conglomeration of all the sounds of a metropolis', while the recurring *allegro con fuoco* depicts the dynamic and rhythm of the traffic in particular. And in order to recreate the totality of the soundscape of the city, Meisel placed the orchestra in different parts of the cinema so as to wrap the audience in sound.[50] Not only was there the visual montage of images, but Meisel produced something similar in sound. Thus the experience of traffic as a 'total experience' (*Gesamterlebnis*) was stated in an artistic style appropriate to early-twentieth-century modernity.

But sound was not always perceived so favourably. During the 1920s, in tandem with theories on nervousness, the noise of the city became increasingly pathologized. The growth in the volume of traffic on the roads and in the air inevitably led to a rise in the overall level of noise from engines.

The police intermittently carried out crackdowns against (mostly youthful) drivers of motorcycles who had removed the silencers from their machines in the belief that this enhanced performance, when in fact all it enhanced was noise. Similarly, the increasing use of low-flying aeroplanes in the mid 1920s led to complaints from citizens who found their daily peace disrupted. In particular, the gratuitous use of the car horn (as noted briefly by Königsberg's police president Schoene in his bulletin quoted on p.219), was a cause of complaint, as one driver from the village of Naunhof near Leipzig, found to his cost. His familial signal on returning home led to a bitter legal fight with one of his neighbours who alleged that indiscriminate use of the car horn was a source of irritation and disturbed the quiet of the evening.[51]

Individual efforts were made in some cities to combat the problem. In September 1932 the city authorities in Stuttgart inaugurated a four-week experiment to combat the clamour generated by the unnecessary sounding of horns and careless driving (the two were thought to be linked), so as to bring about calmer traffic and more considerate street behaviour. The police issued six guidelines, including rules on the proper use of warning signals and the car horn, but extended its remit to urban noise in general. It published the guidelines in the press for a period of a week before setting up controls around the city. For three weeks the public were 'educated' and 'warned', after which miscreants faced stiff penalties. The experiment was to be repeated half-yearly until it was no longer required. The city still found itself exhorting the public in 1935:

> The measure 'Combat Noise' wants to educate the German people in a new morality of composure [Ruhemoral]. It addresses itself therefore to every people's comrade and shows them how they continuously violate the environment in their professional and non-professional activity, partly unconsciously and partly through neglect. The possibility is provided through a functional division of the spheres of factory, house and traffic noise, to enlighten in equal measure the factory engineer, the housewife, the motorcyclist, the car mechanic, the radio listener, the pianist, the worker and the clerical employee, how they in their profession and otherwise, must help to maintain the health of their people's comrades:
>
> Instead of hand on the horn: foot on the brake.[52]

Nonetheless, some progress was registered in the city. Already in 1934 the Stuttgart police reported a general calming of traffic, fewer frayed tempers, the disappearance of reckless speeding over crossroads (where traffic lights were absent), and a fall in casualties in proportion to the rise in road vehicles (Table 6).

Traffic and the national consciousness

Much of the literary discourse on the experience of the modern city refers to its alienating quality. Walser's fictional diarist Jakob von Gunten, describes the sensory imprisonment and loss of identity of the individual in the crowd at the turn of the century thus:

> What shoving and crushing, what a rattle and patter! What yelling, stamping, humming and buzzing! And everything so squashed together.... New crowds press their way into the existing crowd, and it goes, comes, appears and proceeds as one.... And one thinks of unknown streets, invisible new and equally overpeopled neighbourhoods ... what is one really in this flood, in this never-ending stream of humanity?[53]

Indeed, a reading of Ruttmann's montage of the early morning commuters spilling out from the trams, metropolitan train and underground systems en route to work, might suggest that he wished to underline this alienating quality of urban modernity more than twenty years later. In these scenes Ruttmann's cross-sectioning of individual bodies into brief filmcuts of heads, legs, feet, or simply the backs of people, mirrors their displaced experience of the modern city.[54] But the atomization of the individual in the mass of the city was a superficial one. For, like the vehicles, individuals, as we have seen, also form the component parts of city traffic: collectively directed by traffic signs, regulations, and police hand signals. Ruttmann thus orchestrates them into Kracauer's 'mass ornament'.

Commuters, carried by the rail or tram tracks and the arterial roads, advanced upon the city in symmetrical lines and once within the city limits circulated in geometric spheres, both movements forming a grid that contained and controlled the energies of the metropolis that furthered its economic wellbeing.[55] This was visible in cities such as Cologne and Chemnitz where before the First World War fully-developed tram systems were integrated into regional networks configuring the travelling experience into a geometric form (see Figure 12.1).[56]

During the 1920s newer residential areas on the outskirts of cities were linked either by extensions of the underground network, or the tram system, and, from the later 1920s, increasingly by motor buses. Thus in Frankfurt am Main the Römerstadt estate, located on the northern outskirts of the city at Praunheim-Niddatal, was linked to the city centre by the No.18 tramline from 1927; the estate at Riederhof-West was served daily by the No.18 and No. 32 trams and by the new motorbuses; while the No. 2 and No. 34 trams ran on an axis along the Erschersheimer Landstrasse to the centre (Westbahnhof) also linking the suburbs of Bornheim and Ginnheim to the north. In Berlin, the Siemensstadt to the north-west of the city was linked by a purpose-built underground connection, making the Siemensdamm a 'busy urban boulevard a mere 20 minutes from the centre'. And Onkel Toms Hütte (south-west) and the Britzsiedlung (south-east) were also 'developed on extensions of the U-Bahn system.'[57] These transport networks were the nervous sinews of the (sub)urban 'spinal columns' that stretched their 'long fingers... into the countryside' (see Figure 12.2).[58]

Thus the emerging modern transport technology facilitated the easy conquest of space (and time), while the emerging traffic systems, founded on the new science of urban planning, unified the city's fragmented parts, as well as connecting it to its hinterland. In a period when incorporations were producing what Oswald Spengler referred to as 'megapolises' of a never-ending new and foreign landscape, the new rational transport systems also allowed the individual to decipher and map the city, both physically and mentally, in a new way. The modern integrated transport system, it was believed, would achieve the sort of national unity that politics had failed to deliver:

In all areas of modern communications the individual radial transport networks, with their strong concentration around various individual centres,... reveal the transport unity.... People, places and states which through the power-political wills and power-political boundaries, have been until now unnaturally and forcibly hindered in their natural-inclined communal life, have been finally brought closer together again by the technology of our day in a matchlessly modern conquest of space and time. Thus a spatial reconfiguration of the greatest scale has been unleashed over the whole of Germany.[59]

Thus the explicit aim of the modern traffic system in the interwar period was to further the integration of Germany. The 1920s saw the continued rationalization of Germany's urban transport companies into unitary, publicly-owned enterprises that allowed radial traffic systems to emerge.[60] This rationalization paralleled a movement in the economy and meant that the country's social and economic energies could be directed from a nodal point of national purpose. As a result it was not just the physical map of the city and country that altered as roads were widened or developed, pushing back human habitation and nature, or as new industrial technology allowed for the surface flesh to be cut into to allow new underground arteries to come into existence or motorways and bridges to span the landscape. As with steam trains in the nineteenth century, the development of a modern traffic system eventually impinged mentally upon the individual, creating a new consciousness of being a *participant* in a revived Germany.[61]

For the new mental map of the German city was not confined to its immediate borders. In the opening scenes of Ruttmann's *Sinfonie*, the trains, hotels and air transport emphasize Berlin's centrality not only as a *Grossstadt* in Germany, but also as a *Weltstadt*. The new 185-kilometre long Berlin ring road, more than two-thirds of which was completed by December 1938, was not only an achievement of modern technology and planning. The ring situated Berlin at the hub of Germany by linking it via the 2 014 kilometres of new motorway system, to the regions (see Figure 12.3, i, ii).[62] To be a Berliner in the 1920s was to be at the hub of a modern world system, connected through a new national transport network of roads and air, and at whose centre, symbolically, at least, was Alexanderplatz, Berlin's own nodal point (see Figure 12.4).

At the opening of the 7th International Roads Congress, held in Munich on 3 September 1934, Rudolf Hess told those assembled that the architecture and scale of the new motorways reflected a technology that 'corresponded to the level of culture (*Kulturstufe*) of the German people. We hold the simple monumentalism (*schlichte Monumentalität*) and functionalism for that artistic form corresponding to the spirit of the age.'[63] And their intended function was indeed to embody the spirit of the age. The motorways, like the *Land-* and *Schnellstrassen* of the 1920s, held out the expectation that they would 'bind the German tribes' firstly within Germany itself – so that any 'region as a whole can be closely connected to the rest of the Fatherland'[64] – and subsequently, as an emerging national unit, into the larger geography of middle Europe.

Individual drivers could now move beyond the local horizon and connect as individuals within a larger German *Heimat*. Through car and motorway the nation could be served in its discovery of itself as well as mobilized in the conquest of space.[65] For quite apart from the popular emphasis upon driving as a leisure activity, or the obvious implications which road construction had for the economy, the road building programme of the 1930s functioned in much the same way as the development of air traffic in its contribution to a new self-awareness of a national and continental identity.[66] As the *Times* correspondent commented in his report, 'Lessons of the Road' in 1938,

> If an Englishman wishes to begin to understand German instincts in international affairs there is another lesson which he must let the roads of Germany teach him. All of them, except northwards, lead eventually to that curious barrier resembling a level crossing gate, that national fact of which we English have no experience – a land frontier with foreign country beyond.[67]

Conclusion

While in 1927 some cultural critics marvelled at the sheer verve and technical accomplishment of Ruttmann's *Sinfonie*, others found the montage of a multitude of associative, quickly-alternating scenes an alienating and superficial portrayal of Berlin, reducing the city to the sum total of 'soulless ornaments' devoid of living content, as critics from Siegfried Kracauer to Barry Fulks have argued.[68] Indeed, Kracauer, citing the Russian filmmaker, V. I. Pudowkin, who accused Ruttmann of a dilettantist use of montage as a substitute for 'inner order', was scathing about the film for 'showing much' but 'revealing nothing'. According to Kracauer, the *Sinfonie* signalled 'paralysis' because of its 'apolitical nature' (*Haltungslosigkeit*) in adopting an 'ambiguous neutrality', resulting in a lack of comment on the real Berlin of the 1920s, namely the conditions and everyday life of its inhabitants. Instead, Kracauer argues, Ruttmann

> lets thousands of details stand unconnected next to one another and introduces mostly freely thought-up linkages which are devoid of content. At most the film is based on the idea that Berlin is a city of tempo and work – a formal idea which certainly does not provide a content and, perhaps for this reason, intoxicates the German petty bourgeois in society and literature. Nothing is seen in this Symphony because not a single meaningful connection is exposed by it.[69]

To be sure, Ruttmann's apparently arbitrary and hasty montage of automated production processes and office interiors, of streams of anonymous and silent commuters disgorging onto platforms, of street scenes of shoppers and pulsating traffic, of mass leisure activities and the night-time revelry of the big city, suggest the substitution of the individual-oriented *Gemeinschaft* (community) for the commercial and sexual nexus of the atomized *Gesellschaft* (society). The *Sinfonie* on first reading conveys the visible chaos of the metropolis, familiar to us from George Grosz's portrayals between 1917 and 1919, and the silent alienation of Herbert Bayer's collage, *Lonely Metropolitan* (1932).[70] But, as I have argued, rather than being empty of content, Ruttmann's *Sinfonie* addressed the very connections that were emerging in German society in the early part of this century but which critics, such as Kracauer, were unable, or unprepared, to see.

The re-reading of cultural statements, such as the *Sinfonie*, and the social historical analysis of contextualized contemporary concerns, allows us to reconstruct the experience of the city in early twentieth-century Germany as mediated through its traffic. In this chapter I have argued that Ruttmann's film can be re-read as a part of a codex of 'signs' (Benjamin) pointing to how the experience of traffic emerged as a defining paradigm of German modernity in the first half of this century.

Notes

1. For the background to the film and for biographical details of Ruttmann, see Jeanpaul Goergen, *Walter Ruttmann. Eine Dokumentation*, Berlin: Freunde der Deutschen Kinamathek, 1989.

2. William Charles Urrichio, 'Ruttmann's "Berlin" and the city film to 1930', PhD thesis, New York University, New York, 1982; Sabine Hake, 'Urban Spectacle in Walter Ruttmann's *Berlin: Symphony of the Big City*', in Thomas W. Kniesche & Stephen Brockmann (eds), *Dancing on the Volcano. Essays on the Culture of the Weimar Republic*, Columbia SC: Camden House, 1994, pp.127–42.

3. Horst Matzerath (ed.), *Stadt und Verkehr im Industriezeitalter*, Cologne, Weimar, and Vienna: Böhlau, 1996; Erik Eckermann, *Vom Dampfwagen zum Auto. Motorisierung des Verkehrs*, Reinbek: Rowohlt, 1989; Richard J. Overy, 'Heralds of Modernity: Cars and Planes from invention to necessity', in Mikulás Teich and Roy Porter (eds), *Fin de Siècle and its legacy*, Cambridge: Cambridge University Press, 1990; Philip Gassert, *Amerika im Dritten Reich: Ideologie, Propaganda und Volksmeinung 1933–1945*, Stuttgart: Steiner, 1997, pp.151–8; Winfried Nerdinger, 'Modernisierung, Bauhaus, Nationalsozialismus', in idem (ed), *Bauhaus-Moderne im Nationalsozialismus. Zwischen Anbiederung und Verfolgung*, Munich, 1993, pp.9–23.

4. Hildegard Glass, 'Responses to the urban challenge in German utopian literature 1871–1914', PhD thesis, University of Texas at Austin, Texas, 1992. See the illustration 'Zukunftsvision von Arpad Schmidhammer: Münchner Straßenbild im Jahre 1900', in Reinhard Bauer, Günther Gerstenberg and Wolfgang Peschel (eds), *Im Dunst aus Bier, Rauch und Volk, Arbeit und Leben in München von 1840 bis 1945. Ein Lesebuch*, Munich: Piper, 1989, p.77.

5. László Moholy-Nagy, 'Dynamik der Grossstadt. Skizze zu einem Film', in idem, *Malerei, Photographie, Film*, Munich, 1925, pp.114–29; Goergen, *Walter Ruttmann*, pp.28, 61.

6. Goergen, *Walter Ruttmann*, p.92.

7. Dr R. W. Schulte, Leiter des Psychologischen Instituts der Preußischen Hochschule für Leibesübungen, 'Die Psychotechnik im Dienste der Verkehrspolizei', in *Das neue Berlin*, 1929, Heft 11, reprint Berlin, 1988, pp.224–6.

8. A process that one German sociologist, writing in a different context, refers to as *Ordnungschaffend*. Ludwig Neundörfer, *Die Angestellten. Neuer Versuch einer Standortbestimmung*, Stuttgart: Ferdinand Enke Verlag,1961, p.9; David Harvey, *The Urban Experience*, Oxford: Blackwell, 1989.

9. Siegfried Kracauer, *Das Ornament der Masse*, Frankfurt a. Main: Suhrkamp, 1977.

10. See the contributions in Matzerath, *Stadt und Verkehr*.

11. Fritz Voigt, *Verkehr*, Zweiter Band Zweite Hälfte: Die Entwicklung des Verkehrsystems, Berlin, 1965, pp.671–2. Of the 225 streetcars in Germany in 1907, 189 were electric, 14 were steam powered and 22 were horse powered.

12. *Statistisches Jahrbuch für das Deutsche Reich* (hereafter StJBDR), 1938, p.243; *Statistiches Jahrbuch der Stadt Köln*, Vol. 19, 1930, p.111; Voigt, *Verkehr*, 681.

13. *Statistisches Jahrbuch Deutscher Städte* (hereafter StJBDS), 26, Berlin, 1931, p.240.

14. Figures taken and rounded from following volumes of StJBDR: 1926, 1929, 1935.

15. Richard Korherr, in the *Süddeutsche Monatshefte*, 1930, cited in Klaus Strohmeyer (ed.), *Berlin in Bewegung Literarischer Spaziergang*, vol. 2: *Die Stadt*, Reinbek: Rowohlt, 1987, pp.138–9.

16. George W. Goldschlag, 'City', in Robert Seitz and Heinz Zucker (eds), *Um uns die Stadt 1931. Eine Anthologie neuer Grosstadtdichtung*, orig. Berlin 1931, reprint with a foreword by Ulrich Conrads, Der Bauwelt Fundamente 75, Braunschweig, Wiesbaden, 1986, pp.173–4.

17. Peter Fritzsche, *A Nation of Fliers. German Aviation and the Popular Imagination*, Cambridge, Mass.: Harvard University Press, 1992.

18. Staatsarchiv Dresden (hereafter STAD) MdI Nr.1507, Bl. 18: Sitzung des Ehrenausschusses für die Dresdener Flugtage im Mai 1911, [Sonderdruck] 13 Jan. 1911; see also the report by the Chemnitz Verein für Luftfahrt to Staatsminister Dr. Beck, Dresden, 18 May 1911 in the same file.

19. Landeshauptarchiv Koblenz, 403/12121 Luftschiffahrt 1909–14, Bl. 69–89. StJBDS 22 Berlin, 1927, 506–7.

20. STAD MdI 15118, Luftschiffahrt Mitteldeutsche Aero-Lloyd, Leipzig; and Saxony Landtag, Dresden, 15 May 1925.

21. StJBDS 26 Berlin, 1931, p.254.

22. Landesarchiv Berlin (hereafter LAB StB) 142/I 3515: 'Die Subventierung des deutschen Luftverkehrs durch die Kommunen 1927'; Arbeitsauschuss der deutschen regionalen Luftverkehrsgesellschaften Frankfurt-am-Main, 19 February 1930 to the Präsidium des DST, 'Zu Punkt 2 der Tagesordnung: Vertretung des Deutschen Städtetages in der Deutschen Lufthansa'; Deutscher Städtetag, 'Vermerk über die Besprechung am 21. Februar 1930 in München über Luftverkehrsfragen'.

23. Deutsche Lufthansa A.G., *Betriebsmitteilungen*, Vol. 11, No. 3, 31 March 1927: 'Das Streckennetz 1927 der Deutschen Luft Hansa'; StJBDS 26 Berlin, 1931, pp.252–3; *The National Geographic Magazine*, Vol. LXXI, No. 2, Washington, February 1937, 131, 154.

24. Deutsche Lufthansa A. G., *Betriebsmitteilungen*, 'Der deutsche Luftverkehr im Sommer 1927', Table: Die Entwicklung des deutschen Luftverkehrs 1919–26; StJBDR 1926, p.106; StJBDR 1929, pp.163–4.

25. Leo de Laforgúe, *Symphony der Weltstadt: Berlin*, orig. 1939, re-released, Berlin West, 1950; Richard van der Borght, *Das Verkehrswesen*, Leipzig, 1925, p.163, 166; See the opening bicycle scenes in Slatan Dudow and Kurt Brecht's film *Kuhle Wampe oder Wem gehört die Welt*; Richard Bessel, 'Transport', in Colin Chant (ed.), *Science, Technology and Everyday Life 1870–1950*, London: Routledge, 1989, p.163.

26. Georg Simmel, 'Die Grossstädte und das Geistesleben', *Jahrbuch der Gehe-Stiftung zu Dresden*, 9, 1903, pp.227–42, translated as 'The Metropolis and Mental Life', in: Kurt Wolff (ed.), *The Sociology of Georg Simmel*, New York: Free Press of Glencoe, 1950, p.420. Joachim Radkau, 'Die wilhelminische Ära als "nervöses Zeitalter", oder: die Nerven als Netzwerk zwischen Tempo- und Körpergeschichte', in *Geschichte und Gesellschaft*, Vol. 20, 1994, pp.211–41.

27. John Czaplicka, 'Pictures of a City at Work, Berlin circa 1890–1930: Visual Reflections on Social Structures and Technology in the Modern Urban Construct', in Charles W. Haxthausen and Heidrun Suhr (eds), *Berlin. Culture and Metropolis*, Minneapolis and London: University of Minnesota Press, 1990, pp.18–19.

28. Kurt Tucholsky, 'Traffic Regulations' in *Deutschland, Deutschland über alles*, 1929, trans. Anne Halley with an afterword and notes by Harry Zahn, Amherst: University of Massachusetts Press, 1972, p.193.

29. Statistisches Bundesamt Wiesbaden, *Bevölkerung und Wirtschaft 1872–1972*, Stuttgart and Mainz, 1972, p.206.

30. Bessel, 'Transport', p.182.

31. Hermann Glaser, *Das Automobil. Eine Kulturgeschichte in Bildern*, Munich: Beck, 1986, pp.35–6.

32. StJBDR 1938, pp.241–2.

33. *Statistisches Jahrbuch der Stadt Berlin* (hereafter StJBB), Vol. 10, 1934, p.274; StJBDR 1938, p.242.

34. Korherr, cited in *Berlin in Bewegung*, p.139; Walter Kordt, 'Die Kantate der Gelassenheit' in Seitz and Zucker, *Um uns die Stadt*, p.62.

35. Gottfried Feder, *Die Neue Stadt. Versuch der Begründung einer neuen Stadtplanungskunst aus der sozialen Struktur der Bevölkerung*, Berlin, 1939, p.24.

36. STAD MdI 13819, 'Bericht über die Leipziger Verkehrsfragen unter Berücksichtigung der Messe in erster Linies der Technischen Messe', 13 May 1925, p.29; StJBB, Vol. 10, 1934, pp.150–51; Paul Roggatz, 'Die Strasse im Sozialen Wohnungsbau – Ihre Aufgaben und Ihre Kostendeckung', in *Der Soziale Wohnungsbau in Deutschland*, 2 Jg., Heft 3, 1 February 1942, pp.82–8, reprinted in Tilman Harlander and Gerhard Fehl (eds), *Hitlers Sozialer Wohnungsbau 1940–1945, Wohnungspolitik, Baugestaltung und Siedlungsplanung*, Hamburg: Christians, 1986, p.240.

37. *Münchener Neueste Nachrichten*, Nr. 56, 4 December 1907.

38. Excerpted from Goldschlag, 'City'.

39. GSt APK XX HA Rep 240 C58d, NSDAP Kreisleitung Lötzen – an allen OG und St.P. Leiter Lötzen, 15 October 1936. Italics are original. I am indebted to Dr Liz Harvey for this source.

40. *The Times*, 3 October 1938: 'A Picture of Germany'.

41. STAD MdI 14605, Dresden Polizeipräs. 10 August 1931; Staatsarchiv Munich (hereafter STAM) 944, *Frankfurter Zeitung* 357, I Morgenblatt, 24 December 1908.

42. *Deutsche Tageszeitung* Nr. 25, 15 January 1929: 'Die Verkehrspolizei der Luft'.

43. STAD MdI 13819, Bl. 24–57, 'Der Reichsverkehrsminister, L.3.1200/25 in Berlin', 9 May 1925.

44. *Neueste-Nachrichten Generalanzeiger*, Nr.30, 19 January 1911.

45. NSDAP Kreisleitung Lötzen, op.cit.
46. See, for instance, the contributions in *Der Verkehr: Zeitschrift für das gesamte Verkehrswesen*, Vols. 1–7, 1947–53; Thomas Sudbeck, *Motorisierung, Verkehrsentwicklung und Verkehrspolitik in der Bundesrepublik Deutschland der 1950er Jahre: Umrisse der allgemeinen Entwicklung und zwei Beispiele: Hamburg und das Emsland*, Stuttgart: Steiner, 1994.
47. Schulte, 'Die Psychotechnik...', in *Das Neue Berlin*
48. Schulte, 'Die Psychotechnik' op.cit.
49. Gerhard Lamprecht's film of Erich Kaestner's children's story, *Emil and the Detectives*, released in 1931, can also be read in this light.
50. Goergen, *Walter Ruttmann*, p.59.
51. STAD MdI 14605, Verkehrsarbeitsgemeinschaft to Interior Ministry, 20 September 1928; Polizeipräs. Dresden, Traffic Division to MdI, 10 August 1931; Friedrich Wacker, Naunhof, letter of complaint to Kreishauptmann, Leipzig, 8 December 1931.
52. STAD MdI 14605, Richtlinien 'Kampf den Lärm' 1935.
53. Robert Walser, *Jakob von Gunten*, Vol. 6, Jochen Greven (ed.), Frankfurt a. Main: Suhrkamp, 1978, pp.34f.
54. Maud Lavin, 'Photomontage, Mass Culture and Modernity', in Boston Institute of Contemporary Art, *Montage and modern life, 1919–1942*, Cambridge, Mass., and London: MIT Press, 1992.
55. In this respect they are an analogy of the circulation of capital. See in general, Harvey, *Urban Experience*.
56. Verein für Fremden-Verkehr in Chemnitz hrsg, *Chemnitz und Umgebung. Führer durch Chemnitz*, Chemnitz, Dritte Auflage 1914/16, p.119; Kölner Verkehrs-Verein, *Köln am Rhein*, Cologne, (n.d.), 30–31; Voigt, *Verkehr*, p.676.
57. Peter Hall, *Cities of Tomorrow*, Oxford: Blackwell, 1990, pp.119, 121–2; For background on the new estates see Barbara Miller Lane, *Architecture and Politics in Germany 1918–1945*, Cambridge, Mass.: Harvard University Press, 1985 (1968).
58. John P. McKay, *Tramways and Trolleys. The Rise of Urban Mass Transport in Europe*, Princeton University Press, 1976, p.209.
59. LAB 142/I StB 498, 'Zur Deutschen Klein- und Vielstaaterei. Die raumverschiebende Auswirkung der Neugliederung in Südwestdeutschland, dem rheinfränkischen Wirtschaftsgebiet', pp.1–4.
60. Otto Büsch, *Geschichte der Berliner Kommunalwirtschaft in der Weimarer Epoche*, Berlin: Friedrich Meinecke Institut, 1960, p.89; Peter Hüttenberger, *Düsseldorf Geschichte von den Ursprüngen bis ins 20.Jahrhundert*, Band 3: Die Industrie- und Verwaltungsstadt 20.Jahrhundert, Düsseldorf: Schwann im Patmos, 1989, pp.369, 386.
61. Gudrun Brockhaus, *Schauder und Idylle. Faschismus als Erlebnisangebot*, Munich, 1997, pp.68–117.
62. Bundesarchiv Koblenz (hereafter BAK) NS22/493, *Der Grundstein* [Nr. 7], July 1939: 'Kernstück aller Reichsautobahnen: Der Ring um Berlin'; *Frankfurter Zeitung*, 8 April 1938: 'Der Spatenstich'.
63. BAK NS22/493, *Völkische Beobachter*, 4 September 1934: 'Die Straßen des Führers als Bindemittel zwischen den deutschen Stämmen'. To lend authority to his point, Hess drew on the historical Prussian examples of earlier transport and communication projects, namely that of Friedrich Lüders (roads) 1779, and Friedrich List (railways) from the mid nineteenth century.
64. Geheimes Staatsarchiv Preußischer Kulturbesitz, Rep.77/41, Bl. 303 Oberbürgermeister Jarres, Duisburg.
65. Roggatz, 'Die Strasse', p.241.
66. Brockhaus, *Schauder*, pp.78–81; Deutsche Lufthansa, *Lufthansa Betriebsmitteilungen* 11 Jg., Nr. 9 September 1927: 'Luftfilm'.
67. *The Times*, 'Lessons of the Road', 1938.
68. Siegfried Kracauer, 'Film 1928', in idem, *Das Ornament der Masse*, pp.307–8; reprinted in English in his *From Caligari to Hitler. A Psychological History of The German Film*, Princeton University Press, 1949, 5th edn 1974, pp.182–8; Barry Fulks, 'Berlin: Die Sinfonie der Grossstadt', in Nicholas Thomas (ed.), *International Dictionary of Films and Filmmakers*, vol. 1: 'Film', Chicago and London: St. James, 1990, 2nd edn, pp.89–91; Hake, 'Urban Spectacle', p.129.

69. Kracauer, 'Film 1928', my translation.
70. Dawn Ades, *Photomontage*, London: Thames and Hudson, 1976, 99–105, 139.

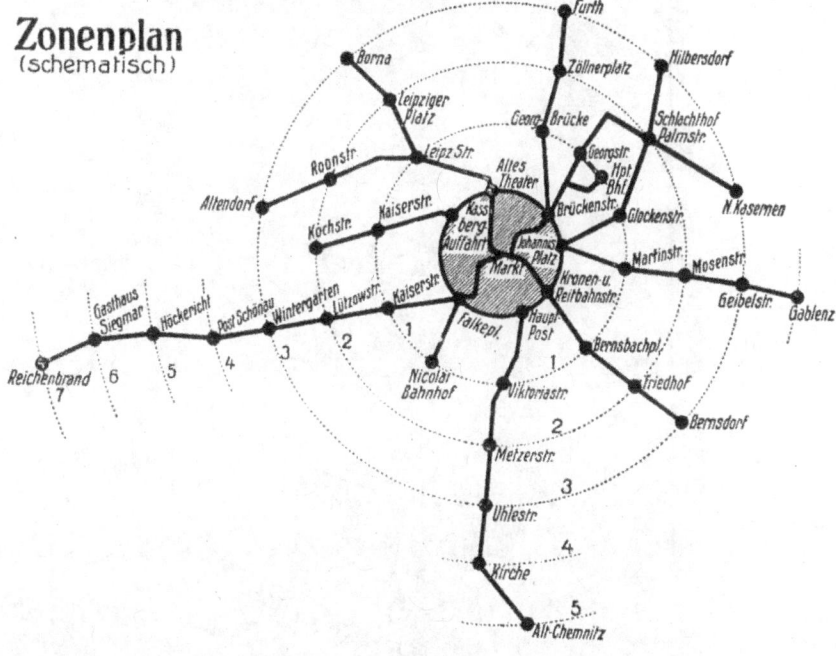

12.1 Chemnitz zone map, 1914–16

12.2 Berlin transport networks, 1931

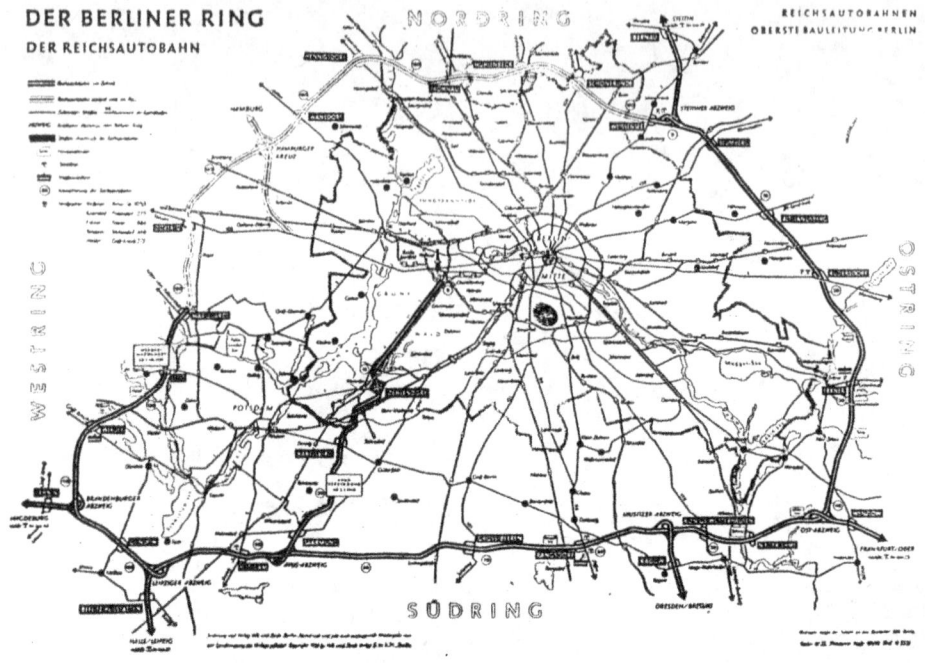

12.3 'Roads of the Führer': i. *Der Grundstein* [No. 7], July 1939: 'Kernstück aller Reichsautobahnen. Der Ring um Berlin'; 12.3

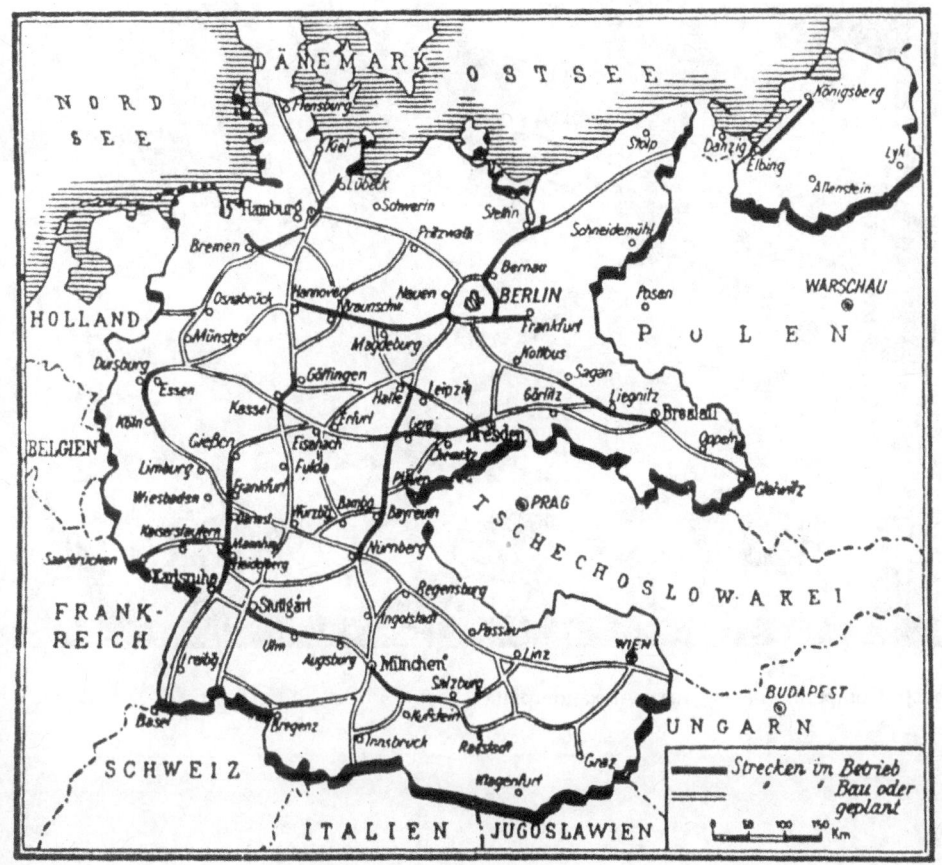

ii. *Frankfurter Zeitung*, 8 April 1938: 'Der Spatenstich'

12.4 Competition entry, 1933: Alexanderplatz

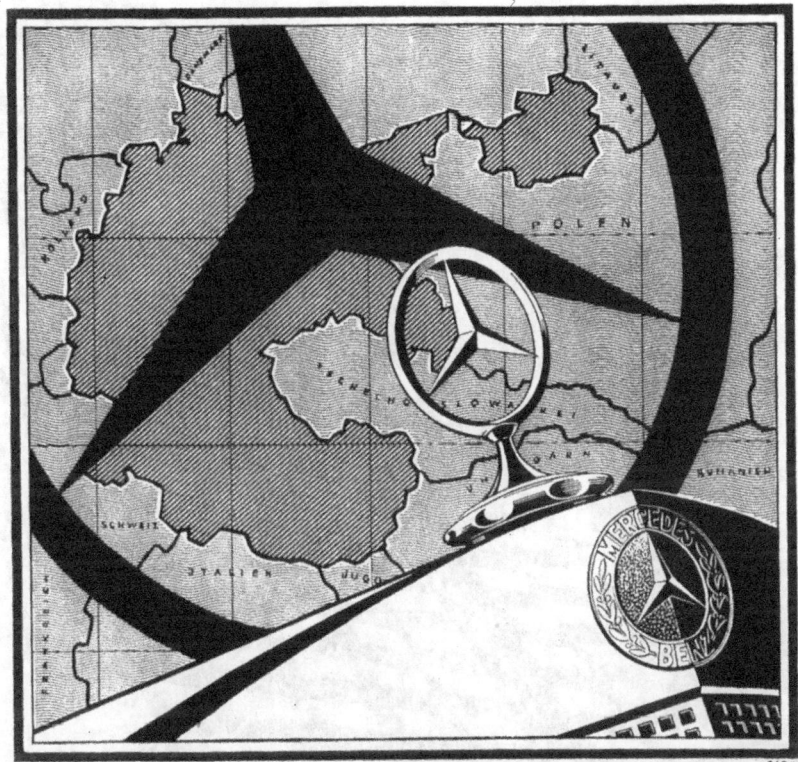

Taten von Weltgeltung
waren und bleiben unser Prüffeld · Der Erfolg:
Spitzenleistungen als preiswerte Serienerzeugnisse!

Auszug aus unserem Bauprogramm 1938:

Personenwagen: u.a.	Lastwagen: u.a. 1,5 to Nutzlast	2 to Nutzlast
Typ 170 V (1,7 Ltr.) .. ab RM 3750.-	als Fahrgestell mit Vergasermotor RM 3490.-	als Fahrgestell mit Vergasermotor RM 4040.-
Typ 230 (2,3 Ltr.) .. ab RM 5875.-	als Fahrgestell mit Dieselmotor .. RM 4990.-	als Fahrgestell mit Dieselmotor .. RM 5650.-
Typ 320 (3,2 Ltr.) .. ab RM 8950.- ab Werk	7fach bereift ab Werk	7fach bereift ab Werk

MERCEDES - BENZ
Verkaufstellen und Vertretungen an allen größeren Plätzen des In- und Auslandes

12.5 'Mercedes Benz, Deeds of World Renown'

12.6 Still from *Berlin: Sinfonie der Grossstadt*

13

Wim Wenders and Berlin

Sabine Jaccaud

This essay considers the role of memory in a cinematic representation of Berlin and explores echoes between a film and architectural developments in this city since 1989. Wim Wenders' portrayal of Berlin in *Der Himmel über Berlin*[1] (*Wings of Desire*) captures the city the way it was in 1987. Berlin appears in its divided stasis and also as a place that contains juxtaposed traces of different historical periods. If Berlin is indeed the quintessential central European example of a city where contemporary history has inscribed a rapid succession of traces, its identity before German unification was imbued with a strong presence of the past. This aspect is portrayed by Wenders in his film and, despite the frozen division of the city during the Cold War, he opens questions about the future of this past. In this respect, this study seeks to explore *Der Himmel über Berlin* in juxtaposition to alterations made to the city's fabric after German unification. It will do so by considering the site of the Potsdamer Platz. Film and architecture meet on this location.

Der Himmel über Berlin is about Berlin as much as it is the story of a romantic encounter between an angel and a trapeze artist or a tale of the crossing of boundaries between infinite and finite time and between observation and experience. In this film, the city is portrayed as a place of change that is deeply connected to a sense of historical process. Berlin is explored by Wenders' camera and he offers a portrait of its gaps and cracks, and of areas where the past is readable. Within these, he locates a story of characters in search of their own stories and of an experience that would endow them with a sense of inscription within history. Even if the characters interact with each other, the film mainly shows their encounter with the city and how personal and urban histories echo each other.

In an interview with the Berlin architect Hans Kollhoff, Wenders discusses the reasons why Berlin was the only possible setting for this film. In his view, Berlin as an urban space reveals questions of memory and identity in the late twentieth century and had become an emblem for the tensions of our time. For Wenders, Berlin is 'a city which constantly throws you back into the past, not just in brief glimpses but as a total sensation'.[2] In this respect, it is neither a museum-city nor a historical theme park where history is commodified, or at least it was not when Wenders filmed *Der Himmel über Berlin*. He perceived the city as a place where history, not only German but international as well, is present every day, in cracks and details rather than in orchestrated monuments. It is a city made of an accretion of superimposed or juxtaposed stories, a palimpsest or a lamination of traces from different historical moments. This is apparent from an early scene when the city is filmed from the air in a panoramic *Flugaufname*, showing the city's TV tower and the highway entering West Berlin.

Old and new buildings are perceived together and new accretions fit into a pre-existing pattern. The palimpsest is an emblem for this urban situation. It brings to mind notions of tracing, inscribing and deleting as well as a central idea of cohabitation of the past and the present. If Berlin is a key example, it is not the only one. In the period in which Wenders directed this film, the city as a representational topos was – and still is – receiving vast amounts of attention. Since the late 1960s, a renewed interest in the fabric of the historical city is apparent on an international level, not only in architectural theory and practice[3] but also in narrative representation. If aspects of contemporary culture and genre can be broadly labelled 'Postmodern', it is because they share a construed distance from a Modernist agenda. After a period where an important focus in architecture was an international, heroic style that expressed concerns about the construction of a new, postwar urban environment[4] architecture turned back to the historical city as a source of solutions to the problems encountered in Modernist practice. The past was thus explored as a persistent and generative force within the present. However problematic in its practical form, this revised architectural agenda examines urban fabric and the density of traces of the past it contains. This situation finds parallels in the field of narrative representation. Indeed, Postmodern narrative could be described as a complex interplay between novelty and heritage, invention and saturation, and a return to traditional form with the mature distance of parody and irony.[5] A central aspect of Postmodern narrative representation, one that is visible within *Der Himmel über Berlin*, is the way stylistic innovation is rooted in references to the past, to previous representations and to their lingering presence as shapers of contemporary culture and perception. If the city is a recurrent topos in both contemporary architecture and narrative representation, it is because it is a space where memory and history are readable and have a visible generative function. The city therefore echoes in its own layered structure the palimpsestic aspect of new developments in these fields. Indeed, they fit within pre-existing patterns and this is apparent in both fictional descriptions of the city and architectural inscriptions on its space.

Wenders views Berlin as a repository of the memory of past events. This reinforces his own statement that, for him, cinema is a medium of expression that involves memory by preserving traces of experience on a reel. City and film both preserve the traces of time on a given place. In the case of Berlin, Wenders encounters and portrays a city where these are omnipresent and which is representative of the tensions characteristic of the period between the end of the Second World War and the end of the Cold War. In a collection of essays and comments on his own experience of cinema, Wenders writes that,

> The thing I wished for and saw flashing was a film in and about Berlin. A film that might convey something of the history of the city since 1945. A film that might succeed in capturing what I miss in so many films that are set here, something that seems to be so palpably there when you arrive in Berlin: a feeling in the air and under your feet and in people's faces, that makes life in this city so different from life in other cities. To explain and clarify my wish, I should add: it's the desire of someone who's been away from Germany for a long time, and who could only ever experience 'Germanness' in this one city. I should say I'm no Berliner. Who is nowadays? But for over twenty years now, visits to this city have given me my only genuine experiences of Germany, because the (hi)story that elsewhere in the country is suppressed or denied is physically and emotionally present here.[6]

Berlin carries within its structure and substance scars of war and political division. After a history of rapid expansion since the eighteenth century, and of devastation, fragmentation and reconstruction in recent times, the city is a space of lasting tensions with no contemporary European precedent. In 1987, these were rooted in the division of the city's space. Wenders wrote that 'the idea that it was once one single city never ceases to overwhelm me'[7] and its present unification gives the city of *Der Himmel über Berlin* its awaited sequel. The film is the portrait of a city at a given moment in time and is now dated. But even though the divided city does not exist any more, it is still so much part of how its identity had been registered for a quarter of a century. Berlin 'offers strange views of the past or of what still remains from the past, witnesses of everything that has happened'.[8] Wenders writes that the city is 'an open history book'[9] where all documents tell a story of loss. The fragmentation that had become associated with postwar Berlin, its rubble, its four sectors and the Wall erected in August 1961 all became emblems of this era, on a wider scale than in Germany as a whole. Within this division of the city into two ideological zones and different sectors, gaps and empty spaces prevail. On the western side, they bear witness to deleted presences. They are either ruins preserved as memorials to Berlin's ordeal during the war, such as the Kaiser Wilhelm Gedächtniskirche, or empty and suspended patches, like the site of the Alekan Circus in Wenders' film, or indeed the Potsdamer Platz.

In *Der Himmel über Berlin*, the city is seen to carry multiple layers of time within its space. The present form of the city stores the memory of past ones. Wenders locates two groups of characters within Berlin, and they are 'living on different time scales. Angels live in enduring and eternal time, and humans live in their own time.'[10] The angels are defined by an ontological complexity, living on the boundary between two realms: the human and the spiritual.[11] They introduce a mystical, albeit unfocused, dimension to this portrayal of Berlin and are construed out of an extensive network of references which bring to mind the Angel of Death, angels in the Christian tradition, as well as sculpted figures of angels which inhabit Berlin, such as the golden Siegessäule monument which appears frequently in Wenders' film. Other references within this allusive density include Rainer Maria Rilke's *Duino Elegies* and Walter Benjamin's angel of history. The latter describes the figure from Paul Klee's painting *Angelus Novus* as caught in the storm of progress with 'his face ... turned toward the past. Where we perceive a chain of events, he sees one single catastrophe which keeps piling wreckage upon wreckage and hurls it in front of his feet.'[12] Wenders' angels oversee the life of the city and are attentive to its details as they read the weight of the past within them. They remember the city from its earliest days as they belong to a space that is wider than a human one. They tell the story of the city, one that starts with the formation of the soil on which it grew. They are a form of vocalized memory or witness to the city. Through their presence, Wenders plays with connections between stories and history as well as with links between the past and the present as both are recorded by these angels. He writes that,

> In the film of course it's not HISTORY
> But A story, though of course
> A STORY may contain HISTORY,
> Images and traces of past history,
> And intimations of what is to come.[13]

In this respect, Berlin in 1987 is represented as a moment in time that has a given shape. It is one moment within a larger history. For instance, the film portrays Berlin's division by the wall as one of its main characteristics. But Wenders does not only film the western side. His camera glimpses across the wall into the no-man's-land, the Prenzlauer Berg and the area around the Museumsinsel. These places are part of Berlin's historical identity and the fact that they were on the 'other' side does not erase this fact. However, if the angels can move freely in space and cross the border at will, they are unable to influence their environment in any way or leave a trace of their presence. But their presence and their mobility offer a comment on the latent union and oneness of Berlin that underlies its division. The title of the film indicates the overriding presence of one sky above the divided city, recalling a memory of its whole history, on a scale wider than the recent past and the present.

Wenders expresses his perception of Berlin as a history book by revealing the past beneath and within the city of the present. He writes that: 'behind the city of today, in its interstices or above it, as though frozen in time, are the ruins, the mounds of rubble, the burned chimneystacks and facades of the devastated city, only dimly visible sometimes, but always there in the background ... [this] yesterday is still present everywhere, as a "parallel world".'[14] If memory is contained within the fabric of the city, it can be brought to light by being confronted with the knowledge of that city's past that lies in an individual. The character of Homer who appears regularly throughout the film represents 'the story-teller, the muse, the potential guardian of collective memory and history'.[15] He first appears in a scene set in Hans Scharoun's library on the Kulturforum of West Berlin. Wenders explains that Homer is 'an old archangel living in the library'.[16] He is conscious of being the storehouse for memory, a witness to the experience of Berlin's history through the twentieth century. He is also conscious of his advanced age and his disconnection from his audience. Wenders describes the origins of this character in his collection of essays and comments on his own films entitled *Die Logik der Bilder* (The Logic of Images). He writes that Rembrandt's painting entitled Homer was a model as it depicts an old man telling stories, alone, cut off from his listener.[17] Homer's name harks back to the role of regenerative cultural landmarks and emphasizes the role of memory in shaping stories.[18] There is a closeness between him and the angels, as both are in touch with 'the latent past'.[19] These angels have 'been in the city since the end of the war', when Wenders points out that God turned away from Berlin, leaving the city to its own chaos.[20] Throughout the scenes where Homer appears, he is alone and silent, closed in on his mental storehouse that only the angels can share by their capacity as listeners and eavesdroppers. He expresses the sense of loss that Wenders associates with Berlin and also represents the spirit of a tired and burnt-out city and mourns the loss of another Berlin; Weimar Berlin (see Figure 13.1).

A significant scene in this respect is when Homer is walking alone along the wall, seaching for the Potsdamer Platz that once was the heart of the city and all that remains on the spot where he is wandering is a weed-filled no-man's-land bordering the wall. Homer compares his memories of the site to what he sees and is unable to accept the contrast. During this scene, fragments from archives appear that show ruins of bombed buildings and rubble-filled streets that bring to mind the postwar *Trümmerfilms*.[21] The script of *Der Himmel über Berlin* – written in association with Peter Handke[22] – tells us that these images have appeared on Homer's inner eye.[23] Past and present are in total contrast to each other and only connected by memory, a memory that is undergoing confusion and disorientation in relation to the brutality of the contrast between then and now. Homer appears to be rattling around in the Berlin of the late eighties, lost and confused and looking inwards to his memories. These are triggered by his return to their original site, the city thus functioning as a mnemonic device. His presence and concerns show the importance for some to keep on telling stories 'even though [they] may in parts be ugly'.[24]

Homer is inscribed within time and can connect its different parts or at least diagnose their disconnection, through references to his own experience. Included in the relics of the past city, he is a voice which is problematic in the sense that his cohesive words remain silent to the population and only accessible to the silent and uninterfering angel, Cassiel. A connection between past and present through memory exists but remains in the form of a monologue. Indeed, in Homer's words: 'nenne mir, Muse, den armen, unsterblichen Sänger, der, von seinen sterblichen Zuhörern ... verlassen, die Stimme verlor ... wie er vom Engel der Erzählung zum unbeachteten oder verlachten Leiermann draussen an der Schwelle zum Niemansdland wurde.'[25] The aspect of Berlin that the Homer scenes bring to light is that the city's past is most powerfully present where it is absent. Homer has lost the monuments in the city that were reference points in his mental cityscape and cannot replace them. If Berlin is attractive to Wenders for its wilderness and for the cracks in its surface, he explains that the mind can grasp hold of broken things better than it can of things whole, on which memory slips away. It is unusual for a city to have such deserted lots and broken or scarred elements in its fabric. This waste space in the city, which was an emblem for political stasis in 1987 and became ephemeral soon afterwards, was full once, however. Homer's memories of the Potsdamer's active years reveal this. By filming cracks and gaps, Wenders shows the traces of a destructive history in a way that avoids an aestheticization of the past or its reduction to familiar clichés.

In *Der Himmel über Berlin*, two ways of representing history are contrasted. Firstly, by showing an old Berliner on a no-man's-land and by sharing his memories, and secondly, through the portrayal of the making of an American television film in Berlin. The latter shows actors at work and extras waiting on the set that is an old bunker on the Goeben Strasse.[26] Using a complex interaction between different levels of time, these scenes are constructed out of a retro pastiche of the past where 'forties clothes, cars and props are being used to stage this making of a film within a film. This stands as a comment on the fact that these aspects of the war are accessible to postwar generations through filmed evidence, such as documentary footage. However, Wenders is also contrasting the recycling of these images and a mass-media re-creation of the past through a form of period nostalgia with Homer's memory and the city's telling of its own history through what is missing or absent. A play with surface imagery is separated from an investigation into the persistence and livelihood of the past within the present. In my view, this is an attempt to find a German vocabulary which could represent its own past in the medium of film, acknowledging the weight and influence of American cinema at the same time.

Der Himmel über Berlin represents Wenders' return to Germany after seven years in the United States. In this respect, it is a homecoming piece. Berlin conveys a sense of 'Germanness' to the director, one he re-explores in the light of his American work.[27] Prior to working in the United States, his early films attempted to grasp the influence of American imagery on German contemporary life and culture. After his return, he alters his focus to consider Germany through its own imagery. As a director who is part of the New German Cinema, Wenders works within the boundaries of defining a cinematic culture that is representative of postwar Germany. Indeed, one of the aims of the New German Cinema was to recreate a film culture perceived as non-existent since the War and to do so by presenting views of the present. Its main directors – Herzog, Fassbinder, Wenders, Syberberg, Kluge and Schlöndorff – have no shared aesthetic but rather share a concern with finding a representational vocabulary which offers an alternative to an American one. A major difference between these two national cinemas resides in the fact that American movies are products of a show business industry subjected to the pressures of a market economy, whereas the New German Cinema is the result of a ' "cultural" mode of production' in which issues of identity, history and cinema itself became a priority.[28]

Der Himmel über Berlin is a mature work in Wenders' career and its setting in Berlin brings forth all these issues of German identity and history. As an example of a cinema of authors, the film is both subjective and personal and seeks to capture impersonal traces of history's mythical dimension in the city. It represents a problematization of German history during the War. Wenders directs a film that portrays a city through its scars and does so by accepting what is already there. In this respect, exploring one's identity in the present involves looking back into the past. The effect of paying close attention to urban space, as Wenders does, is to bring history into the foreground. His film therefore participates in a vast corpus of German cultural production focused on 'coming to terms with' the experience of the Nazi era and telling its impact on German society from within, after the relative silence of the postwar generation.[29] The film gathers elements from previous representations and reconfigures them into a new whole which is constructed on an allusive or meta-level. *Der Himmel über Berlin* is therefore a contemporary representation of questions surrounding memory and identity. It is not a pastiche of the past or a representation solely motivated by nostalgia. Indeed, the film relies on such Postmodern representational strategies as the integration of non-fictional material into its narrative flow, the self-reflexive portrayal of representational problems through the confrontation of two narrative solutions and the allusive density that shapes its moods and characters.[30] *Der Himmel über Berlin* shows representation at work in a manner that emphasizes the exploratory ramblings of memory, its fluctuating and slippery aspect and its crucial role in shaping one's perception of the present.[31] Wenders writes that Berlin appears to him as 'more a SITE than a CITY',[32] as a space where identity can be thought about in relation to reconstruction and the incorporation of the past into the present. This identity will involve accepting the challenge of the past and building a future that is aware of its presence. If the city since German unification appears optimistically as a construction site, it is paradoxically not as open as it was in 1987 when questions about how to enfold history in a contemporary political agenda were still probing for answers. Keeping in mind Homer's ramblings on the Potsdamer Platz, I will outline recent alterations to Berlin's fabric, and consider the answers they provide to these mnemonic concerns.

After German unification, Berlin was designated the nation's capital. In this respect, the city is being rethought to ensure that it will be the political centre of a new nation and bear this resonance more loudly than it will reminiscences of its past as the capital of Germany before and during the Second World War. If this mainly involves issues of rethinking this space as a whole and reconnecting its two parts, it also triggers debates about the place, role and purpose of history and memory within this new fabric. Most sites that called for alteration, such as the Reichstag; or development, such as the area where the Wall used to be, carried heavy historical associations. Certain key parts of Berlin today stage historical awareness within a city that is becoming a synthesis of many layers of its own identity.

The ambitious scope of this urban development followed specific initial outlines and resulted in a dispute between differing schools of architectural thought and practice. It is a dispute about 'directions and individuals',[33] fuelled on one side by advocates of a traditional 'Berliner' direction to new developments and on the other side by advocates of international influences and visionary projects. Hans Stimmann's aim as Senatsbaudirektor from 1991 was to hold on to a

'Master Plan', drawn up for the historical city centre or at least for what is left of it after the War and forty years of the German Democratic Republic. He found the basis for the plan dimensions in the still legible historic street and block pattern dating from before the War, for the elevation in the uniform cornice height of 22 metres and for the structure in the perforated façade of indigenous stone. When dealing with invitations to tender, competition juries and in discussions with investors and their architects, Stimmann arms himself with this set of regulations in an attempt to not lose sight of the goal, the recovery of the traditional city.[34]

If this is the expression of an ongoing clash in architectural circles between, on one side, historicists or rationalists and on the other, deconstructivists and neo-moderns,[35] its occurrence within the framework of Berlin's development since 1989 is of interest in relation to issues of urban memory raised both in Wenders' film and in the Potsdamer Platz project. By turning to history and tradition, this 'Master Plan' explores the generative persistence of the past in a way that reads it out of the city's distinctive features such as building proportions and materials. If it seeks to lay down guidelines to ensure the establishment of solutions to urban development that are not tied to passing architectural trends, it is also restrictive and selective, focused on a particular layer of the city's history. This layer is the nineteenth century, and if this period is a safe one to recall as a time when Berlin was being shaped as an important European city, it is also one where issues of contemporary identity in both political and architectural history can be avoided. If this historicist approach reflects a reliance on urban memory within contemporary practice, it also carries the overtone of a normalization of this memory, through a selective process.

The freedom to imagine the shape the city might take in the future has been replaced by the materialization of this future in a firmly defined form. Open questions surrounding the task of memory suddenly called for specific answers. Berlin was no longer solely representative of Germany's division and the contrasted attitudes to processing and using history in East and West but was acquiring the task of symbolizing Germany as one. The suspended city in Wenders' film was also a West-German show-case where new building followed a specific political agenda. Unified Berlin is being shaped as a German show-case, still as rooted in politics, although the agenda has changed.

The Potsdamer Platz is an example of the process of refurbishing and redesigning unified Berlin. Before 1989, this area, as portrayed by Wenders, was a grassy no-man's-land inscribed by traces of past streets and railway tracks vanishing mysteriously into vertical slabs of concrete. Two hundred and fifty years of growth shaped the adjacent Leipziger Platz and Potsdamer Platz. Since the Second World War, four short periods define this section of the city, and are echoed in other areas. Firstly, the *Trümmermeer* (sea of rubble) after the bombs, when most of the buildings were left in a skeletal form, led either to their reconstruction, their removal, or their persistence as skeletons. Secondly, the erection of the Wall and the gradual dismantling or removal of buildings from its surroundings created an empty buffer between two ideologies. The Potsdamer Platz, in this respect, was a key viewing area where each side displayed itself to the other. A third layer of growth or change occurs through the establishment of a Kulturforum on the western side of this area. Finally, the most recent developments after unification inscribe a new story onto this part of the city. If planners and architects were confronted with an eclectic space when development plans where set in motion, they were also encountering a loaded emptiness as each preceding layer of history left its directive trace on the site.

The Potsdamer Platz is a focal point in Berlin's present construction boom, echoing its lost role as the older city's heart. It was chosen for the first staged opening in the Wall on 12 November 1989, when the mayors of each Berlin exchanged a symbolic handshake.[36] The Removal of the Wall released a site within the city that called for development and will soon be the locus of a large architectural ensemble. Independent submissions for the Potsdamer Platz competition were signed by a large number of Berlin and international architects, including Hilmer & Sattler, Renzo Piano, O.M. Ungers, Josef Paul Kleihues, Arata Isozaki, Richard Rogers, Hans Kollhoff, Lauber & Wöhr, Diener and Diener, and Giorgio Grassi. These projects are published in Thies Schröder's book entitled *Der Potsdamer Platz* and in a *Domus Dossier* on Berlin.[37] If they differ vastly in their architectural expression, a few strikingly similar elements appear in all these projects. They share an awareness of historical traces often erased from sight, such as the octagonal shape of the Leipziger Platz and the line of the Potsdamer Strasse. These projects attempt to restore their presence, thus complying with aspects of Stimmann's 'Master Plan'. The Achteck as well as the tree-lined Potsdamer Strasse are to be revived and will become part of Berlin as a re-established European capital. Through their presence, these elements should assist in reconnecting Berlin with memories of its lost past. The Potsdamer Platz projects reveal that an anchorage in historical roots is exploited as a creative potential rather than as a limitation or constraint. They are not expressions of nostalgia but of contemporary explorations of history, echoing the representational concerns of *Der Himmel über Berlin*. In this respect, Homer's rambling on the Potsdamer emphasizes a portrayal of the way urban space functions as a trigger for memory over a desire to retrieve or replicate the past as it was. The latter, in Berlin, would carry dangerous political implications.

The jury of the Potsdamer Platz competition selected Renzo Piano's project, but the development of the site as a whole will be carried out through a collective work including the participation of Christoph Kohlbecker, Isozaki, Kollhoff, Lauber & Wöhr, J. R. Moneo and Richard Rogers. The result will be an ensemble of buildings that will serve a variety of functions. Juxtaposed with traces of the old Potsdamer Platz and Leipziger Platz, the Kulturforum stands out as a pre-established element in the landscape, playing a decisive role in shaping the site and the form of the new ensemble. If Scharoun's library now defines the western corner or edge of the project, its initially disruptive direction is maintained and integrated.[38] In this respect, the palimpsestic aspect of the Potsdamer Platz will be amplified by this inclusion of references to multiple and even conflicting periods of the Platz's history. This development project answers questions open in many minds over half of this century and epitomized by the character of Homer in Wenders' film. As the old man carries himself and his memories of the prewar Platz around the no-man's-land of the mid 'eighties, he tells himself that 'ich gebe so lange nicht auf, bis ich den Potsdamer Platz gefunden habe!'[39] and later in the film that 'nur noch die Römerstrassen... führen ins Weite, nur noch die ältesten Spuren führen ins Weite, nur noch die ältesten Spuren führen weiter.'[40]

Homer's quest for what the city has lost is being filled by the new construction plans. As we are now in a transitory time, when the choices have been made for the site's future but their construction not yet completed, the outcome of the realization is still suspended.[41] At present no answers have really been given in relation to Homer's puzzled exclamation 'Ich kann den Potssdamer Platz nicht finden.'[42] One wonders how much of the old forms someone like him would recognize in the new ones. One can only underline the integrative and historically conscious or accommodating intent within the plan, one that tries to make a latent past manifest. However, as Alan Balfour notes, part of the essence of the Potsdamer Platz lies in its many changes.[43] If its new shape will guarantee a continuum with this aspect and add to its ability to record the residue of each layer as well as contribute a new one, echoing Berlin's contemporary history, it might also be too rigid in its approach to allow future changes to develop. Urban process in its organic aspect is thus being replaced by large-scale planning. The new Berlin that is being shaped is instigating the end of something, possibly of Berlin's identity as a war-scarred city. The tensions of the Cold War are being assimilated, even though they have left traces in the city's fabric. For Wenders, there will be fewer cracks to hold on to in the new appearance given to the city.[44] They are being built over and built out, as Berlin works towards becoming one city again.

Wenders measured the poetic dimension of the gaps and cracks in the divided city and explored the way they functioned as triggers to historically oriented musings about Berlin's past and future. *Der Himmel über Berlin* captures the eloquence of absence, the absence of a city as one city and the gaps in the city's fabric, most of all in the scenes on the fallow land of the Potsdamer Platz. Wenders establishes in this respect that 'perhaps it is the breadth of possibility that makes a city'.[45] Now, Berlin is becoming a space where presence is being inscribed in a new urban symphony. When most historical landmarks within the city are being integrated into a redefined whole, what might be lost is the emotional presence of the past within Berlin's gaps and cracks, the one which first attracted Wenders to this city.

Notes

1. For the film's script with stills, see Peter Handke and Wim Wenders, *Der Himmel über Berlin*, Frankfurt am Main: Suhrkamp Verlag, 1987. The film itself was released by Road Movies/Argos Films in 1987.
2. In an interview published in *Nova Narració*, April, May, June 1988, p.72.
3. For instance, in the work of Aldo Rossi, Robert Venturi, Kenneth Frampton, Colin Rowe and Fred Koetter and Bernard Huet.
4. Pioneered in the work of visionary architects such as Le Corbusier and Mies Van der Rohe, this International Style of steel, glass and concrete volumes became increasingly widespread after the end of the Second World War. It offered innovative and cheap solutions to urban reconstruction and development.
5. The studies of Linda Hutcheon and Brian McHale explore in detail the complexity of Postmodern narrative and representation. For Hutcheon, see *A Poetics of Postmodernism*, London: Routledge, 1988 and *The Politics of Postmodernism*, London: Routledge, 1989; for McHale, see *Constructing Postmodernism*, London and New York: Routledge, 1992 and *Postmodernist Fiction*, London and New York: Methuen, 1987.
6. Wim Wenders, *The Logic of Images*, trans. Michael Hofmann, London: Faber and Faber, 1991, pp.73–4. (The original German edition is *Die Logik der Bilder*, Frankfurt am Main: Verlag der Autoren, 1988.)
7. *Nova Narració* interview, p.72
8. Ibid., p.66
9. Ibid., p.49.
10. In David Harvey, 'Time and Space in the Postmodern Cinema', p.314, in *The Condition of Postmodernity*, Oxford: Basil Blackwell, 1990, pp.308–23.
11. Closing a talk on 'The City, The Cinema: Modern Spaces' during an event entitled 'The Visual Arena of the City' at Senate House in London on 2 March 1995, James Donald referred to the angels in Wenders' film. Through these figures, he noted a shift from a concern with 'l'Etrange' or the urban uncanny in Modernist cityscapes to 'l'Etre-Ange' [the angel-being], in a Postmodern context of blurred boundaries and ontological complexity. Angels can appear as spiritual lures in a fragmented space, or on the other hand, as spiritual residue or potential.
12. Walter Benjamin, 'Theses on the Philosophy of History', *Illuminations*, IX, ed. Hannah Arendt, London: Fontana Press, 1973, p.249.
13. *The Logic of Images*, p.76. Wenders' capitalization.
14. Ibid., p.80.
15. Harvey, 'Time and Space in the Postmodern Cinema', p.317.
16. Wenders, *The Logic of Images*, p.137, 'eines alten Erzengels, der in der Bibliothek lebt'.
17. Ibid., p.137.
18. The name does not in fact appear in the film – the script thus offers more information and establishes a sense of interdependence between pictures and text.
19. *Logic of Images*, p.80.
20. Ibid., p.80.
21. German films set in devastated cities which were still a sea of rubble, or *Trümmer*, after the war.
22. The Austrian writer Peter Handke and Wenders have often collaborated on cinematic projects, including the adaptation into film of Handke's novel *Die Angst des Tormanns beim Elfmeter*, Filmverlag Der Autoren, 1972. Their collaboration reveals a shared concern with the interdependence of writing and film, image and text and a desire to explore creative innovation within a cultural scene that is saturated with pre-established images.

23. Handke and Wenders, *Der Himmel über Berlin*, p.58.
24. Harvey, 'Time and Space in the Postmodern Cinema', p.317.
25. Handke and Wenders, *Der Himmel über Berlin*, pp.59–60 [name me, Muse, the poor immortal storyteller who, abandoned by the mortals, lost his voice. He who, angel of tales, was ignored and scorned on the border of the no-man's-land].
26. Including the American television series icon Peter Falk whose presence here is associated with his fictional character, Colombo. If the American icon is recognizable in Berlin, his presence is a comment on the powerful presence of American culture and products in postwar Europe
27. The films he directed in America are: *Paris, Texas* (1984), *Nick's Movie: Lightning over Water* (1981), and *Hammett* (1982). *Alice in the Cities* (1974), opens on the Road Movie genre, recalling *Kings of the Road* (1976) but with an American setting which then shifts to Germany. Wenders discusses America and American imagery in 'Der Americanische Traum', in *Emotion Pictures*, Frankfurt am Main: Verlag der Autoren, 1986, pp.141–70.
28. See Thomas Elsaesser's study *New German Cinema: A History*, Basingstoke and London: Macmillan, 1989, most of all pp.3, 6–7, 42. This study also explores the funding strategies involved in maintaining an independent status.
29. For other cinematic references to German narratives focused on memories of the Nazi era, see Anton Kaes, *From Hitler to Heimat: The Return of History as Film*, Cambridge, Mass., and London: Harvard UP, 1989.
30. Wenders is shaping his own picture on a premise of precedence. Many frames are quotes or allusions to other Berlin films such as Joseph Von Sternberg's *Der Blaue Engel* (1930), Walter Ruttmann's *Berlin: Sinfonie Einer Grossstadt* (1927), or the Trümmerfilms. A level of reference that is less explicit and more diffused into the city concerns the Nazi era and its propaganda films such as those of Leni Riefenstahl. Wenders also alludes to American detective movies, and establishes internal references to his own earlier work. His films therefore explore the genre of cinema and its history, as well as its representational strategies. In *Der Himmel über Berlin*, the character of Homer is played by Curt Bois, whom Wenders describes as 'so alt wie das Kino' (as old as cinema), in *Die Logik der Bilder*, p.137, and who thus embodies these concerns.
31. Henri Bergson establishes that memory is a progression from past to present and participates in perception. See *Matière et Mémoire* (1896), Paris: PUF, 1990, pp.274 and 269. This study is echoed in Raphael Samuel's *Theatres of Memory*, London and New York: Verso, 1994, where he presents memory as 'an active, shaping force' (Introduction).
32. *The Logic of Images*, p.74 (Wenders' emphasis).
33. Peter Rumpf, ' "Querelle" architettonica berlinese', in *Domus Dossier: Berlin*, Milan: Domus, 1995, pp.113–14.
34. Ibid., p.114.
35. The architecture critic Charles Jencks establishes a list of labels to fit differing aspects of contemporary architectural practice and outline types within its broad spectrum. See *The Language of Post-Modern Architecture*, London: Academy Editions, 1991; *Late-Modern Architecture*, London: Academy Editions, 1980, and *Post-Modernism: The New Classicism in Art and Architecture*, New York: Rizzoli, 1987. For a more up to date discussion of examples of differing architectural theory and practice on the contemporary scene, see Nan Ellin, *Postmodern Urbanism*, Oxford and Cambridge, Mass.: Blackwell, 1996.
36. For a discussion of this moment of Berlin's history, see Alan Balfour, *Berlin, The Politics of Order: 1737 to 1989*, New York: Rizzoli, 1990, p.246.
37. Thies Schröder, 'Die Chance des Potsdamer Platzes? Ein Platz im Spiegel der Wettbewerbe', in *Der Potsdamer Platz, Eine Geschichte in Wort und Bild*, Berlin: Verlag Dirk Nishen, 1993, pp.151–63. *Domus Dossier: Berlin*, Milan: Domus, March 1995. See particularly the 'Potsdamer Platz' section, pp.68–97.
38. Alan Balfour discusses a voluntary disruption of the historical patterns in the site which would have defined Mies van der Rohe and Hans Scharoun's contributions to the Kulturforum and shaping of the site. See *Berlin: The Politics of Order*, pp.55 and 168.
39. Handke and Wenders, *Der Himmel über Berlin*, p.59 [I will not give up until I have found the Potsdamer Platz].
40. Ibid., p.90 [Only the Roman roads lead far ahead, and the oldest traces lead further].
41. A website allows virtual visitors to keep up with the progress of this construction site. At http://

cityscope.de, documents about urban developments in the new centre of Berlin are available and include panoramic views of key sites, including Potsdamer Platz.
42. Handke and Wenders, *Der Himmel über Berlin*, p.58 [I cannot find the Potsdamer Platz].
43. Balfour, *Berlin: The Politics of Order*, p.46.
44. The sequel to *Der Himmel über Berlin*, released in 1993 and entitled *In Weiter Ferne, So Nah!*, picks up on the closing caption of the first film: 'fortsetzung folgt' [to be continued]. Wenders worked without Handke on its script and the latter, as well as the film itself, follows a rather worn down thread. Handke's absence is felt, and the city has changed, unified Berlin being seemingly less of a challenge to the imagination than the city used to be. This notion is present in a preface Wenders wrote for Mario Ambrosius' collection of photographs of Berlin. Here, he writes that the pictures that capture the Potsdamer Platz, as well as other areas of the city, 'have not robbed the place of its time', suggesting that other representations and works in and on this city are more [obtrusive] in their approach. See *Berlin – Wintermärchen ohne Mauer*, Berlin: Verlag Ute Schiller; Tokyo: Libroport, 1991.
45. *Nova Narració* interview, p.72. Italics mine.

13.1   Still from *Der Himmel über Berlin*: Homer and Cassiel in the library.

Select bibliography

Abrams, L. (1992), *Workers' Culture in Imperial Germany: leisure and recreation in the Rhineland and Westphalia*, London: Routledge
Abramsky, C., Jachimezyk, M. and Polonsky, A. (1986), *The Jews in Poland*, Oxford: Blackwell
Ades, D. (1976), *Photomontage*, London: Thames and Hudson
Alfred Flechtheim, Sammler, Kunsthändler, Verleger (1987), exh. cat., Düsseldorf: Kunstmuseum
Als Hamburg nobel war (n.d), exh. cat., Hamburg
Altenloh, E. (1914), *Zur Soziologie des Kino: Die Kino-Unternehmung und die sozialen Schichten ihrer Besucher*, Jena
Alter, P. (1989), *Nationalism*, London: Edward Arnold
Alter, P. (ed.) (1993), *Im Banne der Metropolen. Berlin und London in den zwanziger Jahren*, Göttingen and Zürich: Vandenhoeck und Ruprecht
Ambrosius, M. (1991), *Berlin–Wintermärchen ohne Mauer*, Berlin: Ute Schiller, Tokyo: Libroport
Anděl, J. (ed.) (1993), *The Art of the Avant-Garde in Czechoslovakia 1918–38*, Valencia: IVAM Centre Julio Gonzalez
Anderson, B. (1983), *Imagined Communities, Reflections on the Origin and Spread of Nationalism*, 2nd edn., London and New York: Verso
Anderson, H. (ed.) (1988), *Rosa Mayreder: Tagebücher 1873–1937*, Frankfurt am Main: Insel
Anderson, N. K., and Ferber, L. S. (eds) (1990), *Albert Bierstadt, Art and Enterprise*, New York: Hudson Hills Press
Arts Council of Great Britain (1987), *Le Corbusier, Architect of the Century*, exh. cat., London: Arts Council
Ascherson, N. (1986), *The Struggles For Poland*, London: Michael Joseph
Augustine, D. L. (1994), *Patricians and Parvenus: Wealth and High Society in Wilhelmine Germany*, Oxford: Berg
Bairoch, P., Batou, J., and Chèvre, P. (1988), *The Population of European Cities. Data Bank and Short Summary of Results*, Geneva: Droz
Balfour, A. (1990), *Berlin, The Politics of Order: 1737 to 1989*, New York: Rizzoli
Baranowski, B. (1975), *Życie codzienne małego miasteczka w XVII i XVIII wieku*, Warsaw: Panstowowy Instytut Wydawniczy

Barea, I. (1966), *Vienna*, New York: Knopf; London: Pimlico, 1992
Bata, *Architectura e Urbanismus 1910–50* (1991), Zlin
Bata. T. (1941), *How I Began*, tr. J. Baros, Batanagar, India
Bata, T. Jnr., and Sinclair, S. (1990), *Bata: Shoemaker to the World*, Toronto: Stoddart
Bauer, R., Gerstenberg, G., and Peschel, W. (eds) (1989), *Im Dunst aus Bier, Rauch und Volk, Arbeit und Leben in München von 1840 bis 1945. Ein Lesebuch*, Munich: Piper
Beiträge zur Geschichte der Städte Mitteleuropas (8 vols) (1981–7), Linz: Österreichischer Arbeitskreis für Stadtgeschichtsforschung und Ludwig-Boltzmann-Institut für Stadtgeschichtsforschung
Beller, S. (1989), *Vienna and the Jews, 1867–1938: A Cultural History*, Cambridge University Press
Bender, T., and Schorske, C. E. (eds) (1994), *Budapest & New York*, New York: Russell Sage Foundation
Benjamin, W. (1973), *Illuminations*, London: Fontana Press
Benjamin, W. (1992), *One-Way Street and Other Writings*, London: New Left Books
Bergson, H. (1896), *Matière et Mémoire*, Paris: PUF, 1990
Berlin um 1900, exh. cat. (1984), Berlin: Berlinische Galerie
Berman, M. (1985), *All that is Solid Melts into Air*, London: Verso, 1985
Berman, R. (1985), *Modern Culture and Critical theory: Art, Politics and the Legacy of the Frankfurt School*, Wisconsin and London: University of Wisconsin Press
Bernecker, P. (1968), *Österreich – 50 Jahre Republik 1918–1968*, Vienna: Institut für Österreichkunde, Ferdinand Hist. Verlag
Berner, P., Brix, E., and Mantl, W. (eds) (1986), *Wien um 1900: Aufbruch in die Moderne*, Munich: R. Oldenbourg
Bettauer, H. (1922), *Die Stadt ohne Juden*, Salzburg: Hanibal, 1980
Bienarzówna, J., and Małecki, J. M. (1979), *Dzieje Krakowa: Kraków w latach 1796–1918*, III, Kraków: Wyd Literackie
Birchall, E. (1985), *Wedding Tour – January to June 1873 and Visit to the Vienna Exhibition*, D. Verey and A. Sutton (eds), Gloucester and New York: St Martins
Blanning, T. C. W. (1994), *Joseph II*, London: Longman
Boberg, J., Fichter, T., and Gillen, E. (eds) (1986), *Die Metropole: Industriekultur in Berlin im 20. Jahrhundert*, Beck
Bogucka, M., and Samsonowicz, H. (1986), *Dzieje miast i mieszczanstwa w Polsce przedrozbiorowej*, Wrocław: Ossolineum
Boissevain, J. (ed.) (1996), *Coping with Tourists: European Reactions to Mass Tourism*, Providence and Oxford: Berghahn
Böröcz, J. (1996), *Leisure Migration: A Sociological Study on Tourism*, Oxford: Pergamon
Boulboulé, G., and Zeiss, M. (1989), *Worpswede. Kulturgeschichte eines Künstlerdorfes*, Cologne: DuMont
Boyer, J. (1995), *Culture and Political Crisis in Vienna. Christian Socialism in Power, 1897–1918*, Chicago and London: University of Chicago Press
Braun, G. and W. (eds) (1993), *Mäzenatentum in Berlin*, Berlin and New York: Walter de Gruyter
Bröcker, P. (1908), *Hamburg in Not!*, Hamburg
Bröcker, P. (1910), *Die Architektur des Hamburgischen Geschäftshauses. Ein zeitgemäßes Wort für die Ausbildung der Mönckebergstraße*, Hamburg
Brockhaus, G. (1997), *Schauder und Idylle. Faschismus als Erlebnisangebot*, Munich: Antje Kunstann

Bullen, R. J., Pogge von Strandmann, H., and Polonsky, A. B. (eds) (1984), *Ideas into Politics. Aspects of European History 1880–1950*, London: Croom Helm
Busch, H., and Sloman, R. (1974), *Das Chilehaus in Hamburg. Sein Bauherr und sein Architekt*, Hamburg: Christians
Büsch, O. (1960), *Geschichte der Berliner Kommunalwirtschaft in der Weimarer Epoche*, Berlin: Friedrich Meinecke Institut
Buszko, J. (1970), *Uroczystości kazimierzowskie na wawelu w roku 1869*, Kraków: Ministerstwo kultury i sztuki
Campbell, J. (1978), *The German Werkbund. The Politics of Reform in the Applied Arts*, Princeton University Press
Carr, G. J. and Sagarra, E. (eds) (1985), *Fin-de-Siècle Vienna*, University of Dublin Press
Chant, C. (ed.) (1989), *Science, Technology and Everyday Life 1870–1950*, London: Routledge
Corbin, A. (1990), *Women for Hire. Prostitution and Sexuality in France after 1850*, Cambridge, Mass.: Harvard University Press
Crankshaw, E. (1983), *The Fall of the House of Habsburg*, Harmondsworth: Penguin
Cross, T. (1994), *The Shining Sands: Artists in Newlyn and St Ives 1880–1930*, Cambridge and Tiverton: The Lutterworth Press, Westcountry Books
Das Zeitalter Kaiser Franz Josephs 1880–1916, exh. cat. (2 vols), (1987), Schloss Grafenegg: NÖ Landesmuseum
De Certeau, M. (1988), *The Practice of Everyday Life*, tr. S. Randall, Berkeley: University of California Press
Deák, I. (1990), *Beyond Nationalism. A Social and Political History of the Habsburg Officer Corps 1848–1918*, Oxford and New York: Oxford University Press
Der Potsdamer Platz, Eine Geschichte in Wort und Bild (1993), Berlin: Dirk Nishen
Der Unverbrauchte Blick, exh. cat. (1987), Berlin: Martin Gropius Bau
Dessauer, A. (1910), *Grossstadtjuden*, Vienna: Braumüller
Die Düsseldorfer Malerschule, exh. cat. (1979), Mainz: Philipp von Zabern
Dienst, H., and Saurer, E. (eds) (1990), *'Das Weib existiert nicht für sich'*, Vienna: Verlag für Gesellschaftskritik
Domus Dossier: Berlin (1995), Milan: Domus
Duby, G., Fraisse, G., and Perrot, M. (eds) (1994), *19. Jahrhundert (Geschichte der Frauen*, vol. 4), Frankfurt and New York: Campus
Eberlein, K. K. (1929), *Geschichte des Kunstvereins für die Rheinlande und Westfalen, 1829–1929*, Düsseldorf: Schriften des städtischen Kunstmuseums Düsseldorf
Eckermann, E. (1989), *Vom Dampfwagen zum Auto. Motorisierung des Verkehrs*, Reinbek: Rowohlt
Ekielski, W. (1908), *Akropolis. Projekt zabudowań wawelu w latach 1904–1906*, Kraków
Ellermeyer, J. (ed.) (1986), *Stadt und Hafen*, Hamburg: Christians
Ellin, N. (1996), *Postmodern Urbanism*, Oxford and Cambridge, Mass.: Blackwell
Elsaesser, T. (1989), *New German Cinema: A History*, Basingstoke and London: Macmillan
Engelsing, R. (1978), *Zur Sozialgeschichte deutscher Mittel- und Unterschichten*, Göttingen: Vandenhoeck & Ruprecht
Evans, R. J. (1987), *Death in Hamburg. Society and Politics in the Cholera Years*, Oxford: Clarendon Press
Feder, G. (1939), *Die Neue Stadt. Versuch der Begründung einer neuen Stadtplanungskunst aus der sozialen Struktur der Bevölkerung*, Berlin

Foltyn, L. (1991), *Slowakische Architektur und die Tschechische Avantgarde 1918–39*, Dresden: Verlag der Kunst
František, Č. (1983), *Studie a materiály* I, Prague: Národní Galerie
Fritzsche, P. (1992), *A Nation of Fliers. German Aviation and the Popular Imagination* Cambridge, Mass.: Harvard University Press
Fritzsche, P. (1996), *Reading Berlin 1900*, Cambridge Mass. and London: Harvard University Press
Gallwitz, S. (1922), *Briefe und Tagebuchblätter von Paula Modersohn-Becker*, Munich: Wolff
Gassert, P. (1997), *Amerika im Dritten Reich: Ideologie, Propaganda und Volksmeinung 1933–1945*, Stuttgart: Steiner
Gieysztor, A., and Roslanowski, T. (eds) (1976), *Miasta doby Feudalnej w Europie środkowo-wschdnieij, Przemiany społeczne a układy przestrzenne*, Warsaw, Poznań and Toruń: Państwowe Wydawnictwo Naukowe
Glander, H., and Venzmer, E. (1963), *Ahrenshoop*, Schwerin: Petermännchen Verlag
Glaser, H. (1986), *Das Automobil. Eine Kulturgeschichte in Bildern*, Munich: Beck
Glettler, M., Haumann, H., and Schramm., G. (eds) (1985), *Zentrale Städte und ihr Umland. Wechselwirkungen während der Industrialisierungsperiode in Mitteleuropa*, New York: Scripta Mercaturae
Goergen, J-P. (1989), *Walter Ruttmann. Eine Dokumentation*, Berlin: Freunde der Deutschen Kinamathek
Good, D. F. (1984), *The Economic Rise of the Habsburg Empire, 1750–1914*, Berkeley: University of California Press
Gordon, D. (1974), *Modern Art Exhibitions*, Munich: Prestel
Grafton, A., and Blair, A. (eds) (1990), *The Transmission of Culture in Early Modern Europe*, Pittsburgh: University of Pennsylvania Press
Grosz, G. (1955), *Ein kleines Ja und ein grosses Nein*, Hamburg: Rowohlt
Gruber, H. (1991), *Red Vienna. Experiment in Working Class Culture 1918–1934*, Oxford University Press
Gruszynski, A. (ed.) (1997), *Museum der Gegenwart – Kunst in öffentlichen Sammlungen bis 1937*, Düsseldorf: Kunstsammlung Nordrhein-Westfalen
Guttmann, R. (1916), *Die Kinomenschheit: Versuch einer prinzipiellen Analyse*, Vienna and Leipzig: Anzengruber, Brüder Suschitzky
Hadamowsky, F. (1988), *Wien: Theatergeschichte*, Vienna: Jugend und Volk
Hall, P. (1988), *Cities of Tomorrow*, Oxford: Blackwell
Hamann, B. (1996), *Hitlers Wien*, Munich: Piper
Hamel, I. (1967), *Völkischer Verband und nationale Gewerkschaft: der Deutschnationale Handlungsgehilfen-Verband 1893–1933*, Frankfurt am Main: Europäische
Hamm, M. (ed.) (1976), *The City in Russian History*, Lexington: University Press of Kentucky
Handbuch des Kunstmarktes: Kunstadressbuch für das deutsche Reich, Danzig und Deutsch-Österreich (1926), Berlin: Antique Verlaggesellschaft Hermann Kalkoff
Handke, P., and Wenders, W. (1987), *Der Himmel über Berlin*, Frankfurt am Main: Suhrkamp
Harler, T., and Fehl, G. (eds) (1986), *Hitlers Sozialer Wohnungsbau 1940–1945, Wohnungspolitik, Baugestaltung und Siedlungsplanung*, Hamburg: Christians
Hartley, H. (1939), *Eighty-five Not Out: a Record of Happy Memories*, London: Frederick Muller
Harvey, D. (1989), *The Urban Experience*, Oxford: Blackwell
Harvey, D. (1990), *The Condition of Postmodernity*, Oxford: Basil Blackwell

Hausmann, M. *et al.* (1986), *Worpswede. Eine deutsche Künstlerkolonie um 1900*, Fischerhude: Galerie Verlag
Haxthausen, C. W., and Suhr, H. (eds) (1990), *Berlin. Culture and Metropolis*, Minneapolis and London: University of Minnesota Press
Hentzen, A., Rave, P., and Thormaehlen, L. (eds) (1936), *Ludwig Justi: Im Dienst der Kunst*, Breslau
Hietala, M. (1987), *Services and Urbanization at the Turn of the Century: the Diffusion of Innovations*, Helsinki: SHS
Hof, I., and Wojtowicz, J. (1972), *Miasto europejskie w epoce oświecenia I rewolucji francuskiej*, Warsaw: Panstwowe wydawnictwo naukowe
Hof, I., and Wojtowicz, J. (1997), *The Enlightenment: An Historical Introduction*, Oxford: Blackwell
Hofmann, W. (ed.) (1978), *Courbet und Deutschland*, Cologne: DuMont
Hornsby, M. (1909), *The Queen 'Newspaper' Book of Travel: a Guide to Home and Foreign Resorts*, London: Cox
Hroch, M. (1985), *Social Preconditions of National Revival in Europe*, Cambridge University Press
Hubchick, D., and Cox, H. (1996), *A Concise Historical Atlas of Eastern Europe*, London: Macmillan
Huret, J. (1911), *En Allemagne: La Bavière et la Saxe*, Paris: Fasquelle
Hutcheon, L. (1988), *The Politics of Postmodernism*, London: Routledge
Hutcheon, L. (1989), *A Poetics of Postmodernism*, London: Routledge
Hüttenberger, P. (1989), *Düsseldorf Geschichte von den Ursprüngen bis ins 20. Jahrhundert*, vol 3: *Die Industrie- und Verwaltungsstadtim 20. Jahrhundert*, Düsseldorf: Schwann im Patmos
Inspiracje sztuka japonii w malarstwie i grafice polskich modernistów (1981), Kraków: Muzeum Narodowe
Jackson, F. (1985), *Sir Raymond Unwin: Architect, Planner & Visionary*, London: Zwemmer
Janák, J. (1981), *Třbíč. Dějiny města*. II, Brno: Blok
Jefferies, M. (1995), *Politics and Culture in Wilhelmine Germany: The Case of Industrial Architecture*, Oxford: Berg
Jencks, C. (1980), *Late-Modern Architecture*, London: Academy Editions
Jencks, C. (1987), *Post-Modernism: The New Classicism in Art and Architecture*, New York: Rizzoli
Jencks, C. (1991), *The Language of Post-Modern Architecture*, London: Academy Editions
John, M., and Lichtblau, A. (1993), *Schmelztiegel Wien einst und jetzt. Zur Geschichte und Gegenwart von Zuwanderung und Minderheiten*, Vienna: Böhlau
Junge, H. (1992), *Avantgarde und Publikum*, Cologne/Weimar/Vienna: Böhlau
Jušek, K. (1994), *Auf der Suche nach der Verlorenen. Die Prostitutionsdebatten im Wien der Jahrhundertwende*, Vienna: Löcker
Kaes, A. (1989), *From Hitler to Heimat: The Return of History as Film*, Cambridge, Mass. and London: Harvard University Press
Kain, R. (1981), *Planning for Conservation*, London: Mansell
Kamphausen, A. (1972), *Der Baumeister Fritz Höger*, Neumünster: Wachholtz
Károlyi, K. (1891), *Budapestnek vesznie kell!* [Budapest must perish], Budapest
Kasinitz, P. (ed.) (1995), *Metropolis. Centre and Symbol of our Times*, London: Macmillan
Kellner, L., Arnold, P., and Delisle, A. (1914), *Austria of the Austrians and Hungary of the Hungarians*, London: Isaac Pitman

Kirsch, H. K. (n.d), *Worpswede. Die Geschichte einer deutschen Künstlerkolonie*, Munich: Bertelsmann
Kliemann, H. (1969), *Die Novembergruppe*, Berlin: Deutsche Gesellschaft für Bildende Kunst
Kloschatzky, W. (1998), *Viennese Watercolours of the Nineteenth Century*, New York: Harry Abrams
Kniesche, T., and Brockmann, S. (eds) (1940), *Dancing on the Volcano. Essays on the Culture of the Weimar Republic*, Columbia SC: Camden House
Koch, A. (1905), *Darmstadt: Eine Stätte moderner Kunstbestrebungen*, Darmstadt: Koch
Kocka, J. (ed.) (1988), *Bürgertum im 19. Jahrhundert. Deutschland im europäischen Vergleich*, Munich: Deutscher Taschenbuch Verlag
Kocka, J., and Mitchell, A. (eds) (1993), *Bourgeois Society in Nineteenth-Century Europe*, Oxford: Berg
Krabbe, W. R. (1989), *Die deutsche Stadt im 19. und 20. Jahrhundert. Eine Einführung*, Göttingen: Vandenhoeck und Ruprecht
Kracauer, S. (1949), *From Caligari to Hitler: a Psychological History of The German Film*, Princeton University Press (5th edn 1974)
Kracauer, S. (1977), *Das Ornament der Masse*, Frankfurt am Main: Suhrkamp
Krejcar, J. (1928), *L'architecture contemporaine en Tchechoslovaquie*, Prague
Kubiczek, F., et al. (eds) (1994), *History of Poland in Numbers*, Warsaw: CSO
Kühnelt, H. (1986), *Österreich: England/Amerika: Abhandlungen zur Literatur-Geschichte*, ed. S. Patsch, Vienna and Munich: Christian Brandstätter
Langewiesche, D. (1979), *Zur Freizeit des Arbeiters. Bildungsbestrebungen und Freizeitgestaltung österreichischer Arbeiter im Kaiserreich und in der ersten Republik*, Stuttgart: Klett-Cotta
Lavin, M., Boston Institute of Contemporary Art (1992), *Montage and modern life, 1919–1942*, Cambridge, Mass and London: MIT Press
Leśnikowski, W. (ed.) (1996), *East European Modernism, Architecture in Czechoslovakia, Hungary and Poland between the Wars*, London: Thames and Hudson
Lees, A. (1985), *Cities Perceived: Urban Society in European and American Thought, 1820–1940*, Manchester University Press
LeGates, R., and Stout, F. (1996), *The City Reader*, London: Routledge
Leitsch, W., and Wawrykowa, M. (eds) (1989), *Austria-Polska*, Warsaw and Vienna: Wyd. Szkolne i Pedagogiczne/Österreichischer Bundesverlag
Lenman, R. (1997), *Artists and Society in Germany 1850–1914*, Manchester and New York: Manchester University Press
Lepetit, B., and Hoock. J. (eds) (1987), *La Ville et l'innovation en Europe 14e–19e siècles*, Paris: EHESS
Lepszy, L. (1912), *Cracow: The Royal Capital of Ancient Poland. Its History and Antiquities*, London: T. F. Unwin
Lichtenberger, E. (1993), *Vienna: Bridge Between Two Cultures*, tr. D. Mühlgassner and C. Reisser, London and New York: Belhaven
Liebermann, M. (1993), *Vision der Wirklichkeit*, Frankfurt am Main: Fischer
Lohrmann, K. (ed) (1982), *1000 Jahre österreichisches Judentum*, Vienna: Roetzer
Lovis Corinth. Eine Dokumentation (1979), Tübingen: Verlag Ernst Wasmuth
Luckhurst, K. (1951), *The Story of Exhibitions*, London and New York: Studio
Lukacs, J. (1988), *Budapest 1900: an Historical Portrait of a City and its Culture*, London: Weidenfeld and Nicolson
Lützow, F. (1902), *The Story of Prague*, Medieval Towns Series, London: J. M. Dent

Maak, K. (1985), *Die Speicherstadt im Hamburger Freihafen. Eine Stadt an Stelle der Stadt*, Arbeitshefte zur Denkmalpflege in Hamburg no.7, Hamburg: Christians
MacCannell, D. (1976), *The Tourist: a New Theory of the Leisure Class*, New York: Schocken
Mączak, A., and Smout, T. C. (eds) (1991), *Gründung und Bedeutung kleinerer Städte im nördlichen Europa der frühen Neuzeit*, Wiesbaden: Harrasowitz
Madurowicz-Urbanska, H. (1978), *Badania nad historią gospodarczo-społeczną w Polsce*, Warsaw:
Mahood, L. (1990), *The Magdalenes. Prostitution in the Nineteenth Century*, London: Routledge
Mai, E., and Paret, P. (eds) (1993), *Sammler, Stifter, und Museen*, Cologne: Böhlau
Manggha wystawa kolekcji Feliksa Mangghi Jasieńskiego (1989), Kraków: Muzeum Narodowe w Krakowie
Markiewicz, H. (ed.) (1973), *Tadeusz Boy Żeleński o Krakowie*, Kraków: Wyd. Literackie
Matěj, M., Korbelářová, I., and Levá, P. (1992), *Nové Vitkovice 1876–1914*, Ostrava: Památkový ústrav v. Ostráve
Matzerath, H. (1985), *Urbanisierung in Preußen 1815–1914*, Stuttgart, Berlin, Cologne and Mainz: Verlag W. Kohlhammer/Deutscher Gemeindeverlag
Matzerath, H. (ed.) (1996), *Stadt und Verkehr im Industriezeitalter*, Cologne, Weimar, and Vienna: Böhlau
Mayer, S. (1918), *Die Wiener Juden: Kommerz, Kultur, Politik 1700–1900*, Vienna: Löwit
Mayreder, R. (1982), *Zur Kritik der Weiblichkeit. Essays.* Reprint Munich: Frauenoffensive
McHale, B. (1987), *Postmodernist Fiction*, London and New York: Methuen
McHale, B. (1992), *Constructing Postmodernism*, London and New York: Routledge
McKay, J. P. (1976), *Tramways and Trolleys. The Rise of Urban Mass Transport in Europe*, Princeton University Press
Melinz, G., and Zimmermann, S. (1991), *Über die Grenzen der Armenhilfe. Kommunale und staatliche Sozialpolitik in Wien und Budapest in der Doppelmonarchie*, Vienna and Munich: Europa
Miller Lane, B. (1985), *Architecture and Politics in Germany 1918–1945*, Cambridge, Mass.: Harvard University Press (1968)
Miodońska-Brookes, E., and Cieśla-Korytowska, M. (1992), *Feliks Jasieński i jego Manggha*, Kraków: Universitas
Moderná Architekturá na Slovensku 20 a 30 Roky (1991), Spolok: Architektov Slovenska
Moholy-Nagy, L. (1925), *Malerei, Photographie, Film*, Munich:
Mollat du Jourdain, M. (1994), *Europe and the Sea*, Oxford: Blackwell
Monroe, W. S. (1910), *Bohemia and the Čechs; The History of the People, Institutions, and the Geography of the Kingdom, together with accounts of Moravia and Silesia*, London: G. Bell
Montane, H. (Franz Höfberger) (1925), *Die Prostitution in Wien, Ihre Geschichte und Entwicklung von den Anfängen bis zur Gegenwart*, Hamburg, Leipzig, and Vienna
Moreck, C. (1925), *Führer durch das 'Lasterhafte' Berlin*, Leipzig: Verlag moderner Stadtführer
Morgenstern, H. (1901), *Das Schubwesen in Österreich.* Special issue of *Statistische Monatsschrift*, NF, 12
Munch und Deutschland (1994), exh. cat., Hamburg: Kunsthalle
Muther, R. (n.d.), *Aufsätze über bildende Kunst*, 2 vols, Berlin: Ladyschnikow
Nerdinger, W. (ed.) (1993), *Bauhaus-Moderne im Nationalsozialismus. Zwischen Anbiederung und Verfolgung*, Munich: Prestel

Neruda, J. (1993), *Aus dem Alltag der Prager Stadtpolizei. Eine Erzählung aus der Zeit der k. u. k. Monarchie* (reprint), Prague: Vitalis
Neundörfer, L. (1961), *Die Angestellten. Neuer Versuch einer Standortbestimmung*, Stuttgart: Ferdinand Enke
Nicolaisen, D. (1985), *Studien zur Architektur in Hamburg, 1910–1930*, Hamburg
Niethammer, L., and von Plato, A. (eds) (1985), '*Wir kriegen jetzt andere Zeiten'. Auf der Suche nach der Erfahrung des Volkes in nachfaschistischen Ländern*, Berlin and Bonn: Dietz
Nolte, H.-H. (1997), *European Internal Peripheries in the Twentieth Century*, Wiesbaden: Franz Steiner
Nolte, H.-H., (ed.) (1991), *Internal Peripheries in European History, Zur Kritik der Geschichtsschreibung* (vol. 6), Göttingen and Zurich: Muster-Schmidt
Olsen, D. (1986), *The City as a Work of Art, London, Paris and Vienna*, New Haven: Yale University Press
Oxaal, I. et al. (eds) (1987), *Jews, Antisemitism and Culture in Vienna*, London: Routledge
Paret, P. (1980), *The Berlin Secession. Modernism and Its Enemies in Imperial Germany*, Cambridge Mass. and London: Harvard University Press
Paszkiewicz, M. (1972), *Jacek Malczewski in Asia Minor and Rozdól*, London: The Lanckoroński Foundation
Paul, B. (1993), *Hugo von Tschudi und die moderne französische Kunst im Deutschen Kaiserreich*, Mainz: von Zabern
Pechstein, M. (1993), *Erinnerungen*, Stuttgart: Anst
Pemmer, H., and Lackner, N. (1974), *Der Prater. Von den Anfängen bis zur Gegenwart. Neu bearbeitet von Günter Düriegl und Ludwig Sackmauer*, Vienna: Jugend und Volk
Peterman, T. (ed.) (1903), *Die Grossstadt*, Dresden
Petráň, J. (ed.) (1990), *Počátky českého národního obrození*, Prague: Academia
Peukert, D. (1987), *Grenzen der Sozialdisziplinierung. Aufstieg und Krise der deutschen Jugendfürsorge von 1878 bis 1932*, Cologne: Bundesverlag
Plagemann, V. (ed.) (1984), *Industriekultur in Hamburg. Des Deutschen Reiches Tor zur Welt*, Munich: Beck
Polišensky, J. V. (1968), *Britain and Czechoslakia*, Prague: Orbis
Pötzl, E. (1884), *Wiener Skizzen aus dem Gerichts-Saal*, Vienna: Rosner
Prigge, W. (1996), *Urbanität und Intellektualität im 20. Jahrhundert. Wien 1900, Frankfurt, 1930, Paris, 1960*. Frankfurt and New York: Campus
Pugh, M. (1997), *A Companion to Modern European History 1871–1945*, Oxford: Blackwell
Pullat, R. (1976), *Gorodskoje naselenije Estonii s konca XVIII veka do 1940 goda*, Tallinn
Pullat, R., and Enn, T. (1980), *Istoria goroda Tartu*, Tallinn: Eesti Raamat
Pulzer, P. (1988), *The Rise of Political Antisemitism in Germany and Austria*, London: Halban
Purchla, J. (1990), *Jak powstał nowoczesny Kraków*, Kraków: Wyd. Literackie
Purchla, J. (1993), *Teatr i jego architekt*, Kraków: Międzynarodowe Centrum Kultury
Ránki, G. (ed.) (1989), *Hungary and European Civilization*, Indiana University Studies on Hungary, Budapest: Akadémiai Kiadó
Rausch, W. (ed.) (1983), *Die Städte Mitteleuropas im 19. Jahrhundert*, Linz: Ludwig-Boltzmann-Institut für Stadtgeschichteforschung
Rauschnabel, K. (1984), *Stadgestalt durch Staatsgewalt? Das Hamburger Baupflegegesetz von 1912*, Arbeitshefte zur Denkmalpflege in Hamburg, No.6, Hamburg: Christians

Reulecke, J. (1985), *Geschichte der Urbanisierung in Deutschland*, Frankfurt: Suhrkamp
Roschitz, R. (1989), *Wiener Weltausstellung, 1873*, Vienna: Jugend und Volk
Rotenberg, R. (1995), *Landscape and Power in Vienna*, Baltimore: Johns Hopkins University Press
Roters, E. (1984), *Galerie Ferdinand Möllers: die Geschichte einer Galerie für moderne Kunst in Deutschland 1917–1956*, Berlin: Berlinische Galerie
Rozenblit, M. L. (1983), *The Jews of Vienna, 1867–1914: Assimilation and Identity*, Albany: SUNY
Rubey, N., and Schoenwald, P. (eds) (1996), *Venedig in Wien: Theater- und Vergnügungsstadt der Jahrhundertwende*, Vienna: Ueberreuter
Samuel, R. (1994), *Theatres of Memory*, London and New York: Verso
Schenda, R. (1997), *Volk ohne Buch. Studien zur Sozialgeschichte der populären Lesestoffe 1770–1910*, Munich
Schiefler, G. (1985), *Eine hamburgische Kulturgeschichte 1890–1920*, Hamburg: Verein für Hamburgische Geschichte
Schnitzler, A. (1968), *My Youth in Vienna*, London: Weidenfeld and Nicolson
Schorske, C. E. (1981), *Fin-de-Siècle Vienna. Politics and Culture*, Cambridge: Cambridge University Press
Schrank, J. (1899), *Die amtlichen Vorschriften betreffend die Prostitution in Wien, in ihrer administrativen, sanitären und strafgerichtlichen Anwendung*, Vienna
Schumacher, F. (1935), *Stufen des Lebens. Erinnerungen eins Baumeisters*, Stuttgart and Berlin
Schwedeler-Meyer, E. (ed.) (1912), *Hugo von Tschudi: Gesammelte Schriften zur neueren Kunst*, Munich: Bruckmann
Seaton, A. V. et al. (eds) (1994), *Tourism: the State of the Art*, Chichester and London, John Wiley
Segel, H. B. (1987), *Turn of the Century Cabaret*, New York: Columbia University Press
Seitz, R., and Zucker, H. (eds) (1986), *Um uns die Stadt: eine Anthologie neuer Grossstadtdichtung* (orig. Berlin 1931), Der Bauwelt Fundamente 75, Braunschweig: Vieweg
Selwyn, T. (ed.) (1996), *The Tourist Image: Myths and Myth Making in Tourism*, Chichester and New York: John Wiley
Silber, Michael K. (1992), *Jews in the Hungarian Economy, 1760–1945*, Jerusalem: Magnes
Sitte, C. (1891), *Der Städtebau nach seinen künstlerischen Grundsätzen*, Vienna.
Slezak, F. (1982), *Ottakringer Arbeiterkultur an zwei Beispielen*, Vienna: Slezak
Sorkin, D. (1987), *The Transformation of German Jewry, 1780–1840*, Oxford University Press
Starzynski, J. (1971), *Aleksander Gierymski*, Warsaw: Auriga
Stewart, R., Ketner, D. J., and Miller, L. A (1991), *Carl Wimar. Chronicler of the Missouri River Frontier*, New York: Abrams
Storch, U. (1993), *Das Pratermuseum*, Vienna: Museum der Stadt Wien
Strohmeyer, K. (ed.) (1987), *Berlin in Bewegung Literarischer Spaziergang*, vol. 2, die Stadt, Reinbek: Rowohlt
Sudbeck, T. (1994), *Motorisierung, Verkehrsentwicklung und Verkehrspolitik in der Bundesrepublik Deutschland der 1950er Jahre: Umrisse der allgemeinen Entwicklung und zwei Beispiele: Hamburg und das Emsland*, Stuttgart: Steiner
Švacha, R. (1995), *The Architecture of the New Prague 1895–1945*, Cambridge, Mass.: M.I.T.

Tábori, K., and Székely, V. (1908), *Az erkölcstelen Budapest* [Immoral Budapest], Budapest
Tadeusz, W., (1971), *Zarys historii budowy miast*, Wrocław: Ossolineum
Tanzer, G. (1992), *Spectacle müssen seyn: Die Freizeit der Wiener im 18 Jahrhundert*, Vienna: Böhlau
Taylor, W. (ed.) (1991), *Inventing Times Square: Commerce and Culture at the Crossroads of the World*, New York: Russell Sage Foundation
Teeuwisse, N. (1986), *Vom Salon zur Secession*, Berlin: Deutscher Verlag für Kunstwissenschaft
Teich, M., and Porter, R. (eds) (1990), *Fin de Siècle and its Legacy*, Cambridge: Cambridge University Press
Thomas, N. (1990), *International Dictionary of Films and Filmmakers* (2nd edn), Chicago and London: St. James
Thompson, E. P. (1991), *Customs in Common*, London: Penguin
Tichy, M. (1984), *Alltag und Traum. Leben und Lektüre der Dienstmädchen im Wien der Jahrhundertwende*, Graz and Vienna: Böhlau
Tucholsky, K. (1929), *Deutschland, Deutschland über alles*, tr. A. Halley, Amherst: University of Minnesota Press, 1972
Uhde-Bernays, H. (1947), *Im Lichte der Freiheit. Erinnerungen aus den Jahren 1880 bis 1914*, Frankfurt am Main: Insel
Üprus, H. (1965), *Tallinn aastal 1825*, Tallinn: Jirjastus Kunsts
Van de Velde, H. (1962), *Geschichte meines Lebens*, ed. H. Curjel, Munich: Piper
Van der Borght, R. (1925), *Das Verkehrswesen*, Leipzig
Venzmer, W. (1982), *Adolf Hölzel, Leben und Werk*, Stuttgart: Deutsche Verlags-Anstalt
Viator, S. (Seton-Watson, R.) (1908), *Racial Problems in Hungary*, London: Constable
Vida, M. (1992), *The Spas of Hungary*, tr. É Vámos, Budapest: Franklin Nyomda
Voigt, F. (1965), *Verkehr, vol. 2, part 2. Die Entwicklung des Verkehrssystems*, Berlin: Duncker and Humblot
Waissenberger, R. (ed.)(1986), *Wien 1815–1848: Zeit des Biedermeier*, London: Alpine Fine Arts Collection UK
Wallerstein, I. (1974–1988), *The Modern World System. I–III*, New York: Academic Press
Walser, R. (1978), *Jakob von Gunten*, ed. J Greven, Frankfurt am Main: Suhrkamp
Wąsicki, J. (1960), *Miasta zachodniego pogranicza Wielkopolski, 1793–1815*, Poznań
Wasilewski, E. (1925), *Poezje*, Kraków: nakładem krakowski spółki wydawniczej
Weinstein, J. (1989), *The End of Expressionism. Art and the November Revolution in Germany 1918–19*, Chicago and London: The University of Chicago Press
Weiss, T. (1987), *Legenda i Prawda Zielonego Balonika*, Kraków: Wyd. Literackie
Weltge-Wortmann, S. (1979), *Die ersten Maler in Worpswede*, Worpswede: Worpsweder
Wenders, W. (1991), *The Logic of Images*, tr. M. Hofmann, London: Faber and Faber
Westphal, C. (1938), *Fritz Höger. Der niederdeutsche Backstein-Baumeister*, Westphal: Wolfshagen-Scharbeutz (Lübecker Bucht)
Wheatcroft, A. (1995), *The Habsburgs: Embodying Empire*, London and New York: Viking
White, W. (1957), *A July Holiday in Saxony, Bohemia and Silesia*, London: Chapman and Hall
Wickham Steed, H. (1919), *The Habsburg Monarchy*, London: Constable and Constable
Wickham Steed, H. (1924), *Through Thirty Years, 1892–1922: A Personal Narrative*, 2 vols, London: Heinemann

Wiegenstein, J. (1978), *Artists in a Changing Environment: the Viennese Art World 1860–1918*, Ann Arbor: University Microfilms Indiana University

Windsor, A. (1981), *Peter Behrens: Architect and Designer 1868–1940*, London: Architectural Press

Wistrich, R. (1988), *The Jews of Vienna in the Age of Franz Joseph*, Oxford University Press

Wittlich, P. (1992), *Prague Fin de Siècle*, Paris: Flammarion

Wobbe, T. (1989), *Gleichheit und Differenz: politische Strategien von Frauenrechtlerinnen um die Jahrhundertwende*, Frankfurt: Campus

Wolff, K. (ed.) (1950), *The Sociology of Georg Simmel*, New York: Free Press of Glencoe

Zeleński, T. (1954), *Boy Słówka*, Kraków: Wyd. Literackie

Ziak, K. (1979), *Des Heiligen Römischen Reiches größtes Wirtshaus*, Munich and Vienna: Jugend und Volk

Zimmermann, S. (1997), *Prächtige Armut. Fürsorgepolitik, Kinderschutz und radikale Sozialreform in Budapest im Vergleich mit Wien 1870–1914*, Sigmaringen: Thorbeke

Index

References to illustrations are given in *italics*.

Aachen, 51
The Abduction of Daniel Boone's Daughter by the Indians, 49
abolitionism, 182
absolutism, 93, 96
academy salons, 51
accidents, 217–18
'acculturation', 146
Achenbach, Andreas, 48
Achtek, 248
Adenauer, Konrad, 215
advertising, 16, 28, 114
aeroplane, 28, 40 n30, 240 *see also* air transportation
Africa, 15
agriculture, 94, 96
Ahrenshoop, 53, 54–5
air transportation, 213–14
alcohol, 161, 169
Alekan Circus, 242
Allgemeiner Nieder-österreichische Volksbildungsverein, 163
Allgemeiner Österreichische Frauenverein, 193 n26
allotments, 36
Alps, 52, 124
Alster Lake, 10
Alte Pinakothek (Munich), 46, 50
Alt-Moabit, 66
Altona, 220
Altstadt (Hamburg), 10, 11, 14, 17
Ambrosius, Mario, 252 n44
Americanism, 46 *see also* United States of America
angels, 242
Angelus Novus, 242
Angestellte (white-collar employees), 200
Anschluss, 198
antiquity, 111
anti-semitism, 78, 114, 150–53
Antwerp, 47
apartment block, 29, 31, 34
applied arts, 56
apprentices, 202

ara patriae, 104
Arbeiterzeitung, 163, 170, 204
archaeology, 112
architecture, 2, 3, 9–20, 28–39, 89–90, 101–3, 108, 112, 240
Architekten und Ingenieurverein Hamburg (AIV), 19 n23
Die Architektur des Hamburgischen Geschäftshauses, 14
aristocracy *see* upper classes
art, 2, 45–60, 63–78, 101–14
artists' colonies, 52–5, 57–8
Art Journal, 125
art trade, 51–2
Asia Minor, 111
assimilation, 146, 148, 152–4
Association of Feminists, 190, 193 n27
Attack on an Emigrant Train, 49
Aufklärung (Enlightenment), 149
Augsburg, 215
Ausgleich, 105, 133
Austria, 51, 92, 101, 114, 135, 159, 197–206
Austria-Hungary *see* Habsburg Empire
avant-garde, 27, 28, 52, 58
Avenarius, Ferdinand, 13
Azbé, Anton, 48

Baba *see* Na Baba
Baden, 127
Baedeker, 126, 128, 130
Baillie Scott, M. H., 31
Balfour, Alan, 249
balls, 87, 127, 129, 130
Baltic States, 48, 86, 90, 92, 96
Bantzer, Carl, 50
Barbizon landscape school, 49–50
Barek, Josef, 33–4
Barkenhoff, 55
Barlach, Ernst, 71, 74
Baroque, 9, 14, 131, 146, 149
Barr, Alfred, 76
Bastien-Lepage, Jules, 50, 53

268 INDEX

Bata, Jan, 35, 38
Bata shoe company, 4, 34–9, 40 n34
Bata, Tomáš, 35–9
Baudouin de Courtenay, Jan, 114
Bauhaus, 27, 56, 209
Baupflegegesetz, 16, 17
Bavaria, 54, 86, 215
Bavarian State Galleries, 50
Bayer, Herbert, 226
Bebel, August, 11
Beckmann, Max, 73, 74, 76
Bedford Park, 32
Beethoven, Ludwig van, 127, 129, 149, 161, 170
begging, 175, 182, 185, 204
Behrens, Peter, 57
Belgium, 49, 52, 56
Belgrade, 133
Benedikt, Moritz, 155–6
Benjamin, Walter, 67, 242
Berlage, Henri, 30
Berlin, 1, 3, 4, 7, 45, 46, 47, 48, 50, 54–5, 63–78, 124, 130, 135, 136, 145, 209–26, 232–3, 234, 236, 239–52
Berlin Academy, 47, 67, 68–9, 76
Berlin Alexanderplatz, 210, 221
Berlin Artists' Association, 69
Berlin National Gallery, 50, 67, 68, 74–8, 81, 83
Berlin: Symphony of a City, 209–26, 238, 251 n30
Berlin Wall, 241, 246, 247–8
Berlioz, Hector, 170
Bernheim, 52
Bettauer, Hugo, 156
Białystok, 91, 95
bicycle, 216
Biedermeier, 161
Dierstadt, Alfred, 49
Bilder der Grossstadt, 210
Bildung, 6, 149, 167, 169 see also education
Bildungsarbeit, 169
Birchall, Emily, 125
Der Blaue Engel, 251 n30
Blaue Reiter, 52
'blue Mondays', 161
Bobrowski, Z., 91
Bode, Wilhelm von, 47, 56, 64
Bohemia, 31, 32, 85, 87, 88, 93, 95, 96, 111, 124, 132, 134, 146, 152, 171
Bohemian Industrial Museum, 134
Bohemian Museum, 134
Bois, Curt, 251 n30
Boisserée collections, 46
Bonn, 47
boulevards, 28, 29, 66, 96, 125, 136
Boy-Żeleński, Tadeusz, 107
Brahms, Johannes, 127, 170
Brandenburg, 52
Braque, Georges, 73
Bratislava, 39 n7, 93
Bremen, 54, 215
Breslau, 145, 211, 212
brick, 10, 13, 14, 15, 17, 18, 37, 89, 90
Brieger, Lothar, 70, 71
Brno, 28, 33, 36, 38, 39 n7, 145
Broch, Hermann, 157
Bröcker, Otto, 16
Bröcker, Paul, 3, 9–20, 23–5

Brożek, Vlastimil, 34
Die Brücke, 45, 52, 64
Brüder Kohn, 129
Brussels Congrès International d'Architecture Moderne (C.I.A.M.), 34
Buda, 93, 98 n24, 133
Budapest, 2, 5, 6, 123, 124, 126, 130, 131, 133, 134, 136, 144, 145, 152, 164, 175–96
Building Cooperative of Public Servants, 32
Burgtheater, 127

cabaret, 5, 107–14
cafés, 4, 28, 66, 67, 93, 107, 130, 162, 188
Cannetti, Elias, 157
capital cities, 93–4, 102–14, 133, 146, 175, 246 see also individual cities
capitalism, 6
cars, 39 see also motor vehicles
cartoons, 108–12
Carus, K. G., 45
Cassiel, 244
Cassirer, Bruno, 50, 64
Cassirer Gallery, 52, 64, 65, 67, 71, 72, 77, 78
Cassirer, Paul, 50, 64, 65, 67
cathedrals, 9, 10, 106, 111, 128
Catherine the Great, 89
Catholic Church, 93, 96, 146, 149, 162
censorship, 109, 165, 171
Central Europe, 2–3, 85–100, 124, 145
České Budějovice, 95
Cézanne, Paul, 71
Chamber of Labour, 202, 206 n16
charity, 203
Chemnitz, 223, 231
Chiemsee, 53
'Chilehaus', 11, 18, 22
chłopomania (peasant mania), 113
cholera, 9–10, 125
Christian Social Party, 160, 166–8, 170, 171, 202, 205
churches, 9, 104, 110
cinema, 2, 7, 28, 33, 128, 164, 165–6, 209–26, 239–52
City Park, 133
city planning see urban planning
The City without Jews, 156
civil service, 199, 200, 203
class, 2, 3 see also working class, middle class, upper classes
class conflict, 17
classicism, 90
clinker, 10, 14, 15
coffee houses see cafés
Cold War, 7, 241, 249
collective housing, 28, 34, 37, 38 see also apartment block
Cologne, 47, 52, 211, 212, 214, 215, 218, 223
colonization, 15
Columbo, 251 n26
commerce, 4, 9, 13, 28, 33, 34, 91, 135, 136
commercialization, 53, 73, 165
Commission for Christian Youth Education, 170
commissiones boni ordinis, 89
Communism, 73
competition, 32
concert halls, 90

INDEX 269

Congress of Vienna, 125, 127
conservationism, 55, 110
Constantinople, 133
Construction Act (Prague), 29
Constructivism, 27, 74
consumerism, 151
Cook, Thomas, 54, 125, 127, 129, 136
Cook's Excursionist, 125, 129, 136
Le Corbusier, 38, 250 n4
Corinth, Lovis, 48, 67–9, 71, 75
Cornwall, 52, 53
corporatism, 205
corso, 130 *see also* Flower *corso*
cosmopolitanism, 35, 49, 50, 55, 73, 156
counter-culture, 171
Courbet, Gustave, 50, 169
crime, 11
Croat, 28
Cromwell Contemplating the Corpse of Charles I, 49
Cubism, 30, 32
cuisine, 132
cultural consumption, 4, 5, 6, 151, 164, 165
'culture of grace', 6
Customs Union (Germany), 10, 12
Czas, 115 n20
Czechish-Slavonic Ethnographical Museum, 134
Czech lands, 91, 92, 93
Czech language, 94, 95, 134
Czechoslovak Decorative Arts Association (Svaz československého díla), 33
Czechoslovakia, 4, 27–39
Czechs, 132
Czernowitz, 145

Dachau, 53
Daily News, 125
Danneberg, Robert, 197, 199
Danube, 124, 134
Darmstadt, 54, 56, 61
Darmstadt-Mathildenhöhe, 57
Daszyński, Ignacy, 107
Debschitz, Wilhelm von, 48
deconstructivism, 247
Defregger, Franz, 47
Dejvice, 29
Delacroix, Eugène, 169
de Laforgúe, Leo, 216
Delaroche, Paul, 49
'Delnicke Kolonie', 31
demography, 4, 87, 116 n34, 132, 150, 157 n2, 162
demolition, 9
Denmark, 52
department stores, 15, 33, 37
Depression, 38, 198–206, 212, 215
Derain, André, 73
Dessauer, Adolf, 153
de Staël, Madame, 146
Deutsche Gartenstadtbewegung (German Garden City Association), 30
Deutsche Kunst und Dekoration, 57
Deutsche Lufthansa, 214, 215
Deutsche Werkbund, 17
Deutschnationale Handlungsgehilfen Verband (DHV), 17, 20 n29
Devětsil group, 27–8
Diener and Diener, 248

Diez, Wilhelm, 47
Dix, Otto, 74
Döblin, Alfred, 2, 210
docks, 10, 11
'A Document of German Art', 57
Domus Dossier, 248
Dornbach, 128
Dortmund, 215
Dresden, 17, 45, 46, 51, 52, 56, 63, 64, 93, 211, 212, 214
Dresden Academy, 47
Dresden Royal Gallery, 46
Dudok, Willem, 30
Duino Elegies, 242
Durand-Ruel, 52
Düsseldorf, 45–6, 48, 49, 51, 52, 53–4, 63, 211, 212
Düsseldorf Academy, 47, 53
Duveneck, Frank, 47, 49
Dvořák, Vilém, 30
Dynamic of the City, 209
Dzieduszycki, Wojciech, 113

Eastern Europe, 49, 50, 85–100
Eberfeld, 54
Ebert, Friedrich, 69
education, 15, 149, 150–51, 159–60, 162, 166–70
Einstein, Carl, 72
Ekielski, Władisław, 106
Elbe, 18
elites, 88, 89, 90, 96 *see also* upper classes
elitism, 68
Ellenbogen, Wilhelm, 159
Emil und die Detektive, 221
Engel, Antonín, 29
England, 4, 12–13, 30, 124
Essen, 215
Estonia, 86, 90, 95
Eulenberg, Herbert, 73
The Execution of Lady Jane Grey, 49
exhibitions, 56, 57, 65, 69, 73, 74, 79 n38, 107, 128, 132, 133, 135, 136
Expressionism, 45, 46, 64, 65, 68, 71, 74
expulsion, 185, 189

façades, 16, 17, 18 n22, 32, 90, 103, 247
Die Fackel, 154
factories, 27–39, 52
factory towns, 40 n22
Fałat, Julian, 103
Falk, Peter, 251 n26
fascism, 205
Fassadenkommission, 16
Fassbinder, Rainer Werner, 245
Feder, Gottfried, 218
feminism, 176
Fiaker-Milli, 130
film *see* cinema
Finland, 48
fire, 9, 10, 12, 90
Flechtheim, Alfred, 72, 77, 82 *see also* Galerie Flechtheim
Fliegende Blätter, 130
Florian Gate, 104
Flower *corso*, 128, 130, 168
folk art, 31, 40 n19, 113
Fontane, Theodor, 2

Ford, Henry, 35
Frampton, Kenneth, 27
France, 49, 50, 51, 52, 64, 73, 77, 93, 124
franchise, 114
Franco-Prussian War, 50, 217
Frankfurt am Main, 47, 50, 54, 211, 212, 214, 215, 223
Franz-Josef I, 105, 128, 131, 136
Franz-Joseph Bridge, 131
Frauenwörth, 52
freedom, 68, 149, 151–2
Freie Sezession, 65, 69
Freiwillige Arbeitsdienst (Volunteer Labour Service), 202
frescoes, 111
Freud, Sigmund, 154, 156, 157
Friedrich, Caspar David, 45
Frycz, Karol, 107, 109, 115 n20, *118–23*
functionalism, 167

gables, 10, 14, 17
Gabriel, 111
Gahura, František Lydie, 36
Galerie Flechtheim, 67, 73, 74, 77
Galerie Möller, 74 *see also* Möller, Ferdinand
Galerie Simon, 72
Galicia, 105, 108, 111, 132, 146, 152
Galicia-Lodomeria, 102
galleries, 9, 46, 50, 52, 55, 67
Gallery Mietke, 129
'Gallery of Living Art', 75
Gängevierteln (Hamburg), 10
Garden Cities of Tomorrow, 29
garden city movement, 4, 29–39
garden factory, 36
gardening, 15, 29
gardens, 27–39, 127
Gasthäuser, 127, 128
Gdańsk, 86
Gedächtniskirche, 213
Gemeindebauten, 207 n40
Gemütlichkeit, 5, 132, 137
gender, 6, 175–97
Geneva Loan, 198
German, 18, 28, 94, 132
German Artists' Protest (1911), 50
German Garden City Association *see* Deutsche Gartenstadtbewegung
Germany, 4, 7, 9–20, 30, 35, 45–58, 124, 125, 209–26, 235
Gierymski, Aleksander, 51
Glaspalast, 46, 54
glass, 37
Gočár, Josef, 30, 32
Goethe, Hohann Wolfgang von, 132, 163
Goldschlag, Georg, 213, 219
Goldschmidt and Wallerstein, 67
Gothic architecture, 9, 10
Göttingen, 54
le gout juif, 155
Graben, 126
Grand Tour, 124
Graner, Ernst, 129
Grassi, Giorgio, 248
Great Britain, 56, 136
Greater Prague Act, 28, 29, 33

Greece, 48, 111
grid plan, 34
Grinzing, 128
Gris, Juan, 73
Grodska Street, 104
Gropius, Walter, 56
Grossman, Stefan, 160, 168, 170
Grossstadt, 7, 146–7, 157, 212, 225
Grossstadtjuden (big-city Jews), 146, 153, 156
Grosz, George, 2, 64, 70, 73, 74, 226
Gründerzeit, 12
guidebooks, 126–7, 130, 135
guided tours, 103–4
Gumpendorf, 159
Gunten, Jakob von, 216
Gurlitt (Fritz) Gallery, 71, 79 n23
Gurlitt, Wolfgang, 71–2
Gymnasien (grammar schools), 151, 153, 167

Habermann, Hugo von, 48
Habsburg Empire, 2, 3, 5, 27, 85, 91, 96, 101–17, 123–40, 146–58, 164, 175–95, 198
The Hague, 31
Hall, Peter, 29, 30
Halle, 215
Hamburg, 1–2, 3, 9–20, 51, 54, 70, 211, 212, 214, 215, 218
Der Hamburger, 15, 16
Hamburger Echo, 12
Hamburger Fremdenblatt, 12
Hamburg in Not!, 11, 12, 15
Hamburgische Correspondent, 12, 15
Hampstead Garden Suburb, 31, 32
Handke, Peter, 244, 250 n22, 252 n44
Hanover, 215
Hanover school, 18
Hansaplatz, 66
Hansestadt, 13
Hanuš, Alex, 34
Hapsburg Empire *see* Habsburg Empire
Harburger Volksblatt, 12
'Haus Glass', 14
health, 37, 53
Heckel, Erich, 74, 76
Heimat, 225
Heimatkunst, 53, 55
Heimatliteratur, 15
Heimatrecht, 207
Heimatschutz, 14, 15, 19 n17
Hellerau, 30
Hellocourt, 38
Hendel, Zygmunt, 105
Herrmann, Curt, 75
Herwarth Walden, 52
Herzl, Theodor, 155
Herzog, Werner, 245
Hess, Rudolf, 225
Hesse, 53
Hesse-Darmstadt, 57
Heurigen (wine taverns), 127, 128
Heydt, Eduard von der, 77
Hilversum, 31
Der Himmel über Berlin see Wings of Desire
Hintertreppenromane, 163
Hiroshige, Utagawa, 110

Hirth, Georg, 56, 57
historical colourism, 49
historicism, 12, 47
Hitler, Adolf, 157, 217
Hoddis, Jakob von, 46
Hoelzel, Adolf, 56
Höger, Fritz, 3, 11, 14, 15, 17
Holland, 31, 47, 50, 52
Holocaust, 157
Holstein, 14
Homer, 7, 243–4, 248, 249
Honzík, Karel, 39, 44
hospital, 105
hotels, 125, 129, 126, 134
housing, 10–11, 199, 200, 201
Howard, Ebenezer, 29, 31
Hrabia Wojtek (Count Wojtek), 113
Hradec Králové, 32
Hübschmann, Bohumil, 31, 32
Hudson River, 49
Humoristische Blätter, 130
Hungary, 48, 124, 133, 135, 136, 146, 164, 165
Hussites, 135
hyperinflation, 198

immigration, 6, 150, 162
immorality, 177–9, 182, 185
Impressionism, 64, 68
Independent Socialist Party (USPD), 65
industrialization, 85, 114, 133, 161, 162
inflation, 65, 70
Insel Verlag, 54
institutions, 48, 85–91
intellectuals, 95
intelligentsia, 103
interior design, 15, 32
International Association Against White Slavery, 190
International Roads Congress, 225
L'Intransigeant, 73
In weiter Ferne, So Nah!, 252 n44
Isozaki, Arata, 248

Jagiellonian dynasty, 104
Jakob von Gunten, 223
Janák, Pavel, 30, 31, 32
Japan, 107, 109–10
Japonisme, 109–10
Jasieński, Feliks 'Manggha', 109–10
Jawlensky, Alexei von, 48
jazz, 146
Jencks, Charles, 251 n35
Jesuits, 91
Jews, 6, 7, 77, 113, 114, 145–58
Jihlava, 95, 96
Jindřichův Hradec, 95
Johnson, Eastman, 49
Joseph II, 132, 146–7, 162
Jugend, 56
Jugend am Werk (Youth at Work), 202
Jugend in Not (Youth in Need), 202
Jugendstil, 47, 154
Jungen, 167
Junkers Luftverkehr A. G., 215
Justi, Ludwig, 68, 74–8
Jutzi, Phil, 210

Kaestner, Erich, 221
Kahnweiler, Daniel-Henry, 72
Kandinsky, Vassily, 48, 52, 58
Kant, Immanuel, 68, 149
Karfík, Vladimír, 37, 38
Karlsruhe, 9, 30, 53
Kärtnerstrasse, 126, 130, 164
Kassel, 215
Katen, 53
Kaulbach, Friedrich, 48
Kautsky, Benedikt, 201
Kessler, Harry, 56
Kierownictwo Odnowienia Zamk Królewskiego (Directorship for the Restorations of the Royal Palace), 110
Kikeriki, 130
Kirchner, August, 220
Kirchner, Ernst, 46, 71, 74, 76
Klee, Paul, 76, 242
Kleihues, Josef Paul, 248
'Klöpperhaus', 14–15
Klopstockstrasse, 65, 78
Knaus, Ludwig, 53
Knirr, Heinrich, 1
Koch, Alexander, 57, 58
Kohlbecker, Christoph, 248
Kohlmarkt, 126
Kokoschka, Oskar, 71
Koła Polskiego (Polish Circle), 110–11, 113
Kollhoff, Hans, 239, 248
Kollwitz, Käthe, 48, 68, 71
Kolportage novels, 163–4
Königsberg, 48, 219, 220–21, 222
Königgrätz (Sadova), 159
Die Königstochter im Irrenhaus, 163
Kordt, Walter, 218
Korherr, Richard, 218
Kotěra, Jan, 30–32, 36, 41
Kouřim, 94
Kracauer, Siegfried, 210, 223, 226
Kraków, 5, 86, 93, 94, 98 n24, 101–17, 123, 145
Kraków Narodowej Sztuce (Kraków – the National Work of Art), 103
Kraus, Karl, 154, 155, 156, 157
Kraus, Max, 74
Krefeld, 54
Kreisstädte (district capitals), 95
Krejcar, Jaromir, 39 n8
Kroměříž, 96
Kronenzeitung, 164
Kuehl, Gotthard, 50
Kulturforum, 248–9
Kulturstufe, 225
Kunst und Künstler, 64, 65
Das Kunstblatt, 65, 71
Künstlerkommision (commission of artists), 15, 16
Kunststädte, 52, 70
Kunstverein, 51
Kupelwieser, Paul, 31
Kurfürstendamm, 52, 58, 66, 69
Kurza Noga (Hen's Leg), 108

labour market, 199–200, 202
'The Labour Movement as a Preparatory School for War', 17
'ladies' academies', 48

272 INDEX

Lamprecht, Gerhard, 221
Lanckoroński, Karol, 110–11, 112
Landeskunstkommission, 75
landscape painting, 52
Langbehn, Julius, 55
Lange, Hermann, 73
Latvia, 86
Lausanne Loan, 198
Léger, Fernand, 73
Lehrter Bahnhof, 66, 69
Leibl, Wilhelm, 47, 52
Leichter, Käthe, 201, 207
Leipzig, 93, 211, 212, 214, 215, 218
Leipziger Strasse, 67
leisure, 6, 36, 160–61
Lemberg, 145
Lenbachplatz, 58
Lessing, Gottfried Ephraim, 149, 163
Letchworth, 29, 31
Leutze, Emanuel, 48, 49
Leva Fronta, 34
Levy, Rudolf, 73
Ley, Walter, 70
Liberalism, 183
liberalization, 96
Liberec, 95
Liberty Leading the People, 169
libraries, 162–3, 169
Lichterfelde, 211
Lichtwark, Alfred, 9, 10, 13
Liebermann, Max, 50, 64–5, 67–70, 71, 75–8, 169
Liegnitz, 54
lifts, 13
literacy, 162
literature, 15, 163–4
Litoměřice, 95
Litomyšl, 96
Livonia, 86, 88
Ljubljana, 165
Lloyd Wright, Frank, 30, 38
loans, 198
local government, 88, 89
Łódź, 95
Logical Positivism, 154
Die Logik der Bilder (The Logic of Images), 243
Loket, 95
London, 2, 29, 30, 46, 51, 124
Lonely Metropolitan, 226
Loos, Adolf, 154
Louny, 31–2, 41
Low Countries, 51
Lower Austria, 162
Lower Austrian Catholic Women's Organization, 166
Lower Austrian Organization for Education and Instruction, 168
Lublin, 86, 91
Ludwig I, 46
Ludwig, Ernst, 57
Luftverkehrs A. G., 215
Luitpold (Prince), 48
Lukásbad spa, 135
Lumière Brothers, 164
Lunn, Henry, 54
Lützow, Franz, 135
Lützow Ufer, 66

Luxemburg, Rosa, 113
Lviv/Lvov, 5, 86, 91, 96, 123

Mackensen, Fritz, 53–4
Mackintosh, Charles Rennie, 31
Magazine of Art, 50
Magdeburg, 215
Mahler, Gustav, 154, 157
Makart, Hans 136
Malczewski, Jacek, 106
Malkasten (Paintbox), 49
Manet, Édouard, 50, 64
Mannheim Gallery, 50
Marc, Franz, 52, 75
Margaret Island, 135
Maria Theresa, 94
Marion Church, 104, 110
markets, 95
Marr, Carl, 49
Martini, Simone, 70
Marxism, 113, 154, 155
Masaryk, T. G., 27, 28
Masereel, Franz, 210
mass culture, 6, 34, 210
Matejko, Jan, 104
May Day, 168
Mayreder, Rosa, 182
Mazowia, 86
Mecklenburg, 53
media, 15–16, 45, 93–4
Mehoffer, Józef, 102, 111
Mehring, Franz, 11
Meidner, Ludwig, 46
Meier-Graefe, Julius, 50
Meisel, Edmund, 221
Memel, 51
memory, 239–52
Merritt Chase, William, 49
'The Metropolis and Mental Life', 216
Metternich, Clemens, 147
Michalikowa, Jama, 107, 115 n20
Mickiewicz, Adam, 104, 107
middle class, 4, 39, 51, 66, 91, 93, 124, 130, 150, 153, 157, 160, 162, 166, 176–81, 191
migration, 2, 87
Mikwa, 114
Millenary Exhibition, 133
Millet, Jean-François, 169
Ministry of Culture and Education, 166
Modernism, 27–39, 71, 73, 74, 76, 77, 103, 106, 111, 155, 160, 209, 240
modernity, 27, 28, 46
modernization, 1, 4, 7, 64, 87, 88–90, 94–6, 124, 147, 155, 191, 205, 215
Modersohn, Otto, 53–4
Modersohn-Becker, Paula, 48, 53–4, 75
Mödling, 127
Moholy-Nagy, Lásló, 209
Moll, Carl, 129
Möller, Ferdinand, 67, 72, 73–4
Mönckeberg, Johann Georg, 11
Mönckebergstrasse, 11, 14, 15, 16, 17, 21
Moneo, J. R., 248
Monet, Claude, 50
montage, 7, 209, 225
monumentalism, 225

morality, 175–93
Moravia, 4, 31, 34, 86, 87, 88, 93, 95, 96, 124, 132, 146
Moreck, Curt, 66
Morocco Crisis, 15
Morris, William, 57
Moser, Koloman, 136, 154
motor vehicles, 213–14
motorways, 225
Mozart, Wolfgang Amadeus, 127, 161
Mueller, Otto, 74, 75
Muhlheim, 215
multi-stories, 37, 38
Munch, Edvard, 51, 75–6
Münchener Neueste Nachrichten, 218
Munich, 2, 15, 46–57, 63, 64, 65, 75, 93, 211, 212, 214, 215, 218, 220
Munich Academy, 47, 49
Munich United Workshops, 56
municipal authorities, 135, 176, 184, 190–91, 195 n75
Münter, Gabriele, 48, 52
Murnau, 52
museums, 4, 90, 127, 134 see also galleries
music, 93, 170 see also individual composers
Muther, Richard, 50, 55, 57

Na Baba, 33, 34, 40 n20
Napoleonic Wars, 45, 51
Náprstek, Vojta, 134
Naprzód (Forward), 114
Naschmarkt, 133, 154
national identity, 5, 32, 223–6, 241, 245
National Socialism, 77, 205, 245
The National Vigilance Association, 190
nationalism, 3, 5, 18, 51, 76, 91, 101–17, 123, 131–4, 135, 137, 170–71, 205
nationalization, 35
Naturalism, 50
Naunhof, 222
Neide, Emil, 48
Neruda, Jan, 178
Netherlands, 91
Neue Abteilung, 75
Neue Freie Presse, 130, 155–6
Neue Sachlichkeit see New Objectivity, 209, 220
Neumann, I. B., 72
Neumann/Nierendorf Gallery, 67
Neustadt (Hamburg), 10
Neuwaldegg, 128
Neuzeit, 149, 150, 152
New German Cinema, 245
'New Lanark', 34
Newlyn colony, 53
New Objectivity see Neue Sachlichkeit
New York, 49, 72, 135
New York Congress of the International Garden City and Town Planning Federation, 30
Nicolaisen, Dörte, 11
Nicholas I, 107
Niedersachsen, 215
'Niemannhaus', 14
noise pollution, 222
Nolde, Emil, 76
Noskowski, Witold, 107–8, 109, 115 n20
Notstandsaushilfe, 201

Nové Město, 32
November Group, 69
Nowe Miasto (New Town), 110
Nussdorf, 128
nutrition, 201, 203

Obrist, Hermann, 48
Óbuda, 133
offices, 11, 13, 14, 18
Olbrich, Josef Maria, 57, 109, 154
opera, 95, 103, 108, 127
Ořechovka, 32, 33, 34, 42
Österreichische Hauspersonalzeitung, 164
Österreichische Kriminal-Zeitung, 164
Österreichische Wochenschrift, 152
Overbeck, Fritz, 54
Owen, Robert, 31, 34

palaces, 9, 75, 76, 77, 131
Palucci (Marquis), 90
Pankok, Bernhard, 56
Paris, 2, 27, 38, 46, 50, 56, 66, 72, 124, 125, 126, 128, 135, 136, 164
Paris Exposition (1937), 38
Parker, Barry, 29
parks, 87, 90, 127, 128, 131, 162, 167
pątnictwem narodowym (national pilgrimages), 103
patriarchy, 4, 34
patronage, 65
pavements, 89–90
Pawlatschenhaus, 129
peasantry, 111–13
Pechstein, Max, 46, 68, 71–2, 74, 76
pedestrians, 216–17, 218
Pellerin, 52
Pendl, Erwin, 129
Pensionen, 126
peripheries, 87
Pernerstorfer, Engelbert, 170
Pest, 2, 27, 98 n24, 133, 134, 178, 183
Peter the Great, 89
Petřín Hill, 134
photography, 102, 129
Piarists, 91
Picasso, Pablo, 73
Piloty, Karl Theodor, 47
Plečnik, Josip, 30
plein-airisme, 45, 47, 50, 53
Plzeň, 95, 96
Podlasie, 86
Poland, 48, 85, 86, 88, 89, 91, 92, 95, 96, 101–17
police, 7, 11, 165, 177–81, 183, 186, 210, 216, 219–22
Polička, 95
Polívka, Karel, 34
Polska Partia Socjalno-Demokratyczna (Polish Social-Democrat Party, PPSD), 113, 114, 116 n36
pomnikomania, 107
Pomorze, 86
pompes funèbres, 104, 106
Popper, Karl, 154
popular culture, 160, 161–4
postcards, 129, 130
Postmodernism, 240, 246
Potocki, A., 89

Potsdamer Platz, 7, 213, 239, 242, 246, 248, 249, 252 n44
Der Potsdamer Platz, 248
Potsdamer Strasse, 67, 248
Pötzl, Eduart, 130
poverty, 6, 175–95, 197–206
Poznań, 86, 91, 96
Prague, 2, 5, 28–39, 91, 93, 94, 98 n24, 123, 124, 126, 133, 134, 144, 145, 152, 165
Prague Architects Association (Společnost Architektů), 30
Prague City Council, 135
Prater, 125, 126, 128, 130, 131, 162, 164
press, 57, 93, 94, 130, 131, 152, 164, 166, 169 *see also* media
Pressburg, 152
prison, 184
prisoners of war, 17
property, 149–50
Protestantism, 135
prostitution, 6, 128–9, 130, 175–96, 202
provincial centres, 94–6
Provinzjuden, 150
Prussia, 4, 47, 58, 75, 86, 92, 101, 159, 210
Prussian Academy of Arts, 68
Przybyszewski, Stanisław, 107
public buildings, 9, 10, 90, 91, 106
public health, 28, 167, 175, 186, 187, 201–2
public order, 180, 184
public space, 4, 177–91
pubs, 4, 161, 203 *see also Gasthäuser*
Pudowkin, V. I., 226
Purchla, Jacek, 108
Purrmann, Hans, 68, 73

railways, 11, 30, 31, 52, 55, 124, 127, 133, 135
Raphael, 46
'Rappolthaus', 14
rationalism, 247
rationalization, 35, 88–9, 199–200, 207 n21, 224
Realism, 50, 52
regional authorities, 135
regional identity, 5, 12, 55
regulation, 6, 89, 90, 175–6, 181–7, 207 n31, 210
Reich Statistical Office, 217
Reichspost, 132
Reichsrat, 111
Rembrandt, 243
Rembrandt as Educator, 55
Renaissance, 9, 50, 104, 111
Renan, Ernest, 101
residency, 184–5 *see also* housing
Residenzstadt, 131, 146, 155, 161
Rethel, Alfred, 51
Reymont, Władysław, 113
Rhenish-Westphalian art union, 51
Rhine, 52, 54
Riefensthal, Leni, 251 n30
Riesenrad (Ferris wheel), 128
Riga, 5, 88, 90, 92, 93, 94
Rilke, Rainer Maria, 55, 242
Ringstrasse, 125, 132, 136, 162, 166
roads, 86
Rococo, 9
Rogers, Richard, 248
Rohlfs, Christian, 74, 75

Romanticism, 112–13
Rostworowski, Emanuel, 92
Ruhr, 52, 71
Russia, 48, 86, 89, 92, 101, 107, 109, 124
Ruttmann, Walter, 7, 209–39, 251 n30
Rygier, Tadeusz, 104
Rynek główny (Main Square), 104
Rzeznia koszerna (kosher slaughter-house), 114

Sailer, Berta, 207 n18
St Petersburg, 51, 92, 114
Salt, Sir Titus, 31
satanism, 107
Saxony, 45, 51, 86, 214
Scandinavia, 48, 50
Schadow, Wilhelm von, 47
Scharoun, Hans, 243, 249
Scheffler, Karl, 65, 70, 76
Schiller, Friedrich, 132, 149, 163
Schliessman, Hans, 130
Schlöndorff, 245
Schmidt-Rottluff, Karl, 68, 74
Schnitzler, Arthur, 123, 156
Schoenberg, Arnold, 154, 155, 157
Schönbrunn, 131
School of Applied Arts (Prague), 31
schools, 95 *see also Gymnasien*
Schorske, Carl E., 6, 153
Schröder, Thies, 248
Schubert, J. P., 170
Schulte Gallery, 52
Schulte, R. W., 210, 221
Schultze-Naumburg, Paul 13, 19 n17
Schumacher, Fritz, 16–17, 18
Schumann, Robert, 170
Schupo, 216
Sckopp, Ferdinand, 14, 15
Secession, 102, 106, 108 *see also Freie Sezession*
  Germany, 50, 51, 54, 56, 64, 66–9
  Vienna, 57, 103, 129, 154
Segantini, Giovanni, 170
Šenkýř, Josef, 32, 33
sewage systems, 87
sexual behaviour, 165, 175–95
shopping, 11, 18, 58
Sichulski, Kazimierz, 113
Siemens, 211
Silesia, 93, 124
Simmel, Georg, 2, 216
Sindelsdorf, 52
Sistine Madonna, 46
Sitte, Camillo, 15, 29
Šlapeta, Vladimir, 40 n20
Slevogt, Max, 75
slum clearance, 10, 11, 12, 16
Sobieski, Jan, 104
Social Democracy, 6, 11, 12, 28, 159, 162–3, 167, 197–206
Social Democratic Workers' Party (Sozialdemokratische Arbeiterpartei, SDAP), 159–60, 167–71
socialism, 7, 11, 18, 111, 113, 114
Society Against White Slavery, 190
Socjal-demokracja Królewstwa Polskiego i Litwy (Social Democracy of the Kingdom of Poland and Lithuania), 113

Solingen, 11
Sorkin, David, 148
South Tyrol, 171
souvenirs, 126, 129
Sozialistische Monatshefte, 12
spas, 125, 134–5
Speicherstadt, 10
Spengler, Oswald, 224
Sperl, Johann, 52
Spořilov, 33–4, 42
sports, 136
Staatsdruckerei, 136
Städel Institute, 47
Stadtbahn, 127, 131
Staffelsee, 52
standardization, 35, 37
Stanislav, August, 89
state, 165–71
State Design School, 56
State Planning Commission for Prague and its Environs, 28, 29
Stavba, 28
Stavitel, 28, 31
steamliner, 28
steel frames, 13, 14
stepped roofs, 18
Stern Josef Luitpold, 170
Sternberg, Joseph von, 251 n30
Stettin, 54
Stimmann, Hans, 246–7
Strauss, Johann, 170
Strauss, Richard, 170
Streifzüge durch die Baukunst (Excursions in Architecture), 15
Stuck, Franz, 47
Sturm Gallery, 72
Stuttgart, 56, 212, 214, 219, 222
Styl, 28, 30
suburbs, 10, 28, 29, 33, 90, 129, 161–2, 180
successor states, 198, 206 n4
Suess, Eduard, 152
Sukiennice (Cloth Hall), 104, 110
Sullivan, Louis, 30
Surrealism, 27
surveillance, 187–8
Švácha, Rostislav, 29
Svaz see Czechoslovak Decorative Arts Association
Switzerland, 51
Syberberg, Hans Jürgen, 245
Symbolism, 47
Symphony der Weltstadt (Symphony of a City) 7, 216
Szinyei-Merse, Pál, 50
szopka, 107
Sztuka (Art), 107

Tábor, 95
Taliesin, 38
Tallinn, 5, 89, 90, 92, 93, 94, 98 n24
Tandler, Julius, 203, 205
Tartu (Dorpat), 90
Tatra Mountains, 112
Tauentziehnstrasse-Kurfürstendamm, 66, 67
taxation, 65
Teatr miejski (Municipal Theatre), 103, 106, 108

technology, 87
Teige, Karel, 28, 34
telephone, 52
Teufelsmoor, 53, 55
theatre, 9, 87, 90, 91, 92, 94, 95–6, 103, 134, 161, 162, 170
Thusnelda in the Triumph of Germanicus, 47
Tiergarten district (Berlin), 67, 72, 82
Till Eulenspiegel, 170
The Times, 127, 220, 225
Tolerierten, 149, 150
Toman, Jindřich, 114
Tönnies, Ferdinand, 2
tourism, 5, 55, 112, 123–40
Tourism and Travel Company, 134
Towarzystwo Miłośników Historii i Zabytków Krakowa (Society of Friends of Kraków's History and Monuments), 102
Towarzystwo Szkoły Ludowej (Society of People's Schools), 103, 105
town planning *see* urban planning
trade unions, 17, 169, 197, 207 n18
traffic, 14, 129, 209–26
trams, 125, 127, 211–12, 223–4
transport, 5, 7, 18, 125, 127, 129, 209 *see also* air tranportation, cars, motor vehicles, railways,
Treaty of St Germain, 198
Třebíč, 88
Třeboň, 95
Trieste, 145, 165
Trümmerfilms, 243, 250 n21, 251 n30
Tschudi, Hugo von, 50, 64, 75, 76
Tucholsky, Kurt, 217
Twain, Mark, 125
'A Typical Day at the Headquarters of the Prague Police', 178
Tyrol, 54

Uhde, Fritz von, 5
Uhde, Wilhelm, 72
Underpass (Spandau), 210
unemployment, 200–204, 207 n17
Ungers, O. M., 248
unions, 51
United States of America, 35, 38, 48, 49, 50, 51, 72, 124, 146, 245, 251 n27
Unter den Linden, 66
Unwin, Raymond, 29, 30, 34, 38
upper classes, 6, 88, 89, 90, 91, 93, 94, 110–13, 127, 128, 130, 161 *see also* elites
urban networks, 53, 86–7, 89
urban planning, 2, 7, 15, 16, 17, 28–39, 89–90
urbanization, 1–2, 191

vagrancy, 182, 185, 187, 191, 204
Vagrancy Act, 1885 (Austria), 184, 185, 194 n47
Vajdahunyad Castle, 133
van de Velde, Henry, 56, 154
Van der Rohe, Mies, 250 n4
Vaterland, 108
Velhagen & Klasing art series, 55
venereal disease, 105, 183, 188, 190
Venice, 10
'Venice in Vienna', 128–9
Verein Wiener Freie Volksbühne, 170
vermin, 178

Verne, Jules, 169
Verschönerungsverein (association for the protection of rural beauty), 128
Vienna, 1, 2, 3, 5, 6, 29, 31, 54, 57, 93, 94, 102, 111, 123–40, 141–2, 145–58, 159–74, 175–96, 197–206
Vienna Opera, 103
Vienna Secession *see* Secession
Viennese Music Week, 136
'Viennese types', 130, 143
villa colonies, 30, 31, 33
villas, 31–2, 134
Vilnius, 91, 93
Vinnen, Carl, 50
Vinohrady Savings Bank, 33
Vision und Baugesetz, 74
Vítkovice, 31
Vlaminck, Maurice, 73
Vogeler, Heinrich, 54–5
Voit, August, 46
völkisch ideology, 17, 18, 218
Volksbund der Katholiken Österreichs, 170
Volksgemeinschaft, 17, 206
Volksheim (municipal adult education), 168
Vondrák, Jaroslav, 32, 33
Vorstadt see suburbs
Voysey, Philip, 31

Wagner, Otto, 29, 31, 116 n23, 167
Wagner, Richard, 170
Wagnerschule, 108
Der wahre Jacob, 11
Walden, Herwarth, 72
Wallerstein collection, 46
Wallraff-Richartz Museum, 47
Wall Street Crash, 38, 198
Walser, Robert, 216, 223
warehouses, 10, 14
Wärmestuben (drop-in centres), 202
Warsaw, 48, 86, 91, 93, 94
Washington Crossing the Delaware, 49
Wasilewski, Edmund, 104
watercolours, 129, 130
water supplies, 87, 91, 127
Wawel Bricks, 105
Wawel Hill, 5, 104–14
Weber, Max, 2
Weimar, 9, 54, 56
Weissenhof colony, 33
welfare policy, 180–81, 189, 199, 202–3, 204
Welt-Reise Zeitung, 129
Weltstadt, 216, 225
Welwyn Garden City, 30, 31
Wenders, Wim, 7, 239–52
Werefkin, Marianne von, 48
Werkbund, 33
Werner, Anton von, 47, 48, 50, 76
Westfalen, 215
Westheim, Paul, 65, 76, 77
Weyersberg, 53
'white slavery', 189, 190

Wickham Steed, Henry, 127, 136, 137
Wielki, Kazimierz, 106
Wielkopolska, 86
Wiener Arbeiterschule (Vienna Workers' School), 168
Wiener Cicerone, 130
Wiener Lieder, 156
Wienerwald (Vienna Woods), 127, 162
Wiener Werkstätte, 129
Wiesbaden, 54
Wilhelm II, 47
Willingshausen, 53
Wimar, Carl, 49
Wings of Desire, 7, 239–52
Winter, Max, 163
Winterhilfe (Winter Relief), 203
Witkiewicz, Stanisław, 112–13
Witt, Francis, 129
Wittelbach dynasty, 46
Wittgenstein, Ludwig, 154, 155, 157
Wittredge, Worthington, 48
Wodzicki, Ludwik, 105
Woerzerich, Hans Werner, 70
Wojkiewicz, Witold, 113
Wolf, Hugo, 170
women, 6, 37, 169, 175–96, 198, 200, 201, 204
wood, 89, 90
Woodville, John Caton, 49
workers' colonies, 31, 33, 36
working class, 30, 159–60, 165–71, 177–95, 198–206
World Exhibition, Vienna, 125
World War I, 2, 31, 35, 36, 50, 51, 57, 87, 126, 136–7, 160, 164, 165, 167, 176, 189, 190, 192, 198, 209, 213, 217
World War II, 241, 250 n4
Worpswede, 52, 53, 55
Wrocław, 93
Wümme-Zeitung, 55
Wunderwald, Gustav, 210
Wyspiański, Stanisław, 102, 106

'Young Vienna', 154
youth, 165, 169, 170, 171, 181, 190, 201–3, 218, 222

Zaběhlice, 34
Zahradní Město, 33, 34
Zakopane style, 112
Zamość, 91
Zamoyski, A., 89
Zawiejski, Jan, 103, 106, 108, 110
Zawiejski's Wawel, 108
Die Zeit, 18
Zentralverein der Wiener Lehrerschaft, 167
Zetkin, Clara, 11
Zielony Balonik (Green Balloon), 5, 107–14
Zille, Heinrich, 2
Zionism, 155
Zlín, 4, 34–8, 43, 44
Zola, Emile, 169
Zukunft (Future), 168